Covenant and Eschatology

Covenant and Eschatology: The Divine Drama

Michael S. Horton

Westminster John Knox Press
LOUISVILLE • LONDON

Scripture quotations from the New Revised Standard Version of the Bible are copyright © 1989 by the Division of Christian Education of the National Council of the Churches of Christ in the U.S.A. and are used by permission.

Scripture quotations from the *Holy Bible, New International Version* are copyright © 1973, 1978, 1984 by the International Bible Society. Used by permission of Zondervan Bible Publishers.

Scripture quotations from the *New King James Version* are copyright © 1979, 1980, 1982 by Thomas Nelson, Inc. Used by permission.

Book design by Sharon Adams
Cover design by Night & Day Design

First edition
Published by Westminster John Knox Press
Louisville, Kentucky

This book is printed on acid-free paper that meets the American National Standards Institute Z39.48 standard. ∞

PRINTED IN THE UNITED STATES OF AMERICA

02 03 04 05 06 07 08 09 10 11—10 9 8 7 6 5 4 3 2

Library of Congress Cataloging-in-Publication Data is on file at the Library of Congress, Washington, D.C.

ISBN 0-664-22501-2

Contents

Acknowledgments

Since I have spent so many hours on this project, there are too many colleagues whose generosity I have abused, too many friends and family members whose patience I have indulged, and too many mentors whose reputations I will embarrass if I implicate them all here.

Nevertheless, special thanks must be given to Yale University and especially the Divinity School for giving me the opportunity to sit in on a work in progress for two years as research fellow. The generosity of spirit was matched by the depth and breadth of assistance I received in class and in conversations. I am grateful especially for the time given to me by George Lindbeck, David Kelsey, Serene Jones, Cyril O'Regan, and, above all, Nicholas Wolterstorff. Thanks also to Paul Stuhrenberg for his assistance and the use of the Divinity School library.

My friends at Yale were (and remain) a source of constant encouragement, dialogue, criticism, and nonsense. I especially want to acknowledge Stuart Davenport, Eric Gregory, Preston and Lisa Graham, Peter and Patricia Anders, George and Katie Levesque, Kyle Farley, James Stout, David Legg, and Greg and Jeannie Ganzel.

I am grateful to Westminster Seminary in California and to my colleagues, especially R. Scott Clark and Steven Baugh, for their critiques, and to Fanie du Toit who fueled my interest in postmodern theologies during our Oxford days together and since. Other friends and colleagues elsewhere whose suggestions at least reduced the number of my errors include Richard Lints, Scott Oliphint, Kevin Vanhoozer, and William Davis. Thanks to Gabe Nave, Joshua Rosenthal, Steve Moulson, Zack Keele, and especially Eric Landry for their assistance.

I am grateful for the opportunity to have prepared and presented chapter 1 of this volume as a paper for the Christian Systematic Theology Group of the American Academy of Religion (AAR) in 1998, which was then published by the *International Journal of Systematic Theology* (March 2000). I also appreciated the helpful suggestions of John Webster and Colin Gunton. Thanks also to Donald McKim and Daniel Braden at Westminster John Knox.

Saving the best for last, I am grateful to my wife Lisa not only for providing the usual support but for being my conversation partner. Far more than a sounding board, she provided invaluable insight and criticism at key junctures in the project.

Introduction

Before the Curtain Rises
Covenant and Eschatology as Theological Method

This book is the beginning of an attempt at a theological project—more specifically, an attempt to integrate biblical theology and systematic theology on the basis of scripture's own intrasystematic categories of covenant and eschatology. Although it is rather different in style and method from a traditional prolegomenon, this work represents an exercise in theology in which theological method is determined by the content of the system instead of being regarded as predogmatic reflection. Probably no area of systematic theology is more frequently criticized and, at the same time, has more monopolized the horizon than theological method—or, to use the more technical term, prolegomenon. By now many have cited Jeffrey Stout's colorful comparison of works on method to clearing one's throat before giving a paper: one or two times is fine, but eventually the audience becomes restless. Hans Frei observed,

> Someone has rightly said, "A person either has character or he invents a method." I believe that and have been trying for years to trade method for character, since at heart I really don't believe in independent methodological study of theology (I think the theory is dependent on the practice), but so far I haven't found that I'm a seller to myself as a purchaser.[1]

As its etymology would suggest (viz., "things said before"), the prolegomenon is the section at the beginning of a systematic theology or dogmatics that lays out the foundations for what will be said in the rest of the work. Our purpose in the present work is not so much to develop a full-fledged prolegomenon, but to take Frei's advice to develop a theological paradigm and method dependent on the content they are intended to illumine.

Medieval and modern systems, despite a wide range of diversity, tended to view this enterprise as "foundational" in the sense of exposing the preexisting axioms of universal reason and experience from which ecclesiastical dogmas, or at least theories, could be extrapolated.[2] By contrast, post-Reformation Protestant systems saw their task as rather different. Instead of regarding questions of method (e.g., epistemology, ontology, metaphysics) as predogmatic axioms that all were obliged to accept and from which dogma could be deduced with considerable certainty, these theologians insisted that this was already an exercise in dogmatics. In other words, the foundations were to be derived not from universal foundations from the light of nature, but from the particular self-revelation of God according to the light of grace.[3] So for these theologians of what has come to be called "Protestant scholasticism," the goal of a prolegomenon was to make explicit the presuppositions derived from the intrasystematic unity of theology. It was a self-consciously circular enterprise, self-consciously nonfoundationalist in the medieval and modern senses.

WHY THE POST-REFORMATION
SCHOLASTICS AS CONVERSATION PARTNERS?

Given our attempt in this proposal to include precritical theology in the conversation, it would be appropriate at this point to defend the sixteenth- and seventeenth-century dogmaticians against the rumor that they constructed a highly speculative theory of scripture that abstracted scripture from Christ.[4] With others who have closely studied the sources on these matters, I contend that conservative evangelical theologies represent "turgid scholasticism" not when they rely on the Protestant scholastics, but precisely to the extent that they abandon or (as is more frequently the case) ignore them.

Even Paul Tillich found this American ignorance of the Protestant scholastics appalling:

> Orthodoxy is greater and more serious than what is called fundamentalism in America. Fundamentalism is the product of a reaction in the nineteenth century, and is a primitivized form of classical Orthodoxy. Classical Orthodoxy had a great theology. We could also call it Protestant scholasticism, with all the refinements and methods which the word "scholastic" includes. Thus, when I speak of Orthodoxy, I refer to the way in which the Reformation established itself as an ecclesiastical form of life and thought after the dynamic movement of the Reformation came to an end. It is the systematization and consolidation of the ideas of the Reformation. . . . Hence, we should deal with this period in a much more serious way than is usually done in America. In Germany, and generally in European theological faculties—France, Switzerland, Sweden, etc.—every student of theology was supposed to learn by heart the doctrines of at least one classical theologian of the post-Reformation period of Orthodoxy, be it Lutheran or Calvinist, and in Latin at that. Even if we

should forget about the Latin today, we should know these doctrines, because they form the classical system of Protestant thought. It is an unheard-of state of things when Protestant churches of today do not even know the classical expression of their own foundations in the dogmatics of Orthodoxy. . . . All theology of today is dependent in some way on the classical systems of Orthodoxy.[5]

Far from the usual caricature, Protestant scholasticism for the most part represents the period of refinement and systematization that ordinarily follows periods of discovery. While we engage in profitable discussions with those outside of our tradition, we might fruitfully add these forgotten resources to our list of conversation partners. It represents a tradition that is only superficially represented in any of the extant theological schools.

The assumption of this work is that this is not only the most accurate conception of theological method, but that it finds a sympathetic corollary in the present milieu, after the critique of rationalism, autonomy, and the fruitful explorations of the "hermeneutical turn." Our goal in this work is not to repristinate the achievements of these classic systems of the sixteenth and seventeenth centuries, but to harvest some of these basic insights in an effort to engage with these contemporary conversations. As Tillich indicates,

> Protestant Orthodoxy was constructive. It did not have anything like the pietistic or revivalistic background of American fundamentalism. . . . One of the great achievements of classical orthodoxy in the late sixteenth and early seventeenth centuries was the fact that it remained in continual discussion with all the centuries of Christian thought. . . . These orthodox theologians knew the history of philosophy as well as the theology of the Reformation. . . . All this makes classical orthodoxy one of the great events in the history of Christian thought.[6]

Remarkably, while few theologians seem to recognize the corollaries, certain philosophers who figure prominently in our conversation (e.g., Gadamer, Ricoeur, Wolterstorff, Polanyi) at least hint at the connection. For instance, after noting that the last time science and theology were on speaking terms was in the era of scholasticism, Michael Polanyi says that "though their enterprise collapsed, it left great monuments behind it, and we are today in an infinitely better position to renew their basic endeavor. The present need for it could not be more pressing."[7]

For a variety of reasons, some of which we will explore in various places, theology has become increasingly fragmented and unsure of its location in academic (or even ecclesiastical) discourse. "In my world," Robert T. Osborn complains, "it is no longer clear what theology is, where it can or should be done, or how. . . . What remains when doubt has eroded all foundations, when criticism has completed the task of deconstruction, is the indubitable doubter, the certain critic: We doubt and criticize and therefore we are."[8] Our project will simultaneously reject the assumption that theology follows a modern eschatology of "the education of the human race," as well as the assumption that whatever has been done well in the past necessarily meets present concerns with nothing more to be said or formulated in a new situation. Treasures old and new will, hopefully, be discovered, judged not by their age but by their adequacy and faithfulness to the divine drama. Our precritical forebears will be treated here as important, though not definitive. Much has happened since Ursinus and Turretin, and these erudite Christian thinkers would be among the first to insist that we take account of progress in relevant disciplines.

Too often in contemporary theology, despite the now almost universal repudiation of modernity, method assumes a remarkably modern critical stance. Although antifoundationalist "foundations" are presupposed in the place of modern ones, in the thriving (if scorned) industry of methodological theology, the distinct voice of scripture and that "great conversation" which is tradition is often still postponed. In other words, theology is increasingly absent from the discipline of theology. What is required—and I think that Frei and others were after this—is a theological method that is already conceived, shaped, and determined by the content of its confession. The more that modern foundationalism is shaken off, the greater the openness to particular confessional theologies. Despite his emphasis on public criteria, even David Tracy has concluded, "Nor is the confessionalist position likely to lack resources from the contemporary intellectual situation to warrant its claims to publicness." In fact, Tracy thinks that "a confessional position in theology can unite with a profoundly modern sense of historical relativity without collapsing into the privateness of either Christian sectarianism or secularist relativism." He adds,

> When joined to a strong biblical sense of idolatry grounded in a Christian theological sense of the sovereignty of God, the public plausibility of the confessional position seems secure. Christian theology, therefore, should not hesitate to begin with its own inner history and reflect upon its own special occasion or illuminating event as the properly self-evidencing reality of its real foundation.[9]

None of this means that theology need not account for its claims, for the church as well as the academy. What are its methods? Its modes? Its models and its governing motifs? A traditional prolegomenon would generally follow a pattern something like this: The Object of Theology (subject matter); the Source(s) of Theology; the Genus and Species of Theology (epistemology: to what sort of "knowledge" does theology lay claim, and what is the relation of faith and reason?); the Criteria of Theology (how is it tested?). We hope to follow the present volume with a variation on this classical approach, but in the present work the goal is to lay out a program of sorts, to expose the animating sources and theory-laden structure of a particular theological scheme that could offer a model for reintegrating our fraying discipline.

Our goal all along will be to defend the definition of theology as *the church's reflection on God's performative action in word and deed and its own participation in the drama of redemption.* To that end, we have suggested the following lines of development.

METHOD: REDEMPTIVE-HISTORICAL/ESCHATOLOGICAL

Kant's query, "For what can I hope?" is regarded in this project as the most fundamental quest of human understanding. Taking advantage of advances in biblical theology, this work will argue that eschatology should be a lens and not merely a locus. In other words, it affects the way we see everything in scripture rather than only serving as an appendix to the theological system. While eschatology in the narrower sense may be left intact at the conclusion, we will be referring to eschatology in the broader sense as the form and shape in which redemptive revelation comes.

This approach already assumes, then, the inadequacy of a merely "cognitive-propositional" approach, in George Lindbeck's taxonomy. Already in the first centuries, Irenaeus, Athanasius, and others responded to the threats of Gnosticism and Arianism by appealing to scripture and theology as a history of redemption. Following a promise-fulfillment hermeneutic, they defended and refined Christian claims, not on the basis of putative givens of universal reason and experience, but by delineating the *plot* whose integral unity reflected a general canonical unity. The history of Israel, sketched in broad outline around Jesus Christ, was redrawn in darker lines by the apostles.

Long before Moltmann's appeal to recover the eschatological perspective of all of theology, various Reformed scholastics of the sixteenth and seventeenth centuries were founding what would come to be known as "biblical theology." With renewed focus given to the unity of scripture around Christ and redemption, a fresh interest in history as the locus of redemption and revelation emerged. While the internecine confessional battles and the rise of pietism and rationalism interrupted this program in academic theology, this trajectory received renewed attention around the turn of the twentieth century among a circle of biblical and systematic theologians who saw themselves as its successors.[10]

We will also contrast our model, which aims at being a theology of the cross, with theologies of glory, particularly with respect to manifestation (vision) over proclamation (hearing), respectively. Tracy is correct in observing that the theologies focused upon proclamation "will intensify the Christian sense, present in Paul, Augustine, Luther and Calvin, that the gracious God can never be taken for granted. God's naked majesty and sovereignty, God's judgment and wrath, remain as radical not-yet reminders to all who would rest easily and complacently in an always-already presence of God's graciousness."[11] At the heart of our understanding of theology as eschatology is the already–not yet dialectic.

By "redemptive-historical," then, is meant the organic unfolding of the divine plan in its execution through word (announcement), act (accomplishment), and word (interpretation). Revelation is therefore the servant of redemption, circumventing any conception of revelation as mere enlightenment, gnosis, information, or full presence. Change is a vital category for this perspective, as revelation exegetes divine action and human response in actual historical contexts. The eschatological aspect emphasizes that the character of this progress is not a straight line of horizontal development. Thus, we note its contrast with dominant modern, especially Hegelian, teleologies, in which the character or progress of this organic development is historically immanent. Rather, this plot unfolds through apocalyptic "irruptions" in the fabric of ordinary history, particularly (though not exclusively) connected with the people of Israel. God's work progresses on the vertical as well as the horizontal plane.

By "vertical" (obviously a spatial metaphor), we recognize the scriptural witness to God's judging and saving acts in terms of "descent" to his garden, his mountain, his ark of the covenant, tabernacle, temple, city, and land. These vertical "irruptions" do not delineate two causal or cosmological realms (a natural order sealed off from divine intrusion), but two distinct types of divine activity (viz., those performed in an ordinary manner, providence, and those performed in an extraordinary manner, miracle). Without these periodical interruptions of providentially governed yet rebellious human history, there could be no "progress of redemption." We are in a better position today to recognize the degree to which eschatological assumptions are used, consciously or not, to underwrite entire theological and practical regimes. Overrealized eschatologies, both secular and religious, have often shaped belief and practice in triumphalistic and excessively apocalyptic directions, while underrealized eschatologies have often generated despair, resignation, and a failure of nerve in the face of evil.[12]

Furthermore, the covenant itself is stable, though hardly static; historical, though not historicist. The vertical "intrusions" keep redemptive history from being "one damned thing after another," while the horizontal stride keeps eschatology from being subsumed into some ahistorical event. The "new thing" is a true novum, yet not "wholly other." The new creation is both new *and* creation—that is, both that which transcends creation and that which renews and therefore has some considerable continuity with it.

In general, "we do not yet see everything in subjection" to the Kingdom of God (Heb. 2:8). But the writer to the Hebrews hastens to add, "we do see Jesus, who for a little while was made lower than the angels, now crowned with glory and honor because of the suffering of death, so that by the grace of God he might taste death for everyone" (v. 9). Even in this age, there is this eschatological in-breaking, the implications of which we will consider more fully in relation to the liturgy of Word and sacrament. The ministry of Word and sacrament itself not only points to but is the means through which the new creation, glorification, and the wedding feast claim us in the present. The ministry of the keys represents the eschatological in-breaking of the last judgment, as the church administers discipline, with the authority given to "bind" and "loose." Similarly, diaconal service not only witnesses to but participates in the restoration of the cosmos at the end of history. Often, the various loci of the *ordo salutis* (order of salvation: calling, regeneration, repentance and faith, justification, sanctification, glorification) have been separated from the *historia salutis*. This is true even of much conservative and Reformed systematics.[13] The result is that we often fail to recognize the revolutionary logic of biblical (especially Pauline) eschatology, in which the future is semirealized in the present and the individual is included in a wider eschatological activity. The cross and the resurrection form the horizon of expectation for the people of God, holding in check overrealized and underrealized eschatologies, respectively.

While the kingdom of God cannot be simply equated with the church, at this moment in redemptive history, in the church God has delivered the "keys of the kingdom" in such a way that through its ministration the new age occupies a foothold in this world. And yet it does so only in a manner consistent with the realization that the kingdoms of this world have not yet been made the kingdom of God; cult and culture continue in their distinct existence, each with its distinct goals, interests, motives, and character. Between the "Christianizing" of culture (which more often amounts to the exploitation of Christianity for secular ends) and Christian passivity toward culture stands the unresolved tension of the already and not-yet. Negotiating that tension will inevitably involve multiple interpretations and programmatic strategies, but its recognition—more than that, the prominence we give to it in our systematic endeavors—may at least challenge our tendencies toward quietism and triumphalism.

Another advantage of this redemptive-historical pattern in scripture itself is that it brings together the personal and corporate dimensions of redemption. Much of modern theology, from pietism to liberalism, has concentrated on individual salvation and the subjective experience of redemption, at the expense of the holistic vision that is found in scripture, which unites the *ordo salutis* to the *historia salutis*. In this model, that which God is doing in the experience of believers will be treated as derivative of that which God is doing in the world, in history. At the outset, this proposal encounters formidable opposition, especially in the light of the criticism of religion by Feuerbach, Marx, Nietzsche, Freud, and some post-structuralist writers. So chapter 1 will examine the possibility of an eschatological method by (a) challenging a Platonizing version of Christian theology (that has been justly criticized) and (b) replacing that version with our formulation as a conversation partner with Ernst Bloch, Jacques Derrida, and Mark C. Taylor.

Realizing that such claims, though advocated with renewed vigor by diverse theologians in our day, are controversial, one of the goals of this work is to provide an account of this hermeneutical lens in the light of contemporary challenges. In doing so, we will be drawing on speech-act theory, particularly in our discussion of divine speech.

MODE: ANALOGICAL

Given this method, how are we to understand the claims that God acts and speaks, so central for a redemptive-historical/eschatological hermeneutic? After exploring the various options, we will offer an analogical account. As we will argue, contemporary theology both on the left and the right seems to have misunderstood the nature and role of analogical discourse.

On both sides, the claim that biblical predication of divine attributes, action, and speech is at least to some extent analogical in nature is credited to the movement away from orthodoxy to liberalism. In fact, however, it was the Fourth Lateran Council in the thirteenth century that countered excessive anthropomorphizing tendencies with the declaration that in all such predications "there is always greater dissimilarity than similarity" between the analogue. In other words, when one says that "God is good" and "Sally is good," the predicate "good" is used neither univocally (i.e., identically) nor equivocally (i.e., with no actual similarity), but analogically. Analogical thinking, then, identifies certain aspects of the unknown in terms of the known and familiar. We can often recognize this in ordinary experience—for instance, when we are at the zoo and hear the guide referring to the animal that has just been relocated. For many of us, it is a wholly unrecognizable name, so the guide begins to explain the attributes of this animal. Immediately, our imaginative memories race back and forth between all of the monkeys, horses, bears, and giraffes we have seen before. It is perhaps a little like rifling through a deck of exotic wildlife photographs to make a positive identification, as the guide provides greater description. As we will see, this becomes more complicated when we are discussing God as the one to whom analogies of the familiar apply. How can we know that the analogies work? After all, God says, "No one can see me and live," so how can we know whether the terms that we apply to God are in fact the right fit? Like the relation of the "sign" and "thing signified" in sacramental theology, the way of divine self-communication unites word and reality by promise and not by the (Nestorian) separation or (Eutychean) confusion of these two aspects.[14]

According to this mode, then, scripture provides the community with authorized analogies, drawing on that which is more familiar in human experience in order to indicate appropriate references to that which is more remote. God is therefore neither "wholly other" nor "wholly identical" to human experience, although the only knowledge of God that could be gleaned apart from God's own gracious initiative would be confused and utterly equivocal apart from God's initiative in self-communication. We will argue that since it is God, after all, who is believed to have appropriated these self-descriptions, the reference range is determined (and therefore not equivocal), but approximate (and therefore not univocal). Appealing to Calvin's development of the notion of accommodation, we will argue that such analogical discourse is appropriate but approximate, allowing us to make assertions concerning God's being and action without allowing access to the inner life (i.e., "hiddenness") of God. After all, it is not God's inner essence but God's revealed character, intentions, and actions made explicit in Christ that concern humanity in its concrete situation.

Analogical thinking is necessarily dialectical thinking, as analogies both are and are not their referent. Univocity is the result of resting in the illusion of pure presence—the *visio Dei*, while equivocity occurs when theology rests in the "is not." This underscores the eschatological dimension of theological epistemology. Much of modern theology has been so determined a priori by Kantian categories that force a choice between univocity and equivocity, hypertranscendence and hyperimmanence, rationalism and irrationalism. That means that a genuinely dialectical movement will resist the temptation to set transcendence against immanence or to collapse one into the other. Further, therefore, if analogical discourse is dialectical, then chief among such examples is the *eschatological* nature of such truth. Just as an analogy represents an "is and is not" operation, the eschatological character of theology will underscore the "already/not yet" dimension of theological language. Never resting, never yielding, this is the epistemology of pilgrims: no final truth-as-vision here and now, but truthful divine accommodation for the purposes at hand, which the church's theology and proclamation exist to serve. The eschatological method and the analogical mode, therefore, are more than complementary: they are correlates.

MODEL: DRAMATIC

If this redemptive-historical method, with its analogical mode, is the best approach to theology, we could expect to find an adequate analogy in the realm of drama. Cultural anthropologist Clifford Geertz has suggested that the analogies of game and drama are less strained than that of text. His thoughts are worth quoting at length:

> The drama analogy for social life has of course been around in a casual sort of way—all the world's a stage and we but poor players who strut and so on—for a very long time. And terms from the stage, most notably "role," have been staples of sociological discourse since at least the 1930s. What is relatively new—new, not unprecedented—are two things. First, the full weight of the analogy is coming to be applied extensively and systematically, rather than being deployed in piecemeal fashion—a few allusions here, a few tropes there. And second, it is coming to be applied less in the depreciatory "mere show," masks and mummery mode that has tended to characterize its general use, and more in a constructional, genuinely dramaturgical one—making, not faking, as the anthropologist Victor Turner has put it " . . . drama as communion, the temple as stage; the symbolic action theory toward those of theater and rhetoric— drama as persuasion, the platform as stage."[15]

The dramatic model is holistic, rather than singling out a particular "faculty":

> "The great impact [of the theater]," Morgan writes, "is neither a persuasion of the intellect nor a beguiling of the senses. . . . It is the enveloping movement of the whole drama on the soul of man. We surrender and are changed." Or at least we are when the magic works. What Morgan, in another fine phrase, calls "the suspense of form . . . the incompleteness of a known completion," is the source of the power of this "enveloping movement," a power, as the ritual theorists have shown, that is hardly less forceful (and hardly less likely to be seen as otherworldly) when the movement appears in a female initiation rite, a peasant revolution, a national epic, or a star chamber.[16]

Social studies are currently following three basic paradigmatic analogies: the text, the drama, and the game. And although Lindbeck draws extensively from Geertz, the latter offers an interesting criticism of a text-centered model:

> Even more than "game" or "drama," "text" is a dangerously unfocused term, and its application to social action, to people's behavior toward other people, involves a thoroughgoing conceptual wrench, a particularly outlandish bit of "seeing-as." Describing human conduct in the analogy of player and counterplayer, or of actor and audience, seems, whatever the pitfalls, rather more natural than describing it in that of writer and reader. Prima facie, the suggestion that the activities of spies, lovers, witch doctors, kings, or mental patients are moves or performances is surely a good deal more plausible than the notion that they are sentences.[17]

It would appear that scientists get a cognitive grip on their proposed theories only after constructing an appropriate model. In philosophy and hermeneutics, root metaphors are not only illustrative but often generative and regulative of meaning, whether one thinks of Gadamer's "horizons," Frei's "narrative," Ricoeur's "world-projection in front of the text," Heidegger's "clearing," Derrida's "text"/ "writing"/"difference," or Lindbeck's "semiotic (cultural-linguistic) system (grammar)." As Rorty observes concerning the "picture" or "mirror" analogy,

> The picture which holds traditional philosophy captive is that of the mind as a great mirror, containing various representations—some accurate, some not—and capable of being studied by pure, nonempirical methods. Without the notion of the mind as mirror, the notion of knowledge as accuracy of representation would not have suggested itself. Without this latter notion, the strategy common to Descartes and Kant—getting more accurate representations by inspecting, repairing, and polishing the mirror, so to speak—would not have made sense.[18]

In theology as well, analogies are powerful things, and if so, then it is all the more important to pick models that will account for the largest amount of input from theology's sources. While theology seems caught between text-centered and history-centered theologies (to a limited extent a replay of the word-revelation vs. act-revelation debate), drama provides the conceptual space for encompassing both—and, we will argue, much else besides. "Game" and "text" are more inclined toward individual subjectivity, while "drama" captures both individual and public aspects of theological discovery and its subject matter.

This dramatic analogy is superior to the picture analogy that has dominated Western thought and theology since Augustine. Nancey Murphy observes, "We imagine that the sentence 'The cat is on the mat' is a picture of a fact, where the cat is represented by the word *cat*, the mat by *mat*, and *on* pictures the relation between them. What the later Wittgenstein offers in place of the 'picture' picture is a *moving* picture. To understand the sentence, ask for a little story that makes sense of what a person might be doing with that sentence in a social setting; for example, answering a question about where to look for Tabby."[19] Modern foundationalism has made theology in its image, withholding from theology its own intrasystematic resources. In our approach, we will argue, the covenant and its canon determine theological method, rather than vice versa. The "first things" are themselves implications of everything else that is said.

As many readers will know, the appropriation of drama as a metaphor for theology is not new with me.[20] In fact, it has a distinguished pedigree. I have mentioned Irenaeus and Athanasius, who, although they do not explicitly employ a dramatic analogy, explain the Christian system of faith and praxis along sympathetic lines, following the plot of redemption. Dante's implicit analogy seems to be that of a drama as well, although his "stage" is more speculative (with the future state as its setting) than historical. As Susan Schreiner and others have illustrated, the dramatic analogy was a favorite of Calvin, who often referred to the world and history as "the theater of God's glory."[21] With the rise of modern theater, the familiarity of this analogy has grown, from Shakespeare's "all the world's a stage" to Beckett's "Waiting for Godot." In fact, playwright Dorothy Sayers was convinced that "the dogma is the drama," and that the Christian creed, together with its narrative emplotment and characterization, represented the most interesting play ever staged.[22]

More recently still, Derrida has appealed to this analogy with great success, and in a manner that elicits in response a like appeal. His use deserves quoting at length:

> The theater of cruelty expulses God from the stage. It does not put a new atheist discourse on stage, or give atheism a platform, or give over theatrical space to a philosophizing logic that would once more, to our greater lassitude, proclaim the death of God. The theatrical practice of cruelty, in its action and structure, inhabits or rather *produces* a nontheological space. The stage is theological for as long as it is dominated by speech, by a will to speech, by the layout of a primary logos which does not belong to the theatrical site and governs it from a distance. The stage is theological for as long as its structure, following the entirety of tradition, comports the following elements: an author-creator who, absent and from afar, is armed with a text and keeps watch over, assembles, regulates the time or the meaning of representation, letting this latter represent him as concerns what is called the content of his thoughts, his intentions, his ideas. He lets representation represent him through representatives, directors or actors, enslaved interpreters who represent characters who, primarily through what they say, more or less directly represent the thought of the "creator." . . . Finally, the theological stage comports a passive, seated public, a public of spectators, of consumers, of 'enjoyers'—as Nietzsche and Artaud both say—attending a production that lacks true volume or depth, a production that is level, offered to their voyeuristic scrutiny. . . . The origin of theater, such as it must be restored, is the hand lifted against the abusive wielder of the logos, against the father, against the God of a stage subjugated to the power of speech and text (235, 239).[23]

Unlike Derrida's binary opposition of stage and speech/text (which hardly allows for an adequate theatrical analogy), our use will seek to integrate them. I am not intending drama as an analogy of how one *does* theology, an alternative to theology as a science, for instance. It is not employed as a method or a mode, but as a model: as the best way of thinking about the practice of theology in ecclesial and academic reflection. Thus, the scriptures as script and double agency as the action that follows that code, uniting divine action and discourse, events and words, seems to me to be better at unifying what is actually there than metaphors such as narrative, text, speech, revelation, manifestation, and so forth. The dramatic metaphor makes it easier to include often marginalized elements while, precisely for that reason, turning down the volume on some of the aspects that have perhaps been too over-determining in both theologies of revelation and theologies of history.

Since revising this manuscript for final publication, I have realized that the analogy has been profitably explored in various disciplines, including theology.[24] Undoubtedly my appeal to drama is spurred by my reading of Geerhardus Vos on the biblical-theological side, and on the philosophical side by Alasdair Mac-Intyre, particularly his singular treatment in *After Virtue*.[25] Although he is working chiefly within the narrative framework, MacIntyre's analysis of how identity emerges is at least as congenial to a dramatic metaphor. Speaking, writing, and acting cannot be viewed in atomistic terms as brute facts, but are specific events by belonging to a certain context or praxis. And that leads us to the fourth methodological criterion.

CONTEXT: COVENANT

Abstraction, the preoccupation of certain philosophical systems that have profoundly shaped modern theology, is like Noah's pigeon, which had great difficulty finding any terra firma on which to light. But, as Geerhardus Vos put it, "The circle of revelation is not a school, but a 'covenant.'"[26] In our estimation, most varieties of modern theology have found divine speech and action in history problematic as a result of misdiagnosing the God-world relation. Consequently, theology swings between the poles of total creator-creature identification and "wholly other" transcendence. Full presence or full absence: these trajectories continue to delineate some of the most dominant theological proposals after Descartes and Kant.

Whereas philosophy looks for first principles outside of scripture, theology is the church's reflection on its own witness to revelation in history. Therefore, theology must be anchored in the substance of its own "first principles." The content, in other words, must provide the resources for its method. Unlike speculative approaches, contextualization of theology in the progress of the covenant helps us to avoid the Scylla of rationalism and the Charybdis of some missiological theologies that stress the regnant cultural patterns of today as normative.

"Covenant"—and not the idea in general, but the specific praxis developed throughout redemptive history—is the culture of the people of God, shaped by the drama of the two cities and the two seeds. This is precisely why accommodation to the powers and authorities of the nations ("this present age") spells not the relevance, but the ultimate defeat of the people of God. This redemptive-historical drama incorporates believers in such a manner that it constitutes its own cultic "culture." This is not to eliminate the believer's dual citizenship and the profound influences of specific cultures. But even these secular cultures are interpreted by the believer in a covenantal light, as even the cities of human-kind are, and evaluated in terms of God's common grace and human rebellion, redemption, judgment, and consummation.

Reflecting a profound Barthian insight elaborated by postliberalism, David Kelsey remarks that much of modern theology, both conservative and liberal, has been in the translation mode, viewing Christian speech as the attempt to make revelation conceptually accessible and relevant to contemporary culture. Gadamer's "fusion of horizons" has been appropriated, usually secondhand, in evangelical homiletics to justify the practice (despite theoretical commitments) of giving equal weight to scripture and culture. David Tracy and other proponents of what Lindbeck calls "experiential-expressivist" views of religious language demand that Christian doctrine pass the bar of human experience.[27] We will, however, follow the Reformers in their insistence that reason and experience are not tests of, but are tested by, God's public address to us as summoned sinners. Peter Berger illustrates this position in *The Noise of Solemn Assemblies*: "In a culture where religion is functional both socially and psychologically, Christian preaching itself ought to call men to a confrontation with the God who stands against the needs of society and against the aspirations of the human heart."[28] We need to recover that sense so pervasive in other periods; namely, that even Christians do not know what they really need or even want—and that attending to their immediate felt needs may muffle the only proclamation that can actually satisfy real needs. Berger judges that "the more general personal consequence of the abandonment of theological criteria for the Christian life is the cult of experience. . . . Emotional pragmatism now takes the place of the honest confrontation with the Christian message."[29]

Adopting the view that "human experience" is hardly neutral but rather culturally and ethically conditioned, our proposal will attempt to challenge the notion of culture's ultimacy or even equality with scripture as a criterion of truth. Gadamer's general hermeneutical theory cannot account for that transformation that Christians call "conversion"—a lifelong process of "putting on Christ." Instead of trying to found preaching and practice on a general hermeneutical theory (the sort of thing that Gadamer himself would reject), distinctively Christian presuppositions must be brought to bear. The hearer/reader's situatedness is defined as "this present evil age that is passing away." This relativizes every "past," "present," and "future," and therefore counters conservative nostalgia as well as the near-fatalistic embrace of the present and the future. It also means that the believing community today in the United States has more in common with the believing community in first-century Asia Minor than it has with the late capitalist culture of Los Angeles and New York. Our identity is preeminently shaped by the role that we play in the drama of redemption ("the age to come" as it has dawned in Christ).

This does not make us inactive in this world—quite the contrary. Rather, it makes us active in a fundamentally different way. Particularly since Pentecost, the drama of redemption unfolds as a play-within-a-play. While dramatic events unfold in world history, captured for most of us on the evening news, the biblical drama unfolds in a manner that those who are outside of its performance only regard as insignificant. This is underscored by the fact that believers are cast in the role of "strangers and aliens," and their message is regarded as "foolishness." It is a strange irony that the play-within-a-play ends up becoming the all-encompassing divine drama that sweeps the entire natural creation and its history into its action and plot. With that in mind, the church ought not to shrink from participating in what in this age is regarded as a marginalized (off-off Broadway) production and should attempt to salvage whatever it can from it in order to appeal to a wider audience. Our model has assumed that much of contemporary Christian practice (if not always theory) has adopted the myth of neutrality in the realm of culture and is dangerously inattentive to the subtle (and not-so-subtle) forms of distortion that are passed off as translation. The alternative is to take more seriously, not less, the situated character of our existence as sinners as well as saints and to recognize the profoundly ethical dimension of both "horizons." The result, we hope, will include a recognition that the horizon of the text should not simply be fused with the horizon of situated interpretation, but that the former will overwhelm, transform, and convert the latter. This is in part what is meant by the Pauline imperative to make "every thought captive to obey Christ" (2 Cor. 10:5).

Barth and his postliberal ("narrative") heirs have indicated the right direction in this whole matter of translation. In the approach we have outlined, however, there is more than a narrative to "absorb" the reader into the world of the text; there is a covenant to reorient one's ultimate loyalties, aspirations, and identity. Further, "absorption" is more passive than "performance," and the latter seems more comprehensive of faith and practice. Critics of narrative theology have rightly challenged the limitations of the metaphor of indwelling a text. As Miroslav Volf points out, "The notion of inhabiting a biblical story is hermeneutically naïve because it presupposes that those who are faced with the biblical story can be completely 'dis-lodged' from their extratextual dwelling places and 're-settled' into intratextual homes. . . . In the New Testament, of course, we read nothing of inhabiting a 'cultural-linguistic system' or 'texts.' Much more prosaically, we are told that Christians live, on the one hand, 'in Corinth' or 'in Rome,' and, on the other hand, in some mysterious way also 'in God' or 'in Christ.'"[30] Christians live in this world, not in a text. That is to say, they live on a public stage and not in a private realm of textual world-projection. More than a script is needed for this transformation. A drama in which the covenant establishes concrete performances generates not only passively transformed readers, but a new reality outside of the text-script in which covenant partners actively participate in the ongoing and unfolding performance on the world stage. Just as the United States Constitution unites a modern American citizen to the War for Independence, the covenant as constitution unites the people of God in every age ("to a thousand generations"). This diachronic unity is established not simply by the convention, however, but by the Spirit's eschatological work of uniting people to Christ as their representative head within this context.

The postliberal school, particularly Frei, has drawn on Calvin's metaphor of "spectacles" in relation to scripture. In contrast, much of modern theology (and some premodern theologies heavily influenced by Augustinian Neoplatonism) seems to have had for its root metaphor a "mirror." Recognizing the difference between spectacles and mirrors is rather easy: one looks *through* spectacles and *at* a mirror. While one must beware of making too much of metaphors (including drama), Reformation theology has substantiated this insight more generally. Accordingly, scripture is to be treated not as a mirror-image of reality, but as a divine interpretation of that reality in the light of the actual situation that obtains between persons within a particular context.

Our model also may help to make the postliberal point that higher-critical methods cannot establish the foundation of Christian theology. Despite the important role of critical research, secular analysis can only observe purely secular cultural influences. And, as John Milbank, Colin Gunton, and many others have recently observed, "secular" cannot be identified with "neutral": higher-critical scholarship was never unbiased or nontheological. The tendency, for instance, to reduce all historical factors to naturalistic explanation underscores how important it is to recognize the diversity of methods peculiar to each discipline. Historians should not be expected to discern the hand of God in providence, since the object of their inquiry concerns secondary causes. (The corollary, of course, is that historians cannot eliminate supernatural explanations or reduce "fact" to naturalistic explanations, since this too is beyond their competence.) But theology has special revelation as its principium. The question, therefore, is not whether God can act or speak. Nor is it a matter of establishing "neutral" criteria for determining what God could have done or said. Rather, it is a matter of attending to what God has in fact done and said that establishes the criteria of faith. This is precisely what makes Christian theology resistant to modern foundationalism. The presuppositions of scripture, not of supposedly predogmatic reflection, must constrain theology.

Our goal here, then, is to demonstrate that God's covenant with his people, through the history of Israel and the church, is the stage on which the divine drama is performed. This is the primary sociocultural location of the play and its performers—rendering it *this* play and not another. While critics have reason to question the apparent disinterest in external reference among some narrative theologies, we are more aware than ever of the situatedness of our existence. We are no longer *res cogitans*, floating minds looking down upon stable objects and discerning their most intimate details as disinterested spectators. Our pre-Enlightenment forebears recognized this and warned sharply against considering God in *esse*, instead considering God as he has covenanted with sinners in Christ. As Calvin demonstrates in his dialectic between the creator and the creature in his opening to the *Institutes*, all knowledge of God—and indeed of all reality— is always a personal knowledge, a knowledge-in-relationship.

No more concrete category can unite history and eschatology, the individual and the community, divine and human agency, than the scriptures' own method of contextualization: the covenant. This is the social location of revelation and redemption. Here, there are no "objects" and "subjects" in the post-Enlightenment sense, but a covenant Lord and covenant servants along with their shared environment of created reality. Absent from this picture are abstract entities. Since the creator of all reality is a person, all of that reality that God voluntarily produces exists in relationship. This means that, on one hand, the divine drama is a God's-eye view of the reality it addresses. Although it is communicated analogically, it is communicated by God for the covenant people and, indeed, for the whole world. This is in part what makes this approach inherently public and evangelistic. On the other hand, it is in some sense an "inside story," like any other narrative of dramatic interest. Few people would find their imaginations sustained by plays consisting of monologues about "Justice" or "Love," "Meaning" or "Theodicy." While there is certainly a place for such theorizing, the drama of redemption is suspicious of the abstract and is at home in the concrete actions of agents. It is not surprising that the Reformed scholastics referred to the knowledge of God and redemption that is possible for us as *theologia viatorum* (the theology of travelers) or *theologia nostra* (our theology).

In *The Meaning of History*, H. Richard Niebuhr compares and contrasts Lincoln's "insider" version of American history and that of the *Cambridge Modern History*.[31]

> Lincoln's Gettysburg Address begins with history: "Four-score and seven years ago our fathers brought forth upon this continent a new nation, conceived in liberty and dedicated to the proposition that all men are created free and equal." The same event is described in the Cambridge Modern History in the following fashion: "On July 4, 1776, Congress passed the resolution which made the colonies independent communities, issuing at the same time the well-known Declaration of Independence. If we regard the Declaration as the assertion of an abstract political theory, criticism and condemnation are easy. It sets out with a general proposition so vague as to be practically useless. The doctrine of the equality of men, unless it be qualified and conditioned by reference to special circumstance, is either a barren truism or a delusion."[32]

Niebuhr points out, "The difference in sentiment is so profound because the beings about which the accounts speak differ greatly; the 'Congress' is one thing, 'our fathers' are almost another reality."[33]

> The inspiration of Christianity has been derived from history, it is
> true, but not from history as seen by a spectator; the constant refer-
> ence is to subjective events, that is to events in the lives of subjects.
> What distinguishes such historic recall from the private histories of
> mystics is that it refers to communal events, remembered by a com-
> munity and in a community. Subjectivity here is not equivalent to
> isolation, non-verifiability and ineffability; our history can be com-
> municated and persons can refresh as well as criticize each others'
> memories of what has happened to them in the common life; on the
> basis of a common past they can think together about the common
> future.[34]

Furthermore, a biblical-theological understanding of covenant ties things
together in systematic theology whose relations are often strained: ecclesiology
(the context of the covenant), theology proper (the covenant maker), anthropology (the covenant partner), christology (the covenant mediator), soteriology (the
covenant blessings), eschatology (the covenant's consummation). These are not
forced relationships, but entirely natural in view of the way the biblical drama
itself meets these various loci. At the same time, it clearly maintains a distinction
between the context in which the loci are framed and a supposed central dogma:
"covenant" serving as the former, rather than the latter. The concept of the
covenant is also a doctrine alongside others in the system, but is not necessarily
central in that role. Once the covenantal context is sufficiently recognized, theological system should have a focal awareness of Christ and all his benefits and a
tacit awareness of the integrating covenantal structure.

Theologies that focus on a central dogma (Theology of Word, Theology of
History, Theology of Encounter, Theology of the Spirit, Theology of Correlation, Theology of the Trinity, Theology of the Community) frequently tend
toward reductionism. In such approaches, the abstract idea often swallows the
particular details whole, and in the process essential features of church proclamation and praxis are marginalized or entirely eliminated. In the process, is it not
often the case that the central dogma itself, inasmuch as it becomes a metaphysical Idea, loses its particularity and concrete definition? It is ironic that in many
of these modern systems the program (i.e., system) overdetermines exegetical possibilities to a far greater extent than at least the better representatives of precritical systems.

Despite differences on essential features of covenant theology, Karl Barth certainly captured the existential importance of the covenant in Christian experience. Wherever this motif has been emphasized, believers have been content to
rest in the promise to which they are actually entitled as God's covenant people.
This does not mean that everyone in the covenant is necessarily converted, since,
as Augustine said, "There are sheep without and wolves within." Yet it does mean
that this mixed assembly is corporately addressed as the people of God. "And
since he is our sovereign Lord," Barth writes of Jesus Christ, "what Luther said
about the Word of God also holds true for Agape. It is a 'passing thunderstorm'
that bursts at one moment here and at another moment elsewhere. . . . Whoever

calls on his name will be saved. That is to say, whether or not the thunderstorm bursts, such a person may live and work with a *promise*."[35]

> He has *promised* that perfect love is the heaven spread out over him, whether or not this love is momentarily clear or hidden from him. Protected and encouraged by the promise of this love, he may pray, study, and serve; and trusting in it, he may think, speak, and finally also die. Once a man knows where to seek and from where to expect the perfect love, he will never be frustrated in his attempts to turn himself to it and to receive from it an orientation which enlightens his small portion of knowledge. This love abides in the one in whom the covenant between God and man is fulfilled. It abides even when theologians come and go and even when things become brighter or darker in theology. It abides like the sun behind the clouds, which more precisely is and remains victoriously above the clouds as "the golden sun." . . . Simply to know about it affords ample occasion to join in the praise of God, the God of the covenant, the God who is love itself.[36]

Although moderns have made far too much out of central dogmas and *termini a quo,* there is an irresistible urge to find a significant core of doctrines to which all else must be related. This, I think, is suggested by the way in which all things in scripture point to Christ, a hermeneutical principle that Jesus himself authorizes.[37] It is not a canon within a canon, but it is a canonical center that Jesus' identity and mission represents. And yet his centrality cannot be accounted for in the abstract. It requires a context, and that context seems to be shaped in scripture by the notion of covenant. It is not Jesus Christ as healer, as guide, as fellow traveler, as ruler, or a host of other things, that this particular story highlights, although it is true that Jesus was and is all of these. It is Jesus Christ as the mediator of the covenant that occupies center stage and unites the drama of redemption in its Old and New Testament acts.

As drama is a wider analogy for the project as a whole, covenant is a sufficiently broad biblical category to encompass the most important aspects of this drama. Far from displacing christology or a particular doctrine, such as justification, from centrality, "covenant" becomes the context in which such crucial and definitive doctrines have their fullest force. For instance, what does "to justify" even mean apart from the biblical context in which it emerges as a situated concept? There, it develops as an arrangement that has been breached by one party but fulfilled by another on the defaulter's behalf. Christology, particularly the doctrine of the two natures of Christ, is enriched by the redemptive-historical development of the covenant lord–covenant servant motifs, especially in the prophets. This covenantal context will play an important role, for instance, in our account of divine speech (especially in relation to the central speech acts of command and promise). It will also figure prominently in our hermeneutical discussions and in the reintegration of such victims of false dilemmas as word and act, personal encounter and metaphysical description, faith and praxis, and the unity of Old and New Testaments.

Thus, the content of theology is already defining its methodology: "method" is not something that one does independent of theology, a salute to whatever branch of the sciences is currently reigning. Rather, the structural apparatus of theological method is already what I take to be the structural apparatus of scripture itself.

In an attempt to make the intrasystematic resources of Christian proclamation more normative for theological reflection, we will test our model on two central Christian claims; viz., that God acts and that God speaks. Our exploration concludes with an outline of how this proposal might address the fragmentation of theology and reintegrate Old Testament and New Testament scholarship, biblical theology and systematic theology, theory and practice, and similar aspects of the enterprise. Overcoming the isolationism and overspecialization that has resulted from a variety of factors obviously cannot be accomplished merely by proposing a model for reenvisioning theology. But perhaps it can assist in that endeavor. Like some expressions of the new urbanism in architecture and city planning that end up merely creating an eerie reproduction of a bygone era, theological repristination may feed nostalgia but cannot feed the soul or maintain a genuine continuity with the *Wirkungsgeschichte* ("effective history") of past fidelity and its effects in the present. Nor has theological Bauhaus, in the form of secular theologies, offered anything beyond the end of theology itself, placing a flat roof even over the church, where human relationships become all that matters. What is needed is a much more complicated and demanding reevaluation of the intrasystematic foundations of Christian self-description, with a rigorous attention to the situated character of our goals as well as our means. It is with that in mind that we begin our exploration.

Chapter One

Eschatology after Nietzsche
Apollonian, Dionysian, or Pauline?

> *The lawless land of erring, which is forever beyond good and evil,*
> *is the liminal world of Dionysus, the Anti-Christ, who calls every*
> *wandering mark to carnival, comedy, and carnality.*[1]

Listing six stages in the "History of an Error," Friedrich Nietzsche describes "How the 'Real World' Finally Became a Fable." First, the real world is regarded as attainable for the wise and virtuous man: "I, Plato, am the truth." Next, the real world is available not in this world, but is promised in the next to the pious: "to the sinner who repents." Eventually, this Christianized Platonism renders the real world "unattainable, unprovable, unpromisable, but the mere thought of it a consolation, an obligation, an imperative." One thinks of Kierkegaard. But then this ideal realm becomes regarded as unattainable, or at least unattained, an unknowable noumenon: "Hence no consolation, redemption, obligation either: what could something unknown oblige us to do? . . . (Break of day. First yawn of reason. Cock-crow of positivism)."

Having no practical or theoretical use, the "real world" is at last abandoned and with it the obligations and imperatives which attached to it. The conclusion:

> The real world—we have done away with it: what world was left? The apparent one, perhaps? . . . But no! *with the real world we have also done away with the apparent one!* (Noon; moment of the shortest shadow; end of the longest error; pinnacle of humanity; INCIPIT ZARATHUSTRA.)[2]

In Hegel's left-wing successors one meets the synthesis of Plato's two worlds—a cosmology, ontology, and metaphysic that has dominated Western thought. In fact, it is not so much a synthesis as it is a repudiation of the "true world" of Par-menides, Plato, and Platonized Christianity. In other words, it is a rejection of Apollo in favor of Dionysus.[3] To the extent that Christian theology has incorporated this Platonist legacy, it has been liable to the devastating criticism of Hegel's students, not the least of whom was Nietzsche himself. The purpose of this chapter is to analyze the revolt against an explicitly Christian eschatology and to distinguish Pauline eschatology from the Platonist trajectory. By setting the New Testament's two-age model against the two-world model, perhaps the Pauline eschatology may receive renewed vigor in current discussions. But before we investigate this Pauline model, we must attempt a dangerously brief account of the problem.

PLATO'S TWO WORLDS

Particularly since Plato sought to harmonize Parmenides and Heraclitus by developing a system in which Parmenidean stasis and Heraclitean flux could be given their own distinct spheres, there has been a tension between the "realms" of the forms and the appearances. Further, the immortal soul—itself a spark of the divine logos—dwelt in the highlands of the eternal forms and had only in this temporal life of shadows to recollect its preincarnate existence in order to find its way back home.[4] A key source for this dualistic picture is, of course, the famous illustration of the cave in Book 7 of the *Republic*. The moral to the story: "The world of our sight is like the habitation in prison, the firelight there to the sunlight here, the ascent and the view of the upper world is the rising of the soul into the world of mind."[5] Like the prisoner, one "must be turned round with the whole soul away from the world of becoming until it is able to endure the sight of being and the most brilliant light of being; and this we say is the Good, don't we?"[6] It is not surprising, then, that the philosopher would have little interest in history or in any kind of intramundane redemptive scheme.

While it is not our purpose here to investigate the extent to which early main-stream Christianity was influenced by Plato or by derivations (e.g., Philo of Alexandria or Plotinus), it is indisputable that early Gnosticism reflected a dualistic ontology with its consequent metaphysical, cosmological, epistemological, and eschatological antitheses. Furthermore, however seminal it may have been, at least a proto-Gnosticism shaped by dualistic ontologies had engendered a speculative tendency even among certain Jewish Christians. The "super-apostles" who were insinuating themselves into the Corinthian church, the dualistic ascetics of Colossae, and the Docetists and perfectionists of John's first letter, already provide a backdrop for this contrast between Plato's two worlds and Paul's two ages. While there is little evidence in the New Testament of a full-blown Gnosticism with the sophistication of something like the Valentinian system, the Hellenistic (notably, Platonic and Stoic) thought, with its sharp ontological dualism, is encountered there in a polemical context. This worldview would have found sympathy with

Bultmann's insistence that it is the "Christ of faith" and not the "Christ according to the flesh" that is of interest; *Geschichte*, but not *Historie*.[7] Especially in Manicheanism, the theme of alienation of the soul from the upper regions by physical embodiment and of redemption by the escape from the realm of nature, matter, and history to that of preincarnate immortality is emphasized.[8] All of this is narrated in a cosmic myth of warfare between the Creator and the Redeemer or, in Marcion's version, between the God of the Old Testament and the God of the New. Just as Plato's art-fanciers, sight-fanciers, and practical agents are inferior to the philosopher meditating on eternal forms, the gnostic separated the sheep from the goats according to "men of flesh" and "men of spirit."[9] An eschatology of escape through either libertine sensuality or ascetic legalism looked backward and forward to the sibling rivalry of Apollo and Dionysus.

However, Christian thought over much of its history (especially in the medieval synthesis) has failed to appreciate sufficiently the revolutionary character of Pauline eschatology precisely to the extent that it has borrowed from Platonizing conceptualities. The reign of Apollo (i.e., Parmenides and Plato) can only heighten the attraction of a Dionysian (or Heraclitean) outlook. Let us then leap to the modern critique.

CHRISTIANITY AS "PLATONISM FOR THE MASSES"

In Ludwig Feuerbach (1804–72) we return to Plato's projection model (viz., realm of appearances as a projection of an eternal realm of forms), but this time the order of projection is reversed.[10] Brian Ingraffia notes that "Nietzsche locates the origin in metaphysics in the distinction between two worlds, a true and an apparent world."

> God serves as the negation and indictment of our life and world; therefore, we must kill this God in order to become free to affirm the actual world. Through the death of God and the abolition of the true world, the metaphysical distinction between a true and apparent world collapse, and along with it collapse all the metaphysical and anthropological dualisms which are dependent upon this distinction. Nietzsche desires to abolish theology's true world because it has served to denigrate the actual world.[11]

In modernism, God is merely a projection of the human self, but in Nietzsche forward, it is "a bad fiction."[12] Ever since Descartes made the *res cogitans* a sovereign subject, modernity has been transferring the attributes that had characterized the nominalist deity (viz., arbitrary and absolute will) to the Sovereign Self.[13] The Sovereign God is replaced with the autonomous moral legislator (Kant), the Absolute/Infinite I (Fichte), Absolute Will (Schopenhauer), or with Nietzsche's Dionysian "Over-Man." This not so wonderful exchange is significant for the problem we are considering, and it has been thoughtfully discussed in many places.[14] The isolated, utterly inaccessible "wholly other" and unknowable noumenon of the *Ding-an-sich,* this voluntaristic *causa sui,* is precisely the early modern presupposition of God. In other words, nominalism's God was the object of Nietzsche's *ressentiment,* the one who must die if the Over-Man is to live. In this account, God was displaced by the self-conscious ego in Descartes and then deported to the unknowable noumenal realm by Kant. Why then retain a "noumenon" that cannot be known? Hegel asked. So, quite sensibly, Nietzsche wiped the "other world" from the horizon to make room for this world, just as his predecessors had removed God from the center of being and knowing in order to make room for the autonomous self. Nietzsche's move, and that of his a/theological successors, is hardly antimodern or postmodern, but is the consummation of modernity's eschatological plot.

Nevertheless, at the heart of the debate is a misunderstanding of the eschatology that shapes New Testament theology. Christianity is indeed "Platonism for the masses" in many of its popular and academic forms. Even when its otherworldly cosmology is discarded as the lingering perfume of an empty vase, as in Bultmann, the older dualism is simply replaced with a rigid neo-Kantian dualism that is just as mythical and arbitrary as Plato's ideal realm. If we follow Mark C. Taylor's version of theological deconstruction, the death of God has involved the death of self and history as well. Taking his cue from Derrida's announcement that "Bataille's atheology is also an a-teleology and an aneschatology,"[15] Taylor states, "From the viewpoint of a/theology, there never was a pure origin and never will be a perfect end. 'All promise, all future hope and expectation, come to an end in the death of God.'"[16] It is the Book (the Bible, that is) that creates the notion of "history," with its promise-fulfillment pattern. "Between the 'tick' of Genesis and the 'tock' of Apocalypse, the history of the West runs its course," Taylor notes. "History, as well as self, is a theological notion."[17] Taking its narrative form, this historical sense is inherently logocentric, regarding "the narrative line as discovered within events rather than imposed upon them from without."[18] Nietzsche opposed Hegel's notion of "world history" because he didn't accept the presupposition upon which it rested; namely, the idea of a telos, purpose, and meaning. "That my life has no aim is evident from the accidental nature of its origin," said Nietzsche. "That I can posit an aim for myself is another matter."[19] The logical conclusion of the autonomy at the heart of modernity is exposed in the constructivism of Nietzsche and his disciples. It is not such a large step after all from Kant's boast that the individual is "meant to produce everything out of himself."[20] Perhaps this makes Kant rather than Nietzsche the first postmodernist.[21] Regardless, the religion of the Bible stood on the sidelines while secular theologies battled over ontological dualism.

While older theology regarded the believer between the two advents as a pilgrim (*viator*), a/theology, with its a-teleology and aneschatology, regards its adherents as nomads consigned (or freed) to aimless wandering (heretical erring, straying, to use Taylor's terms).[22] "The death of the sovereign God now appears to be the birth of the sovereign self," but has led only to the death of the self as well. Thus, naturalistic humanism suffers the same fate as its rival.[23] But for a/theology, this at last opens up the space for writing, the endless interplay of signs, without the interference of an alleged someone or something standing outside the game, outside the crossword puzzle of intersignification. "There is no Logos, there are only hieroglyphs."[24] Without a logos, which would involve looking back to the past in recollection and forward in expectation, there is no transcendent meaning of history. Embracing Hegel's preference for Heraclitean flux, deconstruction nevertheless eschews his teleological view of history. Hegel's rationalism can be attributed to his absolute monism. The One (historical process) demands a single, unified purpose and goal. But this is precisely where Nietzsche objects: "Becoming must be explained without recourse to final intentions," he says. "Becoming must appear justified at every moment (or incapable of being evaluated; which amounts to the same thing); the present must absolutely not be justified by reference to a future, nor the past by reference to the present."[25]

Gone, therefore, is the narrativity of history. Taylor writes, "The disappearance of origin, center, and conclusion points to 'the *seminal* adventure of the trace.'"[26] Here is the Dionysian figure dripping with both blood and semen, death and life, in an endless play of antitheses without synthesis. "Purposeless process" is the name for this. "The wanderer has no certain destination, goal, aim, purpose, or end. While the exile apprehensively pursues the salvific cure of closure, the drifter is 'indifferent to any possible results.' Having 'lost' all direction, the trace becomes a 'purposeless tension.' . . . The lawless land of erring, which is forever beyond good and evil, is the liminal world of Dionysus, the Anti-Christ, who calls every wandering mark to carnival, comedy, and carnality."[27] There is no Sabbath rest, no fixed center, no Alpha or Omega. Everything is dispersed, decentered, and disintegrated. There is no origin and therefore no homecoming, but only an eternal "return" of the trace. Being is swallowed up in becoming.

And yet, despite the aspirations of theological deconstruction, this is no more subversive than Hegel's philosophy of deicide. The only difference is that Hegel's radically centered monism is exchanged for the radical dispersion. As in Hegel, stability gives way to flux. But unlike Hegelian thought, in deconstruction the one is sacrificed to the many, order to chaos, universals to particular, reason to irrationality. Absolute teleology is exchanged for absolute purposelessness. Where is room left for "the ceaseless play of opposites," for the "trace," the intersection between presence and absence? At the end of the day, absence reigns and Dionysus revels in the murder of Apollo. Despite his rhetoric, Taylor's arguments go no further than Hegel's in advancing a genuine *dialectic*. A new monism—the unity of the many and the immutability of process and flux as the condition of existence—emerges to replace older rivals.

In contrast to Hegelian syntheses (including the ostensibly a/theological version), Pauline eschatology remains in an unresolved dialectic—a genuine play, if not of opposites, at least of differences. The theology of the cross demands this "deferral" of ultimate meaning and purpose against all theologies of glory, but it has already seen too much fulfillment of promises on the part of the treaty-making God to despair of a final resolution in the future that the Second Adam will bring to the era of sin and death.

After the post-Hegelian critique (Feuerbach, Marx, Nietzsche, Freud), Christian eschatology was put increasingly on the run, as the world of appearances sought revenge on the supposed real world for despoiling it of its lawful inheritance. The kingdom of God was very much of this world in the thought of Albrecht Ritschl; immanence swallowed transcendence. The only place left for the apocalyptic (i.e., vertical-divine interruption, rather than mere horizontal-human progress) was on the ever-eroding Cartesian islands of individual subjectivity, as in the "eternal Now" of Kierkegaard and his theological successors, especially Barth and Bultmann.

The problem with the critique that culminates in Nietzsche is that it merely substitutes its own dualisms, polarities, and hierarchies. In fact, a Gnosticism that permeates modernity is prominent in Nietzsche as well. For Hegel, Rousseau, and certainly for existentialism—that product of late Romanticism—history represents alienation, particularly the self's alienation from nature. And no wonder, since Descartes's disembodied *res cogitans* hovers over the project. Mark C. Taylor complains that "most of the Christian theological network rests on a dyadic foundation that sets seemingly exclusive opposites over against each other," ending up with a hierarchy.[28] This is certainly true of some aspects of the medieval synthesis, but it is far more consistent with modernity (especially Descartes and Kant) than with the New Testament. But Taylor, like Nietzsche, cannot get beyond Hegelian synthesis, and the result is a new metaphysics, a new metanarrative: everything gets reduced to difference; identity is entirely lost; so it's the reverse hierarchy. (What, for instance, is the "other" without a "self"?) So too with absence: "The duplicitous interplay of identity and difference exposes the absence in all 'presence' by betraying the unavoidable 'presence' of absence." Citing Derrida, "'Embodiment is presence, but it is a presence which is an actual absence, the real absence of a total identity.' The disappearance of the one, a disappearance that is manifest in word and incarnate in writing, is nothing other than the death of God."[29] Gone are the one, identity, presence—sacrificed to their polar opposites. Platonism already sets up the foil: absence as ab'sence, privation; not paradoxical presence in absence and absence in presence. This "writing" is "the arising and passing away that does not itself arise and pass away," Taylor says in citing Hegel.[30] So Heraclitus is correct, and process is God, or the spacing/trace left by the death of God (which is the same thing). There is a logos, a "one," a self-identical and fully present unity to everything after all. Thus it is hardly surprising that Derrida recognizes, "We will never be finished with the reading or rereading of Hegel, and, in a certain way, I do nothing other than attempt to explain myself on this point."[31]

Like Taylor, Derrida demonstrates that he cannot live without a logos or a telos, unchanging universals—however few—upon which one can absolutely depend. First, he refers to a "messianic structure" that is at the heart of deconstruction. No matter how radically different the various options, Hegel's teleological philosophy of history embodied (or rather, disembodied) in Absolute Spirit's becoming-what-it-is; Heidegger's futurity of *Dasein*; Bultmann's "Christ-event" that isn't really an event after all; Derrida's "absolute future" of some "messianic structure," to be distinguished sharply from a particular Messiah and a definite future promised by such, are all equally inconceivable apart from their common Kantian inheritance. For instance, Derrida distinguishes between religions (which are particular and, by the way, dangerous) and "faith" (which is "absolutely universal").[32] Is this not simply Kant's distinction between "ecclesiastical faith" and "pure religion"?[33] Distinguishing "messianicity" from "messianism," he says he wants "to show *that the messianic structure is a universal structure*" (emphasis added).[34] "As soon as you reduce the messianic structure to messianism, then you are reducing the universality and this has important political consequences. Then you are accrediting one tradition among others and a notion of an elected people, of a given literal language, a given fundamentalism." He adds, "There is the general structure of messianicity, as the structure of experience," although he concedes that he is not prepared to say whether the particular versions of messianism "unveil this messianism" or whether one should begin with the general/universal "structure of experience."[35] Either way, of course, the particular is swallowed whole by the universal. Ironically, the grand "incredulity toward metanarrative" (Lyotard) appears to be violated for the sake of the metanarrative of "the universal structure of messianism." Is it possible that Derrida could return in such an obvious way to the idol of modernity, namely, the universal and eternal Logos, the Form or Idea that is sharply distinguished from any of its manifestations in the realm of appearance? The scandal of particularity seems as vexing for Derrida as it was for Kant or Plato. Ironically, even Derrida argues for a split between a true universal Idea that is recognized by universal human experience and particular religions. The universal truth that each particular religion unveils is fine, but to raise any particular religion to the status of truth is to invite reproach. All of this sounds remarkably foundationalist and modern.

What then is the Derridean concept of the "messianic," as opposed to particular messianisms? The former "has to do with the absolute structure of the promise, of an absolutely indeterminate, let us say, a structural future, a future always to-come, *a venir*. The messianic future is an absolute future, the very structure of the to-come that cannot in principle come about, the very open-endedness of the present that makes it impossible for the present to draw itself into a circle, to close in and gather around itself. . . . The non-presence of the Messiah is the very stuff of his promise."[36]

It would seem that Derrida wants to have his cake and eat it too: some sort of eschatological orientation is essential for drawing us toward the future. This is clearly at odds with the a/teleological and aneschatological position, but in order to guard against a projected telos, he insists on this promise as a "structural future" (i.e., an Idea, concept, form, not an actual particular in the realm of appearances and history). Is this *structural* future anything more than a regulative transcendental? With Derrida, Caputo not only distinguishes between "messianic time" and "ordinary historical time," but, in the pattern reminiscent of Bultmann, guards against any attempt to confuse the two. Writing almost as the Marburg neo-Kantian redivivus, Caputo asserts,

> For the coming (*venue*) of the Messiah, the messianic coming, is not to be confounded with his actual presence (*presence*) in recorded history, with occurring in ordinary time, with actually showing up in space and time, which would ruin everything. The coming of the Messiah has to do with the very structure of messianic time, as the time of promise and expectation and opening to the future. . . . The lightness of a messianic expectation, its buoyancy and agility, are not to be weighed down by the lead-footed grossness of the present.[37]

It reminds one of distinctions between the historical and the historic, *Historie* and *Geschichte*, fact and value, the universal idea and the particular event. The "buoyancy and agility" of a self-constructed reality and purpose is set against the externally imposed reality and purpose of God in history. It is Plato's two worlds, the upper register of spirit antithetically (or at least, imperfectly) projected onto the lower register of mere matter and history. Thus, Derrida's "faith without religion," as Caputo asserts, "is something 'universal,' lying at the root of our most everyday practices, not opposed to but forming the very stuff of what we like to call 'reason,' that holy name at the sound of which the knee of every *Aufklärer* and analytic philosopher, from Habermas to Ruth Marcus, must bend."[38] So there is One to whom every knee must bow after all, a Universal Truth to which everyone must submit, a metanarrative toward which we need not exercise incredulity. This indubitable universal experience is opposed to the particular and concrete claims of any particular messianic faith that would announce the arrival of the Messiah in any present/presence. "In deconstruction," Caputo writes, "the constancy of what we call 'my God' goes by other names—names like justice, hospitality, testimony, the gift—and democracy. For God is the name of the other, any other, no matter whom."[39]

But is this not the very humanism that Taylor correctly perceived as merely inverting the order of ontotheology? In other words, the Greek search for the logos, certainty concerning which the modern age made a categorical imperative? These other names of the other, are they not familiar deities in the pantheon of Universal Ideas or the Transcendental Signified? At least Justice, for Derrida, is a *Ding-an-sich*—and, to some extent, it is even a *knowable* noumenon.[40] Deconstruction "does not give content to its faith and hope, but it retains the form of faith and hope. So the 'messianic' is a weak universal."[41] Indeed, it is a universal that renders the particulars little more than expressions which, taken individually, cannot be true in the way in which the universal structure is so. Gregory Bruce Smith offers a typical advertisement for postmodernism when he says that "[p]ostmodernity requires openness to a new synthesis of the universal and the particular such that neither side can gain hegemony,"[42] but in fact deconstruction at least represents the return of the old hegemony of the universal over the particular and the ideal over the historical that is so severely criticized in its ontotheological manifestation.

So it would seem that while deconstruction is a/teleological, it is hardly aneschatological. A messianic future without a messiah, an eschatology without an eschaton: these are gestures that may leave the future open for the endless play of sign, but at the price of a vacuous concept of a "messianic structure" that does bring closure after all, promising infinite and eternal repetition of the same (viz., perpetual change). Romanticism absolutized the past; existentialism the present. And now deconstruction gives to "the future" a mysterious ineffability, a pure Idea with no content—or, at least, with no knowable content in the present. It is an eternal Platonic form or Kantian category: the future—the "messianic future [which] is an absolute future, the very structure of the to-come that *cannot in principle* come about" (emphasis added).[43]

It is Hegel without a logos, telos, or synthesis. Or is it really? Is not Nietzsche's dream every bit as utopian, teleological, synthesized, and logocentric as his rivals? Is not even "endless erring," "wandering," straying, with no particular interest in locating a passage outside of oneself to any New World, a veiled telos after all? Is it now in the self-assurance of a/theology and aneschatology that the disembodied knowing or willing agent recovers his or her precarious balance? John Milbank is correct when he argues that Derrida "remains (as he well knows) also within 'the same' of Hegel."[44] But the "end of metaphysics" is itself a metaphysics. The search for the logos does not end with Derrida, any more than it ended with Nietzsche or Heidegger. We have mentioned Gnosticism as an extreme version of the Platonist heritage and curious resemblance that modern thought—including theology—bears to it. Milbank makes the same observation in connection specifically with Heidegger and Derrida.[45]

In short, the attack on Christian theology under the shibboleth "ontotheology" reflects two misconceptions. The first is that the New Testament eschatology is shaped by, or is at least consistent with, a "Platonism for the masses." The second misunderstanding concerns the extent to which modernity (and postmodernity) often have more in common with ontological-metaphysical-epistemological dualisms than at least New Testament exegesis, if not (admittedly) some aspects of doctrine and piety influenced by Neoplatonism in the medieval synthesis. Having stated the problem, we now turn to the Pauline eschatology.

THE TWO-AGE MODEL

Far more subversive of Platonic-Cartesian-Kantian dualism than the return of Hegelian monism in its many disguises, biblical eschatology disorients and reorients.[46] It does so first by replacing the ontological and epistemological dualisms with dualisms of an entirely different kind: ethical (righteousness/ unrighteousness; sin/grace; justice/injustice) and historical ("this present age" and "the age that is to come"). Thus, it locates the meaning of history in God's purposes for creation and locates the problem of alienation in personal actions concentrated in the drive for autonomy rather than in the denigrated side of the various polarities. The danger of superficial generalization is ever present in attempts to provide contrasting typologies. Nevertheless, when, for instance, Bultmann places the Christ of faith in the category of freedom, spirit, the eternal ("Now"), the noumenal, the historic, the individual, and so forth, it is clear that this is against and not just above the Jesus of history, which belongs in the category of law, flesh, the temporal, the phenomenal, the historical, and the corporate. Even Barth retains a sharp nature-grace orientation, which makes divine activity in ordinary chronological history problematic.[47] There is a certain rigidity to ontological categories that is absent from the ethical/eschatological alternatives, especially given the New Testament writers' polemics against proto-gnostic (or at least Hellenizing) tendencies. When the New Testament writers refer, for instance, to the believer's being "seated with Christ in heavenly places" in the kingdom of grace, it is never meant to convey the impression that they are not also active citizens of the kingdoms of this world. In the scheme we are advancing, one does not have to choose between the historical and the eschatological, since they are coordinated vectors. There is often an antithesis in principle (viz., "this present age" inasmuch as it is dominated by sin) but not in essence. The antitheses that do exist are the result of concrete historical breaches in the divine-human relationship, not the product of the structures of created reality itself. Romans 8 bears this out.

As Geerhardus Vos observes,

> The idea of the creation of the world by God already is incompatible with even that qualified pessimism which is symptomatic of Gnostic speculation. Absolute pessimism would have had to attach itself within the scheme of Paul's thinking to the conception of the *sarx* and there is no evidence whatever either of the primordial origin of the *sarx* in creation or of its lasting persistence in the end. On the contrary, wherever Paul speaks of the two stages of existence he avoids the mention of the *sarx*. The real source of this so-called pessimism lies in the Apostle's acute and pervasive sense of sin. It is the burdensomeness and depressive power of sin that impels irresistibly towards the thought of hope with regard to the eschatological deliverance.[48]

Such terms as "above/heavenly" and "below/earthly" are to be understood in this sense, not in Greek abstractions. So, for instance, to set one's mind on "things above" is not to take flight from this "world of appearances" for the realm of pure spirit, but is to set one's mind on "the things that are above, *where Christ is, seated*" (Col. 3:1, emphasis added). "Above" and "below," like "transcendence" and "immanence," are analogical terms, as classical theology is fully aware when it affirms divine omnipresence. So too, "flesh" and "Spirit" in the New Testament are not to be confused with Greek or gnostic abstractions in which the corporeal is set against the spiritual. Rather, especially in the Pauline corpus, these typical categories are deconstructed and reemployed. Instead of ontological categories, they become radically "eschatologized": "Flesh" refers to self and world under the aeon of sin, judgment, and death, while "Spirit" refers specifically to the Holy Spirit, who has ushered in the era of justification and new life by raising Jesus from the dead.[49] Similarly, "visible"/"invisible" does not refer to ontic realms (i.e., matter/form, respectively), but that which is and that which is to come (Rom. 8:24–25)—*really* to come, and not just in terms of an eternal future (the futurity of *Dasein*, the messianic structure of the future, etc.).

The perspective on Pauline eschatology that I would like to outline briefly is represented best by the Reformed tradition of federal or covenantal theology and its Dutch/Dutch-American "biblical theology" movement.[50] This rise of federal theology in the sixteenth and seventeenth centuries has had a tremendous influence beyond its familiar borders and is often cited by contemporary theologians as a major resource for the recovery of eschatological reflection. Rather than seeing the Bible simply as a sourcebook for timeless truths, it was regarded as a covenant between God and God's people, orienting it to history and dramatic events interpreted by the primary actor in those events. Jürgen Moltmann observes, "This new historic understanding of revelation had its ground in the rebirth of eschatological millenarianism in the post-Reformation age. It was the start of a new, eschatological way of thinking, which called to life the feeling for history."[51] In fact, Moltmann specifically refers to Johannes Cocceius (1603–69), the Reformed theologian noted for emphasizing the historical-redemptive and eschatological structure of systematic theology.[52] Wolfhart Pannenberg has recently written, "Only in the federal theology of Johannes Cocceius does the kingdom of God come into view again as a dominant theme of salvation history and eschatology."[53]

Of these three modern theologians, Barth is the least attracted to the federal theology.[54] This is hardly surprising, given the criticisms of Moltmann and Pannenberg that Barth's own existentialism dehistoricizes eschatology from the outset. The current recovery of interest in eschatology as the very warp and woof of theology, rather than as an appendix to systematics, was anticipated in these sixteenth- and seventeenth-century Reformed thinkers and was already raised again in the Dutch (and Dutch-American) "biblical theology" movement in a highly developed form.

Moltmann has insisted that "[f]rom first to last, and not merely in the epilogue, Christianity is eschatology, is hope, forward looking and forward moving, and therefore also revolutionizing and transforming in the present. The eschatological is not an element of Christianity, but is the medium of Christian faith as such."[55] But long before the theology of hope was announced, Vos had argued, "The Bible is not a dogmatic handbook but a historical book full of dramatic interest." Revelation is subservient to redemption, apart from which the former "would be suspended in the air."[56] Similarly, Ridderbos declared that for Christianity, "it is not a dogma that is central, but the fact of redemptive history itself, which makes such announcements as justification possible. Without minimizing the importance of the former, it is not the *ordo salutis*, but the *historia salutis*, which is primary for Paul." Thus, eschatology becomes "the overpowering certainty" for the people of God.[57] To say that eschatology is the lens through which one reads Scripture is to suggest that "theology is fundamentally Christology. The whole Pauline doctrine is a doctrine of Christ and his work; that is its essence."[58] Furthermore, just as Moltmann picks out the resurrection of Christ as the key to eschatology,[59] Vos states that "through the appearance or resurrection of Christ the eschatological process has been set in motion."[60] In contrast to revelational theologies, whether shaped by positivism or existentialism, Gaffin argues,

> Revelation is not so much divinely given gnosis to provide us with knowledge concerning the nature of God, man, and the world as it is divinely inspired interpretation of God's activity of redeeming people so that they might worship and serve him in the world. . . . The deepest motive controlling the flow of the history of revelation is not instruction but incarnation. Scripture provides no basis for an intellectualistic conception of revelation or theology.[61]

Across the spectrum, preoccupation with the doctrine of revelation must be replaced with an interest in the doctrine of redemption, as it is historically effected. Having introduced the sources of this interpretation of Pauline eschatology, let us turn now to the contrast between its dualism and that of the Platonist-Kantian trajectory.

CONTRASTING DUALISMS

At the outset one may say that Hellenistic dualism is generally ontological and cosmological in nature. The *principium essendi* of this dualism is the eternal One, origin of the real—the sphere of the unchanging forms, in other words, "the true world" in contrast to the realm of temporal and mutable appearances. From this ontological dualism an epistemological dualism emerges in which the knowing subject seeks to transcend the realm of appearances (i.e., time and space) and contemplate the eternal ideas by means of recollection.

In much of modern theology, shaped by the Enlightenment, the ancient cosmology is subjected to demythologizing or deconstruction, but never its categorical framework. Hardly any figure since Plotinus has drawn such a sharp ontological and epistemological antithesis between the eternal realm of ideas (the Christ of faith encountered in the present "now") and the temporal realm of historical events (the Jesus of history) as Rudolf Bultmann. Instead of taking flight into an eternal "beyond," dialectical theology simply reinscribed transcendence within the Kierkegaardian "Moment," the flash (or, as in Barth, the tangent) in which eternity is made present for decision. In this respect, this movement bears much closer resemblance to Hellenistic dualism (including revelation as gnosis) than to Pauline eschatology.

Against Plato's irrepressible "two worlds," accentuated again in Kant, appears Paul's "two ages." Ontological dualism is replaced with eschatological dualism. Instead of the "true world" of eternal perfection versus the "apparent world" of temporal change we find "this present age" and "the age to come." This eschatological dualism appears not only in the Pauline corpus but in the Gospels as well.[62] Nevertheless, this actually becomes the systematic structure of Paul's thought. Specific reference to the two ages is found throughout his epistles. We read of the proclamation of Jesus Christ, "according to the revelation of the mystery that was kept secret for long ages but is now disclosed, and through the prophetic writings is made known to all the Gentiles" (Rom. 16:25–26). "The debater of this age" and "the wisdom of the world" are made foolish by "the wisdom of God" in the gospel. "Yet among the mature we do speak wisdom, though it is not a wisdom of this age or of the rulers of this age, who are doomed to perish. But we speak God's wisdom, secret and hidden, which God decreed *before the ages* for our glory. None of the rulers of this age understood this; for if they had, they would not have crucified the Lord of glory" (1 Cor. 1:20–21; 2:6–8, emphasis added). Satan is "the god of this world" (2 Cor. 4:4) only in an eschatological sense, viz., the "not-yet" of the consummation. After all, after his victory, Jesus Christ is raised "above every name that is named, not only *in this age* but also *in the age to come*" (Eph. 1:21, emphasis added). Before their conversion believers too were "following the course of this world . . . and were by nature children of wrath," but have been claimed by God who, "even when we were dead through our trespasses, made us alive together with Christ—by grace you have been saved—and . . . seated us with him in the heavenly places in Christ Jesus, so that *in the ages to come* he might show the immeasurable riches of his grace in kindness toward us in Christ Jesus" (Eph. 2:2–7, emphasis added). Demas is said to have deserted Paul because he was "in love with this present αἰών" (2 Tim. 4:10). In reality, then, there are three ages to Pauline eschatology: "before the ages" (1 Cor. 2:7), "in this age" (Eph. 1:21), and "in the age/s to come" (Eph. 1:21). The eternal decree ("before the ages") is realized historically in the two ages. "In the present age" believers "wait for the blessed hope and the manifestation of the glory of our great God and Savior, Jesus Christ" (Tit. 2:12–13).

It becomes clear that this two-age model is concerned not with two worlds or realms, but with two ages, one inferior to the other not for any necessary or ontological reasons but for situational and ethical ones. The fall of humankind is in no way located in creation itself, but, in Calvin's apt expression, arises "not from nature, but from the corruption of nature."[63] "This present age" is marked by rebellion against God's reign, while "the age to come" is characterized by the triumph of God over sin, death, and evil. That which happens in the present is not simply for that reason (i.e., being located "in this age") evil, for God's providence or common grace is active in upholding all things and restraining evil, and God's Spirit is creating a community of faith, hope, and love out of spiritual death. It is not "this world" of matter, transience, contingency, and so forth, that is set against "the other world" of pure spirit and apathetic bliss, but "this world-age" of human rebellion, injustice, and irresponsibility in opposition to "the age to come" in which God's reign is uncontested, the cross is transformed fully and finally into glory, and faith and hope are exchanged for sight.

Nowhere is this eschatological dualism more obviously opposed to any ontological version than in the discussion in Romans 8. In verses 1–25 alone, we find much of the list above (the dualisms of Pauline eschatology). "In Christ" there is "no condemnation," since the era of the Spirit of Christ ("life in Christ Jesus") "has set you free from the law of sin and of death." The law, weakened by the flesh, could not save, but God has done this by sending his Son. The Messiah is not "beyond good and evil," but willingly submits to the Father. In his active obedience as the Second Adam, the Servant fulfills the law on behalf of his new humanity, rather than abolishing it; redeems nature instead of eradicating it. This is nothing like the gnostic or even Platonic myth of redemption *from* external law, nature, creation, matter, history, or the like. This has nothing to do with Bultmann's opposition of the realm of the historical (cause-and-effect determinism) and the realm of the historic (existential freedom). Paul continues, "To set the mind on the flesh is death, but to set the mind on the Spirit is life and peace. For this reason the mind that is set on the flesh is hostile to God; it does not submit to God's law—indeed it cannot, and those who are in the flesh cannot please God" (vv. 6–8).

Lest anyone conclude that by "flesh" Paul means natural, physical existence as opposed to heavenly, spiritual existence, he goes on to say, "But you are not in the flesh; you are in the Spirit, since the Spirit of God dwells in you" (v. 9). Clearly, his readers were still physically alive. To be "in the Spirit" is not to be ontologically spiritual as opposed to physical, but is to be "in Christ" rather than "in Adam," to belong "to the age to come" rather than to "this present evil age," to be "children of the resurrection" of whom Jesus Christ is the "firstfruits." Furthermore, Paul has in mind not "spirit" as an abstract ontic principle but "the Spirit of God/Christ." "If the Spirit of him who raised Jesus from the dead dwells in you, he who raised Christ from the dead will give life to your mortal bodies also through his Spirit that dwells in you" (v. 11). The presence of the Spirit is the presence of Christ throughout this present evil age. Through this presence of Christ by his Spirit through Word and sacrament the age to come dawns in this age; and hope not only in God's future, but from God's future, already begins to make all things new, albeit in a sense that cannot be compared to the kingdom's consummation. Further antitheses in this passage include a spirit of slavery leading to fear versus a spirit of adoption leading to childlike dependence (v. 15), and "the sufferings of this present time" versus "the glory about to be revealed to us" (v. 18).

Implicit in Paul's nuanced eschatology is the contrast between a theology of the cross-and-resurrection and a theology of glory (i.e., an overrealized eschatology). Furthermore, not only does the antithesis fail to cut between body and spirit by emphasizing the resurrection of the body; it fails to cut between humanity and nature by emphasizing the cosmic restoration. Human alienation and pain are not due to the nonhuman natural world, but vice versa: the world is in bondage to decay because of human rebellion. But just as it suffers from solidarity with human sin, it will be liberated in solidarity with human redemption. The resurrection of Christ is the beginning of the resurrection of all of the dead and the restoration of the entire creation (vv. 20–23). Because of this, we hope (vv. 24–25).

This is not a hope that clings to the future in any general, intrinsic, or abstract manner—the futurity of *Dasein,* Derrida's "messianic structure of the future," and so forth—as if, again, there is an ontological superiority of the future. Rather, it clings to the promise of the "new thing" that God will do in the future on the basis of God's actions in the past. The age of the Spirit is not contrasted with that of the flesh, says Ridderbos, "first and foremost as an individual experience, not even in the first place as an individual reversal, but as a new way of existence which became present time with the coming of Christ. Thus Paul can say in Romans 8:9: 'But ye are not in the flesh but in the Spirit.' This being in the Spirit is not a mystical, but an eschatological, redemptive-historical category."[64] The "new creation" is not limited to an individual-existential reality, but is eschatological and cosmic throughout.

We can sympathize with Moltmann's assertion that the revelation or manifestation of Christ is an event rather than a quasignostic "eternal moment" in the present. Goethe reflects this romantic notion: "All these passing things we put up with; if only the eternal remains present to us every moment, then we do not suffer from the transcience of time. . . . Past and future it does not know. The present is its eternity."[65] So also said Hegel. Moltmann writes, "Nietzsche endeavoured to get rid of the burden and deceit of the Christian hope by seeking 'the eternal Yea of existence' in the present and finding the love of eternity in 'loyalty to the earth.' It is always only in the present, the moment, the *kairos,* the 'now,' that being itself is present in time."[66] Moltmann says that when we arrive at Kierkegaard's suggestion that "the promised 'fulness of time' is taken out of the realm of expectation that attaches to promise and history, and the 'fulness of time' is called the 'moment' in the sense of the eternal, then we find ourselves in the field of Greek thinking rather than of the Christian knowledge of God."[67] "The Christian believes," says Kierkegaard, "and thus he is quit of tomorrow." Moltmann can only reply,

> This mysticism of being, with its emphasis on the living of the present moment, presupposes an immediacy to God which the faith that believes in God on the ground of Christ cannot adopt without putting an end to the historic mediation and reconciliation of God and man in the Christ event, and so also, as a result of this, putting an end to the observation of history under the category of hope. . . . The God of the exodus and of the resurrection "is" not eternal presence, but he promises his presence and nearness to him who follows the path on which he is sent into the future. His name is not a cipher for the "eternal present."[68]

The question that one may put to Moltmann, however, is whether God's name is a cipher for the "coming future," "a God with 'future as his essential nature' (as

E. Bloch puts it)."[69] Is this not merely to reduce Being to Becoming—once more, a false synthesis founded in the first place on false antitheses?

Regardless, surely Moltmann is correct when he writes that the New Testament believer is different from the Parmenidean or Platonic contemplator: "The 'now' and 'today' of the New Testament is a different thing from the 'now' of the eternal presence of being in Parmenides, for it is a 'now' and an 'all of a sudden' in which the newness of the promised future is lit up and seen in a flash."[70] But is Moltmann's alternative here so future-oriented that it underplays the importance of past and present fulfillment? Is the only alternative to Platonic immediacy in an eternal moment simply an illumination or anticipation of a promised future? Doesn't this mean that eschatology is not really historical after all, but is simply (as in Derrida's "messianic structure of the future") a place-holder for an advent that never arrives, an optimistic version of *Waiting for Godot*? Isn't there a time when we no longer hope because everything will be fulfilled? This appears to be the argument of 1 Corinthians 13: Faith and hope are necessary for pilgrims on the way (a theology of the cross, suited to hearing the preached Word) but will vanish along with knowledge and revelation. "For now we see in a mirror, dimly, but then we will see face to face" (v. 12). A theology of glory corresponds to vision (the direct sight of the One in one's *nous*) rather than to hearing (God's mighty acts mediated in historical and material ways together with the witnessing community). Both crass identification of God with a human artifact (idolatry) and the craving for a direct sight of God in majesty (beatific vision) spring from the same source: the desire to see—without mediation—and not to hear; to possess everything now and avoid the cross. There is for this reason a sturdy link in the biblical text between idolatry and overrealized eschatologies.

Despite their diversity, the biblical writers display unanimity on the tension between the reality of the "new thing" God has done in a particular redemptive-historical era and the horizon of the "already–not yet" that is never transcended in this age. The tendency to reduce eschatology to cultural-anthropological development rendered many theologians in the twentieth century reticent to identify kairos time with chronological history, but once the contrasts are seen as ethical-eschatological rather than ontological, one may be left wondering why the Kantian a prioris ought to be allowed to determine how much of Paul—or the rest of the New Testament— is acceptable. Is there a self-referentially coherent argument for the necessity of preferring such a prioris to those presuppositions of the New Testament?

As Pauline eschatology offers no basis for any developmental utopianism, it cannot be cashed out in existentialist terms. The Parousia is not an eternal moment in the present; but neither is it an always-future event that is never made present in history. Is Moltmann's tendency at this point merely to exchange Parmenides for Heraclitus, regarding the resurrection and return of Christ as a cipher for an always-coming but never-arriving-once-and-for-all? As we have argued, this is made explicit in Derrida and M. Taylor.

In spite of these questions, Moltmann rightly insists that dialectical theology (which he argues was never dialectical, but merely paradoxical)[71] represents a "transcendental eschatology," rooted in Kant and evident in the prominent revelational theologies. For Kantianism, "[t]here can be no such thing as an intellectual knowledge of the 'last things,' since these 'objects . . . lie wholly beyond our field of vision."[72] Barth's famous statement, "Being the transcendent meaning of all moments, the eternal 'Moment' can be compared with no moment in time,"[73] can only be regarded as Gnostic, as far as Pannenberg and Moltmann are concerned.[74]

Given its view of the "eternal moment," it is not surprising that dialectical or existential theology views revelation in manifestational rather than historical terms. For Barth, revelation is "unveiling" rather than the fulfillment of divine promises: "We are all on the way to meet this manifestation of that which is. . . . What is the future bringing? *Not, once more, a turning-point in history, but the revelation of that which is. It is the future, but the future of that which the Church remembers, of that which has already taken place once and for all. The Alpha and the Omega are the same thing*" (emphasis added).[75] It is not the reconstruction of the past (Schleiermacher to Herrmann), but the presence of the past in the existential moment of an individual life that Barth appears to advocate. According to Douglas Meeks, this is precisely the answer that the Marxian thinker Ernst Bloch resisted. "Bloch devotes much of his massive writing to a search in Western and Eastern culture for the new which makes the omega qualitatively more than the alpha."[76]

Moltmann therefore seeks to demonstrate the Pauline emphasis on newness: the novum really is new. He notes,

> But if they know the Redeemer and expect the future of redemption in his name, then neither can the unredeemed state of this world of death become for them, after the fashion of Plato, a part of the insignificant world of appearance in which it is now only a matter of the demonstrating and unveiling of redemption. To be sure, the Alpha and Omega are the same as far as the Person is concerned: 'I am Alpha and Omega' (Rev. 1.8). But they are not the same where the reality of the event is concerned, for 'it doth not yet appear what we shall be' (1 Jn. 3.2) and 'the former things' are not yet passed away, nor are 'all things' yet become new. Thus we must expect something new from the future.[77]

He sees the specter of Plato in dialectical theology, but once more the eschatological "newness" seems to be *entirely* future, relevant to us in the present only as anticipation. This is the heart of his theology of hope. And, to be sure, this is an important aspect of the believer's attitude in the wilderness experience of the already and not-yet: "For who hopes for what is seen?" (Rom. 8:24). Nevertheless, the believer's experience is not all hope or anticipation of future glory for a restored cosmos. It includes incorporation into the newness that has already appeared.[78] Justification and the renewal of the inner self, together with the indwelling of the Spirit as a "deposit," are announced as part of the "already" that not only anticipates but participates in the "age to come."

Moltmann is correct to argue, against Barth and Bultmann, that the "manifestation," "revelation," and "appearance" of Jesus Christ is not merely an unveiling or self-disclosure of God or of divine information, but a new advent of God. This point was made repeatedly by Vos, Ridderbos, and their more recent interpreters, as we have seen. But in the resurrection of Jesus, God's promised future is not merely an eternal moment in the past being somehow repeated in the present (Barth), an illumination of existence (Bultmann), nor is it merely anticipation (Moltmann). It is also not merely proleptic (Pannenberg). In contrast to all reductionism, Pauline eschatology insists that this new age actually *arrives* in Christ as "the firstfruits," the beginning of a full cosmic salvation:

> This is the new, overpowering certainty, that in the crucified and risen Savior the great turning-point has come. This is the main theme of Paul's ministry and epistles. 'Old things are passed away; behold, they are become new' (2 Cor. 5:17). What in very ancient times had been made manifest, brought to light (2 Tim. 1:10; Col. 1:6; Rom. 16:26). And of this 'fullness of the times' (Gal. 4:4), of this *now* of the day of salvation (2 Cor. 6:2), Paul is the herald (Eph. 3:2ff.).[79]

Pneumatology, christology, ecclesiology, theology proper, and all other loci are radically affected (and, as we will pursue in a later chapter, reintegrated) in this eschatological vision.

The manifestation of Jesus "in these last days" is "not, in the first place, made known as a noetic piece of information, but has appeared as an historical event," said Ridderbos.[80] It is ironic that despite Barth's criticism of Bultmann and others for allowing an anthropocentric starting point, the existentialist "Now"—which is the immediate present of the individual self in its innermost subjectivity—takes precedence and is even set over and against the Pauline "now" of historical events with cosmic significance. "When the approach is made from man," Ridderbos observed, "then it is no more the analysis of the history of redemption in Jesus Christ which reveals the real existence of man, but it is the analysis of man in his actual situation which serves as the criterion for what is acceptable in the history of salvation."[81]

It is clear in Paul's writings that the "new" that has come is not merely anticipatory or revelatory, but effective.[82] The resurrection of Jesus Christ has begun to make all things new—not simply to return creation to a pristine origin, but to take a redeemed people and a redeemed creation into a newness that has continuity with the past but is clearly different from anything in the past. In raising Jesus from the dead, the Spirit has granted life to the forerunner who then, by the Spirit, grants this life to his coheirs.[83] The resurrection of Jesus and the resurrection of believers at the end of the age ought not, then, to be regarded as two separate events, but as the beginning and consummation of one single event.[84] In 2 Corinthians 4:16 "the outer man is said to be decaying, while the inner man (cf. Rom. 7:22; Eph. 3:16) is being renewed daily," writes Gaffin. "In effect, then, Paul is saying: the resurrection of the inner man is past; the resurrection of the outer man is still future (cf. v. 14). This should not be understood, however, in the sense of an anthropological dualism. Rather the dual aspect of the *whole* man is in view."[85] The dualism, once more, is eschatological rather than ontological, since the whole person lives "in Christ," "in the Spirit," dominated by the age to come, and yet is still sinful and dogged by voluntary capitulation to "this evil age," which once was the believer's habitat. No less than the soul, the body is called to participate in this new creation even now.[86] The flesh-Spirit antithesis "is not to be taken as a metaphysical or anthropological, but as a redemptive-historical, contrast, namely, as the two dominating principles of the two aeons marked off by the appearance of Christ."[87] The already and not-yet structure of individual salvation (*simul iustus et peccator*) also defines the nature of cosmic redemption: In the resurrection of Christ it is not only the case that the promised future has been anticipated, justified, or proleptically unveiled, but that it has appeared and is already at work in making all things new, from the inside out. Captives freed from sin and judgment are now already justified and are being renewed after the image of the Firstborn from the dead. This eschatological dualism cancels out all rival dualisms that might even employ the same terminology (viz., flesh vs. Spirit). The resurrection of Jesus Christ by the Spirit is effecting a new creation—literally, from the inside out. Thus, there is duality without dualism in the modern sense of antithesis.

Even in supposedly eschatological theologies, it is difficult to find this emphasis. For instance, neo-Kantian theology affirmed Platonic dualism with the strict apposition of *Historie* and *Geschichte*, categories that are entirely absent in the New Testament. Pannenberg seeks to reconcile an alleged apocalyptic and eschatological antithesis. Similarly, Moltmann regards chiliasm (oriented toward a messianic age) and apocalypticism (oriented to eternity) as the two antithetical poles that must be dialectically related in order to avoid either utopian extremism or flights from this world altogether into the transcendent "beyond."[88] But these gestures assume that the Pauline eschatology is far less synthesized than it actually is, as if it required the imposition of external categories to organize the data and keep it in proper balance.

THE HARMONY OF DEVELOPMENT (CHRONOS) AND INTRUSION (KAIROS)

Paul does not regard redemptive-history as a noumenal "history" (i.e., *Geschichte*), nor as a myth that, once deconstructed, illumines our personal existence. Regardless of how one might judge his assertions, Paul is convinced that there is one diachronic time-line leading from creation through the fall and the protoevangelion, on to Abraham and Sarah, exodus, wilderness, conquest, and the Davidic theocracy, through the Babylonian exile, up to the birth of Jesus "in the fullness of time."[89] Note, for instance, the "system" that is already clearly present in Paul, when he introduces the epistle to the Romans with reference to "the gospel of God, which he promised beforehand through his prophets in the holy scriptures, the gospel concerning his Son, who was descended from David according to the flesh and declared to be Son of God with power according to the spirit of holiness by resurrection from the dead, Jesus Christ our Lord" (Rom. 1:1–4). It is not as if Jesus is described as "descended from David according to the flesh" [tou genomenou ek spermatos David kata sarka] but vindicated by the Spirit in any number of nonhistorical "events," as one might have expected in a gnostic use of flesh-spirit, but by a bodily resurrection on the same plane of history (chronos) as the Davidic lineage. Furthermore, this time line connects the past to the present and the future through the gift of the Spirit, whose "new creation" work makes all believers—present and future—in some sense Paul's contemporaries.[90]

Recent theologians have correctly observed that the recovery of interest in the historical and eschatological character of revelation and redemption among the post-Reformation federal theologians, in the hands of pietists and *philosophes,* was transformed into the modern view of history as linear progress. However, this development should not discourage us from the covenantal eschatology itself. For the dialectic that Moltmann and (to a lesser extent) Pannenberg seek, but in our estimation fall short of attaining, was already present and systematized in Paul's thought. So, once more, "heaven" and "earth," "invisible" and "visible," "above" and "below," become eschatologized and "christologized."

Vos argues:

> What gives rise to misunderstanding at this point is the confusion of eschatological two-sidedness with the philosophical bisection of the universe into a higher and lower sphere. . . . Heaven, so to speak, has received time and history into itself. Herein lies the inner significance of the repatriation of Christ into heaven, carrying thither with Himself all the historical time-matured fruit of his earthly stage of work, and now from there guiding with impartial solicitude the two lines of terrestrial and celestial development of his Church. Besides the Christ, the Spirit holds the two aspects of the Christian's double life-process together.[91]

Such a view "stands at a far remove from Greek philosophical dualism. . . . Its mother-soil lies in eschatological revelation, not in metaphysical speculation."[92] While God transcends time, "Paul nowhere affirms that to the life of man after the close of this aeon, no more duration, no more divisibility in time-units shall exist." That would constitute the deification of the inhabitants of the future aeon.[93] So gone is the time vs. eternity antithesis, along with the kindred components of Platonic dualism that have too often been confused with Christian eschatology by friend and foe alike.

So for Paul, history is not steady, rational development, culminating in a golden age that unfolds immanently from the preceding historical epochs. But he is no nearer to Dionysus than to Apollo. If the former represents the immanent-teleological approach to history, the latter is the rather popular denial of meaning and purpose in history altogether after the failures of secular eschatologies. Dionysus announces "the end of history" in the wake of the death of both God and the self. But Paul proclaims the progress of redemption that is not only linear advance (and certainly is not an immanent teleology) but is a real deliverance only because of vertical intrusions.

This is why Vos spoke of the horizontal and vertical dimensions. It is not the eschatological and the apocalyptic, nor the chiliastic and the messianic, nor any other pair of structural opposites whose dialectical imposition upon an otherwise unsystematic body of data brings order out of chaos. It is not as if, for instance, eschatology requires the "already" dynamism of the chiliastic and the "not-yet" transcendent orientation in order to avoid extremes (*pace* Pannenberg and Moltmann). Paul already has a way of talking about eschatology that is neither this-worldly nor otherworldly, neither pure historical progress nor hypersupernaturalism. The progress of redemption moves forward not because of any seeds of progress immanent within history itself, but neither do redemptive events represent existential or purely noumenous tangents that may have, to borrow from Bultmann, historic (i.e., existential) but not historical significance. "Above" and "below" are not superior and inferior realms but, like Spirit and flesh, represent that eschatological newness promised and effected in Christ versus being under the dominion of the old aeon.

The "age to come," then, is not only horizontal/chronological, but also vertical/cataclysmic. As Hans Frei insisted concerning biblical narrative, there is no need to try to get underneath, above, or behind the New Testament eschatology in general or the Pauline treatment in particular.[94]

Moltmann notes Pannenberg's reduction of eschatology to history, while for Barth and Bultmann, "It is not history that puts an end to eschatology; it is eschatology that puts an end to history."[95] Bultmann's demythologization project rested on his audience's assumption that their own individual existence was the center of the universe. Why indeed should there be anything beyond this existential relation? It is hardly any wonder that Bultmann could pit the "Christ of faith" against the "Jesus of history." "This supraindividual horizon of hope can then only be called mythological if one has no concern for the conditions over which this horizon spans its bow. The resignation which confines people to their own selves can hardly be called Christian." This eternal moment paradox, Moltmann concludes, is nothing less than mysticism.[96] Yet, ironically, the modern worldview renders New Testament cosmological assumptions obsolete.[97] "The apocalyptic eschatology which Bultmann considered 'mythical' is more realistic than his faith in the inexorable onward course of world history. The belief that things will 'always go on' and that no end is in sight—at least for us—is one of the fairytales of 'the modern world,' the fairytale of its endlessness and its lack of an alternative. That is secularized millenarianism."[98] Apart from this Pauline eschatology, reversion to traditional dualisms (however much attempts are made to relate them dialectically) is certain. Even Moltmann ends up reinstating Plato's two worlds in his discussion of time and the eschaton: "For Christ surely does not come 'in time'; he comes to transform time. The reduction of eschatology to time in the framework of salvation history also really abolishes eschatology altogether, subjecting it to *chronos*, the power of transience. Is 'temporality' really 'the essence of eschatology' [Cullmann]?"[99]

But why the either-or again? Why must one choose between either the reduction of eschatology to chronos or dispensing with chronos as the linear plane of fulfillment? Does Moltmann's resistance to chronos simply because it is "the power of transcience" reveal a lingering sympathy for Platonic-Kantian categories? We still see signs of the dominance of the modern antitheses, when he places in antithesis advent and chronological history. Paul, on the other hand, uses *kairos* and *chronos* interchangeably.[100] Moltmann regards the eschaton as "neither the future of time nor timeless eternity," but as "God's coming and his arrival." But what does it mean for "God" to arrive if this God's presence in history is only in the future mode, as he insists?[101]

Against Nietzsche's Dionysian eschatology, Moltmann rightly reminds us that any view of eternal recurrence voids hope, the possibility of something genuinely new.[102] Nevertheless, it is not clear whether this novum is more than the mode of God's existence, a new flight to the "other world" under the name of the future or, more precisely, "God's coming." Yet biblical eschatology is not ashamed of chronological, historical time. Without it, "the future" is, like Kierkegaard's "Moment," simply another name for an eternal idea, the "other world"—the "real world"—which is contrasted with the realm of nature, appearances, and history. Gunton is right when he concludes, "As a mere abstraction, empty of actual or promised content, the future is a much overrated realm."[103] Reading Isaiah in the synagogue, Jesus announced, "Today this scripture has been fulfilled in your hearing" (Luke 4:21). The dynamism of the redemptive-historical eschatology is underscored here as elsewhere: the Word *became* flesh; the old really did pass away to make room for the advent of the "new thing"; the shadows gave way to the reality that was not an eternal or static idea, principle, or power, but was the physical descendant of Abraham and Sarah. There is a time for preparation (John the Baptist), a time for deliverance ("these last days"), and a time of judgment and consummation ("the last day"). Revelation, including its doctrinal and ethical deliverances, must be seen as subservient to the temporal history of redemption, not vice versa. The transcience of this stage upon which the drama is played out is precisely what makes it possible for the fading dominance of tragedy to give way to the play—not of aimless drifters in a chaotic realm of purposeless change, but that play which can only belong to "the glorious freedom of the children of God." The last day will end this age with neither a bang nor a whimper, but with a teeming chorus of creation around that image of dialectical irony that persists in the age to come: the triumphant Lamb.

THE POWER OF THE CROSS

In our analysis we have not attempted to exonerate the Christian churches from their captivity to power regimes that subverted human wholeness. Nor are we interested in launching into an argument with Nietzsche's successors over the legacy of Christian conviction and action in the social sphere.

But if Christian eschatology must refuse to be exploited by "the powers and principalities" that dominate the horizon of "this age" in terms of either sanctioning utopia or standing in its way, it must also resist the pressing temptation to abandon history, meaning, purpose, and design by an infinite-personal God who establishes covenantal relationships. It must refuse false antitheses and false syntheses. Hans Blumenberg's observation of the "connection between the modern and Gnosticism" (*The Legitimacy of the Modern*, 99) finds its echo in Hans Jonas (*The Gnostic Religion*, epilogue), and is now repeated in connection with postmodern varieties.

Colin Gunton, for instance, has argued that the displacement of God by humanity and therefore of eschatology by human attainment has left the contemporary person with a "pathological inability to live in the present, while at the same time, as in the consumer culture, it is unable to live anywhere but in the present. Both arms of the paradox alike derive from a gnostic denial of the goodness of creation." Gunton adds the following:

> The anxiety to bring the future about is the cause of the frantic rush that is one mark of the modern failure to live serenely in time. . . . Orientation to a divinely promised future sets human life in context, and is by no means a disincentive to appropriate use of the world. (We should remember Luther's remark that if he knew that the end of the world was coming tomorrow, his response would be to plant a tree.) What mainstream mediaeval eschatology lacked was rather a sense of the interweaving of the times: a way in which the divinely order of destiny of life could, by the work of the Spirit, be anticipated in the present.[104]

If modernity can be characterized by an eschatology of utopia leading to despair, its postmodern successors may find themselves distinguished only by their lustful Nietzschean embrace of this condition rather than the Schopenhauerian resignation that Nietzsche and his disciples have identified with Christianity. Both the modern utopian and the postmodern "active nihilist" share a common metanarrative: "this fading age." The reign of the autonomous self, whether conceived in terms of reason, consciousness, or will, cannot help but end in either resignation or triumphalism.

Only the theology of the cross produces the sort of eschatology that advocates planting a tree (Luther)—neither escaping nature nor conquering nature, but leading the chorus of nature in groaning for the consummation. It begins not from an ontological-cosmological dualism, but an ethical-eschatological one; not from spirit vs. nature, or from any intrinsic fallenness or "thrownness" of human existence, but from the corruption of nature by human rejection of God's reign. In the Genesis narrative, Adam and Eve, along with their progeny, are banished not from the earth, but from Eden. Yet one day, not merely one geopolitical region, but "all the earth shall be filled with the glory of the LORD" (Num. 14:21).

The Christian hope is therefore neither resignation to "the way things are," since God is always on the move, nor mastery, since neither nature nor history is ours to control. The definitive power for the Christian community is neither Apollo (resignation to defeat) nor Dionysus ("the will to power") but the Lamb who was slain for others but now is alive for others. The Savior announced by the prophets and apostles is neither the meek moralist nor the evil genius, but the Creator who redeems. In contrast to the insipid form of Christianity that formed Nietzsche's caricature, the voluntary humiliation of the Servant served an eschatological goal rather than simply exhibiting an eternal principle. If the theology of the cross and its eschatology were mere instances of general sentimentalism concerning weakness over strength, flight from reality into another realm of tranquil apatheia, Nietzsche's charges could be sustained. There is no basis here for a general creed of "power through weakness," a sort of "nice folks finish first" philosophy of life. It is a certain kind of power and a certain kind of weakness defined by the narrative fabric and its specific redemptive-historical, eschatological plot. Throughout the Gospels, the New Adam is tempted with the theology of glory—power and autonomy, Peter himself being identified with Satan for trying to distract Jesus from the cross. No one takes his life; he willingly lays it down in order to take it back up again (John 10).

Nietzsche's description of Christianity may have been accurate not only in terms of the liberal pietism of his day, but in describing the despair and resignation of the disciples after the crucifixion. But, according to the witnesses themselves, their defeatism was due to their broken triumphalism, and in that community gathered around the resurrection of Jesus, the Holy Spirit introduced into the world a new form of power that cannot be reduced to Nietzsche's simplistic categories. It is neither resignation nor self-indulgence, but the power that, precisely in the appearance of its weakness (indeed, failure by the standards of this age), finally breaks the power of that very exploitive dominion that Nietzsche celebrated. In this respect, however, at least Nietzsche was consistent, often unlike his disciples.[105] For Nietzsche, there really can be no ultimate irony to human striving, as one finds so clearly expressed in the New Testament. Like Paul's audience, with whom Nietzsche sympathized, the cross remains "foolishness to Greeks." The irony had already been lost in liberal moralism. Nor, in Nietzsche's proposal, can there be any genuine dialectic, since (for Nietzsche, as a disciple of Hegel) Dionysus simply swallows Apollo whole.

Marx and Foucault have done much to strip the veils of pretension from the face of modernity, exposing the Dionysian and carnivorous character of "the will to power." As Miroslav Volf reminds us, Christianity is not committed to powerlessness, but to a certain kind of power that opposes other kinds of power. "Theology as reflection on the word of the cross must be embodied in the community of the cross whose particular kind of weakness is a new kind of power inserted into the network of the powers of the world."[106] Volf's brief treatment here is highly suggestive of a link between this analysis of power and the interest of this redemptive-historical method in retrieving the theology of the cross in the face of so many versions of the theology of glory. An underrealized eschatology (the cross without the resurrection; Christ without the Spirit; judicial reconciliation

without ethical transformation) may be an unbalanced version of Pauline eschatology and may be corrected by attention to the "already" that has dawned in
Christ's victory. However, a theology of glory cannot be corrected by the internal biblical witness except by contradiction. The dialectic of cross and resurrection, encompassing both advents of the Messiah, never arrives at a synthesis until
the consummation. In that sense, Pauline eschatology is far more dialectical than
so-called "dialectical theology."

From the dawning of the new creation in the resurrection of Jesus, we have
confidence in a final victory of the Other over the genuine source of alienation:
personal and corporate sin and guilt.[107] It is this confidence, anchored in the resurrection, that provides the triumphant indicative for a baptism into the age to
come. Far from embodying resignation or the repudiation of power, the reign of
Christ in grace is just as much of a "power regime" as the reign of Christ in glory.
In Word and sacrament, "the age to come" is not just anticipated, symbolized, or
represented, but already begins to dawn (Heb. 6:5). It is the reality of the cross
and of the bondage of the whole creation to decay because of the curse that keeps
that which already participates in the life of God groaning, longing, straining forward, and hoping for the announcement at the end of chronological history,
"The kingdom of the world has become the kingdom of our Lord and of his Messiah, and he will reign forever and ever" (Rev. 11:15). Whether we call contemporary anxiety Gnosticism, the theology of glory, or "modernity," a fresh interface
with biblical eschatology will invite relief from the burdensome (and dangerous)
pretensions of autonomy ("ye shall be as gods") and escort restless wanderers into
the Sabbath of God.

Taking Romans 8 as our clue once more, we find an eschatology that involves
both the vertical (cataclysmic) and horizontal (chronological), or the synchronic
(irruption from "above") and the diachronic (the fulfillment of redemptive history in an unfolding plot).[108] Unlike the theology of vision, the theology of
pilgrims on the way never surrenders—even to "paradox"—the *dialectic* of transcendence and immanence; grace and nature; miracle and providence; the
"already" and the "not-yet"; the renewal of the individual soul as well as the resurrection of the body and a transformation of the created world even beyond its
origin. Unlike many modern eschatologies, it denies immanent teleologies; but
unlike many postmodern "aneschatologies," it affirms a direction and a consummation whose exact and univocal description remains a divine secret. When theologies of glory buckle under their own utopian weight, it is not surprising that
theologies of despair and, eventually, theologies of a/theology emerge. But not
even Derrida escapes metaphysics or metanarrative, logos or telos. It could lead
to tragic consequences if exploitation of Christian eschatology were simply
replaced with a denial of the dialectic that we have been considering. Without
promises that somehow have a normative, definitive status, and a cognitive,
knowable, constitutive context, there can be neither future nor history, but mere
chronology. There cannot even be the triumph of Dionysus over Apollo, but
merely of Sisyphus over Prometheus.

THE ETHICS OF PAULINE ESCHATOLOGY

Like ancient Gnosticism, there is both an antinomian and a legalistic form of nihilism, which we might associate with Nietzsche's Dionysus and Apollo, respectively. But both are more alike than either is similar to the Pauline eschatology. Both engender irresponsibility toward the other—beginning with the divine Other, but including the human and nonhuman other. Neither selfish flight from "this glorious theater" (Calvin) nor self-indulgence can theoretically coexist with the Pauline eschatology. In an age especially marked by alienation from nature and unrelenting consumption, involving the reduction of God, neighbor, and world to products to be used (eros), the apparent foolishness of the cross and the apparent weakness of its power (agape) bring welcome relief from its messianic rivals. According to Taylor, as we have seen, theological deconstruction celebrates the nomad—endless erring. In contrast to modern optimism, the New Testament eschatology actually concurs, but identifies this as the condition of sin, the dominion of the self opposed to the liberating reign of the Holy Spirit. The new person is not on a pilgrimage from this world to another, but from this world under the reign of unrighteousness to the newness that has already dawned in Jesus Christ.

The new eschatological perspective of those who are baptized into Christ is that of a pilgrim, rather than that of either a settler or a nomad. Joining the *communio sanctorum*, they are confident in the future that they have been promised and already enjoy in a definitive and progressive sense. But while there is a destination that is actually reached in linear time—"at the end of the age"—they never exchange the cross for conquest before that decisive future event when both the Apollonian and Dionysian masses behold that tragicomic incongruity of a lamb who was slain seated triumphantly on a throne.

PART ONE
GOD ACTS IN HISTORY

Brian Hebblethwaite notices, "The topic of divine action in the world has rightly come to occupy centre stage in both doctrinal and philosophical theology."[1] This is not the place for a full treatment of divine providence and the relation of God's sovereignty and human agency. Nevertheless, some meandering into that field is necessary for our account. Our focus is limited to *special* divine action rather than to general providence. This section will (1) state the problem; (2) interact with possible solutions; (3) propose a model of divine action that defends a double agency by especially drawing on speech-act theory; and (4) draw out the hermeneutical implications for theology.

Chapter Two

A God Who Acts?

Perhaps the most important theological affirmation that modern biblical theology draws from the Scripture is that God is he who acts, meaning by this that God does unique and special actions in history. And yet when we ask: "All right, what has he done?" no answer can apparently be given.[1]

The question as to how history and salvation can be related without either being diminished may be regarded as of central importance in contemporary theology.[2]

Some time now has passed since Langdon B. Gilkey's provocative essay in which he observed, "My own confusion results from what I feel to be the basic posture, and problem, of contemporary theology: it is half liberal and modern, on the one hand, and half biblical and orthodox, on the other, i.e., its world view or cosmology is modern, while its theological language is biblical and orthodox."[3] At first, the biblical theology movement seemed to breathe new life into the traditional Christian insistence on divine activity in actual history, even after Rudolf Bultmann's well-known rebuttals. Providing a via media for those who still wanted to affirm something important in Christian historical claims, while continuing to share the higher-critical assumptions concerning the reliability of the biblical reports, biblical theology from Oscar Cullmann to G. E. Wright has affirmed divine action on a single historical time line, but without (at least in Wright's case) affirming what the nature of such action might be. With especially Wright in mind, Gilkey charged biblical theology with double-talk. Although its model is revelation as the recital of divine acts in human history,[4] the movement never could bring itself to affirm that such action—central to its understanding of theology—ever actually occurred.

STATEMENT OF THE PROBLEM

Conceptualizing divine action has been complicated by questions very much at the heart of modern experience: (1) scientific progress, (2) the reality and priority of human agency in modernity, (3) the heightened attention given to theodicy since the Holocaust. In this section we will outline the problem on the first two counts and then discuss the problem of evil in sections two and three.

Bultmann voiced the attitude of many theologians and biblical scholars of his generation when he encountered what he could perceive only as an insurmountable obstacle, namely, the "mythological thinking" that regards divine activity as "an action which intervenes between the natural, or historical, or psychological course of events; it breaks and links them at the same time. The divine causality is inserted as a link in the chain of events which follow one another according to the causal nexus."[5] The modern believer finds himself or herself ineluctably committed to the modern worldview in which such alien causalities are incomprehensible. Sharing Bultmann's fundamental concerns, Gilkey pointed out that the modern worldview rendered the orthodox view of divine self-manifestation problematic on two counts: first, it clashed with the putative sovereignty of natural law (specifically, causation), and, second, "[s]pecial revelation denied that ultimately significant religious truth is universally available."[6] While neo-orthodox theologies have reacted against liberalism's "emphasis on the universal and immanent as against the special and objective activity of God, they have *not* repudiated the liberal insistence on the causal continuum of space-time experience."[7]

The biblical writers and premodern interpreters like Calvin simply take it for granted that God did and said what the Bible says God said and did. But moderns, by and large, don't believe that the Hebrews were on any causal continuum different from our own. Miracles did not and do not happen on the surface of temporal history. So the narratives must be explained as analogical (without any clear definition of that to which they are apt analogies) rather than univocal in communicating what God "said" and "did." Further, our humanitarian ethics render it quite impossible to believe that God could have commanded the destruction of other nations. "Put in the language of contemporary semantic discussion, both the biblical and the orthodox understanding of theological language was univocal."[8]

But in modern theology univocal understanding is traded in for analogical, mythological, or symbolic truth. Biblical theology promised, however, to take theology beyond liberalism. Yet, Gilkey charged, the movement has failed to believe its own claim concerning "God who acts." "First, the divine activity called the 'mighty deeds of God' is now restricted to one crucial event, the Exodus-covenant complex of occurrence."[9] But then, even this founding event is interpreted as Israel's expression of what essentially was a natural event, namely, the crossing of the Sea of Reeds by the serendipitous offices of "the East wind blowing over the Reed Sea."[10] "Thus the Bible is a book descriptive not of the acts of God but of Hebrew religion."[11] "If, therefore, Christian theology is to be the recitation in faith of God's mighty acts, it must be composed of confessional and systematic statements of the form: 'We believe that God did so and so,' and not composed of statements of biblical theology of the form: 'The Hebrews believed that God did so and so.'"[12] Gilkey contrasts early Protestant union of biblical and systematic theology with modern theology:

> At the Reformation, therefore, statements in biblical theology and in systematic theology coalesced because the theologian's understanding of what God did was drawn with no change from the simple narratives of Scripture, and because the verbs of the Bible were thus interpreted univocally throughout. Thus in Reformation theology, if anywhere, the Bible 'speaks its own language' or 'speaks for itself' with a minimum of theological mediation.[13]

But biblical theologians like G. E. Wright assert "the Hebrews knew no miracles" and that these events which they regarded as miraculous were like any other natural phenomenon, but faith interpreted them (*made* them!) supernatural. Here, the "fact" is immaterial to the "value." Neo-orthodoxy attacks the immanence orientation of liberalism.

> And yet at the same time, having castigated the liberals, who at least knew what their fundamental theological principles were, we proclaim that our real categories are orthodox: God acts, God speaks, and God reveals. Furthermore, we dodge all criticism by insisting that, because biblical and Christian ideas of God are "revealed," they are, unlike the assumptions and hypotheses of culture and of other religions, beyond inspection by the philosophical and moral criteria of man's general experience. What has happened is clear: because of our modern cosmology, we have stripped what we regard as "the biblical point of view" of all its wonders and voices. This in turn has emptied the Bible's theological categories of divine deeds and divine revelations of all their univocal meaning, and we have made no effort to understand what these categories might mean as analogies. . . . Consequently, biblical theology is left with a set of theological abstractions, more abstract than the dogmas of scholasticism, for these are concepts with no known concreteness.[14]

From such questions as these raised by Gilkey's landmark essay the so-called "biblical theology" movement never recovered, although it did elicit a cottage industry of interest in theories of divine agency throughout the sixties to the present.[15] As the metanarrative of modernity disintegrates, including the remarkably naïve view of modern science which Bultmann seems to have adopted, the possibility—indeed, need—for a fresh account of traditional Christian claims concerning divine action is in order. Gilkey was certainly correct in suggesting that the ever-expanding rift between biblical and systematic theology has a lot to do with whether one takes the biblical declarations concerning actual historical events in a straightforward manner.

However, Gilkey was wrong to contrast the Reformers of the sixteenth century with modern theologians in reference to univocal and analogical or equivocal

predication, respectively. First of all, it is not as if the biblical writers and orthodox systematicians were naïve with respect to this distinction. If all theological
language is one flat line of univocity, then why is there so much diversity in genre
in scripture? Surely the Psalms know something like that difference as they incor-
porate both matter-of-fact recitals of redemptive history and doxological anthems
with anthropomorphism and other figures. They knew what they were doing and
assumed that readers would as well. As for the orthodox, this very distinction was
stock-in-trade across the Roman Catholic and Protestant lines, and there was a
basic consensus among both that all predications concerning God in scripture are
necessarily analogical and not univocal. It does not help to ameliorate the crisis
if we oversimplify the options. One may still have no interest in thinking or
speaking in the same terms as biblical and orthodox writers, but one should not
overlook the remarkable sophistication of premodern hermeneutics.[16]

Gilkey demonstrates confusion on both the premodern and modern use of
the terms "univocal" and "analogical" when he writes that "the biblical and orthodox understanding of theological language was univocal" and that "the words 'act'
and 'speak' were used in the same sense of God as of men." As we will observe in
another place, this shows a surprising unfamiliarity with the clearly stated positions of medieval scholastics, the Reformers, and their own scholastic successors.
For instance, the rule that in all analogies between creator and creature "no similarity can be found so great but that the dissimilarity is greater" was not generated by a modern rejection of univocity, but was produced by the Fourth Lateran
Council in 1215.[17] So when Gilkey says that "[t]he denial of wonders and voices
has thus shifted our theological language from the univocal to the analogical,"[18]
he can only mean that the denial of wonders and voices has shifted our theological language from the literal to the mythological or symbolic (or some other form
of equivocal discourse). It is clear that he equates *univocal* with *literal*. Given this
assumption, he understandably concludes, "Unless one knows in some sense
what the analogy means, how the analogy is being used, and what it points to,
an analogy is empty and unintelligible; that is, it becomes equivocal language."[19]
More recently, Wolfhart Pannenberg has raised this concern with greater preci-
sion and familiarity with the notion and use of analogical discourse in theology
and has actually concluded that theological language is equivocal.[20] As we will
see when offering our own account, the analogical option has a respected pedigree in theology long before the Enlightenment.

Gilkey apparently concludes with Bultmann that the modern person can no
longer accept the cosmology of the biblical and orthodox worldview and that one
can avoid schizophrenia only by falling out on one side or other of the liberal-
orthodox divide. We recall Bultmann's famous declaration, "It is impossible to
use electric light and the wireless and to avail ourselves of modern medical and
surgical discoveries, and at the same to believe in the New Testament world of
daemons and spirits. We may think we can manage it in our own lives, but to
expect others to do so is to make the Christian faith unintelligible and unac-
ceptable to the modern world."[21] Its non sequitur character has not stunted the

progress of this assumption. Not surprisingly, it is not a theologian but a sociologist who observed the tendency of modern theologians to relativize and historicize the past, but never their own present and its "givens." Berger describes this double standard and then notes that the sociological "is" of any given moment is hardly a criterion:

> In other words, it may be conceded that there is in the modern world a certain type of consciousness that has difficulties with the supernatural. The statement remains, however, on the level of socio-historical diagnosis. The diagnosed condition is not thereupon elevated to the status of an absolute criterion; the contemporary situation is not immune to relativizing analysis. We may say that contemporary consciousness is such and such; we are left with the question of whether we will assent to it. We may agree, say, that contemporary consciousness is incapable of conceiving of either angels or demons. We are still left with the question of whether, possibly, both angels and demons go on existing despite this incapacity of our contemporaries to conceive of them.[22]

Furthermore, critics who argue the incapacity of our contemporaries to conceive of the supernatural do not appear to be terribly aware of the indestructibility of religious consciousness in every culture, including a resurgent supernaturalism (or at least affirmations of divine action in the world) in the scientific West. It is clearly not the case that modern people cannot conceive of such possibilities, but that many are prejudiced against accepting such possibilities. As Nancey Murphy, John Polkinghorne, and a growing circle of scholars on the converging boundaries of science and theology now argue, modern theology has been significantly dependent for its horizons on a scientific paradigm that is increasingly challenged in the light of new discoveries.[23] William P. Alston is correct when he asserts, "Gilkey, again, is typical of theologians of his stripe in simply appealing to the widespread acceptance of the position. . . . A rational person will want to know, not just that the assumption is widely accepted, but what reasons, if any, there are for this widespread acceptance."[24]

Bultmann and Gilkey, however, have accurately summarized the presuppositional difficulties of modern theologians (at once positivists in science and subjectivists in religion) for insisting upon the extramundane intrusion into the causal nexus. Furthermore, they have presented a challenge to both biblical-theological moderates and conservatives that must be addressed. Most of the criticisms leveled against the biblical theology movement of the fifties and sixties could equally apply to narrative or postliberal theologians for whom divine action in history is *thematically* central but also *actually* problematic. It would be quite irresponsible for a contemporary theologian simply to assume the biblical-orthodox outlook (viz., the insistence upon assimilation into "the strange new world of the Bible") without providing some account that takes the criticisms of modernity seriously. To do that, we now turn to the discussion of some of the leading modern candidates for a solution to this impasse. And in concluding we will propose our own analogical account. The modern problem with divine action is at least in part parallel to the modern problem with a caricature of classical ontology in which God is the *ens summum*. A being among beings, a cause among causes. But both problems stem from a misunderstanding or naïveté concerning the classical position, a failure to understand or appreciate the role of analogical discourse.

INTERACTING WITH POSSIBLE SOLUTIONS

At the risk of oversimplifying the options, we will concede to brevity by outlining five general categories of answers to the question of special divine action. Accordingly, the predication of divine action in history is understood in one of the following ways: (1) as the mythological, symbolic, or metaphorical manner of speaking that conceals a revelatory encounter; (2) as the community's interpretation of a natural occurrence; (3) as a reference to the narrative itself rather than to extratextual "realities"; (4) as the ordinary effect of divine embodiment in the world in which all events are simultaneously the products of divine agency and human agency; (5) as the extraordinary effect of divine volition in which God acts either directly or indirectly within the causal structure of human existence. Variations within each category will be noted.

(1) Mythological-Symbolic-Metaphorical Interpretation

"In short, the letter is not the spirit, and the Bible is not religion. Consequently, objections to the letter and to the Bible are not also objections to the spirit and to religion." Such sentiments are hardly surprising, coming from Gotthold Lessing, who made axiomatic for modern rationalists his dictum, "accidental truths of history can never become the proof of necessary truths of reason."[25] In particular, Lessing criticizes the resurrection of Jesus, not for its lack of historical credibility, but for the weakness of history as a category of compelling value for reason.[26] "That, then, is the ugly, broad ditch which I cannot get across, however often and however earnestly I have tried to make the leap."[27]

Modern theology is in large measure a captive to this problem, rooted in a dualism ever present in the rationalist (especially Platonist) tradition of Western thought and brought into sharp antithesis in Descartes. As Henry Chadwick observes,

> Lessing's antithesis between the "accidental truths of history" and the "necessary truths of reason" foreshadows the language of German idealism. For Fichte (deeply influenced by Lessing), "only the metaphysical can save, never the historical." And for Kant before him, "the historical can serve only for illustration, not for demonstration." Lessing is driving a wedge between "event" and "truth" which prepares the way for the divorcing of the Gospel history from the "eternal truths" of Christianity in D. F. Strauss (strikingly anticipated in Schleiermacher's *Christmas Eve*, 1806), and for the high valuation of idea and depreciation of past event which runs through Newman's *Essay on Development*.[28]

"It follows," says Lessing, "that the religion of Christ and the Christian religion are two quite different things."[29] Already there is the distinction between a doctrine's "inner truth" (kernel) and its external (and dispensable) baggage (husk). "The best revealed or positive religion is that which contains the fewest conventional additions to natural religion, and least hinders the good effects of natural religion."[30] Regardless of the extent to which modern theology came to distance itself from a crass Enlightenment encomium for hypertranscendence, especially through the pantheistic tendencies of romanticism, "natural religion" was on every hand given the advantage in a variety of forms. Thus—again, not for historical-critical, but for philosophical-metaphysical/epistemological reasons—the prevailing (though often not explicit) model for interpreting "act of God" was Lessing's ditch and the theological versions of the Platonist/idealist dualism between form and matter, freedom and determinism, faith and history, grace and nature, Gospel and Law, *Geschichte* and *Historie*, the Christ of faith and the Jesus of history, and so on.

As we will see, the antithetical pairing of kerygma and myth arises naturally from these oppositions. Thus, kerygma belongs to the genus of form/spirit, freedom, faith, grace, Gospel, *Geschichte,* and the Christ of faith, while myth is attached to matter, determinism, history, nature, Law, *Historie,* and the Jesus of history. It is no wonder then that at the end of this trajectory (or *is* it the end?) Bultmann would boldly declare, "The Jesus of history is of no concern to me." In fact, "[t]he Jesus of history is not kerygma. . . . So far, then, from running away from *Historie* and taking refuge in *Geschichte,* I am deliberately renouncing any form of encounter with a phenomenon of past history, including an encounter with the Christ after the flesh."[31]

> The hope of Jesus and of the early Christian community was not fulfilled. The same world still exists and history continues. The course of history has refuted mythology. For the conception "Kingdom of God" is mythological, as is the conception of the eschatological drama. . . . The whole conception of the world which is presupposed in the preaching of Jesus as in the New Testament generally is mythological.[32]

Although he argues that this is because of the failure of the kingdom to materialize, one might be justified in suspecting that there are philosophical presuppositions at work that require the demythologizing of claims of special divine action. Let us now briefly summarize the symbolic-mythological-metaphorical option.

A. Ernst Cassirer and the Nature of Myth

Liberal and neo-orthodox theologies have been united in their tendency to interpret at least much of the Bible in terms of myths, sagas, and legends, albeit, usually with some sort of a literal cash value in terms of universal truths of experience, reason, and morality or (for the neo-orthodox) in terms of its kerygmatic core and occasion of encounter. Some current proposals, such as Gordon Kaufman's (*In Face of Mystery*), urge us to abandon supernaturalism chiefly on the basis that it now represents what Tillich would call a "dead metaphor." It cannot really connect with contemporary people and provide meaning for their lives.[33]

Max Müller, an early pioneer of the philosophy of mythology, regarded myth as the clothing of language rather than of thought: "Mythology is inevitable, it is natural, it is an inherent necessity of language, if we recognize in language the outward form and manifestation of thought; it is in fact the dark shadow which language throws upon thought, and which can never disappear till language becomes entirely commensurate with thought, which it never will."[34]

Like the shadows in Plato's cave, myths can often become more "real" than the actual world. The challenge of myth is the problem of appearance and reality and in Müller's thought we see the influence of Feuerbach's critique of religion. Myths are projections of human longings, the cloak of language striving to attain unity with thought.

Indebted to Müller, Ernst Cassirer nevertheless recognized the naïve Platonism of this assertion, as if *reality* were "directly and unequivocally given" and could therefore be so easily contrasted with *illusion*. "From this point of view all artistic creation becomes a mere imitation, which must always fall short of the original."[35] Müller has given a hopelessly unattainable standard that can only lead to linguistic skepticism:

> From this point it is but a single step to the conclusion which the modern skeptical critics of language have drawn: the complete dissolution of any alleged truth content of language, and the realization that this content is nothing but a sort of phantasmagoria of the spirit. Moreover, from this stand point, not only myth, art, and language, but even theoretical knowledge itself becomes phantasmagoria; for even knowledge can never reproduce the true nature of things as they are, but must frame their essence in "concepts." But what are concepts save formulations and creations of thought, which, instead of giving us the true forms of objects, show us rather the forms of thought itself? Consequently all schemata which science evolves in order to classify, organize, and summarize the phenomena of the real world turn out to be nothing but arbitrary schemes—airy fabrics of the mind, which express not the nature of things, but the nature of mind. So knowledge, as well as myth, language, and art, has been reduced to a kind of fiction—to a fiction that recommends itself by its usefulness, but must not be measured by any strict standard of truth, if it is not to melt away into nothingness.[36]

It is interesting to read this in the light of the neopragmatism of Rorty and others in recent debates. A naive realism eventually gives way to a skepticism that can find an adequate justification only in therapeutic usefulness. Cassirer proposes an alternative, however, in his understanding of language, myth, and the real:

> Against this self-dissolution of the spirit there is only one remedy: to accept in all seriousness what Kant calls his "Copernican revolution." Instead of measuring the content, meaning, and truth of intellectual forms by something extraneous which is supposed to be reproduced

in them, we must find in these forms themselves the measure and criterion for their truth and intrinsic meaning. Instead of taking them as
mere copies of something else, we must see in each of these spiritual
forms a spontaneous law of generation; an original way and tendency
of expression which is more than a mere record of something initially
given in fixed categories of real existence. . . . Thus the special symbolic forms are not imitations, but *organs* of reality, since it is solely by
their agency that anything real becomes an object for intellectual
apprehension, and as such is made visible to us. (emphasis in original)

In other words, Cassirer recommends the way of Aristotle over that of Plato.
Instead of trying to find in myth a copy of reality, we should allow the myths themselves to spell out their own logic, their own *semen rationalis*. Thus, the American
flag and the national anthem are not merely imitations of the reality for which
they stand but are "organs of that reality." In other words, symbolic forms become
related to the reality they represent (and in which they participate) in an analogous relation of things seen and heard to the eyes and ears. And language is the
medium that makes this connection. Long before Wittgenstein, Wilhelm von
Humboldt said that "each language draws a magic circle round the people to which
it belongs, a circle from which there is no escape save by stepping out of it into
another," and Cassirer integrated this idealist insight into his view of myth.[37]
   At the heart of Cassirer's thesis is the idea that mythico-religious language is
the original linguistic form. Mythology is united in the priority it gives to "the
Word" as creator of the world.[38] By "naming" someone, significance is conveyed
to that person, and in the mythico-religious realm the name has a certain magic.
Thus, by invoking the name of God, for instance, the people appropriate blessing on themselves and curses on their enemies.[39]
   There is a great deal in Cassirer's influential theory that is helpful, especially
in its critique of the Platonic and nonlinguistic theories of myth. And there is
much in a wide survey of various religions to lend credibility to the thesis that,
for instance, "naming" carries a magical power over the named. But this is hardly
the view of the Old Testament, even in its more primitive stages of redemptive
history. By revealing his name at his own time and in his own way, on his own
terms, God evades capture. Thus, the sacred tetragrammaton is never uttered or
inscribed in the rabbinical tradition. The covenantal structure of even the earli-
est traditions of the Old Testament eliminates any superstitious notions of con-
ferring blessing on oneself or doom on one's enemies. Therefore, as a theory of
religious mythology in general, Cassirer's insights may still be useful, but as a theory of biblical history and language, they fall far short of the actual assumptions
and contexts of the text itself.[40]

B. Rudolf Bultmann

As we have noted, Bultmann's chief problem with a straightforward interpretation of divine action (viz., that God did what the Bible says God did) has to do
with the suggestion of two causalities: one mundane, the other extramundane.

Thus, it is not a matter of historical criticism but of a philosophical commitment to naturalism. Talk of miracles is already and always mythological by definition, since "[i]n mythological thinking the action of God . . . is understood as an action which intervenes" in the world. "In fact, however, a miracle in the sense of an action of God cannot be thought of as an event which happens on the level of secular (worldly) events."[41] But this is not to deny any and all predication of divine action evidently, since he has much to say about the encounter with God in the Word-event that is Jesus Christ mediated through proclamation of the kerygma.[42] According to Bultmann, divine action does not enter the seamless web of natural causes from above, as supernatural links in a natural chain, but is to be seen as "happening within them."[43]

> The real nature of myth is not to present an objective picture of the world as it is, but to express man's understanding of himself in the world in which he lives. Myth should be interpreted not cosmologically, but anthropologically, or better still, existentially. . . . Mythology is the use of imagery to express the otherworldly in terms of this world and the divine in terms of human life, the other side in terms of this side. For instance, divine transcendence is expressed as spatial distance.[44]

A. C. Thiselton has correctly observed, "This definition of myth comes very close to equating myth with analogy, although in some passages Bultmann is at pains to try to maintain a clear distinction between them."[45]

Criticism of myth is hardly imposed from without or reluctantly employed by the theologian, but rather "demands its own criticism—namely, its imagery with its apparent claim to objective validity. . . . Hence the importance of the New Testament mythology lies not in its imagery [i.e., claims to objective validity] but in the understanding of existence which it enshrines."[46] Bultmann himself calls this view paradoxical: "Faith insists not on the direct identity of God's action with worldly events, but, if I may be permitted to put it so, on the paradoxical identity which can be believed only here and now against the appearance of non-identity."[47] With obvious Kierkegaardian influences, Bultmann's emphasis on faith as risk and the necessarily mythological nature of all "objectification" of divine activity deepens the dualisms often associated with modernity. Borrowing on a Lutheran schematization (though not its content), he not only groups nature and history under "Law" and grace and existential freedom under "Gospel," but tends also to group under these categories, respectively, immutability vs. flux, I-It description vs. I-Thou encounter, the Jesus of history (*Historie*) vs. the Christ of faith (*Geschichte*). It is Bultmann's debt to Kierkegaard and especially to Marburg neo-Kantianism, more than historical-critical considerations, that accounts for his apparent inability to recognize in these categories anything but dualistic antithesis.[48] History and nature can be seen only in deterministic terms, as "red in tooth and claw," while the historic (as opposed to historical) realm is utterly free and independent of nature, encountering God in the Now (Kierkegaard's eternal Moment) of one's own personal existence.

Paradox is the only way then of comprehending these two facts. And yet what is actually presented by Bultmann is not a paradox at all, but a contradiction. The objective bystander does not see anything "miraculous" in any events tradition-ally identified as special divine action. As Lutheran Law-and-Gospel categories are reemployed with neo-Kantian substance, so too is Luther's theology of the cross (*Deus absconditus*). God reveals himself by hiding himself, Luther was fond of saying. But Bultmann interprets this to mean that God cannot be known or observed in nature or history except according to faith. These are never integrated or dialectically related, but held in paradox (or, more likely, contradiction).

> In faith I realize that the scientific world-view does not comprehend the whole reality of the world and of human life, but faith does not offer another general world-view which corrects science in its state-ments on its own level. . . . This is the paradox of faith, that faith "nevertheless" understands as God's action here and now an event which is completely intelligible in the natural or historical connec-tion of events.[49]

Bultmann himself raised the question as to whether, given his approach, one might fall back into mythological speech after all. But he is bravely insistent, against all who urge that Christian language is necessarily mythological, that it ought not to end up that way. Demythologization is the only way out. All pred-ication of divine action must be radically criticized historically, to expose its mythological character, and then the interpreter will recognize that all statements about God acting are really statements about oneself. "When we speak of *God* as acting, we mean that *we* are confronted with God, addressed, asked, judged, or blessed by God" (emphasis added).[50] Now *this* sort of predication is not mytho-logical, but the refined residue of demythologized assertions. Indeed, says Bult-mann, this discourse is analogical, rather than mythological or symbolic.[51]

As Schubert Ogden intimates, the Platonic mind tended to regard "mythos" and "logos" as categories of "false" and "true," respectively. Modern science accepted this but included the Bible under the category of myth. Today, however, myth expresses existential orientation, not a "true/false" situation. Myth is now widely regarded as a vehicle of truth, while not itself being true.[52]

C. Paul Tillich and "Symbols of Faith"

Although it is somewhat out of fashion in its pristine form, Paul Tillich's innov-ative appropriation of existentialist and Jungian thought continues to represent a powerful strand in theology and, specifically, the nature of theological language. In his *Dynamics of Faith* (1957), Tillich identified the relationship of symbolic language to his central locus, ultimate concern:

> Man's ultimate concern must be expressed symbolically, because symbolic language alone is able to express the ultimate. . . . Symbols have one characteristic in common with signs; they point beyond themselves to something else. . . . A red light and the stopping of cars

> have essentially no relation to each other, but conventionally they are
> united as long as the convention lasts. The same is true of letters and
> numbers and partly even of words. . . . Sometimes such signs are
> called symbols; but this is unfortunate because it makes the distinc-
> tion between signs and symbols more difficult. Decisive is the fact
> that signs do not participate in the reality of that to which they point,
> while symbols do.[53]

A symbol "participates in that to which it points: the flag participates in the
power and dignity of the nation for which it stands" and "opens up levels of reality which otherwise are closed for us," unlocking "dimensions and elements of
our soul which correspond to the dimensions and elements of reality." However,
"[s]ymbols cannot be produced intentionally—this is the fifth characteristic.
They grow out of the individual or collective unconscious. . . . Symbols do not
grow because people are longing for them, and they do not die because of scientific or practical criticism. They die because they can no longer produce response
in the group where they originally found expression."[54]

Symbolic language is therefore indicative rather than disclosive:

> Religiously speaking, God transcends his own name. This is why the
> use of his name easily becomes an abuse or a blasphemy. Whatever
> we say about that which concerns us ultimately, whether or not we
> call it God, has a symbolic meaning. It points beyond itself while par-
> ticipating in that to which it points. . . . The language of faith is the
> language of symbols. . . . But faith, understood as the state of being
> ultimately concerned, has no language other than symbols. . . . Again
> it would be completely wrong to ask: So God is nothing but a sym-
> bol? Because the next question has to be: A symbol for what? And
> then the answer would be: For God! God is a symbol for God.[55]

Thus, Tillich risks reducing theology to psychology, God to a human feeling
(ultimate concern). Drawing from ordinary experience, myths put "the stories of
the gods into the framework of time and space although it belongs to the nature
of the ultimate to be beyond time and space."[56] To "demythologize," as Bultmann urged, is as impossible in religion as it is destructive of it. At the same time,
idolatry results when the ultimate is reified *as* the symbol:

> A myth which is understood as a myth, but not removed or replaced,
> can be called a "broken myth." Christianity denies by its very nature
> any unbroken myth, because its presupposition is the first com-
> mandment: the affirmation of the ultimate as ultimate and the rejec-
> tion of any kind of idolatry. All mythological elements in the Bible,
> and doctrine and liturgy should be recognized as mythological, but
> they should be maintained in their symbolic form and not be
> replaced by scientific substitutes. For there is no substitute for the use
> of symbols and myths: they are the language of faith.[57]

"Literalism" is, according to Tillich, the result of taking the myths and symbols too seriously, which amounts to idolatry. It is this philosophical and religious

presupposition, Tillich says, and not "rational criticism of the myth which is deci-sive."[58] Tillich's widely influential concept of textual meaning or sense is that one must read the Bible in ways that are counterintuitive. The immediate meaning veils the real meaning imbedded in the myth, a meaning that can be attained only by breaking the myth.

On one hand, it would seem that Tillich's point reflects a valid concern with idolatry. One hardly needs to be reminded not only of the recurring warnings against idolatry in scripture, but of the determination of divine self-disclosure not to yield to one dominant and explanatory metaphor. (It is the doctrine of divine simplicity, by the way, that, at least theoretically, keeps at bay the idolatrous con-fusion of God with words and pictures.) Tillich was concerned that one will sur-render oneself to the symbols or, in "the second stage of literalism," to the church or to the Bible, idolatrously worshiping the creature instead of the Creator, the symbol instead of the ultimate.[59] But Tillich hardly resisted his own root metaphor: "God is the Ground of Being" or "Ultimate Concern." In fact, this was not even really metaphorical or analogical. Tillich meant us to understand these statements as univocal, propositional truths. Thus, we are meant to take at least these statements (or rather, definitions) at face value; that is, in their "immediate meaning," although we are not allowed to do this for any scriptural statements.

Paul Edwards criticized Tillich's symbolic interpretation as philosophical con-fusion. Making the same mistakes as metaphysicians in the past who have thought that invoking "metaphor" and "symbol" might cover a multitude of lin-guistic sins, Edwards writes,

> The concession by an author that he is using a certain word metaphorically is tantamount to admitting that, in a very important sense and a sense relevant to the questions at issue between meta-physicians and their critics, he does not mean what he says. It does not automatically tell us what he does mean or whether in fact he means anything at all. When Bradley, for example, wrote that "the Absolute enters into . . . evolution and progress," it is clear that the word "enter" is used in a metaphorical and not a literal sense. But realizing this does not at once tell us what, if anything, Bradley asserted.[60]

This is not to say that metaphorical language is somehow inferior, much less inimical, to univocal speech. "Often indeed when words are used metaphorically, the context or certain special conventions make it clear what is asserted." Uni-vocal meaning or sense is no more determined by the use of nonmetaphorical than by the use of metaphorical language.

> Thus, when a certain historian wrote that "the Monroe Doctrine has always rested on the broad back of the British navy," it would have been pedantic and foolish to comment "what on earth does he mean—doesn't he know that navies don't have backs?" . . . In these cases we know perfectly well what the authors mean although they are using certain words metaphorically. But we know this because we

can eliminate the metaphorical expression, because we can specify
the content of the assertion in non-metaphorical language, because
we can supply the literal equivalent.[61]

Such an example (viz., the navy) is a "reducible metaphor," and such
metaphors are replete in our ordinary language. But Tillich's "metaphorical" or
"symbolic" expressions are hardly reducible:

> Now, Tillich and many other metaphysicians fail to notice the dif-
> ference between metaphors which are reducible in the sense just
> being explained and those which are not. When a sentence contains
> an irreducible metaphor, it follows at once that the sentence is devoid
> of cognitive meaning, that it is unintelligible, that it fails to make a
> genuine assertion. For what has happened is that the sentence has
> been deprived of the referent it would have had, assuming that cer-
> tain other conditions had also been fulfilled, if the expression in ques-
> tion had been used in its literal sense.[62]

Edwards pursues his argument by referring to Berkeley's critique of Locke's
belief that the sense qualities are "supported" by the material substratum. We
know what it is for pillars, for instance, to support a building.

> He then pointed out that since, according to Locke, the material sub-
> stratum is a "something, x, I know not what" whose characteristics
> are unknown and indeed unknowable, and, since, therefore, it is not
> known to resemble pillars in any way, Locke could not possibly have
> been using the word "support" in its "usual or literal sense." "In what
> sense therefore," Berkeley went on, "must it be taken? . . . What that
> is they (Locke and those who share his view) do not explain." Berke-
> ley then concluded that sentences in question have "no distinct
> meaning annexed" to them.[63]

Tillich's "Being-itself" is like Locke's material substratum, Edwards argues.
Neither is accessible to observation. "We do not and cannot have a stock of literally meaningful statements about it at our disposal which would serve as the
equivalents of Tillich's 'symbolic' statements. The metaphors in Tillich's sentences
are, in other words, irreducible and hence, if my general argument has been correct, the sentences are unintelligible."[64]

The approach taken by Tillich is quite similar to that taken not only by metaphysicians, as Edwards observes, but by the *via negationis* and especially by the
mystics, in which a great deal is said about God in the process of saying that nothing can be said about God.

Tillich's "modest side" concedes that one can have no literal knowledge of
Being-itself, Edwards notes.

> He then seems to be jotting down in a matter-of-fact way the char-
> acteristics of Being-itself, much as a doctor might jot down descrip-
> tions of the symptoms displayed by a patient. He then writes as if he
> had a completely unobstructed view of the Ultimate Reality. Thus

we are told as a plain matter of fact and without the use of any quotation marks that "God is infinite because he has the finite (and with
it that element of non-being which belongs to finitude) within himself united with his infinity. . . ." Again, we are told, without the use
of any quotation marks, and I do not think their absence is a mere
oversight, that God "is the eternal process in which separation is
posited and is overcome by reunion" (*Systematic Theology*, 242).[65]

Dogmatic statements characterize much of Tillich's work, but on what basis?
"Tillich, the dogmatist, does not hesitate to offer translations or what I have
called reductions of his 'symbolic' statements about God. We can also express literally, for example, what we mean 'symbolically' when we say that God is living.
'God lives,' the reduction runs, 'insofar as he is the ground of life' (*Systematic
Theology*, 242)."[66] But the reader is not given any indicators that this is what
Tillich is actually doing. It is possible that Tillich himself did not realize that he
was, at the end of the day, making the same dogmatic statements while denying
in theory the possibility of doing so. Even here, says Edwards, "Tillich never
seems to have noticed that even in his basic statement, when elaborated in terms
of 'ground' and 'structure,' these words are used metaphorically and not literally."

Tillich is here in no better a position than the supporter of Locke
who substituted "hold together" for "support." That Tillich does not
succeed in breaking through the circle of expressions *lacking* literal
significance, *i.e.* lacking referential meaning, is particularly clear in
the case of the "translation" of the sentence "God is his own destiny."
By this "symbolic" characterization, as we just saw, we "point" among
other things to "the participation of God in becoming and in history." But a little earlier . . . we were informed that "God's participation is not a spatial or temporal presence" and twice in the same
paragraph we were given to understand that when "applied to God,"
participation "is meant not categorically but symbolically." In other
words, one metaphorical statement is replaced by another but literal
significance is never achieved. Tillich constantly engages in "circular"
translations of this sort. Again and again he "explains" the meaning
of one "symbolically" used expression in terms of another which is
really no less symbolic.[67]

So, says Edwards, it makes sense for us to speak of God as "king," and not as,
say, a "waiter." Why? Because the referent can be known descriptively in some
fashion. "Similarly, if it were known or believed that God is "concerned with the
welfare" of all human beings in the literal sense of this expression, then it would
make sense to speak of him as our "father" and it would be right to prefer this
symbol to symbols like 'daughter' or 'soprano' or 'carpenter.'" While hardly
eschewing mystery, the believer accepts anthropomorphism on its own terms.
But for Tillich, "Since the 'comparison' between fathers and kings on the one
hand and the infinitely transcending, infinitely mysterious, indescribable Being-
itself, on the other, is a bogus comparison, God may no less appropriately be said
to be a soprano, a slave, a street-cleaner, a daughter, or even a fascist and a hater

than a father or a king."[68] There is absolutely no determination of which metaphors or symbols are appropriate or why, since there is no access to the referent. Thus, Tillich's symbolism is a species of equivocal language.

Paul Edwards's critique is, I think, devastating. There cannot be a symbolic theology. That is not to say that there cannot be symbols, but it is to suggest that without a nonsymbolic referent, there can be no symbolic efficacy. This is not to reduce language to propositions, as we will see below, but it is to say that there must be *some* cognitive purchase for the metaphors and symbols. They must mean something, and that "something" can be at least partially *stated*. Furthermore, in the absence of an observable referent, there must be some criteria for determining the aptness of one metaphor or symbol over another. This, of course, is the same problem that analogical discourse encounters. However, I hope to demonstrate in another chapter that this has a greater chance of succeeding where myth and metaphor have failed.

So far, I have cursorily suggested that, ironically, much of modern theology has surrendered Christian language to various forms of hypertranscendence that reduce that language to symbol and metaphor, thereby returning full circle to hyperimmanence. Furthermore, we have seen how, in the light of linguistic analysis, language thus reduced without remainder cannot even pass as genuinely metaphorical, analogical, or symbolic. It is simply meaningless.

D. Models and Metaphors

Alternatives have been sought between symbolism and literalism throughout church history. What many advocates of "metaphorical theology" share with Bultmann is the confusion of what they regard as a consensus of educated people in the West with an *argument for* the ineluctability of rejecting the biblical and orthodox interpretation of reality. However, one of the most fruitful and interesting projects along these lines is the work of Sallie McFague. In *Metaphorical Theology*, McFague has argued that we are more aware of the discontinuities between God (or the sacred realm) and ourselves (and natural existence) today than in the past. Unlike societies in which the sacred was symbolized or sacramentally re-presented in everyday life, our world is decidedly secular. "If we experience God at all it tends to be at a private level and in a sporadic way," she writes.[69] So McFague finds in the mystical tradition a precedent for a "metaphorical theology" in which nothing is univocal, much less literal. "For instance, I have not found it possible as a contemporary Christian to support an incarnational christology or a canonical Scripture; nevertheless, I have found it possible to support a 'parabolic' christology and Scripture as the Christian 'classic.'"[70]

Without any argumentation, McFague offers her intuition as to how symbols become literalized into the "idolatry" whose danger Tillich signaled. Living in this world in which the divine seems so foreign, "and hence afraid that our images refer to nothing, we literalize them, worshiping the icon in our desperation."[71] Unfortunately, McFague's reductionistic approach to historical theology renders Protestantism inherently "metaphorical," while Catholicism is "symbolic/sacramental" or "analogical."[72] This is epitomized for her in Barth's denial of the *analogia entis* in favor of the *analogia fidei*. "For in symbolic or sacramental thought, one does not think of 'this' *as* 'that,' but 'this' as *a part of* 'that.' The tension of metaphor is absorbed by the harmony of symbol."[73] But does McFague provide, for instance, any account for *how* Jesus participates uniquely in the divine life? And if there is none, how can Jesus even be a symbol in Tillich's sense which she adopts?

McFague radically applies the concept of metaphor even to Jesus: "In such a theology *no* finite thought, product, or creature can be identified with God and this includes Jesus of Nazareth, who as parable of God both 'is and is not' God."[74] For this is the nature of metaphor: it "is and is not" that to which it refers. But more important in this seminal statement than the strictures of metaphor appears to be her bias against the possibility of the finite being identified with the infinite (which is understandable, given her rejection of an incarnational christology). Thus we meet up again with the dualistic legacy of modernity, despite the putative "harmony of symbol." Despite its modern form, we meet here with the same Neoplatonist assumptions as fourth-century Arianism.

Nevertheless, McFague does make the point that has been emphasized in recent literary theory: "Far from being an esoteric or ornamental rhetorical device superimposed *on* ordinary language, metaphor *is* ordinary language. It is the *way* we think" (emphasis in original).[75] Christian metaphors have reference to the external world and although they do so without literal access to that reality, in actual fact there is no language game that has this privileged access. Since all language is metaphorical, the law of gravitation has nothing over religious language in this respect.[76] What is not metaphorical, it seems, is one's own experience. This *is* literal, a direct encounter, according to McFague.[77] So, as with Tillich, there is a univocal core after all.

Despite the many criticisms that could be offered of this position, she is surely correct in reminding us, "In no sense can systematic thought be said to *explain* metaphors and models so that they become mere illustrations for concepts; rather, the task of conceptual thought is to generalize (often in philosophical language, the generalizing language), to criticize images, to raise questions of their meaning and truth in explicit ways."[78] Theological language, as that of other disciplines, moves dialectically between metaphorical and conceptual poles, what one might be warranted to call first-order (doxological) and second-order (doctrinal) reflection. However, McFague's rejuvenation of Tillich's "symbolism" (only now under the term "metaphor") is subject to the same criticisms.

A recurring tendency is to confuse "metaphorical" with "equivocal," and this equivocity is what some theological proposals are really after in their commitment to metaphor. In other words, such things as "metaphorical theology" or "symbolic theology" arise not out of a sense that this best accounts for the community's founding identity—its text, its practices, its second-order reflection— but are due largely to the perceived need to find an alternative to biblical and orthodox belief in the face of modernity. However, the biblical and orthodox use of metaphor or symbol, though self-consciously employed (pace Bultmann), expresses literal predication. No biblical writer believed that God possessed nostrils, a mouth, or that God literally rides upon cherubs and flies upon the wings of the wind, although the psalmist declares,

> Smoke went up from his nostrils,
>   and devouring fire from his mouth;
>   glowing coals flamed forth from him. . . .
> He rode on a cherub, and flew;
>   he came swiftly upon the wings of the wind.[79]

But in representing God as enfolding Israel in his wings (Ps. 36:7) or in everlasting arms (Deut. 33:27), the biblical writer was literally saying thereby that God cares for and protects his people. Although God's being angry is not the same as my being angry, scripture picks out such analogies as being appropriate to the situation. Recalling a point that we made earlier in connection with Gilkey's conflation of univocal and literal, we are also reminded by R. M. J. Dammann that "a word is used metaphorically as opposed to literally, not as opposed to univocally."[80] This is an especially vital point in view of the uninhibited use of "metaphorical" as a weasel word in theology and philosophy, especially for theologians who wish to discard the notion of special divine action while retaining a trace of its meaning.

At the end of the day, even the modern theologians who most eschew the cognitive-propositionalist model (to borrow Lindbeck's categorization) find that they have to offer an irreducible core-proposition in order to have something to which "myths" and "symbols" can legitimately refer. For Tillich, it is "God is being itself" (*Systematic Theology*, 1:238). But despite his reluctant acceptance of at least one univocal dogma, Tillich advanced a symbolic theory of truth and language, holding that (unlike signs) symbols participate in that to which they refer. So the religious person regards claims and discourse about God, humanity, sin, salvation, hope, and the like, as essential to one's faith, although they are meant to be "broken myths"—that is, not discarded for their mythological character, but embraced precisely because of and in full knowledge of their mythological efficacy.

On the other hand, Bultmann sees "myth" as problematic and seeks to peel away the veneer of symbol and myth in order to arrive at the kerygma, which is to say, a propositional statement or series of statements about human existence. The myth of the resurrection, for instance, is not to be abandoned, but is to be "demythologized," which can be taken to mean that it must be translated from literal description of external reference (in which case it would, according to Bultmann, be untrue) to nonliteral description of human existence. In the published exchange with Bultmann, Austin Farrer voiced his concern that his interlocutor takes the Bible more seriously than it takes itself when employing figurative language. "Angels above the blue and devils underground fitly frame the setting of man in the spiritual hierarchy, but excavation will not reach the one or aeronautics the other."[81] Bultmann especially seemed not to have thought that the biblical writers had the slightest self-consciousness about their use of tropes and figures of speech. And, as we have seen, Gilkey and others make that same mistake concerning premodern interpretation in general. But such modern hubris is easily remedied by familiarity with these sources. For instance, Calvin's notion of divine accommodation is widely known, and we will include a fuller discussion of this in another place.[82]

So in demythologization, such "myths" *point to* a new way of being-in-the-world characterized by genuine existence. As even the casual reader of Bultmann's work will recognize, everything "mythological" can be reduced to a nonmythological core of propositions concerning human existence. Some univocal residue always remains in these proposals. Regardless of its content, no theological program has been able to liberate itself from direct (even if analogical) propositions to which religious language and experience is somehow oriented. Religious language calls for a reference and reference calls for propositions and assertions. Not all of those assertions are taken to be shorn of metaphorical veils, nor have they been regarded as always (or even largely) univocal, but from the very beginning Christians have wanted to say certain things about God that could be taken literally. Thus far at least, representatives of this approach have not provided an account of "God acts in history" (and not simply in individual or communal experience) precisely because the approach presupposes that such action is literally impossible.

(2) Communal Interpretation of a Natural Occurrence

The same concerns about identifying reference energize the "mighty acts of God" theology, as expressed by G. E. Wright:

> Thus the covenant at Sinai is clearly a human event, but is it a Divine act in history? The deliverance of Israel from Egyptian slavery at the time of Moses is a fact, but is it also a historical fact that God had chosen Israel for his special possession? The death of Jesus on a cross is certainly an event in history, but is his resurrection and exaltation to God's right hand also a definite and actual event? We today insist that facts should be verifiable, but in Biblical history the primary meaning seen in events, and many matters which are considered events, are not verifiable. They are a projection of faith into facts which is then considered as the revelation of the true meaning of the facts.[83]

Wright says that the kernel-husk approach is "not only to demyth the Bible, but to de-historize it also."[84] He refers to a "docetic view of the Bible" on the part of those who think that it can by shorn of its historical veracity and still yield true inner principles of reason, experience, or ethics.[85] "In some theological quarters one gets the impression that the historical criticism of the Bible has left the faith on such shaky and unprovable historical foundations that we need to find another and firmer basis. . . . Now in Biblical faith everything depends upon whether the central events actually occurred."[86]

Why is the Bible in contradistinction to all other "bibles" centred in the story of the life and historical traditions of one people? . . . The national literature of other people of the time exhibits no such interest in history. To be sure, the ancient kings and nobles of Egypt, Canaan and Mesopotamia had many historical inscriptions and records inscribed on stelae, and on temple, tomb and palace walls. Such annals, however, were concerned almost solely with the personal glorification of those for whom they were prepared. . . . The Biblical point of view is concentrated, not merely on the individual exploits of heroes and kings, not merely on the court annals like the Babylonian Chronicle which were especially important for the calendar and the royal archives, but rather on the unity and meaningfulness of universal history from the beginning of time until the end of time. It is in the framework of this universal history that the chronicles of individual events are set and ultimately receive their meaning.[87]

To be sure, there are minor errors and discrepancies, but "the so-called destructive nature of Biblical criticism has been exaggerated and misrepresented."

On the contrary, we today possess a greater confidence in the basic reliability of Biblical history, despite all the problems it has presented, than was possible before the historical criticism and archaeological research. Theologians, somewhat impatient with detailed historical work, find it simpler to assume that actually it is not especially important, except to add to the sum total of our antiquarian knowledge. Yet in any way to admit a disinterestedness in history or to assume it all to be mythical is certainly a strange way of dealing with Biblical theology, not to speak of the fact that it revives the ancient heresy of docetism.[88]

And yet, it is obvious that the authors/editors were not present at creation, which they nevertheless describe, nor did they have firsthand knowledge of the eschaton, since we are closer than they to that event in history. (The possibility of explaining this in terms of God's being the "omniscient narrator" or at least author in some sense is not even posed.) "Consequently, one cannot maintain the historical value of all parts evenly."[89] The biblical writers "knew nothing of limitless space; their universe was a comparatively small place surrounded by the watery deeps. The revelation of God occurred within the conceptual life of the people then. Yet the absence of a modern scientific view of the universe scarcely makes the literature in itself mythology."[90] But just at this point, he distinguishes again between fact (revelatory historical event) and value (the Bible as merely human interpretation by faith). Biblical faith is "history interpreted by faith," rather than by mythology.[91]

Frank Dilley will not let such an account off the hook easily:

The modern "Biblical Theologian" is in a quandary about what to say. His view of man and of history centers upon his assertion of a "God Who Acts," yet he seems unable to communicate what it is that he means by the actions of God. Unwilling to endorse the conservative view of a God Who Acts through outright miracles or the liberal doctrine of a God restricted to universal actions, he speaks about a God who acts specially in history, but without giving any concrete

content to his assertions, and he seems unable to distinguish his position from that of the liberalism he rejects.[92]

Wright places the whole weight of his proposal on the Exodus and Sinai
events, but "one searches [his work] in vain for any clear description of what God
actually did. He asserts that God acted but never does he attempt to say what
concretely took place in that Divine act."[93] Echoing Gilkey's criticisms, Dilley
observes a particular example:

> Having denounced such modern theologians as Rudolf Bultmann
> and Reinhold Niebuhr for having compromised the Biblical notion
> that God really acts, and having defended the claims that the Bible
> is the "story of what God once did," and that in Biblical faith every-
> thing depends upon whether the central events are really facts or not,
> Wright presents the following account of the resurrection:
>   "The process, the how of Christ's transition from death to the
> living head of the new community, and the language used to describe
> that transition ('raised the third day,' . . .)—these are products of the
> situation. They are the temporal language of the first-century Chris-
> tians. To us, they are symbols of deep truth and nothing more,
> though they are symbols that are difficult to translate."[94]

Dilley replies,

> What is this language symbolic of? If it is symbolic of the raising of a
> physical body, then the language is really literal and not merely sym-
> bolic. . . . And how does one justify the retention of the symbol "res-
> urrection" for what took place if there was no body? Surely Wright
> must offer some clue as to what he is describing if he is to justify speak-
> ing of the resurrection as a fact and as an act of God. What is resur-
> rection that is only symbolically a raising, a resurrection body which
> can only symbolically be called a body? If the Biblical content is to be
> negated in this way, then some other content must be supplied. . . .
> Once content is supplied, either conservatism or liberalism enters in.[95]

Dilley opts for the liberal content, with Whitehead as a major source.

Werner Lemke, a student of Wright's, concurs with some of the criticisms of
biblical theology (especially Barr's). For one, the movement has tended to be one-
sided in its emphasis: acts without words, marginalizing God's self-disclosure
through creation and the words of scripture. "Basic honesty" is at stake in asserting
that "God acts" or "God speaks" while one actually does not accept the factual character of the specific instances that report such events. Personal commitments must
be made at some point, Lemke insists, beyond the merely descriptive analysis in the
form of something like, "According to the preexilic community, God did thus and
so." "Biblical theologians in general need to be more explicit about their ontological and theological assumptions when doing biblical theology."[96]

What critics from Gilkey to Dilley have shown applies to theologies beyond
Wright's. Furthermore, defining "special act of God" in terms of the community's
interpretation of otherwise quite natural (though perhaps extraordinary) events
draws sympathy from nearly every quarter of modern and contemporary theology.

On one hand, Wright does not think that very much in historical criticism has dealt a fatal blow to the Bible's central historical claims. (Similarly, while Lemke is quite open to historical-critical analysis and revision in the light of such analysis, he maintains, "Today we have no good reason to doubt that there is a significant measure of congruence between the actual events of Israel's history as critically reconstructed and the way they were remembered in the sacred traditions."[97]) Despite all of this, Wright is reticent to part with the modern objection to special divine action. Even where there might appear to be a reassessment of the historical-critical damage, philosophical a prioris seem more definitive in rejecting traditional assertions of special divine action. Despite their widely divergent views, theologians from Bultmann to Wright seem united by a presupposition that special divine action does not actually occur but is the product of a community's self-understanding, and for this community, therefore, such events are constitutive and perhaps even regulative. Quite apart from historical-critical conclusions, theology appears to still be mired in Lessing's "ugly ditch," with its equally unattractive dualisms.

(3) Narrative Interpretation

"Narrative is the form in which we render in a coherent fashion the agent's actions across time and thus the agent's character. So if God is an agent who acts in the world so as to disclose divine character and purpose, then narrative is the appropriate form in which to render God's identity"[98] F. Michael McLain's definition shows promise for a narrative approach that can somehow reintegrate act and word, event and interpretation, divine and human agency. While many narrative theologians are reluctant to relate intratextual predications of divine action to extratextual reality, McLain's approach offers an account of double agency in which the idea of "miracle" or a special act of God is rendered more plausible. Part of the problem is that so much of this discussion has failed to make use of distinctions within philosophical theories of agency. First among those distinctions is basic and nonbasic actions, McLain writes. "A basic action is one that is performed not by or in simultaneously performing some other action. A nonbasic action is done *by* performing a basic action."[99]

> By this route we arrive at the not implausible view that bodily movement is part of the meaning of *human* action concepts. Does it follow that things must be this way *in general* with action concepts? Intuitively, no. We can readily distinguish the questions: (1) How do human beings bring about the actions they perform, and (2) Is movement of an agent's body part of the concept of action?[100]

McLain clearly sees through the sociological "argument": "Gilkey does little in this essay to characterise our alleged belief in a causal continuum or to examine reasons which might be given in support of it. He simply assumes, as so many theologians do, that contemporary reflection has, should and/or must accept this belief as central to the context in which we do theology."[101] In fact, McLain says that "it is not the merely subjective response of the believer that is involved in picking out such events"—but then, in the very next sentence, says, "Rather it is *her belief* that *she has discerned* something more of divine purpose such *that she can act* appropriately in relation to it" (emphasis added).[102] While his appeal to basic and nonbasic actions offers a promising analysis of incorporeal action, McLain surrenders the entire notion of miracle by locating the idea of divine action under the category of human interpretation. While interpretation is essential to one's perception of divine action, it should be distinguished from the account of divine action itself. I'm not at all certain how McLain's version is any less subjective than its rivals, after all. While he does not go so far as to say that Easter is what happened to the disciples rather than to Jesus, McLain does not provide us with an account for a literal use of action predicates in relation to God.

In much of narrative theology, this notion of "miracle" as communal or individual, historical or existential, *interpretation* of an otherwise natural event seems to prevail. To be sure, Hans Frei, George Lindbeck, Brevard Childs, and other representatives of the "Yale school" have insisted upon the necessity of belief in the bodily resurrection of Jesus. And yet Frei emphasizes its irreplaceable significance *within the narrative* and Lindbeck *within the semiotic system* of Christian grammar. Lindbeck writes,

> The affirmation of the resurrection, for example, cannot easily be an enduring communal norm of belief and practice if it is seen primarily as symbol of a certain type of experience (such as that of the spiritual presence of Christ as the power of the New Being) that can in principle be expressed or evoked in other ways. Similarly, what Lonergan calls "classical" propositional views of doctrine will be disregarded. These tend to take a particular formulation of a doctrine (e.g., a particular description of the resurrection) as a truth claim with objective or ontological import, and thus have difficulty envisioning the possibility of markedly different formulations of the same doctrine.

Such doctrines "affirm nothing about extra-linguistic or extra-human reality" and are "intrasystematic rather than ontological truth claims."[103] Later he writes, "The physical details of what, if anything, happened on Mount Sinai, for example, are no longer of direct interest for typological or figurative purposes, as they often were for the tradition."[104] How far is this comment from Bultmann's that the Jesus of history ("the Christ according to the flesh") is of no importance? Postliberals of Lindbeck's stripe (cultural-linguistic) eschew a purely subjective view of religion, categorized as experiential-expressivism. Nevertheless, it seems that there is little interest in specifying what they think happened at Mount Sinai or in the tomb of Jesus. To be sure, there are more general descriptions (such as the ones that we find in the resurrection accounts) and narrower descriptions (such as the extent of continuity between the preresurrection and postresurrection state of Jesus' body). But surely a believer will want to confess "a particular description of the resurrection" at least in general terms—and to do so "as a truth claim with objective or ontological import." At least in the case of George

Lindbeck, ecumenical ends have priority over means, since the goal is to allow for "markedly different formulations of the same doctrine."

It would appear that such versions of narrative theology run the risk of simply substituting Kantian categories with narrative intertextuality. But the real question is whether God acts in history—not just according to myth, symbol, communal interpretation, or narrative, but whether God acts at all. Critics of Christian claims are correct to insist upon some response to this question, especially since these claims to extratextual reference are intrinsic to the very narrative that is given priority. Do claims of divine action in history serve a merely regulative rather than constitutive function? If not, Feuerbach's analysis of God-talk seems entirely justified.

A final example from the perspective of narrative is taken from Thomas F. Tracy. "The faithful," he says, "do not undertake a life of devotion to the main character of what they take to be a purely fictional story."[105]

> But given the epistemological and theological problems with miracles, it is ill-advised to tie one's account of God's action primarily to divine interventions that disrupt the regularities we have come to expect among natural events. The more important point at which to resist Bultmann is in his claim that any talk of God affecting the course of nature or human history *constitutes* an appeal to miracle. (emphasis added)[106]

So all that's left of "divine action" (traditionally considered) is actually providence. The rest of his essay is dedicated to demonstrating how God can be said to act in this world while excluding the miraculous (i.e., special divine action). What does this do to the resurrection claim? Tracy's account renders divine action little more than the shaping of influences within an otherwise airtight web of natural cause and effect. Sharing modernity's fear of the possibility of "disrupting the intelligible order of events in the agent's life," Tracy's proposal allows for no in-breaking, no real novum, no vertical, apocalyptic intervention. Rather, God here is truly a factor among factors, contributing to the ordinary causal network within which the agent acts. Miracle is reduced to providence.

It is difficult not to notice a link between views of divine action (and revelation) and views of divine agency (and grace). The tendency to favor human freedom at the expense of divine sovereignty shows itself open to certain related tendencies to sacrifice gracious irruption to mundane human improvement: "If God's action is to be an intelligible development of tendencies at work in the agent's life, then the range of possibilities open to God will be limited in certain ways. In this respect, God's action in us is like our own free acts, i.e. it is a novel development of given resources."[107] Here we would do well to heed Ronald Thiemann's emphasis on the link between the denial of divine revelation and the denial of prevenient grace.[108] "God acts *in* us," Tracy argues, "by contributing to the background from which we act, and in so doing God acts *through* us toward the rest of his creation."[109] What is missing from this account is how (or whether)

God acts *upon* us and the rest of his creation. The question is, does God act upon us and for us in the world? That is a very different question from whether divine activity can be discerned within ourselves and our own experience. This evades the philosophical problems such a view poses by simply reducing "divine action" to psychological or similar actions that—by virtue of their being individual rather than corporate, private rather than public, and subjective rather than objective—can be protected from criticism.

(4) Immanentist Interpretation

Grace Jantzen's *God's World, God's Body* (Westminster, 1984) advances the thesis that the relation of God to the world (and to human agency) is like that of the soul to the body. God is "embodied" in the world. In sharp contrast to the dualistic thought that has created such a problem for modern theology, panentheism seeks to repair antinomies with a monist scheme. One might regard this as the revenge of Aristotle and Hegel over Plato and Descartes. So for Jantzen, every action that occurs in nature and history is *God's* action.[110]

We have already referred to Sallie McFague in connection with metaphorical theology. But since these categories are descriptive of certain common tendencies and not of individuals or schools, it is worth referring once more to her work. As is well known, radical theology of the feminist variety has drawn heavily on process thought and neopagan spirituality. It is not surprising, then, that some of the most interesting representatives of an immanentist interpretation of divine action would be offered by representatives of this community. McFague wonders, "What if, we are asking, the 'resurrection of the body' were not seen as the resurrection of particular bodies that ascend, beginning with Jesus of Nazareth, into another world, but as God's promise to be with us always in God's body, our world?" She emphasizes that such models are not descriptions, but "what-if" or "as-if" experiments.[111]

McFague even speculates that if Christianity had been born in a less Hellenistic milieu it would have been less dualistic and more oriented toward the notion of the world as God's body. While the monarchical metaphor verges on deism, McFague agrees that the body metaphor comes close to pantheism.[112] She admits that it is at least monist and panentheistic. "Nevertheless, though God is not reduced to the world, the metaphor of the world as God's body puts God 'at risk.' If we follow out the implications of the metaphor, we see that God becomes dependent through being bodily, in a way that a totally invisible, distant God would never be."[113] God acts in and with the world as humans act in and with their bodies. Here, the mind-body dualism of modernity does not seem discarded as much as synthesized. But in good Hegelian fashion, it would appear that the One swallows the Many whole; action, whether predicated of human persons or God, is at best an *appearance* of diverse causes, agents, and ends. But does this do justice to the uniqueness of agents? Furthermore, couldn't it serve as a model for totalitarianism and oppression?

Not all proponents of this broad approach are feminists. According to Avery Dulles, for instance, "The best created analogy is the form-matter relationship which occurs, for instance, when the soul animates the body, making it into a human body."[114]

Immanentist approaches strive to ameliorate the chasms of modern dualism. Thus, they are often quite insensitive to the charges of Bultmann and Gilkey concerning the impossibility of divine intervention in the causal nexus by identifying God with the causal nexus. As such approaches find increasingly hospitable ground in the various sciences, the day will surely come when Bultmann's inconceivability of divine action in nature and history will be just as inconceivable for another generation. Still, this approach does seem to partake of the same anthropomorphizing mistake as process thought and panentheism. It reinforces the mind-body dualism and threatens to sacrifice divine transcendence on the altar of immanence. As with Hegel's thought, the dialectic is often lost to a totalizing, final synthesis in which unity will always overcome diversity and spirit will always triumph over matter.

One exception to the mind-body analogy within process thought is John Cobb's suggestion that "[t]he appropriate analogy must be found in the influence of one experience or another rather than in that of the body."[115] An angry feeling can be an efficient cause, but anger itself is not observed.[116] This does have the merit of meeting Hume's objections, at the heart of which was his observation that one cannot see an efficient cause, but only an effect. We see successive events, but not their necessary relations. Cobb notes that recent theology interacts with the question of divine causality at the level of one or more of Aristotle's causal categories: formal cause, material cause, and final cause. For Henry Nelson Wieman, for instance, "God is that process in which human good grows"— an example of God as Formal Cause.[117] Tillich, Whitehead, and Aristotle tend toward God as Material Cause (Ground of Being, World Process, Prime Matter),[118] while Pannenberg and Moltmann favor God as Final Cause, viewing causality as somehow leaping from the future, the *telos*, or end of things, to create effects in the present.[119] But Cobb notes that all of these positions still have some recourse to *efficient* causality.[120] Upon analysis, Cobb concludes that Hume's criticism does not apply "when efficient causality is understood as influence."[121] Just as kindness may be said to be the efficient cause of one person giving another person some money for a meal, although it cannot itself be observed, God's loving influences can be efficient causes without regarding such divine causality in traditional terms of one agent acting upon another.

Cobb's proposal is less reductionistic in some ways. Furthermore, it may account for *some* events, but not the most interesting ones. How does affectional influence account for creation ex nihilo, the dramatic exodus from Egypt, and the resurrection of the dead? Isn't evil too great, too pervasive, to be overcome by such a passive actor?

In the next chapter we will turn to our own proposal.

Chapter Three

Accounting for Divine Action

Hermeneutical Implications

As we have seen, the metaphysical landscape is crowded with competing theories concerning divine agency. Of course, this is nothing new, despite the modern caricatures of a monolithic consensus in the so-called Age of Faith. But today it is complicated by modern views of nature and causality as well as by postmodern views of playfulness and pointless flux. Among fairly mainstream theologians in our day are those who suggest that God does literally act within the chain of human events. Furthermore, within this ambit are those, on one hand, who would argue for some version of a traditional predestinarian position and, on the other hand, those who would propose divine involvement in all events on the basis of a panentheistic perspective. In this chapter we will offer our own analysis of the claim that God acts in history.

The reader will recall that "literal" is not synonymous with "univocal." In analogical language particularly, as applied to interpreting scripture, certain characteristics ascribed to God are meant to be taken literally. Whether one in fact takes them in that way, one hardly needs to reconstruct the original situation or plumb the psychological depths of authorial intention in order to see that the text itself says that God literally rescued the Israelites from Egyptian bondage, brought them into the promised land, filled the temple, judged, redeemed, and so forth. To pick a more mundane example, the statement, "My new car is a lemon," is literally true. Even metaphor (a compressed simile) is not necessarily nonliteral in reference. This is why, for instance, Luther and Calvin insisted on the *sensus literalis*—not as a literalistic hermeneutic, but understood as synonymous with phrases that they actually preferred: the *sensus normalis*. In other words, that determination rests on the goal of the text. What really counts is not what signs or even genres "mean" in the abstract, but how they are used. In direct oral speech, my interlocutor (assuming that he or she is fluent in American usages) would not normally raise objections to such an assertion about my car being a lemon. It is not equivocal. But it is also not univocal, in which case my interlocutor might have said, "Don't you realize that lemons and cars have nothing in common?" Of course, lemons and cars may not have anything in common ontologically (except, on occasion, color), but a disappointing car may be classified as a lemon if, for instance, both are sour, although "sour" is understood differently as well as similarly in each case.

We will discuss analogical referential discourse more fully elsewhere. It was necessary to raise it here only to distinguish "literal intervention" from univocal description; the former we affirm, the latter we deny. God acts in the world: this statement is understood as literally true, analogically interpreted. Description predicates concerning divine action may be taken, depending on the form of speech in which they are found, as literal or metaphorical. But in either case it is analogical. This will satisfy neither champions of univocity[1] nor equivocity. Therefore we will not survey the spectrum under this rubric, but will rather provide an alternative account for special divine action in the world in response to the difficulties raised. Our previous chapter offered a summary of the leading approaches to the God-world relation generally. Before we elaborate our own account we must confront the challenges that we will have to meet with respect to two issues: divine intrusion and double agency.

THE PROBLEM OF DIVINE INTRUSION

Having stated the problem, we will now attempt to address it with our own account of special divine action. I don't think, first of all, that we can provide a justification, much less a proof, for preferring this account to those who do not presuppose the biblical narrative as the definitive parameters of investigation.

First, there is the horizon of the interpreter to consider. Our tendency to generational narcissism perhaps blinds us to the fact that resistance to divine intervention in worldly affairs has a pedigree long before the acme of modern science. One theologian writes, "Those who do not think that God controls the government of the universe will say that this [deliverance of Jonah] was *outside the common course*. Yet from it I infer that *no wind* ever arises or increases except by God's express command" (emphasis added).[2] The writer is John Calvin. While the sentiments may not be surprising, it is at least interesting that he feels obliged to respond to an objection that we normally identify with a post-Newtonian outlook. That which Bultmann insisted was "incomprehensible" to moderns has always been an obstacle for those who—not by observation, but by a priori conviction—presuppose a closed natural system.[3]

For Bultmann and even still for Kaufman and others, an increasingly outmoded cosmology, which for them (and for us) has been so compelling, is being overcome by a far richer and open ethos within the various natural sciences. This has made it possible for the first time since the turn of the eighteenth century to transcend what appeared to be an ever-expanding chasm. Changes in science, which we will observe more closely elsewhere, have altered the "problem" of divine involvement, from the viewpoint of the interpreter's horizon. It stands to reason that one could easily move from a "God of the gaps" metaphysics in the Newtonian worldview to Laplace's famous conclusion that we no longer needed that hypothesis. Even while upholding it in theory, deism rendered divine providence superfluous, and science, in turn, has ever since closed those "gaps" by filling in mystery with natural explanation. As Ian Barbour states it, "God's special action as a cause producing effects on the same level as natural causes was replaced by *law-obeying natural causes in each area of scientific advance.*"[4] But, of course, much has changed. While some theologians remain under the spell of a bygone positivism, Barbour notes that "[p]hilosophers today are cautious about the extension of specific scientific findings into over-all cosmic principles, metaphysical systems, or ethical norms. An argument between a theist and an exponent of naturalism need be viewed no longer as a conflict between religion and science, but rather as a confrontation between 'alternative world-views.'"[5] So too, if theologians wish to insist that God acts in personal existence but not in world history, they can no longer claim ineluctable scientific givens but must join everybody else in *recognizing* their basic beliefs *as* presuppositions, prejudices that already establish their horizon of expectation.

Similarly, Cambridge theologian-physicist John Polkinghorne adds, "Science cannot exclude the possibility that, on particular occasions, God does particular, unprecedented things. After all, he is the ordainer of the laws of nature, not someone who is subject to them. . . . God can't be capricious. He must be utterly consistent. However, consistency is not the same as dreary uniformity."[6] Thus, rather than seeing God as the source of uniformity, there is a greater openness in the current environment for seeing God as the source of genuine novelty and change. As John Searle has observed, the "brute fact" way of picturing reality is as naively objectivist as idealism is naively subjectivist. Rather, he says, we should recognize that "X counts as Y in context C."[7] But, as Polkinghorne observes, theology has not kept up with these changes in science. "Moreover, much twentieth-century theology has been either fideistic (Barth) or existential (Bultmann) in tone, conducted from within ghettoes walled off from scientific culture."[8] This is an ironic verdict concerning someone like Bultmann, so committed to the "scientific culture," albeit of a now bygone era. After quantum theory, assigning probabilities is more common in scientific practice than establishing laws.

Another discovery is chaos systems.[9] The scientific world dominated by Newton possessed calculus, with its corollary in geometry, "the well-behaved curves we can sketch with our pens upon a sheet of paper." While such well-behaved entities do exist, there are "the celebrated fractals, exhibiting roughly the same character on every scale of investigation, saw edges whose teeth are saw-edged, and so on down in an unending proliferation of structure that never settles to a tame unbroken line."[10] "The world is stranger than Newton had enabled us to think."[11] And yet, not even the behavior in quantum physics or chaos systems is totally random.[12] Polkinghorne rightly points out that Gordon Kaufman's "timeless deism" not only excludes the possibility of prayer and other fairly obvious aspects of religious life, but "has not commended itself to those scientist-theologians who have written on these matters," such as Barbour and Peacocke, as well as Polkinghorne himself.[13] Such scientists "do not suppose that modern science condemns God to so passive a role."[14]

For one thing, change and unpredictability are more obvious in contemporary scientific investigation. Barbour adds,

> Moreover, in quantum physics an electron does not have position and velocity; its wave function is an abstract symbolism from which certain correlations among observable quantities can be derived. These somewhat technical developments, which need not detain us now, cast doubt on the commonsense "realist" view that a scientific theory is a picture or replica of the real world as it exists apart from the observer, and gave some support to the view that a theory is simply a scheme for correlating experimental data.[15]

The Christian complex of doctrines (divine order, providence, rationality, and intelligibility, etc.) gave rise to the predictability that was an indispensable presupposition for the rise of modern science in the first place, according to many historians of science.[16]

But two important things happened to undermine this working consensus. First, William of Ockham went one step further than Duns Scotus by snapping the cord holding together God's absolute and ordained power, an essential bond to preserve for Calvin as well as Aquinas.[17] Calvin attacks this nominalist "dogma that ascribes to God absolute power" separated from justice. God would be juggling human beings like balls in the air. "One might more readily take the sun's light from its heat or its heat from its fire, than separate God's power from his justice."[18] By separating the will (divine or human) from nature, modernity introduced an anxiety into both science and metaphysics that helped to trigger the infamous obsession with apodictic certitude. As a consquence, chance-determined laws rather than providentially directed regularities established the criteria by which agential action in the world could be determined.

Once the divine will was conceived as at least potentially capricious, Descartes invented an autonomous (and equally capricious?) self as a storm wall against the crashing and unpredictable *Deus absconditus*. Those Christians who would contribute to the rise of modern science in the sixteenth through eighteenth centuries had to side with traditional theology over against nominalism in order to have a basis for their enterprise. In other respects, nominalism did contribute to the rise of modern science, particularly in its due attention to the particular. But with certain forms of postmodernism representing certain affinities with nominalism (indeed, taken to more radical extremes), the pendulum in the philosophy of science (if not in science itself, which still has to go on working in the laboratory) has swung from absolute determinacy to absolute indeterminacy.[19]

While we cannot naively return to a putative golden age of early modern "integration" and collaboration, there may be no time like the present to reassert the equilibrium which that consensus contributed to some of the most stellar growth in both theology and the natural sciences.

More decisive perhaps than science, says Polkinghorne, has been the philosophical-theological popularity of understanding divine action almost exclusively in terms of influence on individuals in their inner life.[20] It is this trajectory that Feuerbach, Marx, Nietzsche, and Freud correctly critiqued for the most part. But this view of religion is not only anthropocentric; it is highly individualistic and dualistic, as we have argued. Polkinghorne observes that "God cannot interact with the psyche without also interacting with the physical process of the world, since we are embodied beings. There is no totally separate realm of spiritual encounter."[21] While process theology attempts to clear this hurdle with a monistic account, Polkinghorne explains his reservations on scientific as well as theological grounds.[22] As to the latter, process theology seems to place God "too much at the margins of the world," as a panpsychic influence, "with a diminished role inadequate to the One who is believed to care providentially for creation and to be its ultimate hope of fulfillment."[23] This is an ironic outcome for a system that sets out to reduce practically all events to divine activity.

Grace Jantzen's alternative strategy within this panentheistic paradigm is inadequate:

> First, the universe, though it certainly does not look like a machine, does not look like an organism either. It lacks the degree of coherence and interdependence that characterises the unity of our bodies. To put the matter bluntly, if the world is God's body, where is God's nervous system within it? Second, in our psychosomatic nature we are constituted by our bodies, and in consequence we are in thrall to them as they change, eventually dying with their decay. The God of Christian theology cannot be similarly in thrall to the radical changes that have taken place within cosmic history and which will continue to happen in the universe's future. Whatever suggestiveness the idea of God's embodiment in the universe might appear to have as a metaphor, it seems that it cannot successfully function as a putative account of divine action.[24]

"It is possible, however," Polkinghorne says, "to seek to employ the analogical possibilities of relating divine agency to human agency in a more subtle and nuanced manner."[25] While appreciating aspects of Farrer's position, he concludes that one cannot simply call the "causal joint" a mystery (despite its distinguished heritage in theology) without falling into "a fideistic evasion of the problem."[26]

Instead, Polkinghorne speculates on the basis of a whole-and-its-parts view of reality, which involves both bottom-up and top-down causality. After examining this relationship in quantum physics, he concludes, "As embodied beings, humans may be expected to act both energetically and informationally. As pure spirit, God might be expected to act solely through information input. One could summarise the novel aspect of this proposal by saying that it advocates the idea of a top-down causality at work through 'active information.'"[27] Appealing especially to Bohm's version of quantum theory, he argues that "it is possible to maintain a clear distinction between energetic causality and 'informational' causality, in the sense of the model under discussion."[28]

At the end of all this, Polkinghorne advances a variation of process theology's dipolar deity. "The atemporal God of classical theology has the whole of history present to simultaneous view in a way that has no analogue in human experience. Our modes of agency could, therefore, be expected in this case to be of little analogical significance in the search for an understanding of divine action."[29] And yet Christians (assuming, however tacitly, this classical theology) have for a very long time been remarkably capable of understanding divine action analogically. Perhaps he is striving for something more akin to univocity here, but in any case Polkinghorne too closely identifies divine atemporality and divine action. While it is certainly true, according to classical theology, that they are related, it is far more nuanced than his discussion suggests. In such thinking, God's eternal decree is not equivalent to its execution, nor does the former preclude the latter or render it superfluous. Divine action occurs on two levels, in eternity and in time, and it need not be the case that divine ontology has to be therefore dipolar. There are analogies for this, of course, in ordinary human agency, as when an agent plans to hire an employee, marry someone, or go on vacation, and then also actually executes the myriad actions that either contribute to or constitute hiring, marrying, and vacationing.

Another problem with Polkinghorne's account is that, like many who verge on process theology, he takes the incarnation as the paradigm for theology proper: "The religion of the Incarnation seems to imply a divine participation in the reality of the temporal."[30] But does this not imply a non-Trinitarian—indeed, unitarian—conception of God? It is not the Trinity that became flesh, but the Word. The incarnation is too precise a theological point, too particular and specific within the Christian grammar, to be used as a cipher for some general conception of divinity. And if the incarnation is paradigmatic for what it means for God to be God, what is the point of the actual, historical incarnation of Jesus? How does this add anything to the story beyond an illustration of what is already the case, namely, becoming over being? Polkinghorne does not seem to be an exception to the general rule that one either has to live with the mystery of the causal joint or engage in a form of reductionism that can never account for every particular instance of double agency. Polkinghorne's proposal is that human beings act in the world through a combination of energetic physical causality and active information, and that God's providential interaction with creation is purely through the top-down input of information.[31]

By contrast, the primary/secondary causality schema of Catholic and Protestant scholasticism accounts for both order/predictability and what, from our perspective as agents, can only be regarded as "chaos"/randomness/exceptions to the case. Applications were drawn by the post-Reformation scholastics, both Lutheran and Reformed, as Barth observes in connection with the Lutheran Calov, who accepted "chance" in relation to secondary (relative), though not to primary "absolute" causality.[32] Calvin said precisely the same.[33] Thus, instead of reducing the entire account to what divine action is either *for us* (Bultmann, Tillich, Wright) or *for God* (Whitehead, Cobb, Polkinghorne), the wiser path is to acknowledge both, insofar as we are able—that is, insofar as our normative text answers this question in its own way and on its own terms.

Predictable patterns rather than inviolable laws comport better with both biblical theology and contemporary science. But for the former rather than the latter, there must be an active, intelligent, omniscient, and ever-vigilant provider. Even aside from special divine action, novelty and order must be coordinated, as Calvin observes: "Nothing is more natural than for spring to follow winter; summer, spring; and fall, summer—each in turn. Yet in this series one sees such great and uneven diversity that it readily appears each year, month, and day is governed by a new, a special, providence of God."[34] (This was, of course, before the realm of providence was increasingly surrendered to naturalism and divine action was identified almost exclusively with the spectacular or irregular.) Even given the problem of evil, which we shall consider below, there is too much to account for that is great, noble, surprisingly benevolent, and undeservedly rewarding in nature and in history for us to settle for either mechanistic naturalism (a twist on Stoicism) or chaotic randomness (a version of Epicureanism).

It was with representatives from both of these ancient schools that Paul gave his famous speech in the Areopagus.[35] For some present, God was entirely distant; for others, God was in the world or even perhaps one with the world, living, moving, acting, and having the world as its mode of being. But Paul daringly cites some of their own poets to turn the tables. Rather than God living and moving, growing and acting, in and through the world, "In [*God*] we live and move and have *our* being," he says. It is God who has established the very space in which human freedom can exist. Freedom is not intrinsic to creaturehood but is itself a gift of the creator. Debates about divine and human freedom often fail to begin with that assumption, so that already they are thought of by both sides as antagonistic: either God wins, or humans win. But this is to presuppose human autonomy from the outset, as if human beings created themselves. Calvin carefully steers a course between Stoicism and Epicureanism, fate and chance. We need not pursue the full outlines of the doctrine of providence, but will focus his comments on our topic. First, against the Stoics he writes,

> We do not, with the Stoics, contrive a necessity out of the perpetual connection and intimately related series of causes, which is contained in nature; but we make God the ruler and governor of all things, who in accordance with his wisdom has from the farthest limit of eternity decreed what he was going to do, and now by his might carries out what he has decreed.[36]

The reformer will not even grant the substitution of *permissio* for God's decretive purpose. A redemption-oriented theology will necessarily concentrate more on God's works than on God's being; more on action than essence. The God of scripture is, above all, an *actor*: the Living God. Like Luther, who accused Erasmus of turning God into an absentee landlord while human freedom ruled the world, Calvin warns against conjuring "a God who reposes idly in a watchtower."[37]

Analogous to human agency in relation to divine agency is the relation of natural processes to divine intervention. William P. Alston has every right to demand, "Just what have we learned in the last four hundred years that rules out direct divine production of worldly effects?"[38] Science itself tells us today that the category "natural laws" is interpreted as being more like regularities, space enough for predictability without materialistic determinism.

> Thus a law of hydrostatics might specify as a sufficient condition for a body sinking in still water (of sufficient depth) that the body be of a density greater than the water. A man standing upright in the middle of a deep lake without sinking would be a violation of that law, and so would be impossible. But in fact we are never justified in accepting laws of this sort. The most we are ever justified in accepting is a law that specifies what will be the outcome of certain *conditions in the absence of any relevant factors other than those specified in the law.* (emphasis added)[39]

In our account, God works miraculously, not against "laws" (i.e., nature) that he himself has established and upholds in any case, but against regularities. Such direct divine action is therefore irregular, but not a violation of natural laws. Once this distinction is stated, we can already see how unnecessarily captive we have been to the tendency to reify "the way things usually go" into a *thing*, a structure with almost a real ontic existence before which God must bow. But when we are talking instead of regularities, questions otherwise halted are now given free reign: for instance, if order is not an airtight sphere, secured by observable causal necessity, then why is there *any* regularity in nature? Why don't things just come together with *utter* randomness? Perhaps we can account for specific observable causes in our own experience for this or that, but what about the myriad instances in which it is obvious to our experience that there was no observed agent responsible for bringing order out of chaos? At this point we must avoid repeating a "God of the gaps" mistake, but rather press these questions to the point of opening conceptual space for the notion that God is necessary to the order (primary causality) that prevails finally over even the randomness which is attributable to the genuine flux and freedom within nature and human agency (secondary causality).

A further point must be addressed in relation to the claim concerning special divine action. Alston raises the question in the following statement:

> Is the raising of Jesus from the dead an "act of God" in any sense in which the motion of a leaf in the wind outside my window is not? . . . Why is that leaf moving in just the way it is? . . . God knows. And I don't. But in the case of the resurrection we think we have some idea of what He is up to. Nor does this attach only to the 'mighty acts of God in history.' If I take something to be a message from God to me, by understanding the content of the message I take myself to have some idea as to what God was up to in sending the message, viz., getting me to take account of this content in my future behaviour. It is

true that, on this account, what leads us to highlight certain events for special treatment is subjective, viz. the degree of our (presumed) insight into the divine purposes. But that doesn't mean that these events are acts of God only in some subjective sense. . . . It is only our selecting them for special notice that is subjective. And even this may involve a nonsubjective element, viz. God's informing us of His purposes in these instances.[40]

So how do we know that we have selected the right ones? Alston rejects publicity as a necessary criterion for predicating divine action in the world.[41] He has developed this more fully elsewhere.[42] But is this to conflate ordinary divine activity (providence) and special divine activity (miracle)? And is this conflation warranted?

I think it raises more problems than it solves and in the process points up the difficulty of trying to hitch the theological wagon to any currently plausible scientific theory. He correctly realizes that in providing no distinct account for both, discerning the significance of a leaf's movement, a personal communication from God, or the resurrection of Jesus is left to human subjectivity. There are no criteria for distinguishing God's having spoken through the prophets in scripture from God's having spoken through Virginia in the office lunchroom. But surely this not only erases distinctions between inspiration and illumination, but—even more importantly—distinctions between discerning God's ordinary activity through secondary causes and God's "mighty acts" as intrinsically significant landmarks in the dramatic employment of biblical narrative and history.

Alston tacks onto this thesis the possibility of "God's informing us of His purposes in these instances" as a "non-subjective element." But how is this any different from God's informing Virginia of his purposes in the lunchroom? Even if the scriptures are what Alston has in mind (and given his arguments in *Perceiving God*, the notion is not so restricted), can't one be expected to tell the difference between the birth of a baby and the resurrection of someone who was dead only three days prior? To suggest that these "mighty acts" are intrinsically significant is not to say that their entire significance in terms of meaning can be read off the surface of the events themselves (as in some extreme versions of the theology of history),[43] but it is to argue that they are not "selected for special notice" above other events simply because of personal or communal subjectivity. Alston's analysis comes too close at this point to the first position above, in which G. E. Wright and others insist that it is the believer's or community's faith that "sees" the miraculous in otherwise nonmiraculous events. The line between providence and miracle in divine action (as between illumination and inspiration in divine speech) continues to exercise an important function in keeping us from transforming the Bible's straightforward claims to miraculous activity into descriptions of benign, orderly events that can be reduced to a purely natural *explanation*, albeit without losing their supernatural *interpretation*. David Ray Griffin correctly observes, "By definition, a revelation must be a revelation to someone, whereas an act of God is what it is independently of any person's recognition of it."[44]

Finally, our discussion of the conceptual coherence of the notion of special divine agency must include a brief treatment of the problem of ascribing action in the world to an incorporeal agent. It is a question we encounter as children when we ask how it is that God could be said to have healed our illness, especially in cases in which the doctor's activity was observed but God's was not. As Eugene TeSelle observes, "There are some who argue that it is meaningless to speak of any agent which is not embodied, indeed, which is body acting in certain ways. But it can also be argued that organic unity is not a necessary condition for conceiving of an agent, because many of our own acts are not bodily movements but are 'intentional actions,' linked through meanings, not through reference to data of experience or objects of external action,"[45] a point made also by Thomas F. Tracy.[46]

Again we encounter the importance of distinguishing univocal from analogical predication. An apt analogy picks out literal predicates, but God's acting and God's embracing or loving (or, for that matter, God's being good, just, etc.) are both like and unlike an embodied (or for that matter, nonembodied creaturely) agent's. Of course, writes Rodger Forsman,[47]

> God cannot be identified as a subject of discourse in the way in which a physical object can; but it is then asserted that certain events, e.g., the deliverance of Israel from bondage in Egypt or the raising of Jesus from dead, have been brought about by divine activity; and so God can be identified as the agent of these effects. . . . Indirect identifying reference, then, will be identifying reference to something which in the determinate circumstances cannot be directly identified, but can be identifyingly referred to only because of a relation in which it stands to something which can be directly identified as a subject of discourse.[48]

Everyday examples of this include: "the cause of the noise," "the author of the book," or "the builder of the fence." "In each case there is an identifying reference to something by reference to something else."[49] This also should include the distinction which Owen Thomas borrows in this connection between basic and nonbasic actions.[50] But even God's nonbasic action is literally action. Thus, whenever basic action-type predicates occur in relation to God, they are literally, but analogically, descriptive. God can act even specially (i.e., miraculously) through the actions of other (embodied) agents, and often this is an acknowledged element of biblical narrative. In fact, this is what defeats the frequent identification of God's special action with direct action without remainder. Often (perhaps even usually) God is represented in scripture as acting in a miraculous manner (i.e., suspending ordinary natural processes) indirectly (i.e., through secondary causes and agents). Conversely, God's activity may be direct without involving miraculous intervention, as Alston points out: "If God wills, and hence brings it about, that certain thoughts form in my mind together with the conviction that these thoughts constitute His message to me at this moment, that is as full-blooded a case of direct divine action in the world as the miraculous production of audible voices."[51]

In summary, then, the "problem" of miracles is not what it once was, but then our understanding of "miracle" itself must change as well. If a quasideistic, Newtonian worldview led us to think of special divine action in the world as an interruption of natural laws that were increasingly hardened into something akin to Stoic fate, a quasipanentheistic-process worldview may be inclined to lead us toward something akin to Epicurean chance. Just as Bultmann's theology fit well with positivistic science, process theology is the ally of various scientific approaches that are self-consciously "mystical." Both extremes are in marked contrast to the much more balanced perspective of the seventeenth century, where, generally speaking, (a) action did not have to be considered special (i.e., miraculous) in order for it to be considered divine action; (b) natural order *and* novelty were products, not adversaries, of divine supervision; (c) analogical interpretation of divine action-predicates was consciously used without denying the literal character of such assertions. It is not surprising that during this period scientists and theologians cooperated and, in many cases, were one and the same person. Now, for the first time since Newton, the conceptual space for developing this position in newer and fuller ways appears to be opening up, without persons having to resort to mystical theologies and their scientific counterparts that confuse the creator with the creation and reduce diverse agency to a totally unified theory of action. But that promise is more easily made than fulfilled. We turn now to this problem.

THE PROBLEM OF DOUBLE AGENCY

If the "problem" of divine action in the natural world is no longer the problem it once was, the perennial issue of double agency is as intensely debated as ever. Frank Dilley aptly summarizes the issue:

> In short, the dilemma is this: if there is genuine unity of action, two parties doing exactly the same act at the same time, then there is no duality of causes; and if there is duality of causes, then there is no unity of action. . . . If it is not possible to conceive of two sets of free causes operating conjointly in exactly the same action, then it is not possible to satisfy the conditions by which one would be able to say that both naturalistic (and human) and theological explanations are valid. . . . Hence the seeming plausibility of the joint-cause solution breaks down. The alternative to conservatism and liberalism turns out to be a delusion.[52]

On the question of how the divine and human actors can both serve as agents in the same event, we are reminded how easy it is to find bad analogies even for a good theory. For instance, Alston writes, "When I split a log with an axe, it is true both that the axe splits the log and that I split the log."[53] But the axe isn't a personal agent, much less one who possesses genuine freedom and responsibility. Surely Alston would not want to say that the relation of divine and human agency is analogous to that of a human agent and an inanimate tool. According to Barth, echoing the Reformed tradition more generally on this point, "we can take as our starting-point the statement that God rules creaturely occurrence by ordering it." He adds:

> In this context the concept order does not have the passive sense of the permanent structure of a thing, its qualities and circumstances, but the active sense of a continuing operation by which an occurrence in time takes place in accordance with a definite plan, and is determined and formed and directed through constantly changing situations and stages. . . . The rule of God is the order of God in this active sense, His ordering of all temporal occurrence. . . . [F]or certainly we must say that everything which occurs in the temporal course of that history [of the world] is ordered and determined and overruled by God. . . . If God orders world-occurrence, then this includes at once the general fact that He controls creaturely activity. This does not mean that He suspends it as such, substituting for it His own activity. . . . The fact that He controls [the creature's sphere] means that He is the Lord of the creature even while it has its own activity.[54]

I would want to add to that last statement that it is only because God—this particular God—is Lord of the creature that the creature *has* its own activity in the first place. This point is underscored in the Westminster Confession:

> God, the great Creator of all things, doth uphold, direct, dispose, and govern all creatures, actions, and things, from the greatest even to the least, by his most wise and holy providence, according to his infallible foreknowledge, and the free and immutable counsel of his own will, to the praise of the glory of his wisdom, power, justice, goodness, and mercy. Although in relation to the foreknowledge and decree of God, the first cause, all things come to pass immutably and infallibly, yet, by the same providence, he ordereth them to fall out according to the nature of second causes, either necessarily, freely, or contingently. God, in his ordinary providence, maketh use of means, yet is free to work without, above, and against them, at his pleasure.[55]

One of the weaknesses of the contemporary discussions of double agency is that, for the most part, they do not take bearings from the "great conversation" of historical theology. At this point, therefore, I wish to outline briefly some distinctions from this conversation that may prove helpful in understanding the relation between divine and human agency. We shall have to limit ourselves to seminal contributions from the Reformed tradition, for the sake of brevity as well as my own limitations.

Following Luther, Calvin has a developed notion of divine hiddenness undergirding a theology of the cross, as opposed to a theology of glory.[56] Much of what happens in our experience is, to us, fortuitous, since such things "lie hidden in God's purpose." Furthermore, it is not in our power to unlock these sacred precincts. "As all future events are uncertain to us, so we hold them in suspense, as if they might incline to one side or the other. Yet in our hearts it nonetheless remains fixed that nothing will take place that the Lord has not previously foreseen."[57] Such providence sometimes "works through an intermediary, sometimes without an intermediary, sometimes contrary to every intermediary."[58] While in "the law and the gospel" mysteries have been revealed, "his wonderful method of governing the universe is rightly called an abyss, because while it is hidden from us, we ought reverently to adore it."[59] Thus Calvin exercises considerably more restraint than medieval scholastics in probing the intricacies of divine sovereignty, anticipating Austin Farrer's "learned ignorance" concerning the causal joint of double agency. God has decreed the actions of free agents: this statement unearths the location of the *problem* of the causal nexus, without revealing the nexus or its solution. "Nevertheless," says Calvin, "a godly man will not overlook the secondary causes," and eschew any procedure that portrays God as the sole and immediate cause of every event.[60]

With Roman Catholics and fellow Protestants (including the Remonstrants), Calvin and the Reformed tradition generally affirmed the doctrine of *concursus,* which was based on the assumption that "no second cause can act until acted upon."[61] But, following Augustine, Thomists, and Dominicans, the Reformed went a step further than granting this general concursus: "that is, not only exciting to action, but sustaining, guiding, and determining the act. . . ."[62] And yet, the act produced in a concursive event is referred to the second cause.

> When the fire burns, it is to the fire, and not to God that the effect is to be attributed. When a man speaks, it is a man, and not God who utters the words. When the moon raises the tidal wave, and the wave dashes a vessel on the shore, the effect is to be attributed, not to the moon, but to the momentum of the wave. . . . The doctrine of concursus does not deny the efficiency of second causes. They are real causes, having a principium agendi in themselves. The agency of God neither supersedes, nor in any way interferes with the efficiency of second causes.[63]

The locus classicus for illustrating double agency or primary-secondary causality is Acts 2:22–24, where Peter tells the crowd that they sent Jesus to his death, but that he was "handed over to you according to the definite plan and foreknowledge of God" and then in 4:27–28, where John and Peter are praying before the assembly after being released from prison. They pray, "For in this city, in fact, both Herod and Pontius Pilate, with the Gentiles and the peoples of Israel, gathered together against your holy servant Jesus, whom you anointed, to do whatever your hand and your plan had predestined to take place." This sort of double agency is what gives the biblical narrative so much of its dramatic action.

> Absalom, polluting his father's bed by an incestuous union, commits a detestable crime; yet God declares this work to be his own; for the words are: "You did it secretly; but I will do this thing openly, and in broad daylight." Jeremiah declared that every cruelty the Chaldeans exercised against Judah was God's work. For this reason Nebuchadnezzar is called God's servant. . . . The Assyrian he calls the rod of his

anger, and the ax that he wields with his hand. The destruction of the Holy City and the ruin of the Temple he calls his own work.[64]

Owen Thomas is right to remind us that many of the recent attempts have been hampered by poor analogies.[65] Understandably, he points to Jesus as the clue to God's actions in relation to double agency. "The words and works of Jesus are the words and works of God (John 5:19, 19:10, etc.). Christ is the power and wisdom of God in action (1 Cor. 1:24)."[66]

This is where we link up again with our discussion of analogy. An account of divine action (especially *special* divine action) cannot be content with an abstract divine actor. Jesus said, "Whoever has seen me has seen the Father" (John 14:9). Consequently, we could say that Jesus was and remains the univocal core of divine action, discourse, and being. Elsewhere, Jesus is called the "image [eikōn] of the invisible God. . . . For in him *all the fullness* of God was pleased to dwell" (Col. 1:15, 19, emphasis added). God's self-revelation in Christ is not comprehensive: here God still reveals himself by hiding himself. Nevertheless, it is no longer merely analogical to assert one thing of both God and a human being—in this particular case. "Good" as a predicate of both God and Betsy is used analogically, but as a predicate of God and Jesus it is used univocally. Thus, to say that Jesus has acted in a particular way is to say that God has so acted. It is not merely an instrumental christology, either: God acts not only in and through Jesus, but Jesus who acts *is* God in action.

Despite this identity with God, Jesus submitted to the service, obedience, and humiliation that God's justice required for winning redemption of the world. Here therefore we have a sublime example of double agency, in which the Father's sovereignty and the Son's free actions retain their respective integrity. In reply to accusations of breaking the Sabbath, Jesus said, "My Father is still working, and I also am working" (John 5:17). But the Father's working was not identical to the Son's working. Each "working" was the effect of a distinct agent, even though they were working toward the same specific ends in each case. "Thy will, not mine, be done," is not a surrender of Jesus' ego (his identity as agent). Rather, it is his self-surrender to the Father's revealed purposes despite his human fears. And although this is a special case, given the uniqueness of Jesus' unity with the Father, this does give us a biblical model for understanding not only divine agency, but human agency as well. It is the Son who is working and, indeed, is willing to have the success of this work attributed to himself and his mission. But then we also find him attributing these works to his Father.

While Jesus' unity with the Father is sui generis, precisely the same language is used of believers in relation to the Godhead, although we take this to be used in this case analogically rather than univocally. Thus Paul exhorts, "[W]ork out your own salvation with fear and trembling; for it is God who is at work in you, enabling you both to will and to work for his good pleasure" (Phil. 2:12–13). At this point it is important, however, to distinguish between double agency vis-à-vis divine providence and vis-à-vis redemption. It is easy in these discussions to confuse double agency with the debate over sin and grace, or free will and pre-destination. Properly speaking, the doctrine of *concursus* is not necessarily con-nected with the issue of grace and free will. In other words, we are not discussing the relationship between divine grace and human choice or action toward the attainment of salvation, but the general matter of double agency. Hence, Hodge writes, "That [agents] act at all is due to the divine efficiency, but the particular nature of their acts (at least when evil) is to be referred, not to that all-pervading efficiency of God, but to the nature or character of each particular agent."[67] He adds in parentheses, "at least when evil," in order to bracket the case in which a righteous decision or action is attributed to divine grace.

When Paul writes, "But by the grace of God I am what I am. . . . I worked harder than any of them—though it was not I, but the grace of God that is with me" (1 Cor. 15:10), we must first determine whether this represents a reference to agency generally or to credit. It is the latter, of course, which is central for Paul's soteriology: God alone deserves the glory for human redemption. The apostle should not be interpreted as saying generally of human agency, "I am not really the active agent," but rather, "I am not the unmoved agent who deserves the credit."

The difficulties with the traditional doctrine of divine predestination and providence are well known, but they are not treated as difficulties in the scrip-tures. That God is active in caring for the world and leading history to specific ends by governing every specific natural and human event is never regarded as problematic for human responsibility in scripture. Our difficulty is due in large measure to the remarkable anthropocentricity, individualism, and autonomy that are apparently as ineluctable to many modern theologians as the acceptance of causal naturalism.[68] For the people of Israel, divine providence—even when it was recognized as a rod upon their back—was a sign of God's presence and nearness, not of a radical distance and power that could instill only fear and resentment.

Attempting to circumvent the causal debate altogether, Ronald Thiemann does provide an excellent example of double agency, even if one does not fully concur with his account: namely, the example of liturgical absolution. Here, God acts and the minister acts, each performing distinct operations and yet ultimately the efficacy is referred to God. And Thiemann's proposal, which we will discuss in connection with the claim that God speaks, takes the matter one great step forward by introducing the rubric of the gospel as "narrated promise."[69] As we will discuss later, the model of "narrated promise" is certainly moving in the right direction. And yet, this is a piece (albeit, a significant piece) of the larger *covenan-tal* model that incorporates more data and provides for richer explorations of the ways in which God acts and speaks. Owen Thomas also appreciates Thiemann's illustration from liturgical absolution. "Here the divine and human agents are fully active in the one event of pardon." Yet Thomas chides, "I am surprised that the Lutheran Thiemann did not also use the example of Christian preaching in which the hearer relying on the promise of God trusts that the human word becomes the vehicle of the word of God." Thomas cites the Second Helvetic

Confession, a Reformed symbol of 1566, which declares that the preached word is especially the Word of God (*Praedicatio verbi Dei est verbum Dei*).[70]

It seems that this view succeeds where the alternatives fail, particularly in that it accounts for both divine agency (in a robust and thereby meaningful sense) and genuine human freedom. Scripture nowhere suggests that, because a single event is described simultaneously as the act of God and the act of human agents, there is a clash or an overwhelming of one agent by the other in the production of the event. Distinct actors perform distinct acts, although both may be regarded as causes (one primary, the other secondary). Austin Farrer cites an obvious example to which Calvin alluded above:

> Isaiah was convinced that the Assyrian invasions were the scourge of God, a Father's correction of his sons' rebellion. But he knew that the Assyrians were not somnambulists under a divine hypnotism. The Assyrian was a rod in the hand of God's indignation, but he had no notion of being anything of the kind. . . . Isaiah does not begin from speculation into the mystery of Assyrian motives, but from the divine act of scourging Israel's back with an Assyrian rod. His reference of the effect to its divine cause does not go by way of the Assyrian's choices even though he turns aside to muse upon them.[71]

The causal joint is unknown to us: "not knowing the modality of the divine action we cannot pose the problem of their mutual relation," says Farrer.[72] Restraining the urge to speculate beyond this point, Farrer chooses the course of Christian theology over its many centuries, despite the lure of and sometimes even seduction by speculative philosophy. Knowing the precise nature and site of this causal joint would be more interesting and satisfying, but it is not essential for providing a sufficient account of double agency for the divine drama in which we are engaged.

So let us take up Frank Dilley's statement of the problem again:

> In short, the dilemma is this: if there is genuine unity of action, two parties doing exactly the same act at the same time, then there is no duality of causes; and if there is duality of causes, then there is no unity of action. . . . If it is not possible to conceive of two sets of free causes operating conjointly in exactly the same action, then it is not possible to satisfy the conditions by which one would be able to say that both naturalistic (and human) and theological explanations are valid. . . . Hence the seeming plausibility of the joint-cause solution breaks down. The alternative to conservatism and liberalism turns out to be a delusion.[73]

But, in our account, there is no "unity of action" between the two agents. It is one thing to decree the safe passage of a ship in time to be carried out through secondary agents and quite another to guide the ship to its destination as its captain. Hence, there is a genuine duality of causes. How then does this not dissolve all *unity* of action, as Dilley suggests? Of course, it does dissolve such unity of action. But why is that problematic? Dilley demands too much of *concursus* by insisting that it must preserve a unity of action (despite dual causality) that, as we have already seen, is not only unnecessary but impossible, given the distinction between creator and creature. The effect of a concursive event (note "event," not "action," since the argument here is that there are many "actions" involved, on the part of two or more agents) is referred to the secondary agent precisely because it is that agent's actions that are most directly recognized as producing it.

A similar objection is put forward by David Griffin. As Thomas summarizes, Griffin holds that "the primary-secondary cause version of double agency assumes the sufficiency of each cause and that the idea of two sufficient causes for one event is self-contradictory."[74] But the doctrine of *concursus* does not assume the sufficiency of each cause. In any case, the response to Griffin is essentially the same as that made to Dilley: primary and secondary causality each entail subsidiary actions that are proper to each agent. One must not confuse the totality of a produced event (whose diversity is itself discernable upon reflection) with a unity of action or sufficiency of each cause.

Diverging from this fairly traditional account of *concursus* in terms of *primum* and *secundum agens*, Karl Barth says that it would "obviously have been better to refer to the relation between Creator and creature revealed in the Word of God, the relation between the Creator who is gracious and the creature which receives grace."[75] But this reveals the downside of collapsing all of creaturely reality into grace. Barth's account risks reducing anthropology to soteriology, nature to grace. Do we really want to say that all human action is a case of "the creature which receives grace"? Beyond philosophical questions of human freedom, that seems theologically far too restrictive to account for the wide diversity of human action that we actually find exhibited in the Bible itself.

The notion of a divine upholding of the world in general, a universal reign in which nothing *in particular* is willed or accomplished by God in history is the corollary of the belief that God "acts" in the world "universally," while refusing to affirm a single instance in world history in which God has so acted. This includes both "deistic" (hypertranscendent) and "panentheistic" (hyperimmanent) versions of modern theology. By contrast, we maintain the position expressed by Vernon White: "God acts personally, universally, with priority and sovereign efficacy; he acts in relation to particular events."[76] Furthermore, White agrees with Farrer's insistence that the "causal joint" is unknown to us: *that* God and humans are both agents acting in history is clear from the biblical text, but *how* this double agency exists remains a mystery.

Speech-act theory suggests one final point on this matter. Among others, Searle has pointed out the importance of promising as an illocutionary act. Among his conditions for this speech act is the following: "I cannot promise that someone else will do something (although I can promise to see that he will do it)."[77] Relating this to the question of divine agency, we can only conclude that if God cannot fulfill this parenthetical condition (i.e., promising to get the job done, either directly or through other persons), then God cannot be considered as a candidate for promising. As we will argue in part 2, the biblical text itself (especially within its covenantal framework) provides an account of divine speech and action through human agents as well as through ordinary and extraordinary natural and historical events. Biblical theology assumes a richer account of agency than either a supernaturalistic or naturalistic occasionalism.

THE PROBLEM OF EVIL

As we have seen, the question of double agency raises all sorts of questions related to theodicy. If God is the primary efficient cause of everything that happens, why is there evil in the world?[78] But, of course, if God is capable of *any* action in the world (even at the benign level of influence), the problem of evil is just as acute as it is for a full-bodied notion of divine sovereignty. But if God does *not* act in the world, even greater problems emerge. Whether God is too feeble to act in the world or is for some reason aloof or disinterested, accepting the absence of divine action would hardly ameliorate difficulties with God in the light of evil. If God cannot act in the world, he is too weak to be worshiped; if God will not act in the world, he is too callous and unjust to be worshiped. In either case, a retreat into divine passivity will not resolve the vexing issues surrounding theodicy.

Issues related to theodicy have been directly confronted for accounts of divine sovereignty from at least the days of Job. In Western philosophy as well as theology, Stoic fate and Epicurean chance have represented the Scylla and Charybdis between which reflection and action had to steer its course.[79] While some religious and philosophical perspectives, both Eastern and Western, downplay or even deny the reality of suffering and evil in the world, the biblical narrative does actually offer a consistent, though hardly comprehensive, account. *If God acts at all, why doesn't he act more?* This is a good question, but as an abstraction it does not have much to do with the divine drama. In many theodicies, such practical but nevertheless abstract questions fail to recognize the treatment of divine sovereignty over evil that one meets in the biblical text. Here, it is part of a story, a plot. Apart from this plot, there is no context for a Christian response to evil.

Our question, therefore, could be transposed in the following manner: If God is a player at all in this drama, much less the playwright, why doesn't he reduce the problems the characters encounter? In the "divine drama" model, the problem of evil needs to be reconfigured. Without determining the possible positions in advance, the root metaphor nevertheless resists metaphysical speculation. Here, the question is, given the facts of *this* play. It is a drama with its own plot: creation in the divine image, forfeiting the consummation by rebellion, a promised Messiah and a typological kingdom of God, the advent of the second Adam to rescue fallen image-bearers, and his return "at the end of the age" in order to consummate the forfeited kingdom forever. Its central actor is an unsubstitutable character, as Hans Frei would say. And its answer to evil is practical (acted out) rather than theoretical. No other story could be substantiated to make basically the same point.

General metaphysical questions may be interesting, but it seems that a *Christian* theodicy will offer an account in the form of historical narrative. This narrative or dramatic plot is not somehow illustrative of the Christian response, but constitutes it: "This is what has happened, this is where things are now, and this is where they are going." It is impossible to be exposed to the performance of this drama for very long without realizing that evil is treated as the consequence of misused freedom. Sinners and sinned-against, humanity lives "east of Eden," in a wilderness of social constructions that are attempts to flee the presence and reality of God. We noted above that the very idea of special divine action in the world is a "problem" only if one presupposes a worldview in which the ordinary course of nature and history is predestined by either causal fate or chaotic chance. If one begins with the conviction that God is creator and provident lord of all that God has made, then special divine action will be understood as surprising exceptions to God's ordinary rule. But if one begins with the belief that God is an absentee landlord who works in individual psyches but not in nature or history, such special action will be regarded as impossible, incredible, and downright intrusive.

It is the same with the problem of evil. If one begins with the biblical drama, in which a broken covenant lies at the very center of a crime scene, the problem takes on deeply personal and historical overtones. According to this plot, God was in no way obligated to rescue the creature, who had rejected a noble role as divine representative and caretaker of creation, in order to seek autonomy. Such a quest for the supercreaturely freedom to construct oneself and one's world, rather than receive selfhood and otherness as gifts, led to the disintegration of every relationship. And yet, according to this drama, God not only preserved nature, history, and culture (even after the arrogance and brutality of Cain), but executed a redemptive strategy. But even here, God triumphs over evil in the end, not by canceling out the human agency that was misused, but by renewing and restoring the divine image and finally restoring the entire creation, so that together humankind and the world subjected to sin will be liberated to enjoy the consummation that never arrived in Eden. A broken covenant is at last repaired and its conditions fulfilled by the second Adam, who will make all things new in the likeness of his own resurrection.

So when *this* drama is the context for theodicy, the tables are turned. Instead of God being on trial, it is the creature who is arraigned and questioned. Now we begin to see ourselves cast in the role of Adam and Eve, demanding autonomy and self-sufficiency even as we are surrounded by signs of our noble status, which has been assigned to us by a good creator. And now the problem of evil, though not solved in our minds, is overwhelmed by the problem of good. In other words, given this particular drama, one would expect evil and suffering as consequences of the actions of the leading characters. But one would not expect good and blessing as a response of the play's central figure thus wronged. For theology, then, there can be no general, metaphysical theodicy. Every abstract theoretical account founders under the reductionisms of hyperimmanence/hypertranscendence, antitheses or syntheses. Christian theology asserts a practical, not a theoretical, solution to the problem of evil.

Finally, there are practical considerations as well that lead us to affirm special divine action precisely because of, not in spite of, the problem of evil. Jeffrey Eaton has defended the importance of this notion in his defense of liberation theologies. "If God is not an agent engaged in the making of a world," he says, "then God is simply a metaphor for the way the one who uses that metaphor would like the world to go."[80] "Indeed, it is only if God is agent that theology has a God worth having."[81] Eaton too is concerned to steer a course between univocal and equivocal understandings of divine action: "The analogy of divine agency allows one to conceive of God; the realisation that this conception is analogical prevents the idolatrous fixation on the image."[82] Actual divine action in the world is the only genuine safeguard against the pretended rulers of world history, and while members of the theological establishment in our day may not be terribly interested in the idea of divine intervention (especially in judgment), the suffering and oppressed find such assurances empowering. Idolatry is "the sin which most liberation theologians contend is at the root of human oppression," says Eaton.[83]

Eaton does not dismiss the logical problems in asserting divine action, as we have examined them. However, he does not regard paradox as the same thing as contradiction. He writes, "The elusiveness of the causal nexus is the very heart of the paradox of double-agency."[84] But the paradox is what makes genuine divine and human agency meaningful. To attempt to unravel the paradox is to reduce either the self to the other or the other to the self, divine to human agency, or vice versa. Eaton also warns against devising a theodicy-proof account of divine action that ignores the particularity of the biblical account: "One of the sophistications of modern theology is that theological inquiry can be carried on independent of a commitment to the God of theism. This view owes as much to Barth as it does to Hegel."[85] In process thought, God is identified with the world, and this negates some of liberation theology's greatest concerns. For its vision of justice, liberation theology has to insist upon "the theistic assertion of creative omnipotence." God must stand "outside of" the creation, we might say, in order to judge and rescue. God cannot be subject to the same powers and principalities that must be overcome if justice is to prevail. Eaton finds in a robust notion of divine sovereignty a source for the impulses of liberation and therefore wonders why it is that some versions of liberation theology look elsewhere: "It is difficult to imagine that so activist a witness could construe God in terms that are not activist, could be satisfied with the conception of God that is less than that of perfect agency, an agent who, for freedom, creates significantly free creatures."[86] However, it is precisely this awareness of an active God that has motivated prominent liberation theologies.[87]

Serene Jones has observed that Calvin and his sixteenth-century refugee followers also read divine sovereignty as hope for the oppressed.[88] Such a strong view of divine action in the course of human events may not be as favorably received by those who are tempted more by autonomy and ruling than by liberation from the powers and principalities. And, as Calvin reminds us, such a strong account reminds us not only of divine judgment, but of divine patience, instilling "peaceful moderation of mind upon us." "If Joseph had stopped to dwell upon his brothers' treachery," Calvin reasons, "he would never have been able to show a brotherly attitude toward them. But since he turned his thoughts to the Lord, forgetting the injustice, he inclined to gentleness and kindness, even to the point of comforting his brothers and saying: 'It is not you who sold me into Egypt, but I was sent before you by God's will, that I might save your life.' 'Indeed, you intended evil against me, but the Lord turned it into good.'"[89] This is how it seems to go in the divine drama.

CONCLUSION

This chapter has attempted to make the case that, at the end of the day, every theological program that we have considered does in fact affirm a core of set propositions. This is not to justify the position described by George Lindbeck as "cognitive-propositionalism," in which Christian faith and practice can be reduced to timeless principles. Nevertheless, it is to make the point that there must be at least some literal predicates in any system. Bultmann's core propositions include the univocally understood kerygmatic kernel after separation from its mythological husk. Tillich really does believe that God is the ground of being rather than a being.

We do live in a secular environment, as Sallie McFague reminds us, "and hence [are] afraid that our images refer to nothing, [so] we literalize them, worshiping the icon in our desperation."[90] This fits with dramatic tension in the biblical text between Yahweh and even the icons that Israel establishes on the "high places." Even in the episode of the golden calf, Aaron, capitulating to the desires of the people, declares, "Tomorrow shall be a festival to the LORD," feasting and reveling around the idol (Exod. 32:5–6). At least in Aaron's mind, the act could be justified in that it was Yahweh who was being worshiped, albeit through the vehicle of this gilded image. Thus, it was a violation of the second rather than the first commandment. But God commanded the people not only to worship the correct God, but to worship that God correctly; namely, as that God had condescended in self-disclosure. There is a danger of making even good things—the Bible, tradition, the church—ends rather than means, the ultimate object of faith being confused with the ways in which people are incorporated and preserved within the community of faith. But in substituting a "parabolic" for an "incarnational" christology,[91] McFague fails to recognize that in *this* drama the whole point was holding off univocal identification of God with an observable creature until the advent of Jesus Christ, "the eikōn of the invisible God" in whom "all the fullness of God was pleased to dwell" (Col. 1:15, 19). Like the literalists whom she criticizes, McFague trades in the dramatic movement of redemptive history for static principles or symbols. So "idolatry" becomes any identification of the divine with the human, finite, or worldly. This is an odd position to argue for one so committed to a panentheistic picture.

G. E. Wright's biblical theology project has shown much more promise in taking the drama seriously on its own terms, but finally could not bring itself to overcoming the problem of historical reason. Advocating a theology of "God Who Acts" is quite different, it seems, from identifying specific instances in which God actually has so acted. Communal or individual interpretation (or faith) cannot be the source of predicating special divine action. For faith would have no warrant for reaching the conclusion that God was acting here in this or that particular event unless it was in fact the case, quite apart from one's noticing it, that God had acted. All of the faith in the world cannot raise the dead, judge the world, and deliver the earth from corruption.

In the narrative approach, the point is not to get behind or above the text, but to allow oneself to be absorbed by it, to indwell it. "Narrative is the form in which we render in a coherent fashion the agent's actions across time and thus the agent's character," we will recall from F. Michael McLain.[92] But the dramatic model includes this aspect as well as many others that the narrative paradigm does not seem to accommodate. For instance, it would seem that in the most obvious examples of narrative theology, certain dichotomies are unnecessarily extended. For example, reader-text and intratextual reality–extratextual reference. By contrast, performance (in the dramatic mode) transcends these dichotomies by rendering author and reader both characters in the same play. And while "text" can easily become a frozen metaphor, drama includes the essential elements of textuality (as both action and script) while giving more serious attention to the dynamic character of even the text itself. In this respect, Yale postliberalism is perhaps not postliberal *enough*. The sovereign self is still the center of knowing (*principium cognoscendi*), for scripture is normative and events such as the resurrection of Jesus are essential due to their function within the community. While modernity enshrined the sacred self, postliberalism seems to enshrine the sacred community. What is needed, however, is a way of transcending the mind-set of modern autonomy altogether, whether of a Kierkegaardian-individualist or Hegelian-communal variety. By arguing that God has actually acted on the stage of human history, and not merely within the narrative text, we are able to provide legitimate space for both the individual and the community, but as both are seen to be created and supported by the drama, and not vice versa.[93] It is divine *action*, not individual or communal *decision*, that scripts the convictions and conventions of the people of God.

Immanentist approaches share in common with the preceding views a tendency toward the "seeing-as" or, to borrow Cobb's expression, "experiencing-as" in reference to divine action. It is how one describes the event that gives it a sacred or supernatural character, although the event itself is the result of natural causes. But this perspective does not critique naturalism the way it critiques supernaturalism. To be sure, "natural" and "supernatural" explanations may be accounted for in terms of divine dipolarity. Nevertheless, the event is regarded as objectively natural and subjectively supernatural. In other words, God did not become incarnate, bear away sin, and rise again the third day—at least not in the straightforward sense with which Christians have read and been shaped by the gospel. Divine action is reduced to one flat line of ordinary world-embodiment (Jantzen) or influence (Cobb). In all of these proposals, the radical interruption of ordinary expectations by a genuine reversal, a real novum, is absent. As Ernst Bloch reminds us in his inimitable language, "Ultimately, therefore, a public as well as central conception (though in no way a concept) of the beginning of a new life (the *incipit vita nova* formula) came into the world only through the Bible."[94] By contrast, immanentist approaches merge the one and the many, giving priority to human agency while restricting divine agency to affective influence.

None of these proposals provides a satisfactory account for the Christian assertion that God acts in history. However, in a dramatic model, performance is both public and yet textually determined (in scripted form) and interpreted by a particular body of characters before those who as yet can only see themselves as spectators in the audience rather than players. That "God acts in history" is an obvious feature of the performance and is hardly surprising, given the definitive role that this character has in this play. Perhaps in other scripts, but not in this one, this divine character comes off as an intruder. Perhaps in other plots, but not in this one, Yahweh's action in history fails to make sense. This drama justifies our speaking as we do of God's action in the world, not a formal theory of "agent" and "action." God *can* do whatever God in fact *has* done.[95] Thus, we have attempted to lay out an explicit account for the claim that God acts (even specially) in history. God does so in the context of a *covenant*, by means of *Christ*, a point that will be more fully developed in our account of divine speech.

We have seen the challenge before an analogical approach. Near the beginning of this chapter we cited Langdon Gilkey's point: "Unless one knows in some sense what the analogy means, how the analogy is being used, and what it points to, an analogy is empty and unintelligible; that is, it becomes equivocal language." Our proposal has already built so much—namely, the claim that God has acted and does act in the world—on the notion of analogical discourse. Is that sustainable in the light of Gilkey's observation, though?

Without a univocal core, critics have correctly insisted, there is no way of determining whether the analogies we use for an unknown God are apt. But the New Testament represents Jesus Christ as the univocal core of God, "the exact imprint of God's very being" (Heb. 1:3), "in whom are hidden all the treasures of wisdom and knowledge" (Col. 2:3).[96] While redemptive history and revelation cannot be simply reduced to the career of Jesus Christ, the latter is the hidden yet univocal presence of God in the world. According to this divine drama, then, when Jesus acts, God acts. To see Jesus is to see God: "God was in Christ reconciling the world to himself" (2 Cor. 5:19). Even in translation one may detect the writer's enthusiasm:

> We declare to you what was from the beginning, what we have heard,
> what we have seen with our eyes, what we have looked at and touched
> with our hands, concerning the word of life—this life was revealed,
> and we have seen it and testify to it, and declare to you the eternal

life that was with the Father and was revealed to us—we declare to
you what we have seen and heard so that you also may have fellowship with us. (1 John 1:1–3)

A demand for miracles Jesus associated with unbelief, and repeatedly in Israel's history the temptation to idolatry is supported by an overrealized eschatology in which the people demand that patience give way now to immediate gratification, hope to sight, faith to realization, promise to fulfillment. But equally disastrous is an underrealized eschatology, in which the hiddenness of the kingdom under the form of the cross, like the hiddenness of God in Christ as the suffering servant, leads the community to conclude that the Parousia did not come and that God has not acted in history. In contrast to both gilded Ba'als and laments such as "The harvest is past, the summer is ended, and we are not saved" (Jer. 8:20), the apostolic eyewitness of "the word of life" announces a genuine novum, anticipated but greater than anticipated, an event in which God acts visibly and in full view of the audience.

In Jesus Christ, then, God proves the appropriateness of all of the analogies that have been authorized for faithful speech and action by his people before (patriarchs and prophets) and after (apostles). At the same time, proving the appropriateness of revealed analogies is not the same as revealing the precise nature of God's essence. While "good" in reference to Alice may still be different from "good" in reference to God, this adjective has precisely the same meaning in reference to both Jesus and God. It is univocal, not because the autonomous self (or community) has determined its aptness, nor because of how such an affirmation functions within the life of the individual (or community), nor because of any general "univocity of being." Rather, it is univocal because of the unique identity that Jesus both is and enacted as the "only-begotten," the "express image of the invisible God." Unlike the prophets and apostles, when Jesus acts, he is not only the instrument of the Father's secret will, but the divine actor himself, "Immanuel: God with Us." This is how Jesus' role plays itself out in this drama, or, to invoke Frei's suggestive exploration, it is how Jesus enacts his identity.[97] At the same time it is essential to add that although the relation between God and Jesus Christ is univocal in terms of predicates, our knowledge of God—even in Christ—remains analogical and ectypal, which is fitting for pilgrims on the way.

But even if one were to accept the claim, "God acts in history," based on the empirical identity of God and Jesus, what about the reports themselves? Since those now living were not present to experience Jesus directly, how can this claim have any meaning for a community of interpreters today? At this point, action is not a sufficient category to comprehend divine revelation. It is therefore to the world stage and, more specifically, to the relationship of redemption to history, that we now turn.

Chapter Four

All the World's a Stage

*Are there to be no signs of the superabundance of grace outside of
the interior life, or only in a few small and isolated communities?
No signs of this on the great stage of the world?*[1]

*Christ aggregated to his body that which was alienated from the
        hope of life:
the world which was lost
and history itself.*[2]

Hegel had a point when he said that if we had no access to the noumenal we
should not even bother talking about it. In a celebrated discussion with Bultmann, Julius Schniewind put the question now before us in bold relief:

> Has the invisible ever been made visible, and if so, where? The
> inescapable necessity of thinking in picture language derived from
> the world of space and time leaves us with exactly the same ques-
> tion—has the invisible ever been made visible, and if so, where? And
> the only answer is the Christian answer—the invisible God has
> entered into our visible world. . . . Here is the only solution to the
> question of God, the question which underlies every thought which
> enters into the mind of man.[3]

Christianity makes that claim and, in doing so, stakes its entire existence and
credibility on it. Since the claim that God acts, at least for Christian theology,
includes all of redemptive history in its wake, surely the penultimate claim that
God has acted in Christ is the summit and defining criterion for a Christian
account of divine action. More than that, it is the foundation: we could not

assert, much less describe, divine action unless God's own concrete action was the criterion.

While many religious texts are predominantly collections of moral wisdom, the truth and validity of which is independent of any narrative or historical events, both the Old and New Testaments even weave moral wisdom and law in a rich tapestry of narratives that serve as their historical prologue and justification. In a striking passage, Ricoeur claims that there is a specific link between Christian theology and narrative form:

> Not just any theology whatsoever can be tied to the narrative form, but only a theology that proclaims Yahweh to be the grand actor in a history of deliverance. Without a doubt it is this point that forms the greatest contrast between the God of Israel and the God of Greek philosophy. The theology of traditions knows nothing of concepts of cause, foundation, or essence. It speaks of God in accord with the historical drama instituted by the acts of deliverance reported in the story.[4]

In other words, it is "a theology in the form of *Heilsgeschichte*."[5] It is not, we might add, a *Heilsgeschichte* above, behind, *or even in front of* either the text or history, but the divine interpretation of history itself in textual form. Ricoeur is relatively correct in his contrast between biblical and speculative approaches, although the theology of traditions did, of course, concentrate a good deal of attention on the issues that give legitimate rise to questions of cause, foundation, and essence.

According to Pannenberg, the "eclipse" of universal history in hermeneutics is rooted in Schleiermacher's enterprise, which was interested in interpreting scripture in the light of universal consciousness rather than universal history.[6] Because of this course, mediated through Humboldt, Ranke and Dilthey, modern theology had to choose at first between historical criticism and the religious consciousness that was somehow mediated through these texts. By the end of the trajectory leading up to Bultmann (where the dilemma creates a certain degree of schizophrenia), theology was looking for a way out. While one branch has sought repeated revivals of the quest for the historical Jesus, Barth turned to "the strange new world" of the Bible. Since then, a theologian decides whether his or her hermeneutic will be historical-critical or literary-textual. Francis Watson identifies the weakness of this false dilemma:

> Both approaches share the assumption that historical reference and narrative form are incompatible. The theological effect of these current paradigms for gospel interpretation is disastrous. The gospels cease to be gospel if they merely preserve scattered traces of a historical reality qualitatively different from its narrative rendering, or if they merely render an intratextual character whose extratextual existence is a matter of indifference. The tendency of these methods is towards a christological agnosticism or minimalism that willfully overlooks the fact that, for Christian faith, Jesus—the real Jesus, attested in the fourfold gospel record—is the Christ, in whom God reconciled the world to himself.[7]

What is so astonishing is that "it is not clear that the methods and results of contemporary gospel scholarship are so decisive as to compel the abandonment of the central Christian truth-claim. On the contrary, the methods and therefore the results of this scholarship are fundamentally flawed. What is required is a more searching and less superficial account of the relationship between history and narrative," instead of ideology.[8]

Furthermore, if the stage on which this drama is acted out is not simply a text but also a history, then viewing Christian claims and the theology that they generate as a cultural-linguistic, semiotic system is too restrictive a metaphor. History is simultaneously particular and universal, local and global, individual and communal. This approach was also signaled by Wittgenstein, even though it is to him that appeals are often made for incommensurable language games. Norman Malcolm observed,

> The historian, Sir Herbert Butterfield, writing on the subject of military battles in his book *Man On His Past,* says that "every battle in world history may be different from every other battle, but they must have something in common if we can group them under the term 'battle' at all." Notice the striking similarity between Butterfield's assumption and the assumption of Wittgenstein in the *Notebooks* that in regard to the "elementary propositions," *"there must be something common to them; otherwise I could not speak of all of them collectively as the 'elementary propositions.'"*[9]

Pannenberg rightly regards the choice between narrative and history as a false dilemma. "If a text refers to an event, it is pointing away from itself to the event," he says in response to narrative theology. Nevertheless, "[a]s a universal-historical conception of events, historical investigation cannot represent the events it seeks to reconstruct in going behind their texts as something merely past, but, on the contrary, must grasp them in the continuity of meaning in which they stand, which connects them with the present age of the historian."[10]

Pannenberg acknowledges a debt to Gadamer on this point, recognizing distance and prejudices as necessary prerequisites for understanding rather than as insurmountable problems or obstacles. Gadamer correctly argues that the interpreter's horizon is never fixed, but is capable of expanding to include that which is alien to it. Nevertheless, Pannenberg sharply diverges from Gadamer by regarding history rather than language as the bridge. We cannot "conceive of the unity of truth as a timeless identity of a given essential content," says Pannenberg. "It can be conceived only as the whole of a historical career."[11] It is not *die Sache,* but *die Historie,* that provides the universal horizon for hermeneutics.

But doesn't Pannenberg's preference for Hegel force him at crucial points to separate history and eschatology too rigidly? For instance, is it not the case in the New Testament that this problem of distance is bridged not by a general theory of universal history or hermeneutics, but by the redemptive-historical intrusion that marks the period encompassing both Paul and Pannenberg as "the last days"?[12] It is not the fusion of horizons, but the sharing of horizons already fixed (yet still flexible to expansion) that our model presupposes. Accordingly, not only are horizons shared (first by creation and providence, then reestablished in redemption), but they are in tension and even contradiction (by virtue of the noetic effects of sin). Thus the horizons are set not merely by *nudus historicus*, but by the *salus historicus*. One need not turn to an absolute future as the source for a proleptic anticipation of the meaning of history in this age, but need only follow the already-integrated pattern of history and eschatology in the biblical drama.

For post-Kantians of all stripes, an event like the resurrection of Jesus is either historical or subjective (ethical, emotive, existential-eschatological). In our proposal, it is both. Carl Braaten well expresses the unity:

> For history and eschatology are united in the one person of Jesus, like the two natures, human and divine, without division and without separation. The resurrection is to be considered an historical event because it is the subject of reports that locate it in time and space. It happened in Jerusalem a short time after Jesus was crucified. But the resurrection is not merely an historical fact situated in a nexus of interconnected events on the same level. For it is a new beginning; it puts an end to one series of events heading toward death, and inaugurates a new order of life that dies no more. So it is also an eschatological event.[13]

The significance of past and future for the present is determined "from above," as God acts and speaks in history, event-revelation and word-revelation united in a dramatic text and rendered effective by the Holy Spirit.

Scandalized by the particular, the turn to the subject in theology is also driven by epistemological and soteriological universalism. Criticizing liberation theology's emphasis on place, Gareth Jones has attempted to rehabilitate Bultmann's contention that the resurrection of Jesus has to do with time and eternity, not place. "Correctly understood, such an emphasis upon time rather than space becomes the foundation of contemporary theological pluralism, simply because understanding God's action as temporal action means that anyone in time can have a valid perspective (and an invalid one) upon that action."[14] But can theology be predetermined in this manner, when the particularity of space as well as time is so essential to both the narrative and the theological implications that are drawn in scripture from it?

For reasons to which we will refer in the next chapter, Pannenberg rejects the analogical model and turns to his paradigm of revelation as proleptic, at least in part to avoid both relativism and absolutism—the latter identified with any premodern understanding of biblical inspiration. In this way, the general truthfulness of Christianity can be read off the surface of history (autonomously), although Pannenberg recognizes that the meaning of the resurrection of Jesus is realized only in the context of Old Testament expectations. Both the interpreter's autonomy and the general reliability of the chief Christian claim are thus affirmed, Pannenberg insists.

But if God is the ultimate author-actor in this drama, do we need to put off the question of whether this is the way things will turn out? To anticipate a point to be developed in another chapter, one need not choose between absolutism and relativism. There is a third way: to regard the communication of divine action in terms of *divinely authorized analogical discourse within the context of a covenant that plays itself out in a world-historical drama.* According to that model, the *sensus plenior* relates not only to the biblical writers, for whom the ultimate fulfillment of their prophecies was not necessarily comprehended fully, but to us as contemporary readers. We are in a better position than Moses in redemptive history, viewing the future from a higher vista in that progress of salvation, but we are still in a less direct line of sight than those who have passed from the theology of pilgrims to the theology of glorified saints, or those who will be witnesses of "the end of the age." Surely this is enough, in addition to a sober anthropology and an analogical account of divine discourse, to proscribe absolutism without retrenching ourselves in autonomy.

Rather than pitting manifestation (or act-revelation) and discourse (or word-revelation) against each other, the dramatic (i.e., redemptive-historical) approach would regard revelation as the final cause and speech as the instrumental cause of divine communication. Scripture cannot be reduced to either manifestation-revelation *or* discourse any more than a play can be reduced to either the dialogue or the acting. In response to the former, we concur with Wolterstorff's and Ricoeur's incisive critiques. Nevertheless, not only in unique, specific cases, but in every case of divine discourse, that which was hidden is (partially) revealed. When God speaks, God reveals. Here we turn to Luther's (not Barth's) dialectic of divine hiddenness and revelation. Even in self-revelation, God conceals himself, though neither the revelation nor hiddenness is total.[15] Mysteries hidden in the past are not revealed by projecting possible worlds for oneself any more than by a private *gnosis.* Rather, they are revealed by both divine discourse preceding divine acts and then following them in interpretation. *Pace* Pannenberg, God does not leave the interpretation of these historical events to the autonomous mind, will, or experience of the creature, but both discourse and event cohere in an account of revelation that is always the witness to and interpretation of redemption.

Despite wide differences, the directions we have been considering converge in their interests on points that are integral to the redemptive-historical model and that may only be fully integrated within it. These include the reversal of the fragmentation of biblical hermeneutics by paying attention to the textual sense, interpreting for divine discourse, recovering some version of canonical unity, and the *sensus literalis* with its concomitant notion of the *analogia fidei*, or what Ricoeur calls "intertextuality." "So read," he says, "the Bible becomes a great living intertext."[16] But if the Kantian captivity is to come to an end, it will also involve a renewed concern with historical truth claims that have justified the Christian's audacious and often politically subversive confession, "*Christos Kyrios.*"

WHERE THE ACTION IS:
GESCHICHTE AS *HISTORIE*

In his history of the Peloponnesian War, Thucydides distinguishes his account from that of poets (who embellish the facts) and chroniclers (who simply want to flatter their local audience). Sticking to the facts, Thucydides insists on relating only that which he has himself experienced or been able to reconstruct from interviews with participants. Of course, strict accuracy is difficult in every case, Thucydides writes.

> Therefore the speeches are given in the language in which, as it
> seemed to me, the several speakers would express, on the subjects
> under consideration, the sentiments most befitting the occasion,
> though at the same time I have adhered as closely as possible to the
> truth of what was said. But as to the facts of the occurrences of the
> war, I have thought it my duty to give them, not as ascertained from
> any chance informant, nor as seemed to me probable, but only after
> investigating with the greatest possible accuracy each detail, in the
> case of both the events in which I myself participated and of those
> regarding which I got my information from others. And the endeavor
> to discover these facts was a laborious task, because those who were
> eyewitnesses of the several events did not give the same reports about
> the same things, but reports varying according to their championship
> of one side or the other, or according to their recollection. And it may
> well be that the absence of the fabulous from my narrative will seem
> less pleasing to the ear; but whoever shall wish to have a clear view
> [of the events] to judge my history profitable will be enough for me.
> And, indeed, it has been composed, not as a prize-essay to be heard
> for the moment, but as a possession for all time.[17]

As has been done before, we can compare this account of historical procedure to that of the author of Luke-Acts.[18] Not being an eyewitness of Jesus himself, Luke was nevertheless an eyewitness of the apostolic ministry and set out to investigate the reports from eyewitnesses. Addressing his patron, a Roman nobleman, Luke writes,

> Since many have undertaken to set down an orderly account of the
> events that have been fulfilled among us, just as they were handed on
> to us by those who from the beginning were eyewitnesses and ser-
> vants of the word, I too decided, after investigating everything care-
> fully from the very first, to write an orderly account for you, most
> excellent Theophilus, so that you may know the truth concerning the
> things about which you have been instructed. (Luke 1:1–4)

Evidently, Thucydides and Luke were in similar positions. Writing from their limited firsthand experience, they saw themselves as reporters of a sort. Surely they were more: both told the story from a certain point of view, and from within a larger narrative—one Hellenic, the other Jewish. Like the Greek historian, Luke acknowledges that many had undertaken similar accounts. For his part, Luke will compose "an orderly account" based on the most reliable and widely accepted stories. He had been taught these stories from "eyewitnesses and servants of the word," and there were living sources who could correct or refute his reports. He emphasizes a method of careful, precise reporting.[19] Of course, the Gospel of Luke is more than this, but is surely not less. Regardless of what one thinks about his success, the writer set out to present to his patron a carefully researched narrative of the life and times of Jesus of Nazareth in the style of the classical biography.[20] In spite of their diverse interests and foci, all four Gospels relate these events as historical occurrences in calendar days. In Acts, the author of Luke's Gospel reiterates this goal to his patron:

> In the first book, Theophilus, I wrote about all that Jesus did and taught from the beginning until the day when he was taken up to heaven, after giving instructions through the Holy Spirit to the apostles whom he had chosen. After his suffering he presented himself alive to them by many convincing proofs, appearing to them during forty days and speaking about the kingdom of God. (Acts 1:1–3)

According to Luke, then, the early Christian community was formed around the risen Jesus during the period between the resurrection and his ascension. There is no doubt in Luke's mind that this is real history, Jesus presenting "himself alive to them by many convincing proofs." Similarly, approximately a decade earlier, Paul invited skeptics to call on eyewitnesses in Palestine who were still living (1 Cor. 15:3–7). In his first epistle (most likely written toward the close of both his life and the first century), John writes,

> That which was from the beginning, which we have heard, which we have seen with our eyes, which we have looked upon and touched with our hands, concerning the word of life—the life was made manifest, and we saw it, and testify to it, and proclaim to you the eternal life which was with the Father and was made manifest to us—that which we have seen and heard we proclaim also to you, so that you may have fellowship with us; and our fellowship is with the Father and with his Son Jesus Christ. (1 John 1:1–3 RSV)

From the very beginning, Christianity was announced as a public phenomenon, a narrative of historical events and therefore susceptible to refutation. The early community approached these events, at least on that narrative level, as Thucydides approached the Peloponnesian War. These were particular historical events of such significance that they bore a universal urgency. In the case of Jesus, this universal significance was all the more impressive because of the claims made about and by him, especially as these claims had as their referent the Old Testament promises of the visitation of God in the last days. "We did not follow cleverly devised myths when we made known to you the power and coming of our Lord Jesus Christ, but we had been eyewitnesses of his majesty" (2 Pet. 1:16). If these specific events actually did occur in history, these claims are vindicated: this is the missionary strategy of the early church. In the case of John especially, it would seem that the proto-gnostic (Docetist) threat provided a theological rationale for his polemical appeal to the corporeal and historical character of the Christ event. With polemical seriousness, John charges that those who embrace a spiritual Christ rather than an incarnate, historical redeemer are antichrists (1 John 2:18–23, 12–16; 5:9–13).

It is certainly true that some apologetic efforts to defend the historicity of these accounts have exaggerated the businesslike character of the reports and have undervalued the theological agenda of each Gospel. No account—not even Thucydides'—is neutral; every account is always already an interpretation of events in the light of prejudices. Far from being naive in this respect, the evangelists themselves make these prejudices explicit. But there is no question that these are claims concerning things that happened, not just to the community, but to Jesus in Palestine while Pilate was governor of the region.

Thus, Christianity is unlike any other religion; the relationship of faith and history is *the* Christian question, as Julius Schniewind observed in our opening. As C. Stephen Evans states in relation to the Creed's clause "crucified under Pontius Pilate," "Though Pilate himself would otherwise surely bask in well-deserved oblivion, he is immortalized by the need early Christians felt to link the passion of Jesus with secular history."[21] Had the early Christians adopted an interpretation of Jesus as an instantiation of universal, spiritual, rational truths, or simply of new existential possibilities, their redeemer would have been gradually accepted within the wider Hellenistic pantheon. However, their insistence upon Jesus as the single, particular, historical manifestation of God in the flesh, and his crucifixion and resurrection as therefore the basis for the claim of universal lordship, was precisely the *skandalon* that brought reproach to the early community. Had they accepted the Docetist compromise with Hellenism, the followers of the Way could have been assimilated rather than persecuted.

It was precisely this historical dimension with its universal implications (rather than vice versa) that gave them their subversive reputation. They did not begin with a theodicy, a metaphysic, an ontology, an ethic, or a teleology, but with an event. It was this event—whose anticipation most of the disciples failed to recognize in the Jewish narrative itself during the ministry of Jesus—that became the anomaly that provoked the radical paradigm shift in their thought. Only in its further elaboration (i.e., in the formation of the canon, especially as the epistles interpret these founding events) does a "whole" emerge more clearly from the "parts." Aside from the Pharisees (who had a quite different conception), resurrection was not part of their plausibility structure initially. Those influenced by the Sadducees denied its very possibility. As for the activists, revolution rather than resurrection was the framework. But things change. Their frameworks, webs, paradigms, plausibility structures, horizon, noetic web—whatever we wish to call it—could not account for this anomaly. Hence, the crisis.

The goal of this chapter is to carry through our analysis of modernity's binary antitheses in an effort to establish theological presuppositions on the nonfoundationalist foundation of the incarnation and resurrection as universal truth. Part of the argument is that these events are capable of resolving such dualisms into complementary distinctions, rather than antitheses in which Christian theology is commonly identified with the realm of idea, noumena, value, *Geschichte*, myth, and the subjective. The claim here is that the Noumenal became Phenomenal; the Universal became Particular; the transcendent Other became an immanent Other; *Geschichte* became *Historie*. Our purpose is not to limit this to the Incarnation, since the Word created, sustains, and enters our world through divine revelation throughout redemptive history. But it is to single out the central claim of this dramatic narrative.

First, the claim that the Noumenal became Phenomenal should not be confused with the notion of the categories themselves somehow being ontologically dissolved in the incarnation, but that the "ditch" was bridged by a universally significant historical event. As for our definition of "historical," we will assume, with Evans, that "an event or series of events qualifies as historical if it can be assigned a date and if it enjoys meaningful relations, including causal relations, with other events in that stream of datable events that includes human doings and sufferings."[22] We are not here concerned with apologetics per se. In other words, our purpose here is not to make the case for the resurrection or incarnation, but to make our methodological commitments explicit. But in order even to accomplish this goal, it is necessary to recognize some of the modern commitments that render this methodologically problematic.

CHRISTIANITY AND HISTORY: THE PROBLEM STATED

Although a cosmological/metaphysical monist, Plato was an epistemological dualist, and this is essentially the rationalist tradition that has produced Lessing's ditch. As we have seen, Kant was predisposed against Christian orthodoxy, but in some respects retained his pietism with respect to the dualism between the objective and subjective in religion, leaving the latter to theology. Yet even there, for him, Christianity was less a matter of religious experience than a version of universal religion, essentially morality, and was useful insofar as it could be enlisted to support a sense of duty to one's inner law. Without offering an empirical critique of Christian claims concerning Jesus Christ, he simply regarded them as irrelevant: "We need, therefore, no empirical example to make the idea of a person morally well-pleasing to God our archetype; this idea as an archetype is already present in our reason."[23] Even when directly addressing theological topics, Kant avoids reference to the place of Jesus in religion or history. The historical particular is quite irrelevant in the light of universal religious duty.

This omission is hardly innocent, but points up the theological (especially anthropological and soteriological) presuppositions of Kant's epistemology.[24] In Book 2 of *Religion*, he offers a Spinozan Christology as the "idea of God."

> Christ is the representation par excellence of the good principle, as the idea of a humanity agreeable to God: "This ideal of a humanity pleasing to God . . . we can represent to ourselves only as the idea of a person who would be willing not merely to discharge all human duties himself and to spread about him goodness as widely as possible by precept and example, but, even though tempted by the greatest allurements, to take upon himself every affliction, up to the most ignominious death, for the good of the world and even for his enemies."[25]

How is the life of Christ "for the good of the world"? We can see how his life might *serve* the world by example, but what does his death *achieve for* the world according to Kant's Christology? The person on the street in a modern city might well reply that Jesus' exemplary life has only marginal significance. Does the average person, anywhere in the world, obtain a radically different mode of being-in-the-world simply because of this one man's exemplary life? Even if this may be the case for some here and there, doesn't Kant claim too much for his Christology if exemplification of an idea is the point? Surely other great moral figures represent the universal idea of good in the world, and yet they are not lavished with the universal significance that Kant applies to Jesus Christ. Furthermore, how could the death of Christ be significant if he is not who he claimed to be? How indeed could it be, as Kant claims, "the most ignominious death, for the good of the world and even for his enemies," if it did not actually achieve anything for them?

"First," Ricoeur correctly states, "Kant manifests no interest for the Jesus of history, as we would put it today."[26] Because of his notion of analogy (which is quite different from our own), Kant sees "a mighty chasm" between the concept and "the objective fact itself . . . , the overleaping of which leads at once to anthropomorphism."[27] (But why not say, "the overleaping of which leads at once to incarnation"?) What then of Christ's identity? First, as Ricoeur says of Kant, we cannot treat "the humiliation of the Suffering Servant as a historical event." "The presence of this archetype in the human soul is in itself sufficiently incomprehensible without our adding to its supernatural origin the assumption that it is hypostasized in a particular individual. But there is also the conception that will be Hegel's, that is, the inclusion of *kenosis* in the coming to be of God as absolute Spirit."[28]

This also will not do: "Practical reason has no need of religious symbolism to account for this exemplification."[29] Clearly, in these pages, Kant's overriding concern is to guard his deontological ethics, which a high Christology and consequent theories of sin, expiation, and justification might threaten.[30] Hardly reticent to make constitutive theological judgments, Kant elaborates his creed of "pure moral religion" as opposed to "ecclesiastical faith":

> [S]urely we cannot hope to partake in the appropriation of a foreign satisfying merit, and thus in salvation, except by qualifying for it through our zeal in the compliance with every human duty, and this must be the effect of our own work and not, once again, a foreign influence to which we remain passive. For since the command to do our duty is unconditional, it is also necessary that the human being make the command, as a maxim, the basis of his faith, i.e., that he begin with the improvement of his life as the supreme condition under which alone a saving faith can occur. . . . We must strive with all our might after the holy intention of leading a life well-pleasing to God, in order to be able to believe that God's love for humankind (already assured to us through reason) will somehow make up, in consideration of that honest intention, for humankind's deficiency in action, provided that humankind strives to conform to his will with all its might.[31]

While contemporary scholars, including many theologians, may be inclined to dismiss the debate over nature and grace, in Kant's time it was of signal importance. For Kant to champion an explicitly Pelagian scheme was as risky as it was intentional. And the importance of this question for everything else—including hermeneutics and epistemology—cannot be overestimated. For Kant, as Ricoeur summarizes, "faith in a forensic absolution" apart from works "is to corrupt the motives for morality."[32]

Leaving to one side for the moment whether Kant is wrong, it is important for us to realize that, at least in terms of historic Christian preaching, confession, practice, and theology, such guiding attitudes are not scientifically neutral.[33] The method is in the madness of autonomy. In terms of Christian self-identity, Kantianism is modern Pelagianism. While that does not itself disqualify the theory in the minds of many readers, it at least exposes the presuppositions of his epistemology and hermeneutics in relation to Christian claims. His hermeneutical a prioris are neither axiomatic nor demonstrable, but make sense only within a shared naturalistic bias. And before such naturalism reaches broader dimensions in Kant's thought, it is a soteriological commitment. As Ronald Thiemann has demonstrated, soteriological assumptions cannot be separated from the rest of the theological enterprise (including views of revelation).[34]

Throughout its history, Christianity has argued that God became flesh and that this entrance of the transcendent Other into the immanent world-historical situation has universal significance. The formula, "to the Jew first and then to the Greek," or "to Jerusalem, Judea, Samaria, and the uttermost parts of the earth," or "all people everywhere," attests to the early community's conviction that Jesus is the key to understanding the history of Israel and, from that narrative core, the key to understanding the history of the world. Old Testament prophecy anticipated the day when not only would the nations stream to Zion, but Zion would be "exported" to the nations.[35] In fact, this movement may even be discerned within the Gospels themselves, the Synoptics oriented chiefly around the Jewish narrative, while John identifies Jesus as the Logos. Faced with an apologetic crisis after the collapse of Rome, Augustine in his *Civitas Dei* was the first Christian thinker to attempt a full-scale account of the universal-historical significance of Jesus Christ. But the medieval synthesis, to which Augustine in no small measure contributed, tended (especially in its more Neoplatonic expressions) to stress a Hellenistic concern with universal, eternal forms and ideas, as opposed to the particular, temporal events in world history. One of the assumptions of our approach is that this tendency, which Augustine's biblical outlook did not sufficiently overwhelm, is largely responsible for the very foundations of modern historical understanding that have contributed to the dualistic thinking that Christianity confronts as a new Gnosticism. As we have already explored the epistemological insights of Lessing and Kant on this point, we will briefly analyze Hegel's approach to history in an effort to untangle the modern bias against the unity of *Historie* and *Geschichte*.

THE SEARCH FOR THE HISTORIAN'S JESUS

Whereas Kant sought to make room for faith (and delimit metaphysics) by emphasizing the unknowability of the noumenal *Ding-an-sich*, Hegel synthesized the antinomies. However, their antithetical character, hardly abandoned, was essential to the dialectic. We may observe the roots of this absolute idealism in medieval mysticism, especially that of Boehme, Eckhart, and Tauler.[36] Rather than Kant's theological deism being the product of his epistemological transcendentalism, the reverse is the case, and this is true of Hegel's pantheism as well. The *principium essendi* (ontology) is the basis of one's *principium cognoscendi* (epistemology). A collapse of the creator-creature distinction entails the collapse of the archetypal knowledge of God into the system of the autonomous self.

Hegel's *Leben Jesu* (1795) anticipated the historical-critical enterprise. "Spirit" (*Geist*) in general, not the Holy Spirit as worshiped within traditional Christianity, dominated the Hegelian "synthesis." Further, Hegel's "Christology" is decidedly docetic or gnostic, and this is true largely of modern theologies—even those which are more Kantian (or even Kierkegaardian), in which ontological-metaphysical dualism prejudges the possibility of the incarnation. Given the Enlightenment premises, it is hardly surprising that those who were still interested in the historical Jesus might want to determine how to find him hidden in the underbrush of supernaturalism. The first "quest" launched by D. F. Strauss's *The Life of Jesus* (1835) and successive attempts to uncover the historical Jesus above or behind the text itself yielded little more than the mirror reflection of the investigators. As James Robinson put it, "'The historical Jesus' comes really to mean no more than 'the historian's Jesus.'"[37]

While historical-critical investigation is not in itself problematic, the truth is that everyone in the conversation has a stake in the outcome and in a real sense has something to prove. Liberal theology, says Pannenberg, basically concluded that "the person and history of Jesus, is no longer to be found in the texts themselves, but must be discovered behind them."[38] The existentialist and neo-orthodox theologies of the twentieth century attempted to redress the imbalance in favor of the kerygma over history. Thiselton highlights Bultmann's debt to the philosophy of history associated with R. G. Collingwood's idealism, according to which a historian of Julius Caesar is not "trying to *be* Caesar," but seeks to "relive" Caesar's experiences "at the level of *thought* in *the mind*." Collingwood writes,

> The way in which I incorporate Julius Caesar's experience in my own personality is not by confusing myself with him, but by distinguishing myself from him and at the same time making his experience my own. The living past of history lives in the present; but it lives not in the immediate *experience* of the present, but only in the *self-knowledge* of the present. This Dilthey has overlooked.[39]

Thus thought submerges action and events, and interpretation drowns out the very thing that is to be interpreted. Even Heidegger seems to have been under the influences of neo-Kantianism in his antithesis between the objectively historical and existentially historic. Just as Bultmann was worried that referring faith to historical events would somehow "objectify" it into a form of works righteousness, Heidegger asserts, "*Dasein* can *never* be past . . . because it essentially can never be *present-at-hand*."[40] There is an obvious circularity in Heidegger's argument.[41] Gadamer, I would argue, appropriating aspects of Droysen's analysis, marks an important advance with his insistence that the goal of historical understanding is not reconstruction but the continuous effects of past events and communities (*Wirkungsgeschichte*).[42]

Pannenberg wishes to recover the historical side (although the question remains as to whether he has returned to the broken cisterns of the nineteenth-century quest in too many important respects).[43] The "search for the historical Jesus" never did quite provide any clear account of "the historical community." After all, if the historical Jesus was the "pale Galilean," itinerant Sophist, Cynic, or sage, purveyor of moral wisdom and esoteric insight, or social revolutionary, how does one explain the first Christian centuries, which are known to have been characterized by two paradoxical facts: rapid growth and widespread persecution and martyrdom? Pannenberg observes,

> Only the resurrection of Jesus . . . renders intelligible the early history of Christian faith up to the confessions of Jesus' true divinity. If the resurrection of Jesus cannot be considered a historical event, then the historical aspect of the primitive Christian message and its different forms, both of which have crystallized into the New Testament, fall hopelessly apart. . . . The gulf between fact and significance, between history and kerygma, between the history of Jesus and the multiplicity of the New Testament witnesses to it, marks one side of the problem of theology today.[44]

Pannenberg's point is confirmed by Paul's famous speech in Athens. In this address, the apostle to the Gentiles begins with the most universal and abstract, the Athenians' altar to an unknown God, and then begins to identify this universal God with concrete attributes. It is this God who alone is God, who has determined history in its most universal and particular manifestations.

The identification moves from abstract to concrete until finally we get to the practically photographic concreteness of the resurrection: "Because he has fixed a day on which he will have the world judged with righteousness by a man whom he has appointed, and of this he has given assurance to all by raising him from the dead" (Acts 17:30–31).

AFTER HISTORICISM . . . WHAT?

Despite the superficial affinities, Pannenberg's analysis of "universal history" is not, at least on this specific point, Hegelian. Because the goal of history is only provisionally known (i.e., proleptically, because of the resurrection), the future is truly open. I am not as convinced by this argument as Pannenberg, since it is difficult to conceive of such a past event as proleptic of anything that is not already certain. Perhaps Pannenberg is too acutely aware of his affinities with Hegel elsewhere to open himself up to charges of a deterministic teleology here. But Hegel's immanentistic account seems rather different from the biblical view of divine sovereignty. The fact that things will turn out the way the scriptures predict in the end does not exclude contingency and secondary causes. God will so conduct history that it will lead to this end. But just as the first advent was so rich that its fulfillment burst the skins of expectations, so will the second, although it will not take place in contradiction to prophetic utterances. So the future, despite its prophesied details, is as "open" and contingent as the past and the present are in the context of divine providence. The future does not *have* to happen in a certain manner (*de potentia Dei absoluta*) but *will* happen in a certain manner (*de potentia Dei ordinata*), since this is what God has promised to accomplish, either directly or indirectly through secondary agency.

The mystery of double agency may not be as intellectually satisfying as the certainties of absolute determinism and immanent progress, but it is less susceptible to ideological tyranny. As Ricoeur recognizes, this latter approach searches out the geniuses in the history of philosophy, and, not surprisingly, the conclusions of its patchwork enterprise converge on the "the historian's personal philosophy," which is then "privileged and placed at the end of history as the goal toward which all past efforts were aspiring. History marches toward me; I am the end of history. . . . This quite patent vice in eclecticism is that of Hegelianism."[45] By subjectivizing the particulars, one absolutizes his or her own world-historical interpretation. By recognizing Jesus Christ as the key actor in history, all things being "summed up in him," the hubris of projecting oneself as the meaning of history is precluded from the outset. And yet, one can only say that Jesus is the meaning of history, both Israel's and the world's, not because of any universal idea, but because of the particular events that only taken together lead inductively to that conclusion. This equilibrium between universal and particular is precisely what "is sacrificed in Hegel." "In the *Phenomenology of Spirit* one still finds a certain history, but it is, however, 'ideal.' This history is made up of the 'forms' of the Spirit. But when we move on to Hegel's *Logic,* we no longer find 'forms,' but 'categories'; there is no more history at all. The ultimate goal of historical understanding involves, therefore, the suppression of history in the system."[46]

If all of this depends on a universal-historical horizon, is such a view possible? Pannenberg thinks it is possible.

First, even the smallest cultures are related to outside influences. "It is the horizon of world history which first makes it possible to appreciate the full significance of an individual event." Why else, for instance, do we engage in periodization?[47] Like Gadamer, Pannenberg appreciates the insights of R. G. Collingwood, who countered the historical positivism which, under the pretense of a pure scientific method, maintained that historical research was a matter of simply piling up random details and then showing the laws governing them. In truth, the historian conjectures possibilities at the beginning of the project. In fact, "data" can only be understood in terms of their relationships to other facts.

Pannenberg endorses this analysis.[48] But this hardly licenses the historian to come up with just any hypothesis or conjecture: the whole cannot disregard the parts, any more than the parts can disregard the whole, without distortion. It is, once more, the problem of the one and the many applied to hermeneutics. Particulars are essential, but so is unity, but rarely in modern thought is the latter sought without losing the former.

> A Christian will find empirically confirmed even the fact that Jesus Christ is the "axis" of history because the end of history has already appeared in him. He will trust that the course of history will further strengthen his conviction. And there will be a day when the empirical confirmation of the Christian knowledge of Jesus Christ as the fulfillment of history will be acknowledged by all men, either joyfully or against their will. It already has validity for all men, however; the validity of the mission of the church depends on this.[49]

But more important than the validation of the mission of the church, which could and in fact has often masked a quite this-worldly will to power, this world-historical significance of Jesus Christ exists because "that which has been hidden in times past *has now been made known*" (Eph. 3:1–13). God acts and demonstrates sovereignty over all of creation not merely in the resurrection, but throughout redemptive history. The one last stand for divine intervention in history, the resurrection (and apologetics for it) is often treated as the basis for authenticating the whole of the Christian faith. Given the "proof" that, according to scripture, the resurrection of Jesus constitutes, this makes some sense. However, one who does not accept the divinity of God in scripture will not likely see the resurrection of Jesus as proof of that which their presuppositions do not tolerate. To assume non-Christian premises in defending the resurrection often engages in two errors: first, to assume that any reasonable person will be compelled to accept the evidences, and second, to assume that these non-Christian premises are neutral and do not have anything to do with the content of what is being asserted. This does not make evidences unnecessary, but it does require a postfoundationalist paradigm within which to operate. A determinism to end all determinism, the predication of a free, personal, and triune God as the source of both unity and diversity, continuity and contingency, expectation and surprise, wrests sovereignty from the either-or dilemma.[50] The resurrection proves that God alone is God and that this God's sovereignty is the source and environment of human freedom.

It is this inductive approach, beginning with the "main events" (among which the resurrection obtains center stage) and then working dialectically between the whole and the parts that leads finally to a unified view of history. Just as redemptive history itself unifies the biblical canon, which otherwise frays and disintegrates into a thousand pieces, it unifies history itself. This one who died and now lives lends his authority to the entire narrative, so that we ourselves can be written into the script and know our relation to God, as well as—and only in that light—who we are, where we came from, what our real needs are, and where we are going. Our limit-situations are not even truly discerned apart from this divine interpretation of reality. As Pannenberg and others have reminded us, "This claim will appear less astonishing, perhaps, if one considers that it was Israel's history of God and the fate of Jesus which first disclosed to man the understanding of the world as history."[51] On this much, at least, Mark C. Taylor would agree, although with a considerably different appraisal.

Thus far we have argued the possibility of *Geschichte* actually belonging to *Historie* and have contested the programs that have assumed a foundation that is no longer credible even in their more proper domains. But it is one thing to argue that the incarnation and resurrection could have been actual historical events; it is quite another to suggest that these particular, contingent, temporal events actually possess the key to universal history itself.

However, if the reader finds it difficult at first to embrace the Hebrew view of history over the Hellenistic, perhaps it will at least help if we employ Aristotle as therapy against Plato.[52] Without accepting Hegel's deterministic teleology, it is at least a useful metaphor to suggest that as the essence of the oak is in the acorn, the meaning of history is in the appearance and victory of Jesus. Just as in the case of the acorn and the oak, the "accidents" of the events of Jesus' life, death, resurrection, and ascension do not seem to exactly match their "substance." And yet, despite all accidental appearances to the contrary, God has hidden God's majestic essence in the humiliation of the cross. It is no wonder, then, that even Jesus used the paradoxical figure of a tiny seed producing from its own inner essence a giant tree whose sprawling branches enfold the globe. We have already referred to the internal movement of the Gospels, from seeing Jesus as the fulfillment and center of Israel's history (Synoptics) to proclaiming him as the clue to the meaning of life and of world history (John).

Much has been said in the last two centuries about the "Hellenization" of the Jesus movement, but more needs to be said about the Christianization and biblicization of the Gentile world in the first centuries. Both Pannenberg and Ricoeur contribute to this question of Christianity and the meaning of history. So here we reopen that investigation first launched by Augustine's *Civitas Dei*.

CHRISTIANITY AND THE MEANING OF HISTORY

The Greeks knew that their *mythoi* were far from chronicles, and even in the Homeric literature, history and myth never quite converge. Herodotus and Thucydides write histories, but these are more like chronicles. In contrast to the Greek civilization, it was the Hebrew culture, mediated through the scriptures, that yielded a genuinely "historical" consciousness. There is a pre-destination (proorizō—"fore-horizon"), not an immanent teleology, but a divinely governed history appointed to a certain end, but through the agency of free and responsible creatures. So Ricoeur does not seem to overstate things when he suggests that

> Christianity made a violent entry into the Hellenic world by introducing a concept of time containing events, crises, and decisions. Christian Revelation scandalized the Greeks through the narration of those "sacred" events: creation, fall, covenant, prophetic utter-

ances, and, more fundamentally, "Christian" events such as incarnation, cross, empty tomb, and the birth of the Church at Pentecost. In light of these exceptional events, man was made aware of those aspects of his own experience which he did not know how to interpret. His own life was also made up of events and decisions and marked off by important alternatives: to rise up in rebellion or to be converted, to lose his life or to gain it. At that moment history acquired meaning, but it was concrete history in which something happens, in which people themselves have a personality which may also be lost or won.[53]

If, as Ricoeur says, "History is historical because there are unparalleled actions which count and others which do not count,"[54] then surely the repetition of "time" and "times" (as in "the fullness of time") in scripture indicates its historical preoccupation. Old Testament believers are not called to repeat the past, or simply to memorialize it in frozen reverence (a form of idolatry), or to replace the past with a timeless present ("eternity in time"), but to recall the past as the history of God with his people, in the light of the redemptive plot that unites past, present, and future. The success of this strategy depends on the work of the Holy Spirit, both in inspiration and illumination. Thus the goal of all historians, even social historians who eschew the universal for the particular, is some criteria for telling the one from the other. Christianity provides such criteria, not because the incarnation and resurrection exhaust the meaning of history, but because they expose the meaning of history *as meaningful*, the result of a divine plan executed in time.

To Derrida's and Taylor's charge that the Bible gives rise to the very idea of ultimate meaning, selfhood, history, and the like, Christian theology can only plead guilty. Jesus is presented in the Gospels as the temple, the land, and the Sabbath rest. He is the Passover lamb, the second Adam, the true Son of David, and faithful Jacob (Israel). But he is also the eternal creator-logos made flesh, the savior of the world, the sovereign judge before whom "every knee shall bow" on the last day. At last, Israel's Yahweh will be vindicated as God of all gods and Lord over all lords.

In its demand for epistemic certitude, the Enlightenment (like the Platonic tradition) could not appreciate history as a meaningful source of truth. Not only was it contingent, as opposed to an ostensibly necessary and incorrigible reason; it was, by definition, concerned with the past. And the past belonged to an "authority" that the vanguard of the *Aufklärung* simply could not countenance. The static, law-governed, unified, and universal realm of reason was much safer and more certain than the dramatic, plot-governed, diverse, and particular realm of redemptive-history. "A dramatic vision of history has much more affinity with Christian theology than the rationalism of the 'Enlightenment' which destroyed the very ground upon which a theology may be propagated—the ground of ambiguity."[55]

It is the hermeneutical turn that now gives us a wider opportunity to make the case for this distinctly biblical, as opposed to a Platonizing approach to history.[56] As we have argued, the "problem" of divine action in history is the result of modern appropriations of classical dualism. But what if we just do not accept those presuppositions? The "two histories" problem that Bultmann correctly saw resting on a "two causalities" scheme itself rests on the foundation of Kantian dualism that already renders God a distant and unknowable observer of his own creation.

Where we would differ from Ricoeur at this point is in our insistence that faith *is* a "firm assurance" of what we hope for, and that epistemological certainty (Cartesian incorrigibility) is not to be confused with this eschatological and existential certitude. Certainty of a promise is of a different order from certainty of theories and axioms. The writer to the Hebrews defines faith as "the assurance of things hoped for, the conviction of things not seen" (Heb. 11:1). Accordingly, "the age that is to come"(to borrow New Testament terminology) breaks into the present through Word and sacrament, especially in the proclamation of the gospel, creating this faith. Through his historical victory and present intercession, and in the power of the dispatched Spirit, Jesus Christ mediates God's grace in such a manner that believers *now* taste "the powers of the age to come" (Heb. 6:5). Of course, none of this can be demonstrated from either analytic axioms or synthetic demonstration, but the resurrection (which *is* open to synthetic falsification) provides an entry-point, the "particular" from which we can then infer the "whole" that it validates. The resurrection itself cannot *establish* this unity (*pace* Pannenberg), but it is represented in the NT as certifying the entire narrative plot.

Our proposal agrees with Ricoeur that "[a]n important task of present-day Christian theology is to reflect jointly on an eschatology of truth and an eschatology of history."[57] While Ricoeur does not take his own suggestions as seriously as he might, he has provided a sympathetic model for (a) reformulating the unity of *Geschichte* and *Historie*, replacing these with *particular* and *universal* respectively, and (b) reintegrating history and eschatology, which theologians such as Bultmann have set in opposition. Ultimately, however, as Ricoeur himself implies, this will have to rest upon a presupposition of the biblical rather than dualistic ontology of history.

In addition to the various other factors, Bultmann's interpretation of the New Testament as a narrative of a failed Parousia (inherited from Weiss and Schweitzer) is significant in the textual-critical support of his otherwise quite philosophical approach. "For John the resurrection of Jesus, Pentecost, and the *parousia* . . . are one and the same event," Bultmann wrote.[58] But, drawing upon the work of Geerhardus Vos and Herman Ridderbos, Richard Gaffin offers a persuasive alternative to Bultmann's theory. In the Pauline eschatology especially, the resurrection of Jesus, Pentecost, and the Parousia are distinct aspects of a single event. The resurrection of Jesus "is not simply a guarantee; it is a pledge in the sense that it is the actual beginning of the general event." "In fact," Gaffin argues, "on the basis of this verse it can be said that Paul views the two resurrections not so much as two events but as two episodes of the same event. At the same time, however, he clearly maintains a temporal distinction between them."[59] Jesus is so federally identified with his people, and vice versa, that he is regarded as "the first-fruits" of the general resurrection. His resurrection does not merely proleptically anticipate, but actually *commences* the eschaton. Thus, the "already" element of the Resurrection-Parousia-Consummation event is the resurrection of Jesus and the consequent raising to life of the believer from spiritual death, while the "not yet" includes the bodily resurrection of the dead in Christ (his body) and the restoration of the cosmos (his kingdom environment).[60]

IS REDEMPTIVE HISTORY REAL HISTORY?

Despite his emphasis on the Christ event as meaningful only in connection with Israel's narrative, Pannenberg insists that the "burden of proof" for the thesis "that God had revealed himself in Jesus of Nazareth" necessarily "falls to the historian."[61] Furthermore, "This requirement, which a few decades ago in the era of positivistic theories of science would have been simply scandalous, can in fact hardly be avoided."[62]

Do we want to take the unity of *Geschichte* and *Historie* this far? While we must no longer set fact and value in antithesis on these points, there is an opposite danger in conflating them. When Ernst Troeltsch (or his contemporary disciples, such as Van Harvey) argues that historians *cannot* introduce divine or supernatural causality into their interpretations, it seems to me that he is correct up to a point. Just as physicians work in the realm of natural causes and effects in providing a cure, historians do not have at their disposal the tools that could identify the hand of God. Can the historian discern any more than the plausibility of one account of the evidence over another?

Even the factual datum of the resurrection is not as yet a sufficient basis for faith: that is simply historical faith. While dialectical theology eliminated *notitia* and *assensus* from the definition of faith, it would be just as tragic to eliminate *fiducia* from the triad. Despite his conviction that the resurrection is self-interpreting and transparent to historical investigation, Pannenberg does also add that the historian's realm "does not in any case provide sufficient basis for meaningfully raising the question of whether a God has revealed himself here in contrast to all other occurrences in nature and in human history."[63] It is true, says Pannenberg, that the relationship of Jesus to the history of Israel is key. The redemptive-historical approach was right to insist upon "Jesus' connection with the history of Israel," against Schleiermacher's and Herrmann's focus on "the isolated person of Jesus."[64]

If all of this depends on a universal-historical horizon, however, is such a unity of *Geschichte* and *Historie* possible? First, even the smallest cultures are related to outside influences, Pannenberg replies. "It is the horizon of world history which first makes it possible to appreciate the full significance of an individual event." The historian, of course, is involved, but can't just come up with any conjecture about the relationships. So we encounter again the problem of the one and many.

Particulars are essential, but so is unity, but rarely in modern thought is the latter sought without losing the former. This is why modern theology has not been methodologically equipped to handle anomalies, whose very particularity is capable—or should be capable—of upsetting paradigms.

But this is where a more confident biblical-theological approach appears superior to Pannenberg's program. As we have seen, redemptive-historical events even disrupt the expectations of the very audience to which they are connected. Furthermore, the biblical writers are not (for the most part) chroniclers, but witnesses. Their purpose is to proclaim Christ, not merely to provide a historical record, although the latter cannot be severed from the former. Even the genealogies (especially Matthew 1) demonstrate this in the extreme.[65]

Also, there are real changes in Israel's history—often (especially in the prophets) contradicting the expectations and false interpretations of prophecy. If the prophets themselves surprise the Israelites with the "twists" and "turns"—one thinks of Amos 5 ("You who long for the day of the Lord, do you not know . . . ?")—we can hardly place the burden for false expectations (for instance, of a restoration of the theocracy or an immediate Parousia) on the texts themselves. These discrepancies between Israel's prophetic texts and her apocalyptic expectations are not contradictions of Israel's true history, but only of its presumed history and false confidences. If this is so, then surely Jesus' contradiction of the expectations of the Jews of his day concerning the messianic kingdom is of a similar kind. It is the prophetic anticipation, not the contemporary expectations of the people, that confirms or denies Jesus' claim to that title. God's faithfulness to redemptive history, therefore, and not a fatalistic "development" of history in terms of a noncontingent teleology, preserves the fragile bond between the contingent and particular on the one hand and the universal plan of redemption on the other.

CONCLUSION

Throughout our investigation, we have argued that the trajectory of the medieval synthesis most closely identified with Platonism and Neoplatonism received a renewed impetus in the modern project, as evidenced in such representatives as Descartes, Lessing, Hume, and Kant. To the extent that modern theology accepts the fundamental antitheses of phenomenal/noumenal, fact/value, *Historie/ Geschichte*, and so forth, it really is, as Nietzsche declared, "Platonism for the masses," a projection of a "real" (i.e., ideal) world in contrast to the world of appearances and contingent historical events. The most extreme versions of this approach, such as one finds in Bultmann's thought, are at least structurally Gnostic (and, more specifically, Manichean). It is Plato's antithetical "two worlds" that lurk beneath the surface of the antithetical "two histories" and "two causalities" of modern thought (including theology). But set against Plato's "two worlds" is Paul's "two ages."[66]

The biblical account of divine action in history resists Nietzsche's caricature of "platonism for the masses." There is enough for one to dislike about Christianity (for instance, its particularism, which also scandalized postmodernism's ancestors) to add this straw man to its critique. For in its aversion to Platonism, the critique of ontotheology has been justified. Nowhere does this hypothesis find a more compelling example than with respect to the approach to history. Ricoeur contrasts the Christian and Neoplatonic visions in relation to the church father Irenaeus's courageous battle with Gnosticism:

> Let us think about the scope of the revolution in the history of thought that this text [from Irenaeus] represents in relation to that Neo-Platonism in which reality is a progressive *withdrawal*, an ineluctable beclouding that increases as we descend from the One, which is formless, to the Mind, which is bodiless, to the World Soul, and to souls which are plunged into matter, which itself is absolute darkness. Are we sensitive to the distance between this text [and Neoplatonic accounts]? (emphasis in original)[67]

Irenaeus's *Adversus haeresis* advances an embryonic redemptive-historical hermeneutic that grounds the revelation of God in this world and in the service of redemption.[68] He is thoroughly Pauline on the extent of the restoration at the end of history and the centrality of Jesus Christ for the meaning of history as a whole. It is no wonder that this church father was a favorite of Calvin's. In fact, one hears echoes of Irenaeus in the reformer's expression, "Christ aggregated to his body that which was alienated from the hope of life: the world which was lost and history itself."[69] Contrast this line of thought with the expression of Harnack: "I have tried to show what the essential elements of the gospel are, and these elements are 'timeless.' . . . Secondly, the Gospel is based—and this is the all-important element in the view which it takes of the world and history—upon the antithesis between Spirit and flesh, God and the world, good and evil. . . . It is by self-conquest that a man is freed from the tyranny of matter."[70]

And are we sensitive to the distance between a traditional perspective and Bultmann's opposition of the "Christ after the Spirit" to the "Christ after the flesh"? A full-bodied incarnational theology demands a public defense of the Christian claims. Despite the importance of preserving ecclesial identity without surrendering to the spirit of the age in an apologetic enterprise, Christianity knows of no secret societies of the *gnostikoi*. It stands in the public square, on the steps of the temple, on the stage of the Areopagus, and in the synagogue, announcing God's deeds in history, which were promised and fulfilled in the person and work of Jesus of Nazareth. Ricoeur's query is on the mark here: "Are there to be no *signs* of the superabundance of grace outside of the interior life, or only in a few small and isolated communities? No signs of this on the great stage of the world?"[71] In contrast to the gnostic tendencies of much of modern theology, including aspects even of neo-orthodoxy, Christianity meets this challenge directly.

The turn to history that we have been exploiting in this chapter anchors the biblical narrative not in alien stories (viz., the recurring questions of metaphysics, ontology, epistemology, and the natural sciences)—however important and even related to faith at certain points—but in the historical events to which the narrative itself witnesses. On this point, even the later Barth and his postliberal successors seem to be too reticent to accept the union of *Geschichte* and *Historie*, "narrative" substituting for the former, with continued ambivalence toward the latter. Surely C. Stephen Evans is justified in saying, in reference to Hans Frei's identification of the Gospels as "history-like," "If the narrative is history-like, one possible explanation of this fact is that it was written as history."[72]

And that leaves us where we began, with Thucydides and Luke. Both at least attempted to write accurate historical reports of epoch-making events, and both were at least committed to rigorous attention to detail in eyewitness accounts. Both sought to place their reports within a larger series of events and interpretive narratives. But only one even claimed to tell a story that could effect the redemption of readers in distant places and times far from the originating events, and it is that account that created a community of women and men who were willing to give up everything in exchange for their participation in the new creation, the drama of redemption.

PART TWO
GOD SPEAKS

Assuming that God acts in history, we have already concluded that the divine role is not merely that of a playwright, much less of a spectator in the audience. God is also the central character on the stage. And this role also includes the most significant speaking part.

Just as part 1 divided up the topic of divine action into the statement of the challenges, a proposal, and an analysis of hermeneutical implications, part 2 will also follow this strategy.

When we come to the matter of divine speech in scripture, more distinctly biblical-theological notions, such as covenant and eschatology, become especially formative. The category of "speech" is not meant here to prejudge questions related to oral vs. written discourse, but is intended as a broad category for communicative action. Chapter 5 will summarize the problem of divine speech, while chapter 6 will concentrate on developing a proposal in the light of current hermeneutical debates.

Our purpose in this section is not to develop a thorough theory of revelation or inspiration, but is to provide an account for (1) the claim that God speaks, (2) the context in which and conditions under which God has spoken, (3) the means employed in divine discourse, and (4) the hermeneutical implications of this account.

Chapter Five

Divine Rhetoric
An Account of the Claim

We have offered an analogical account of the claim that God *acts* in history. Here we will explore an analogical account of the claim that God *speaks* in history. In either case, as we have seen, the objection arises that in analogies one must be able to compare, and theology is in the unfortunate position of not being able to compare the analogy to God for an analysis of adequacy. We have thus far tried to meet this challenge by (a) pointing out that the nature of analogical discourse allows us to affirm things, not to comprehend them and by (b) arguing that Jesus Christ is the univocal core of both God's being and revelation (albeit veiled).

Inasmuch as speech is a subset of action, the claim that God has spoken is faced with many of the same challenges, and quite a few of its own. Nevertheless, the analysis of divine discourse provides an additional argument in support of both claims. Isn't there another way of accepting an analogy, other than knowing for oneself how well it corresponds with reality? What if such analogical discourse were adopted and authorized by the one to whom the analogies putatively apply? In such a case, the unknown party revealing himself or herself by means of the more familiar would be in the best position to decide on the aptness of the analogies. If scripture involves divine discourse, then one need not possess independent knowledge of God in order to accept and assert that such analogical discourse is literally true of God. It is God's own speech, God's own self-disclosure, that interprets divine action and character. Just as children accept the analogies offered by their parents, believers trust God to communicate truthfully. If we could compare such analogies, we would not need them in the first place. This, of course, bars all pretensions of "autonomous" knowledge or "objective neutrality," but it does secure genuine knowledge. How close? Close enough. That is the answer that an analogical account of divine discourse provides. In this chapter we will attempt to explore the possibilities of such an approach.

CHALLENGES TO THE CLAIM THAT GOD SPEAKS

As the assertion of divine action in history raises questions about universality and access to such salvific events for those outside the community, predicating divine speech meets with similar objections. Whether appearing in the form of rationalism's pure reason, idealism's consciousness, or romanticism's emotive intuition, modernity has often dismissed Christian claims due to the so-called "scandal of particularity." Why would God speak to and through Moses and not apparently to or through an oppressed slave in some other part of the world at the same time? Why do some people hear God speak and others do not? What, if anything, makes one group's claim to divine discourse more privileged than another's? Is not such particularity a recipe for exclusion and violence?

Lessing said that whatever one finds in scripture to substantiate universal reason and experience, so much the better. Kant insisted that humanity did not need an archetype of the perfectly moral person (viz., Jesus Christ), since that archetype formally inheres in the human mind. And in Romanticism the good god of pure spirit communicates directly with the innocent self of pure spirit, as one deity to another. Inwardness and feeling, not publicity and historical demonstration, were hallmarks. But throughout the history of this era, it is the self (absolute, autonomous, pure presence) that is the lord and master of "reality."[1]

Although with quite different influences and proposals, Karl Rahner's view of revelation seems just as indebted to a post-Kantian perspective in which hypertranscendence comes full circle to hyperimmanence:

> When we speak of God's self-communication we should not understand this term in the sense that God would say something *about* himself in some revelation or other. The term 'self-communication' is really intended to signify that God in his own most proper reality *makes himself the innermost constitutive element of man*. We are dealing, then, with an ontological self-communication of God.[2]

Just how central the redemptive-historical narrative, in all of its christocentricity, remains in Rahner's system is unclear. After all, the foundation for faith seems to be an ahistorical ontological grounding. Revelation swallows redemption: "It could be objected against the possibility of speaking about the free and forgiving self-communication of God at this point that this insight comes only as a result of the history of salvation and revelation which has its irreversible climax in the God-Man, Jesus Christ. *But we shall not discuss this until the fifth or even the sixth chapter in our reflections*" (emphasis added).[3] For Rahner, God as "the innermost constitutive element of man" (raising the specter of Neoplatonism once again) is known and knowable—even in an evangelical manner, apart from Christ. Further, since God's self-communication must be carefully distinguished from (and contrasted with) God's saying "something *about* himself in some revelation or other," one wonders what role commands and promises—indeed, covenant in general, could play in Rahner's doctrine of revelation. (Even Barth's theology of the Word falls under this objection.) It is within this context that many find it difficult to say that God speaks, even if it may be possible that God acts. Although we cannot attempt a full analysis of theories of inspiration here, this idea of revelation is inseparable from the claim that God speaks.

While summarizing massive systems is a risky business, Avery Dulles provides a useful overview of the most significant notions in his *Models of Revelation* (Orbis, 1992). The first model is Revelation as Doctrine. Here God is thought to reveal timeless propositions and the Bible (or, in its neoscholastic Roman Catholic form, the Bible and tradition) is regarded as a deposit of these doctrines. Carl Henry and Hermann Diekmann are singled out as representatives of this model.

The second model, Revelation as History, associated with G. E. Wright, C. H. Dodd, Oscar Cullmann, and Wolfhart Pannenberg, centers on divine *acts* (as opposed to divine *words*) as the bearer of revelation. Dulles's third model, Revelation as Inner Experience, regards Christian revelation as a species of a universal religious sense. The presence of many different religions testifies to the universality of religious experience. While in Schleiermacher, for instance, there is a counterweight to a solipsistic view of religion (namely, his emphasis on the church/ community), the tendency of this model (which Lindbeck labels "experiential-expressivism")[4] is to individualism and subjectivism.

In the fourth model, Revelation as Dialectical Presence, neo-orthodox theologians insisted that revelation is to be identified with a personal encounter and not a book, a system of theology, history, or the church. While Barth and Bultmann flesh this out in quite different ways, both regard revelation as an unsettling confrontation in which the Wholly Other addresses individuals. For this to happen, according to Bultmann, scripture must be demythologized and interpreted along the lines of Heidegger's existential analysis.

Finally, model five, Revelation as New Awareness, is associated with those theologies that stress divine immanence in the world process. In this model, revelation does not provide one with new news, but with a new orientation, a new awareness of what has always been and of what is now the case, namely, God's universal activity in the evolution of the cosmos. This view is associated with Pierre Teilhard de Chardin and process thinkers.

What the last four models share is a rejection of (often contempt for) the first. As will become clearer, our proposal does not neatly fit the first model either. In fact, there is no comfortable fit with any of the models that Dulles summarizes, and this impinges quite directly on our account of the claim that God speaks. We will discuss this in our analysis below.

Other challenges contribute to the a priori rejection of divine discourse. Some are theoretical questions about the authenticity and reliability of the documents themselves: What sort of criteria could there be for discerning whether God had spoken, as opposed to some other explanation? What is the relationship between divine and human discourse in the predication of certain books (like the Bible) being "inspired." Other questions are more practical: How does a disembodied agent speak? Can it be just for God to speak to a particular community without speaking to everyone? We will attempt to address these questions in their course.

"THUS SAYS THE LORD" . . . BUT HOW?

Before discussing the covenantal context of divine discourse in scripture we need to cobble together some account for saying that God speaks in the first place. Remember, this is not an attempt at demonstration or an invitation to meet in some supposedly neutral space where things can be decided on the grounds of universal principles upon which every sane person can agree. Rather, as the Reformed scholastics said even before Wittgenstein, the purpose of philosophy is merely to clean up our language and to let us say more effectively and persuasively what it is that we are claiming. To that end, I would like to borrow from the insights of speech-act theory, particularly as it is expressed by J. L. Austin[5] and John Searle.[6]

A. Speech Acts

Every speech act involves the stringing together of sounds or scribbling of signs (or some other means of communicative action). At its bare minimum, then, an utterance is a locutionary act. But locutionary acts may also be illocutionary acts. By means of a locutionary act, one does further acts: promising, warning, asserting, asking, wishing, and so forth. In a locutionary act, one says something, while in an illocutionary act, one does something in saying something. What one happens to be doing in such an act (promising, warning, etc.) is called its illocutionary force.[7] There is still a third category for speech acts: perlocutionary. In this case, an utterance does something yet further, this time not only doing something with words, but doing something to the hearer: convincing, persuading, angering, pleasing, and so forth.[8] As Austin says, "We can similarly distinguish the locutionary act 'he said that . . .' from the illocutionary act 'he argued that . . .' and the perlocutionary act 'he convinced me that. . . .'"[9]

While John Searle does away with the "locutionary act," he is in general agreement with Austin's line of thought. And since he seems to use different words for the same idea, we will retain Austin's term. First, Searle argues, "To take the token as a message is to take it as a produced or issued token," emphasizing the connection between utterances and their speaker.[10] Like deconstruction, speech-act theory is interested in action and not in blithe contemplation or independently meaningful and referring words, as in the mimetic or picture-model of word and reality. But unlike deconstruction, speech-act theory locates the activity in actors (sayers) and not in signs (the said). The meaning of a sentence is in the speech act itself, and while I may not *in practice* be able to say exactly what I mean (due to limited understanding of the language or the language's lack of just the right expression), I am *in principle* capable of coming to say exactly what I mean.

So, for speech-act theorists, "talking is performing acts according to rules."[11] Speech acts are performed by speakers, not by words, so the goal is to discover the illocutionary stance or force. It is not what words are doing, but what speakers are doing in uttering their sentences, and not all utterances are assertions. In an assertion, however, one takes responsibility for, commits oneself to, the propo-

sition. Not all language is descriptive or propositional in the sense of being assertory, Austin argues, in opposition especially to positivism.[12] Speech acts involve
three things: (1) uttering words (Austin's "locutionary act"), (2) referring/predi-
cating (propositional acts), and (3) illocutionary acts.[13] And an illocutionary act
may lead to a perlocutionary act in the same utterance: "For example, by arguing I may *persuade* or *convince* someone, by warning him I may *scare* or *alarm*
him, by making a request I may *get him to do something*, by informing him I may
convince him (enlighten, edify, inspire him, get him to realize). . . . Propositional
acts cannot occur alone; that is, one cannot just refer and predicate without making an assertion or asking a question or performing some other illocutionary
act."[14] There is a further distinction between *referential* statements ("A man
came") and *predicative* statements ("John is a man"). Furthermore, sentences do
not propose, speakers do.

So how can one pick out the particular illocutionary stance or force being performed? "Often, in actual speech situations, the context will make it clear what
the illocutionary force of the utterance is, without its being necessary to invoke
the appropriate explicit illocutionary force indicator."[15] We will recall Searle's
principle that "talking is performing acts according to rules." He distinguishes
here between *constitutive* and *regulative* rules, which we may call (somewhat
loosely) *analytic* or *indicative* and *synthetic* or *imperative*. (These are my suggestions, which, hearing no objections, I will gratuitously follow below.)

In baseball, a "home run" is *constituted* and not merely *regulated* by hitting a ball
a sufficient distance to allow for one to run all of the bases. Within such constitutive conventions (i.e., Wittgenstein's language games), there are rules that govern
how one behaves. Here Searle links illocutionary acts to their institutional context:

> Thus, for example, some philosophers ask, "How can making a
> promise create an obligation?" . . . "How can scoring a touchdown
> create six points?" As they stand both questions can only be answered
> by citing a rule of the form, "X counts as Y". . . . X counts as Y in con-
> text C. . . . In the case of speech acts performed within a language . . .
> it is a matter of convention—as opposed to strategy, technique, pro-
> cedure, or natural fact—that the utterance of such and such expres-
> sions under certain conditions counts as the making of a promise.[16]

Finally, Searle provides his analysis of the structure of a particular illocutionary act to which we will appeal in our covenantal model of divine discourse:
promising. The rules are given, with detailed explanation, for fulfilling the conditions of this particular speech act.[17] In the following section we will use his conditions as a checklist for a particular instance of divine discourse.

B. Divine Speech Acts: An Instance of the Promise

At the outset, biblical religion rules out a manifestational-representational model
of revelation. It is not *gnosis*, enlightenment; nor is it a direct vision of God. "God
reveals himself by hiding himself," Luther's formula reminds us. For that reason,

God is as near as the *word* that is preached (Rom. 10:8). It is precisely for that reason that divine discourse is best likened to acts of *speaking* rather than to acts of *showing*, although the latter are not entirely excluded. So let us take an example of divine promising in scripture and apply to it the criteria that John Searle recommended for the happy execution of a promise.

In Genesis 15 we encounter God's covenant with Abraham, an instance we will take up again below. Abram and Sarah, late in years and childless, were promised a great inheritance by Yahweh. Understandably, Abram was somewhat disinclined to believe this promise and requested some sort of verification for his hope. God said, "[N]o one but your very own issue shall be your heir" (v. 4). In addition to saying so, God "brought him outside and said, 'Look toward heaven and count the stars, if you are able to count them.' Then he said to him, 'So shall your descendants be.' And he believed the LORD; and the LORD reckoned it to him as righteousness" (vv. 5–6). Abram still unpersuaded, Yahweh reasserted the promise and then in a vision enacted a legal ceremony in which, according to ancient Near Eastern treaties, the partners would assume full responsibility for their end of the deal. Walking between severed halves of animals, the partners would assume the curses of breaking this covenant: "May the same end befall me if I should fail to keep this oath." But in this vision, God was the sole partner walking between the severed halves, assuming the burden of the covenant's obligations (v. 17). Later, of course, God would add to the spoken promise the rite of circumcision, to be observed throughout all generations: "You shall circumcise the flesh of your foreskins, and it shall be a sign of the covenant between me and you" (17:11).

How does this representative instance fare in terms of Searle's qualifications for a promise? First, do "the normal input and output conditions obtain"? Already it would appear that there are problems with divine promising. For if God is not endowed with vocal cords, a hand for writing, or some sort of apparatus for communicating verbally, how are humans, who *are* so constituted, going to receive this news? In other words, how can one refer a speech act to a being who does not really speak? But we have encountered this objection in our discussion of divine action. Here, as there, we appeal to analogy. What does it mean to say that God "does not really speak"? Is "really" intended as a way of identifying speech itself with the movement of air through vocal cords and the movement of a hand on some surface? Yet we would have to qualify this even in reference to human speaking. Surely smoke signals, the shipwrecked person's arrangement of stones on the beach, the hand motions of a baseball coach or of sailors with signal lights on the deck of a navy carrier, are examples of communicating. "You shouldn't have *told* me to steal the base," the player tells the coach. But is that an inappropriate manner of speaking? Not at all, since we realize that telling or speaking is broader than the medium it takes. The important thing is that someone communicated to someone. The question is whether the speaker's intentions were realized. The officer on a navy carrier signals the pilot not to land yet because there are too many planes on deck. Somehow, *S* produced in *H* the belief that *Y* was the state of affairs, even though flashing light-signals and uttering sentences are *analogically* related (as indeed even written or spoken words are analogies).

Here the emphasis of speech-act theory on the intentions of speakers and the constitutive rules of given contexts is crucial. What *counts* as speaking? Examples of alternatives to the most familiar forms (uttering sentences orally or in writing) are not intrinsically matters of speaking, but are *constituted* as speaking precisely because conventions are created in which X counts as Y in context C. We can conceive of God acting in the world without being embodied just as we can conceive of ordinary human acts that are not physical in nature (viz., intending, planning, imagining, etc.). Similarly, we can conceive of God acting in the world without being equipped with vocal cords or hands because we can conceive of ordinary human speech acts which are not limited to these operations.

So the real question is what *constitutes* God's saying thus and so? As we will see more fully below, in covenantal discourse the authorizing party speaks through his or her lawyers. Here the convention is the covenant. To the extent that we understand the scriptures as a covenantal document—a treaty of some sort—we recognize that it is a divinely ordained legal convention that regulates this speech act. In other words, X (the utterances of a prophet or apostle) counts as Y (the utterances of God) in context C (the biblical covenant/canon).

While this may work for prophets and apostles who wrote the Bible, what of Abraham? Can we say that he fits with this convention? In this narrative, Abraham is not speaking for God; rather, God is speaking to Abraham, and Abraham is responding. A prophet was authorized and enabled by God to recount this ancient narrative as an essential feature of the covenant's founding. Abraham was addressed by Yahweh in a vision (of course, a common mode of revelation in the scriptures) and this illustrates at least one mode in which God has spoken, even apart from ordinary human modes of discourse. If God may be said to speak through such media, then the first condition of promising seems to be met.

Searle's second condition for promising is that the speaker (S) "expresses the proposition that p in the utterance of T." By uttering T, something else besides uttering T is accomplished. Is our biblical example consistent with this condition? We read, "After these things the word of the LORD came to Abram in a vision, 'Do not be afraid, Abram, I am your shield; your reward shall be very great'" (Gen. 15:1). By uttering the sentence God expresses the proposition that he will be Abram's "shield" and that Abram's "reward shall be very great." The second condition would appear to be fulfilled.

Third, "In expressing that *p*, S predicates a future act of A of S." A promise necessarily links speech and action, word and deed. In our example, the speaker promises to give the addressee an heir—but beyond a personal destiny, promises that all nations will be blessed through his "seed." Viewed canonically, "the promises were made to Abraham and to his offspring; it does not say, 'And to offsprings,' as of many; but it says, 'And to your offspring,' that is, to one person, who is Christ'" (Gal. 3:16). The speaker promises to do something in the future.

Fourth, "*H* would prefer *S*'s doing *A* to his not doing *A*, and *S* believes *H* would prefer his doing *A* to his not doing *A*." A promise is not an invitation. In order to make a promise, both speaker and addressee must already believe that the latter would prefer the execution of this promise. In our example, it is clear that *H* would be overwhelmed with happiness if *S* did *A*. In fact, *H* resists hoping in this promise at first because it seems too good to be true. There is no question as to whether *S* believes *H* would prefer this action.

Searle's fifth condition for a felicitous promise is that "[i]t is not obvious to both *S* and *H* that *S* will do *A* in the normal course of events." In other words, there is no necessity involved. A promise becomes an obligation only after it is made. So a promise cannot be the fulfillment of an obligation, but must be treated as a gift. In Abram's case, there is no expectation of an heir. "But if it is by grace, it is no longer on the basis of works, otherwise grace would no longer be grace" (Rom. 11:6).

Conditions six and seven touch on the matter of sincerity and intention. "*S* intends to do *A*." That is evident in our example. Further, "*S* intends that the utterance of *T* will place him under an obligation to do *A*." In fact, this Searle calls "the essential condition."[18] One can scarcely conceive of a better example of this than the covenantal motif in general and the covenant with Abram in particular. Invoking the language of an ancient Near Eastern treaty (context *C*), Yahweh seals his promise with a solemn ritual (itself a speech act, though with signs other than words) in which he takes full responsibility for the success of the covenant. Now Yahweh knows that, as the suzerain or great king, he may be invoked by the vassal or lesser king and that this invocation will *obligate* Yahweh to rescue the vassal. As we saw in condition five, promises are not based on obligation. Yahweh is utterly free to enter or not enter into a covenant with creatures. But upon choosing to do so, God *creates* and *accepts* an obligation for the future.

In condition eight, "*S* intends (*i-1*) to produce in *H* the knowledge (*K*) that the utterance of *T* is to count as placing *S* under an obligation to do *A*. *S* intends to produce *K* by means of the recognition of *i-1*, and he intends *i-1* to be recognized in virtue of (by means of) *H*'s knowledge of the meaning of *T*." Here is the heart of speech-act theory in linking the meaning of a sentence to the speaker's intention. It also applies the rule concerning institutional conventions: "*X* counts as *Y* in context *C*." Both the speaker and addressee must be familiar enough with the relevant convention to know that what is being done is *counting for* a promise. According to the narrative, Abram knew precisely what God was doing; namely, that these words and deeds expressed in visions were counting as covenant ceremonies, at the heart of which is a promise. Closely associated with this is the final condition, that "[t]he semantic rules of the dialect spoken by *S* and *H* are such that *T* is correctly and sincerely uttered if and only if conditions 1–8 obtain." Searle elaborates, "The meaning of the sentence is entirely determined by the meaning of its elements, both lexical and syntactical."[19] It is not unspoken intentions (psychological divination), but uttered sentences, that count here. It is a straightforward condition, and it would seem that it is sufficiently fulfilled in our example. If these conditions are obtained, the claim that God promises appears to be coherent and at least logically possible. And if God *promises*, there is nothing against this agent's engaging in other illocutionary acts.

COVENANTAL DISCOURSE

As stated in the preface to this section, we are not deciding for speech over writing, but are appropriating speech-act theory for our account of the claim that God speaks. A special kind of divine speech concerns us here: *covenantal* discourse. The covenant concept brings together the various threads thus far considered: double agency, the importance of history (and the relation of redemption to history), and mediated discourse.[20] Just as "history" emerges in Israel (the nations meanwhile preoccupied with nature), the notion of "covenant" attains its clearest expression in that same history. First, let us define this covenantal form of existence and then relate it to the notion of discourse.

As Walther Eichrodt shows, "the covenant-union between Yahweh and Israel is an original element in all sources, despite their being in fragmentary form."[21] From the very beginning, the Israelites were a coalition of tribes who were not committed to nationalism or bound by political aims, but regarded themselves as "called out" by God to belong to God by means of a covenant. Thus, "God's disclosure of himself is not grasped speculatively, not expounded in the form of a lesson; it is as he breaks in on the life of his people in his dealings with them and moulds them according to his will that he grants them knowledge of his being."[22] The promissory character of this covenant "provides life with a goal and history with a meaning":

> Because of this the fear that constantly haunts the pagan world, the
> fear of arbitrariness and caprice in the Godhead, is excluded. With
> this God men know exactly where they stand; an atmosphere of trust
> and security is created, in which they find both the strength for a willing surrender to the will of God and joyful courage to grapple with
> the problems of life. . . . In this way history acquires a value which it
> does not possess in the religions of the ancient civilizations. . . . Their
> view of the divine activity was too firmly imprisoned in the thought-
> forms of their Nature-mythology. In Israel, on the other hand, the
> knowledge of the covenant God and his act of redemption aroused
> the capacity to understand and to present the historical process, at
> first only in the limited framework of the national destiny but later
> also universally, as the effect of a divine will.[23]

It was chiefly the concept of covenant (with its corollary, election) that guarded against a civil religion and made Yahweh's will rather than national aspirations the basis for life.[24]

In a certain sense, the idea of divine revelation was much more difficult for an Israelite to accept. After all, the creator-creature distinction was essential. For nature religions (much like romanticism in our own history), divinity permeates creation. It would stand to reason that if the divine were *immediately present* to the community, every creative impulse or illuminating experience could be regarded as revelation. In such an approach, it would be fairly easy to manipulate the deity's communication or to identify one's own thoughts and intentions with those of the god or gods. (Feuerbach's critique aptly fits natural religion.)

A case of Israel's capitulation to this sort of immanentism/syncretism is evidenced in Jeremiah 23: "I did not send the prophets, yet they ran; I did not speak to them, yet they prophesied. But if they had *stood in my council*, then they would have proclaimed my words to my people. . . . Am I a God near by, says the LORD, and *not a God far off*? . . . See, I am against those who prophesy lying dreams, says the LORD . . . when I did not *send* them or *appoint* them" (vv. 21, 23, 32, emphasis added). Besides the prophets, the people also prefaced their own utterances with the announcement, "The word of the Lord." And in this way God's word becomes "everyone's own word, and so you pervert the words of the living God, the LORD of hosts, our God" (v. 36). Perhaps in the religions of the nations revelation is given on demand (i.e., by knowing the technique), but not in Israel; nor is it even given to individuals for their own personal benefit. Revelation is given in moments of redemptive-historical significance, and it is given through individuals who are called by God and sent by God to the people. They are emissaries of the covenant; thus it is in their office and not in their person that they speak for God. They are not religious geniuses or more sensitive than normal to spiritual realities, but are called and sent. They stand in the council of a God who is not present at hand. As Eichrodt recognizes, to the extent that Israel accommodated to paganism, it always involves "the weakening, if not the loss, of one indispensable presupposition of the covenant concept and opens the door to the misinterpretation and misuse of the covenant for the purpose of harnessing God to human requirements."[25]

Thus, according to the biblical pattern, divine speech is limited to the activity within the divine covenant, in which the clear superior (the suzerain) is determining the terms and conditions for the inferior (the vassal).[26] Meredith G. Kline observes that such covenants are made between unequal partners and they cannot be emended by secretaries. New covenants may be drawn up but are never corrected.[27] Extant ancient Near Eastern documents of this treaty type, a form that became widely used in international diplomacy by the time of Moses, universally demonstrate this impossibility of emendation or alteration on the part of the vassal. For instance, one such treaty declares, "Whoever . . . changes but one word of this tablet . . . may the thousand gods of this tablet root that man's descendants out of the land of Hatti."[28] This form is followed in the Deuteronomic form of the biblical covenant: "You shall not add to the word which I command you, nor take from it; that you may keep the commandments of Yahweh your God which I command you" (Deut. 4:2 RSV). The same covenantal judgment is found in John's Apocalypse: "I warn everyone who hears the words of the prophecy of this book: if anyone adds to them, God will add to that person the plagues described in this book; if anyone takes away from the words of the book of this prophecy, God will take away that person's share in the tree of life in the holy city, which are described in this book" (Rev. 22:18–19). In fact, Revelation 2–3 reflects the covenant lawsuit pattern of the prophets.

Von Rad writes,

> Complete freedom of action, and therefore the freedom to decide, that is, to take the oath or not, is in this case possessed only by the superior—the lesser is simply a recipient. This arrangement is to be understood on the assumption that the recipient will certainly not act against his own interest, for by rejecting the covenant he would only exchange a protection which was to his advantage for an extremely hazardous legal insecurity.[29]

Thus even from the beginning, while "the nations" gathered around their deities who *manifested* themselves in creaturely forms, Israel gathered around Yahweh whenever and wherever Yahweh *addressed* the assembly in judgment and mercy. In other words, Israel's covenant theology is intrinsically discourse-oriented as a mediated encounter between the covenant lord and the servant people. "The covenant is therefore a legal relationship, and comprises the firmest guarantee of a relationship of human communion. In consequence, it was entered upon to the accompaniment of solemn ceremonies, invocation of the deity, a sacral meal, the calling down of curses upon oneself, etc. (cf. Gen. xxvi. 30, xxxi. 46, 54)."[30]

Shalom—peace that is not merely the absence of hostility but the presence of trust and communion—is the goal of the covenant. Unlike their neighbors, who believed that they enjoyed a natural relationship with their deities (expressed in myths), Israel was made aware that her relationship with Yahweh was covenantal. This meant, among other things, that this union was legal *and* relational (contrary to modern tendencies to see these in antithesis), not ontological and natural; historical and mediated, rather than ecstatic and direct. Further it was a voluntary relationship initiated by God.

Some of the biblical covenants are of this suzerainty type, some conditional, others unconditional. The covenant with Abraham as "the father of many nations" is clearly unconditional (Gen. 15), especially as interpreted in the New Testament (cf. Rom. 9:6–8; Gal. 3:1–29). In contrast, the Mosaic covenant is dependent on Israel's obedience. Like the covenant servant in Eden, Israel must resist the temptation of autonomy and serve only the living God. But the prophets are sent as attorneys for the prosecution, with such ominous courtroom announcements as, "Hear the word of the LORD, O people of Israel; for the LORD has an indictment against the inhabitants of the land" (Hos. 4:1). They bring this word, sometimes reluctantly, when the covenant is being violated or when Yahweh insists on extending the ethnic boundaries (as in the case of the prophet Jonah). Jesus also appropriates this prophetic stance, invoking covenant curses (Matt. 21:18–22; Luke 11:37–54; Rev. 2–3) and blessings (Matt. 5:1–12; John 20:29; Rev. 2–3).

Even before the exile, then, the prophet, as the prosecutor of the suzerain's intention to invoke the covenant sanctions, occupies a central role. The prophet's curse is God's curse; the prophet's blessing is God's blessing. In short, the text assumes that when the prophet says, "Thus says the Lord," it *is* God who actually says what the prophet says.

The new covenant is anticipated as a renewed Abrahamic (rather than Mosaic) covenant, for instance, in Jeremiah 31: "It will not be like the covenant that I made with their ancestors when I took them by the hand to bring them out of the land of Egypt—a covenant that they broke, though I was their husband, says the LORD." Rather, God will act unilaterally in salvation, to the end that "I will be their God, and they shall be my people" (vv. 31–33). The Abrahamic covenant is fulfilled because Jesus (who also fulfills the conditions of the Mosaic covenant by his obedience) is the "seed" in whom all the nations are blessed. Jesus is the promised son of Abraham. The Mosaic covenant is not altered in any way; rather, it is fulfilled by Jesus so that in Jesus the children of God may receive the inheritance on the basis of the Abrahamic covenant:

> Brothers and sisters, I give an example from daily life: once a person's will has been ratified, no one adds to or annuls it. Now the promises were made to Abraham and to his offspring; it does not say, "And to offsprings," as of many; but it says, "And to your offspring," that is, to one person, who is Christ. My point is this: the law, which came four hundred thirty years later, does not annul a covenant previously ratified by God, so as to nullify the promise. For if the inheritance comes from the law, it no longer comes from the promise; but God granted it to Abraham through the promise. (Gal. 3:15–18)

All of this brings us to the connection between speech-act theory and covenant theology. Here we recognize the unity of word and deed, act-revelation and word-revelation, event and interpretation, letter and spirit.

"When the LORD saw that he had turned aside to see, God called to him from out of the bush, 'Moses, Moses!' And he said, 'Here I am'" (Ex. 3:4). Like the bare hands lifted in worship (the palms, dirtiest part of the body, held up before God in recognition of both one's creatureliness as well as sinfulness), this response is the epitome of an appropriate creator-creature relationship. Here, there is no attempt to treat God as an object to be conquered, used, or comprehended for one's own purposes, but a simple acknowledgment that one is a lesser being addressed by a greater. God is not being made manifest by tangible or mental representation; rather, God is engaging in discourse. In a sense, even the term "revelation" is too close to the manifestation-model, since, besides the acts of judgment and liberation, God is known in and by what God *says,* and this is itself an action—rather than a concept or idea to be captured, frozen, manipulated, and worshiped in the place of the God who reserves the right to privacy. "Here I am" is a different response from "I see," the latter model dominating Western epistemologies. In the covenantal approach, what dominates is the ear, not the eye; God's addressing us, not our vision of God. The other has priority over oneself. This reply shares some affinities with the thought of Emmanuel Levinas, although he uses it more as a general type than seeing it as a concrete historical encounter between Yahweh and specific individuals. Here is discovered an order, "in the 'here I am' that brought me out of the shadows, where my responsibility could have been eluded."[31]

The diverse Old Testament literature coheres in a covenantal pattern, with Genesis and Exodus serving as a historical prologue for the covenant. With God's mighty acts in history made known, the suzerain justifies the assertion of his rights over those whom he has liberated. The covenant proper is then stipulated, rehearsed in confessional praise (in the Psalter), and its curses invoked against wayward Israel in the prophets; the same prophets promise the Messiah more clearly and definitely. The New Testament, by its very designation, is understood as a ratification of this gracious covenant and the inauguration of its new covenant administration, with the apostles as "ministers of a new covenant" (2 Cor. 3:6) who have, unlike the false prophets of Jeremiah 23:21, "stood in the council" of the Lord during his earthly ministry. Like the historical books, the Gospels expose the founding events that will establish a "new Israel" redrawn around the heavenly temple who has come down to earth. Thus these apostles are sent out as legally authorized witnesses and representatives of the divine court.

EVALUATING THE COVENANTAL DISCOURSE MODEL

The Reformers and their successors broke from medieval system by regarding theology as chiefly practical rather than theoretical—which is to say, by directing all metaphysical reflection to the formal principle of scripture and the material principle of justification in Christ, rather than vice versa. Theology, then, was not regarded by these theologians as a comprehensive and general science of being and things, but as the speech about God as he has revealed himself in word and act, especially in the person of Jesus Christ as he is offered to us in the gospel. Understandably, history, rather than philosophy, increasingly stood in the center of the horizon (without eclipsing its conceptual appartus).

It is hardly surprising that in this "strange new world" of the biblical narrative it would make far more sense to think about commands and promises than theories and speculations. If narrative theology has made contemporary reflection more sympathetic to the redemptive-historical method, then perhaps it is not asking too much to court friendship from the quarter of speech-act theory for helping us to conceptualize the covenantal understanding of the *habitus credendi*.

Covenantal discourse, like most of discourse in general, is primarily concerned with illocutionary speech-acts. In other words, the goal is to determine the stance of a particular speaker—not the author's unstated intentions, nor meaning behind, in front of, or above the text. What was she doing when she said, "Hummingbirds, like unicorns, appear in moments of unexpected delight, only to take flight to safety"? Was she asserting something about unicorns, or just hummingbirds? What was she doing? What sort of speech action was it?

Within the context of the covenant, one can distinguish two subsets of divine discourse—two distinct illocutionary forces or stances: commanding and promising. This is one of the insights of the Reformers and their successors. Both Luther and Calvin insisted upon the distinction (though not separation) between law (command) and gospel (promise). In defending this distinction, Melanchthon points out that it is sanctioned not merely by an observation of the whole, but by explicit exegetical references.[32] While in the law God promises eternal life on the condition of perfect obedience, in the gospel God promises the same on the basis of Christ's perfect obedience. Melanchthon unfolds this argument by means of a summary of redemptive history and its covenants, including the one that we have considered.[33] These categories do not coincide with Old Testament and New Testament, as if the former were "law," while the latter were "gospel." Rather, as Theodore Beza put it,

> We divide this Word into two principal parts or kinds: the one is called the "Law," the other the "Gospel." For all the rest can be gathered under the one or the other of these two headings. What we call Law . . . is a doctrine whose seed is written by nature in our hearts. . . . What we call the Gospel is a doctrine which is not at all in us by nature, but which is revealed from heaven (Mt. 16:17; Jn. 1:13), and totally surpasses natural knowledge. By it God testifies to us that it is His purpose to save us freely by His only Son (Rom. 3:20–22), provided that, by faith, we embrace Him as our only wisdom, righteousness, sanctification and redemption. (1 Cor. 1:30)[34]

According to the Reformed and Lutheran scholastics, law and gospel are actually the means by which the Holy Spirit effects what is promised. "The letter kills, the Spirit makes alive." "Law" creates terror in the hearer because of the awareness of sin it engenders, while "gospel" actually brings life: "By it, I say, the Lord testifies to us all these things, and even does it in such a manner that at the same time he renews our persons in a powerful way so that we may embrace the benefits which are offered to us (1 Cor. 2:4)."[35] Here it seems to me that we have, as in Ezekiel 37 and Romans 10, an example of a *perlocutionary* speech act. In the discourse of judging and justifying, individuals are actually judged and justified.

This is amply demonstrated throughout scripture: "This is my comfort in my distress, that your promise gives me life" (Ps. 119:50). "So shall my word be that goes out from my mouth; it shall not return to me empty, but it shall accomplish that which I purpose, and succeed in the thing for which I sent it" (Isa. 55:11). Jesus adds, "It is the spirit that gives life; the flesh is useless." But he was hardly pitting the Spirit against the word and the ordinary means of grace, adding, "*The words* that I have spoken to you are spirit and life" (John 6:63). The words spoken are themselves life-giving, not because there is a magical power inherent in a string of utterances, but because of the efficacy of the Holy Spirit working through the faith-creating promise. By this word God actually performs what is threatened in the law and what is promised in the gospel.

At this point our model shares affinities with Ronald Thiemann's proposal in *Revelation and Redemption* (Notre Dame, 1985). In his model of revelation as "narrated promise," he argues, "Surely there is no natural or innate connection between human language and God's reality, but Christian faith demands that once God has claimed a piece of creaturely reality as his own and bound himself to it, then we are warranted in accepting the God-forged link between the human and the divine."[36] So why do we think we can interpret God's speaking? Nicholas Wolterstorff correctly responds, "The conviction that God speaks and that we can interpret that speech presupposes that God is not *ganz anders*."[37] It was Barth's rejection of any *analogia*, perhaps a Kantian-Kierkegaardian transcendence, that accounts for the fact that he virtually ignores the notion of divine speech. If so, this may have contributed to his reticence (like that of Brunner and Bultmann) about identifying revelation with words and designative content.

Wolterstorff has offered a redolent account that I have found quite helpful in developing a covenantal model. At the heart of his *Divine Discourse* is the claim that (a) God speaks and that (b) his discourse can be discerned by us. As in our proposal, Wolterstorff attaches divine discourse to the Christian scriptures. But can we say that the Bible is a medium of this discourse? Are we *entitled*? For Barth, God is speaking in the *events* of Christ's doings and sayings, but the biblical writers are *reflecting* on these events. God is not speaking in scripture for Barth, but the biblical writers are "communicating what God revealed to them and others."[38] Asserting divine inspiration is not enough to support the notion that God speaks, for this can happen without saying that the Bible consists of acts of discourse.[39] Even dictation would not guarantee who is the author of a given discourse, as the one who signs the document authorizes it as the medium of his or her speech.[40] These are salutary reflections on the doctrine of inspiration and have in fact been argued along similar lines throughout church history. As far as I am aware, not a single well-known biblical exegete has interpreted the speeches of Job's counselors as divine speech, though it has been traditionally regarded as belonging to the canon of inspired scripture.[41]

How then do readers or hearers come to recognize divine discourse in the Bible? With the Reformed tradition, Wolterstorff reflects on Calvin's *testimonium Spiritus Sancti*. In the reformer's words, "Credibility of doctrine is not established until we are persuaded beyond doubt that God is its Author" and "the highest proof of Scripture derives in general from the fact that God in person speaks in it."[42] Wolterstorff makes ingenious use of Calvin's point here by suggesting that in the process of interpreting the divine discourse mediated by the human discourse of scripture, one comes to realize that God is saying that he is this book's author. Beyond this inner illumination, "the likelihood that it is true depends very much on the trustworthiness of the relevant documents."[43]

This, indeed, is the heart of the question. Textual sense interpretation or theories that collapse divine discourse into a revelation event do not necessarily require such demonstrations, but the claim being made here is that God *said* something to someone at some time and place. Such an inquiry would, first of all, take into account the claims of the early church concerning the biblical narratives. The early church clearly believed that the apostles spoke for God. In fact, Paul believed this about his own case, and, says Wolterstorff, "so far as I can tell, no New Testament writer diverges from Paul in this understanding of the status of an apostle."[44] But was Paul entitled to hold this belief? His miraculous encounter with the ascended Jesus convinced him that this was so, and the early church believed it was so. How about the commissioning of the others? Was this *God* commissioning the eleven? If so, why? "Because those who believed that Jesus was resurrected—there were doubters—believed, on that ground, that by way of Jesus acting, God was acting. Eventually the church would come to the view that Jesus's actions *just were* God's actions."[45] Thus, Wolterstorff concludes that the disciples "were commissioned to be *witnesses to*—that is, *witnesses concerning*—Jesus Christ. For that, they had to have known Jesus, recall the major outlines of his life and words, be able to say who he was."[46]

So how do we come to conclude that *these* books—the New Testament books—form the book to which we can apply the designation "God's speech"? Wolterstorff recognizes that this question turns on external and not merely subjective criteria, viz., the matter of canonicity. "To be accepted into the canon, the book had to possess *apostolicity*. . . . There's a canonical impulse within the New Testament books; canonicity is not some fate which befalls them from outside."[47] Thus, Wolterstorff summarizes:

> Let us gather the strands together. Suppose the apostles were commissioned by God through Jesus Christ to be witnesses and representatives (deputies) of Jesus. Suppose that what emerged from their carrying out this commission was a body of apostolic teaching which incorporated what Jesus taught them and what they remembered of the goings-on surrounding Jesus, shaped under the guidance of the Spirit. And suppose that the New Testament books are all either apostolic writings, or formulations of apostolic teaching composed by close associates of one or another apostle. Then it would be correct to construe each book as a medium of divine discourse. And an eminently plausible construal of the process whereby these books found their way into a single canonical text, would be that by way of that process of canonization, God was authorizing these books as together constituting a single volume of divine discourse.[48]

I concur with Wolterstorff's points thus far, including his cursory description of canonicity. Nevertheless, it would seem that *covenant* provides a broader and more definite context for discourse (that God speaks) and canonicity (that God speaks *here*).[49] Regardless, both of our proposals will surely be liable to the charge that they turn Christianity into a "religion of a book" instead of a religion of Jesus Christ. "But why would that be?" he asks. "The focus of the Christian scriptures is of course on Jesus Christ. Why is it that if we interpret God as telling us, by way of the scriptures, about God's entrance into our history centrally and decisively in Jesus Christ, we have turned the Christian religion into a 'religion of the book'—worse yet, into *bibliolatry*?" Similarly, Brevard Childs reminds us that in actual practice the health of the church has always been measurable in terms of its recognition that in scripture God actually addressed them:

> Genuine rebirth in the history of the church has always been accompanied by a rediscovery of the central role of the Bible as the vehicle for encountering the living God. Moreover, spiritual renewal has usually resulted in greater intensity in wrestling with God's word. In sum, there has never been a serious form of Christianity that has divorced itself from scriptural authority. . . . To speak of moving beyond the Bible always signals a return to the wilderness and a loss of divine blessing.[50]

As a final consideration, Wolterstorff notes that more could, and ought to be, said concerning God's speaking in Jesus Christ, as well as appreciating "the conviction, shared alike by rabbinic Judaism and classic Lutheranism and Calvinism, that by way of authorized interpretation of the sacred text, God speaks anew: the line between divine discourse and interpretation is breached."[51] At this point, we once again recognize a robust theology of the Spirit emerging, which Barth's understandable but tragic reaction (against especially Hegel's "Absolute Spirit," perhaps?) undervalued, at least in the outworking of the system. Combined with this pneumatological-christological orientation is an eschatological perspective and the concrete form of the covenant canon, all together serving to move us beyond the antinomies of modern theology.

COMPARISON WITH ALTERNATIVES

Once more, the static view of textual meaning (reducing meaning to timeless texts or truths) is challenged—not only by a redemptive-historical method, but by a method of authorial discourse interpretation.[52] What is God *doing* by means of a given passage? This blurs the sharp line between word and act. This is the question that such a method poses at every turn. Subjectivity and objectivity are not *realms*. They are not universals or particulars; substances, accidents, or essences. Rather, they are *stances*. "Here I am" is an example of a subjective stance, not of subjectivity-in-general. There is therefore no reason to forbid propositions "about God" as part of revelation (*pace* liberalism, neo-orthodoxy and postliberalism), nor any reason to reduce all of revelation to true propositions (some forms of conservatism). While disclosure of God's attributes may be an intention of the divine author in a given discourse, there are always other interesting things that God is doing in speaking besides proposing or asserting. Further, given the fact that revelation follows the temporal pace of redemption (rather than vice versa), even propositions are rarely statements of eternal truths; they are more frequently declarations that are contextually made under the categories of command and promise. Some of these commands and promises (viz., those related to the Mosaic theocracy) change, while others remain valid forever (viz., the Abrahamic covenant).

This redemptive-historical and covenantal character of the biblical narrative shapes the nature of the human response. While it is part of human practice since the fall to regard autonomy as normal instead of sinful, covenantal epistemology is simply the divinely enabled recognition of reality as divinely constructed and regulated in relationship. It is neither antirational nor even suprarational, but the right use of reason in covenantal obedience. Given this background (which we cannot sufficiently explore here), it is no surprise that the sort of knowledge we are taking about is best illustrated in the response, "Here I am."

Knowing God is an existential way of knowing. It does not occur apart from knowledge of certain facts about God (any more than it can in ordinary human relationships). Nevertheless, the Hebrew understanding of knowledge in general was covenantally determined by its own dramatic history and narrative of redemption, in contrast to the ideal of *scientia* or the *gnosis* of speculative philosophers and first-century sects. It was knowledge oriented toward a person and for a particular reason involving (but not reduced to) one's own existence. But because this person is more unlike than like the human persons with whom we are familiar, it is analogical. Further, it is personal-analogical knowledge supernaturally acquired through redemptive history and discourse. But it is not only a knowledge of a personal God who acts in history for the redemption of a people, but a knowledge that one living now, even outside of that original community, may have, by covenantal incorporation into the eschatological community of the Spirit.

As Wolterstorff has pointed out, this divine discourse model describes what actually takes place in the biblical narrative much better, for instance, than manifestational theories. According to the latter, knowledge of God is acquired chiefly by divine *disclosures* rather than by divine *discourse*. It is the tyranny of the eye once more, the temptation to idolatry through mimetic representation, whether such representation is identified as "symbol," "encounter," "*visio Dei*," "metaphor," "ontological self-communication," or some other option. According to the model that we have been defending, what is given in scripture is not *primarily* doctrine or universal moral principles (although these are important elements in the text) demanding assent (although this is included in the appropriate response). The accent rather falls on the revelation of divine commands and promises in historical contexts. In fact, all of the doctrine and ethics that one finds in scripture may then be related as loci under these two headings and illocutionary acts. In the face of such discourse, the appropriate response is, "Here I am." Pretensions to autonomy are surrendered to the priority of the Other, thereby receiving back the authentic "I" thus surrendered.

At this point I would like to return to Dulles's models of revelation. There have been attempts to mediate this apparent confusion of rival theories. Gabriel Fackre mounts an impressive attempt to build ecumenical bridges between these models by regarding each as a moment within a comprehensive account.[53] So, for instance, there is the moment of "preservation," a "universal human experience—moral, affective, rational," to which "inner experience" and "new aware-ness" correspond. "Action refers to revelation in definitive historical deeds of God, the election of Israel and incarnation in Christ," to which "revelation as his-tory" and as "dialectical presence" would point. Furthermore, "[i]nspiration has reference to privileged accounts and interpretations of the deeds of God in scrip-ture," to which an evangelical version is committed. Finally, "[i]llumination is a rubric for the light given on all the foregoing in sequel acts of disclosure."[54]

But while attempts to overcome differences are likely to bear some fruit along the way, it seems that it is not merely the case that these different models have a different component that they overstress, ignoring other elements, but that each model has different answers to many of the same questions across the spectrum of issues related to revelation. While not quite incommensurable language games, these distinct models not only fail to affirm or emphasize certain important aspects of the other models, but in fact deny what is essential to them.

However, in the covenantal model we have supported here, there is neither antithesis nor synthesis. That is because this model, quite apart from attempting to reconcile each model, already has a vested interest in some of the chief points that each model makes, but cannot make adequately, because of what it denies. In our approach, revelation is inseparable from what God says, what God does, what one experiences, what encounter one has with God, and the new awareness of even the ordinary providence or common grace activity of God in the cosmos.

To be sure, the model of covenantal discourse does not, for instance, identify revelation and experience the way the experiential model does, nor encounter the way dialectical theology does, and so on. Nevertheless, no elaboration of this model can be attempted without doing justice to each of these aspects. As we have hinted at all too briefly here, the covenantal model emphasizes divine action (events) and divine discourse (words), without pitting one against the other. In fact, the words only occur as events (speech acts). Furthermore, it emphasizes the I-Thou encounter that upsets our orientation and aspirations, rather than merely confirming them. We are addressed, judged, justified, and incorporated into a community of discourse founded by divine initiative. Dialectical theologians are correct to insist that "[t]he word is not simply 'information,' but a call, a pledge, a challenge, and a promise."[55] And far from being reluctant, the covenantal dis-course model emphasizes that point, but without the existentialist reductionism. It is rather difficult, after all, to conceive of encounters by means of illocutionary acts that would not involve knowing something *about* the character and inten-tions of the one encountered.

While the covenant cannot be altered, it can be encountered in startling new ways even by those who have spent their entire lives in this community. For one person, the proclamation of God's righteousness can be utterly devastating and disheartening (as when Luther read of "the righteousness *of* God" before under-standing "the righteousness *from* God"). This encounter is not a parenthetical aspect of our account, therefore. We would concur with Gadamer's observation:

The gospel does not exist in order to be understood as a merely historical document, but to be taken in such a way that it exercises its saving effect. This implies that the text, whether law or gospel, if it is to be understood properly—i.e., according to the claim it makes—must be understood at every moment, in every concrete situation, in a new and different way. Understanding here is always application.[56]

The last comment reminds us of the indispensability of a strong pneumatology as well as Christology. At its heart, then, this model is concerned with the *ethical* divide between creator and creature, rather than with ontological or epistemological decoys that allow us to divert attention from our personal responsibility. The distance of this covenantal dimension from certain prominent and traditional theories of natural revelation is underscored by a comment from G. C. Berkouwer:

[In traditional Roman Catholic theology] the knowledge relation between Creator and creature is ontologically fixed. It results in knowledge of the formal aspects of God's being, in an independent natural theology of the first article (God as Creator) which has nothing to do with the knowledge of God in the reality of his grace and mercy. . . . What is the significance of this true knowledge of God who is here known as the Being "which exists in and of itself," as "the Prime Mover, the first cause, necessary being, the uncaused being, the true and the good, the rational designer, who is his own goal"? How is it possible that such considerations derived from the natural light of reason can be connected with the name, which God himself revealed to Moses when he said: "I am that I am"? Can one really be satisfied with this identification of the "natural" conception of "God as being" and this covenant name expressing his faithfulness to his people?[57]

And this is another reason that such knowledge must not only be covenantally related to a Thou who addresses us, but to the community in which we find ourselves addressed. Thus, the church becomes the environment for the *habitus cognoscendi*. Liberals and evangelicals alike have tended to underappreciate the ecclesial context for any genuine knowledge of God. In such alternative models, coming to faith is often regarded chiefly in voluntaristic, moralistic, or merely cognitive terms. Not only is the individual disembodied from the body of Christ, but the self is disembodied and reduced to human willing and thinking. But in a covenantal approach, knowledge of God that is useful (i.e., pertaining to redemption and faithfulness) can ordinarily be acquired only within the visible covenant community: "In Judah God is known" (Ps. 76:1). It is not surprising therefore that Calvin's ecclesiology appears under the section of the *Institutes* entitled "The Means of Grace."

In our approach, the speaker and the intentions of that speaker that are expressed, confirmed, and fulfilled in history, and not merely propositions about what is and has always been, have priority. And inner experience of God's justice, goodness, and righteousness fill human beings with awe and with fearful dread when they contemplate the lives actually led in response to this "general revelation." Finally, none of this can be considered to have revealed anything if it is not statable, that is, if it is not proposed, asserted. In this model, revelation is neither identical to doctrinal and ethical propositions nor set in opposition to them.

A covenantal epistemology will focus on what God is doing, by means of what God *says* and *does*, and not chiefly on what God *is* and *shows*. According to the former, one is called, interrupted from one's ordinary routine, judged, blessed, held accountable, put in question, and assured. By themselves, manifestational approaches will allow the hearer to remain aloof, judging instead of being judged, merely observing, theorizing, speculating. Instead of reducing divine revelation to a Platonizing (and Cartesian) model of communicating one idea from one mind to another, we must recover the biblical (i.e., covenantal) epistemology that calls not only for observation, reflection, and description, but for trust and obedience to a Thou. It is not a matter of merely assent or unbelief, but of obedience or autonomy.

Divine revelation as manifesting what God *is*, as opposed to discourse concerning what God has *done* and will *do* in the future, represents a real polarization whose opposites cannot be harmonized. The diverse theologies that rely heavily on Mircea Eliade's analysis of myth can only reduce theology to the very nature mysticism of the nations against which Israel was called to stand in contrast. Ricoeur emphasizes proclamation over manifestation in a way that to some extent parallels Wolterstorff's preference for discourse over manifestation. According to the manifestation model, says Ricoeur, "the sacred" is central, and seeing it is as important. Furthermore, those who regard revelation primarily as the "manifestation" of the sacred or God/the gods usually regard the correspondence between heaven (sacred) and earth (profane) as normal. In other words, there is no sense of God disrupting the earthly order. Miracles take place, for instance, because they are part of the normal course of religious life. Everything becomes miraculous; the whole cosmos itself takes on a magical (or at least mystical, numinous) air. (Affinities with process theology might be suggested here.) On the other hand, a hermeneutics of proclamation is disruptive precisely because the universe is not divine, miracles are not ordinary, and God is absolutely unconditioned by the creature:

> We need to begin with the Hebraic domain. There, in effect, the rupture is consummated. Indeed, one cannot fail to be struck by the constant, obstinate struggle against the Canaanite cults—against the idols Baal and Astarte, against the myths about vegetation and agriculture, and in general against any natural and cosmic sacredness—as expressed in the writings of the Hebrew prophets. . . . I will say first of all that with the Hebraic faith the word outweighs the numinous. Of course, the numinous is not absent from, say, the burning bush or the revelation at Sinai. But the numinous is just the underlying canvas from which the word detaches itself. This emergence of the word from the numinous is, in my opinion, the primordial trait that rules all the other differences between the two poles of the religious.[58]

Drawing on von Rad, Ricoeur argues, "The whole of Israel's theology is organized around certain fundamental discourses."[59] On one hand, there is the confession of the liberating acts, but then there is the prophet's disorienting speech against Israel's presumptions and over-confidence in terms of these founding events. "Other forms of discourse—the hymn, wisdom, and so on—are grafted onto this polarity of tradition and prophecy. In every manner, the religious axis passes through such speech-acts."[60] Hierophanies (such as the burning bush, pillar of fire, cloud, ark of the covenant) are overwhelmed by instruction, as Torah smashes the potential idols. "A theology of the Name is opposed to any hierophany of an idol. . . . *Hearing the word has taken the place of a vision of signs*. . . . Although there is still sacred space and time, the emphasis is ethical and theological rather than aesthetic" (emphasis added).[61]

At this point, something needs to be said parenthetically about the place of "signs" as "visible words" (Augustine). There are clearly sign-events throughout Old and New Testament epochs and when the patriarchs, prophets, and disciples ask for signs, they are sometimes given them, though never on demand. To say that hearing has replaced seeing is not to eliminate the visual from eschatological hope, but is to give the word priority over sight in the logic of eschatology (promise as distinct from possession). The visual is included in redemption and revelation (particularly in the sacraments), but even there, is effective not in abstract terms, but only as God's word of promise is attached to its use. Later on, more will be said about the role of the sacraments in this drama.

Furthermore, ritual is "no longer founded on the correlation between myth and ritual as in the sacred universe," as the sacredness of nature "withdraws before the element of the word, before the ethical element, and before the historical element. In particular, a theology of history could not accommodate a cosmic theology. The battle had to be merciless, without any compassion," and the prophets waged this with sarcasm toward those who used the same wood with which they started their fires as objects of worship. In the place of a logic of correspondences is a new logic of limit-expressions.[62] In other words, the primary mode of revelation is telling rather than showing. That is to say that scripture is chiefly prophetic: promise and fulfillment, and (forth-)telling is the mode of prophetic revelation. As Fackre expresses it,

> But more than that, the Bible is a book that tells an "overarching story." While imaginatively portrayed, it is no fictive account, having to do with turning points that have "taken place" and will take place, a news story traced by canonical hand. Its "good news" is about events in meaningful sequence, unrepeatable occasions with a cumulative significance internal to their narration (in contrast to "myth" that dissolves uniqueness, expressing what is always and everywhere the case).[63]

Ironically, then, modern theology, in its preference for "showing" (symbolism, illustration, mythological or allegorical indicator of a hidden universal or existential truth), has more in common with the religion of "the sacred" than that of scripture. This should not be surprising, given that the Jewish-Christian suspicion of "the sacred" earned the early Christian community the reputation for being atheists. A theology of vision corresponds to a *theologia gloriae*, while a theology of promise corresponds to the *theologia crucis*. The former craves an unmediated encounter with the sacred in a realized eschatology, while the latter patiently and joyfully receives the mediated encounter with a personal God in the "already" and "not yet" tension that belongs to faith rather than sight.

While this model is motivated by exegetical concerns first and foremost, it would seem that there are wide areas of possible convergence, even if the rival models are not simply treated as pieces of the comprehensive puzzle. According to Ernst Fuchs, "The so-called Christ of faith is none other than the historical Jesus."[64] This is a far cry from the neo-Kantian antithesis that has reigned even all the way up through dialectical theology. And Gerhard Ebeling argues, "The Kerygma . . . is not merely speech about man's existence. It is also a testimony to that which has happened."[65] Such advances among Bultmann's own students indicates perhaps a more open atmosphere for relaxing reductionism. The same evidence is apparent among those who have advanced the model we have been proposing, who, while affirming the authority of scripture, protest against reducing it to timeless propositions. Instead, they insist on regarding revelation as subservient to redemption, not vice versa, with the implication that the history of redemption, and not *merely* doctrine, is the content of divine communication.[66] As a representative of this position, Richard Gaffin writes, "Revelation never stands by itself, but is always concerned either explicitly or implicitly with redemptive accomplishment. God's speech is invariably related to his actions. It is not going too far to say that redemption is the *raison d'être* of revelation. An unbiblical, quasi-Gnostic notion of revelation inevitably results when it is considered by itself or as providing self-evident general truths. Consequently, revelation is either authentication or interpretation of God's redemptive action."[67] In fact, George Hunsinger refers to this school as an important conversation partner for narrative theologians who have in the past been wary of an almost "positivist" version of revelation that they have identified with conservative evangelical method: "If I am not wholly mistaken about the continuum that seems to run from the likes of Calvin through the likes of Kuyper and Bavinck to the likes of Frei and Lindbeck, then it would not seem amiss to suggest that a similar possibility [for genuine dialogue] exists also for evangelicals and postliberals today."[68]

To sum up, we have argued that God speaks, analogically understood. Like the causal joint in the matter of double agency, we cannot possess the archetypal knowledge of God's being that could indicate just how, on the divine side, such analogies hold up. But, as with the former question, it is enough that God, who does possess this exhaustive self-knowledge, has selected and authorized certain analogies and not others as appropriate. We have advanced this claim along the lines of the covenantal context in which the speaking of a human representative counts as divine speech (command and promise). This has not accounted for the notion of inspiration, since that is beyond the range of our interest here.

With the assistance of speech-act theory, we have exhibited a particular speech act, promising, as being conceptually coherent in its application to divine speech.

The question raised concerning analogy from Scotus to Pannenberg, namely, how one could affirm analogy without knowing to what extent the analogy actually corresponded to what we might call the *Ding-an-sich*, would appear to have an adequate resolution. This problem—and the problem that drives both Kantian skepticism and Hegelian idealism in metaphysics—is overcome finally by the surrender of autonomy. Never—not even through scripture—does a creature possess a God's-eye view of even oneself. This archetypal knowledge is unavailable in this life or the next, according to classical Roman Catholic and Protestant theology. But the alternative is not equivocity and relativism, since there is a trustworthy revelation (albeit ectypal and analogical) appropriate to pilgrims on the way. By authorizing this particular covenantal discourse, Yahweh has determined that it adequately expresses his character and intentions. That authorization in turn authorizes contemporary readers to assert that they have truly, though not univocally, grasped this character and these intentions. God has spoken to them through authorized discourse. And we hope that we have indicated how this model could better comprehend the multifaceted character of revelation, while avoiding reductionism.

There is one final question, though. If *drama* is the suggested root metaphor in this project, doesn't the rubric of divine *discourse* represent something of a diversion? Not really. We have argued that modern theology has depended on false dilemmas: revelation is either doctrine or encounter, either act or words, as if "revelation" through discourse in any other interpersonal context could survive such reductions. Why should it be necessary to say, for instance, that "[t]he Bible thus is not primarily the Word of God, but the record of the Acts of God, together with the human response thereto"?[69] We know only that in a given event God is doing *x* (judging, liberating, promising, warning) and not *y*, because the same God interprets it for us as such in the context of covenant. Thus, language and action must be seen together. In other words, revelation and redemption are coordinated, with the former serving the interests of the latter, rather than vice versa.

Even in general literary theory, there appears to be growing appreciation for getting beyond the reduction of a text to one thing (viz., a text, a narrative, writing, speech). Umberto Eco, for example, distinguishes between discourse, plot, and story.[70] In our model, revelation is the servant of redemption; divine saying serves divine saving. So, as a script is essential but not sufficient for a drama, so too divine discourse. We now turn to the hermeneutical method implied in this notion.

Chapter Six

Interpreting for Divine Discourse

This presupposition of the textuality *of faith distinguishes* biblical faith ('Bible' meaning book) from all others. In one sense, therefore, texts do precede life. I can name God in my faith because the texts preached to me have already named God.[1]

Practice *gives the words their sense.*[2]

Paul Ricoeur put a fine point on an emerging consensus on the unity of speech and action when he observed, "I think we are at a moment that I would qualify as being beyond the linguistic turn. . . . Two factors, I believe, have facilitated this surpassing of the linguistic turn: on the one hand, the recognition that discourse is an action; on the other hand, and in a contrary sense, the recognition that human action is a speaking action."[3] We have already appropriated speech-act theory in other respects and now we are able to deal more directly with this step "beyond the linguistic turn." Our goal in this chapter is to tease out the hermeneutical implications of our account for the claim that God speaks. But we begin once more with the particular challenges facing this part of the proposal.

THE HERMENEUTICAL CHALLENGES TO OUR ACCOUNT

According to Gadamer, modern hermeneutical theory and its interpretive practice were on a mission, aiming at "the liberation of interpretation from dogma."[4] This, by the way, corresponds also to Descartes's concern to discover a method that could provide certainty beyond the parochial loyalties of confessional strife.[5] This point should not be underestimated in its significance: the hidden prejudices of modern hermeneutics, arising in the context of theological liberalism, are already deeply imbedded in the dualistic trajectory we have been noting throughout this work. Like foundationalism, modern hermeneutics emerged as a means of overcoming theological orthodoxy. Gadamer observed that "[t]he historical critique of Scripture that emerges fully in the eighteenth century has its dogmatic basis" [faith in reason], just as medieval and Reformation hermeneutics had their own.[6] Mark C. Taylor has emphasized the theological implications of deconstruction.[7] Similarly, Kevin Vanhoozer has carried forward the case that the death of the author and related results of some postmodern theory are motivated by theological (or rather, a/theological) ambitions.[8] Like the relationship between a mother and her wayward child, theology, which gave birth to hermeneutics, has become the target of radical hermeneutical theory.

The breakdown in the rather straightforward approach to biblical interpretation, in which whole and parts interact dialectically to form the *analogia fidei*, was at least in part occasioned by the assertion of epistemological and ethical autonomy. John Webster points this out in relation to Spinoza's formative impact:

> Undergirding Spinoza's construal are a number of features which prepare us for the insignificance of Christian doctrine for much modern hermeneutics: an idealisation of reading the Bible as an instance of general hermeneutical operations (what Spinoza calls 'inquiry'); a construal of the hermeneutical situation in such a way that the judging self is fundamentally important; a conviction that the invocation of theological doctrine is an impediment, since questions of interpretation are pre-doctrinal, to be settled prior to entry into the sphere of the Credo; a presupposition that the world of the Bible is a problem, since we both pre-exist and transcend the world, entertaining an attitude of distance toward it. Indeed, such is Spinoza's account of the hermeneutical situation that it can hardly be called a situation at all, at least not in the sense that we are "situated" within it, for its most fundamental axiom is that of the aseity and transcendence of the interpretative act.[9]

As Kurt Mueller-Vollmer explains, the rationalistic philosopher Christian Wolff divided texts into historical and dogmatic, the latter weighed "on the strength of their arguments, their truth content, and the knowledge of the subject matter displayed" (all of which should be obvious to the unbiased reasoner), while historical works were "judged according to the 'completeness' of the historical account which they offer and according to their 'truthfulness' and 'sincerity,' since we no longer have access to historical truth once the events referred to are past."[10] Enlightened readers could be expected to divine not only the subject matter but the mind of the author. At first, this was a search for the objective point of the author, depending on the use of words and genre, but this became increasingly subjectivized and psychologized. This was especially in vogue in Romanticism, with Schleiermacher arguing that a text in general and authorial intent in particular are expressions of the individuality of the authorial subject.

In the Romantic movement, especially in the first decade of the nineteenth century, texts became regarded as works of art and in that sense expressions of

the author's subjectivity.[11] Art is symbolic, and just as there are as many interpretations of a master-painting as there are interpreters, so too with texts. Romantic hermeneutics follows Plato's *mimesis* (*Republic*, book 2), as Gerald Bruns puts
it, "slipping into the feeling or delusion that we are someone else (Achilles, say,
or some other heroic or maybe not-so-heroic character)."[12] Further, speaking is,
for Schleiermacher, the inverse of thinking.[13] Thus, interpretation holds together
the two movements of understanding what is said and the subject matter itself as
it exists in the speaker's mind. The "great divisions" here, according to Schleiermacher, are *grammatical* and *psychological.* So the goal of historical and linguistic
knowledge is to remove the obstacles between the original readers and us. Interpretation begins only after we've established similarities. "The rules for the art of
interpretation must be developed from a positive formula, and this is: 'the historical and diviniatory, objective and subjective reconstruction of a given statement.'"[14] Thus, "The task is to be formulated as follows: 'To understand the text
at first as well as and then even better than its author.'"[15] Sympathetic understanding is the criterion of interpretation.[16]

Wilhelm Dilthey (1833–1911) gradually moved away from psychologism
toward culture and language. Understanding (*Verstehen*) as "disclosing a world"
first becomes articulated explicitly, and in opposition to the positivistic historians he distinguished the method of the human sciences from those of the natural
sciences. There is no such thing as "laws of history," for instance. Instead, he
would find a foundationalist grounding for his enterprise in psychology, an
attempt that came to be universally regarded as a failure. Nevertheless, Dilthey
at least liberated understanding from its Cartesian captivity to thought. Instead,
"lived experience" became the habitation in which thought and language flour-
ished. Yet, in contrast to Droysen, Dilthey emphasized the Romantic theory of
projection and consequent historicism that seem to have had such a decisive
influence on the various attempts at reconstructing the historical Jesus. Gadamer
expresses the weakness of this position, inasmuch as it relativizes the past, but not
the present.[17]

In *Being and Time* (1927), Heidegger claimed that the abandonment of
Descartes's *cogito* requires also the rejection of the author/creator-reader/audience
dualism. Thus, understanding becomes ontologically grounded, as *being-in-the-
world* is substituted for the ordinary subject-object category. Appropriating
Humboldt, Heidegger brings language and speech to the foreground again. With
this in mind we can better appreciate Bultmann's motive in his demythologizing
program, where the goal of interpretation is to penetrate beyond what is *said* to
what is *meant* (not authorial intent but the existential meaning for us).[18] It is not
a shared historical consciousness (*pace* Romanticism), but a shared existential orientation that Bultmann champions.[19]

Heidegger's other famous pupil, Hans-Georg Gadamer, with this hermeneutical tradition generally, locates hermeneutics in understanding. But instead of
seeing this as a matter of overcoming the alienation of historical distance, he
argues for the historical nature of understanding itself. Neither the historicist's

distanciation nor the romanticist's naive claim to have overcome this gulf does justice to the "horizoned" character of historical consciousness. This rootedness means that the interpreter always comes with prejudices, many of them tacit, but these are not evils to be avoided. Rather, they are necessary conditions of understanding. This continuum between the historical event/author and the interpreter is "effective history" (*Wirkungsgeschichte*).

Medieval interpretation had been shaped by dogmas, a priori judgments, but the Reformation replaced this with a concern with the text, says Gadamer.[20] So instead of seeing doctrine itself as the be-all and end-all of interpretation, Protestant interpretation called for the extraction of doctrine from the text. Thus, the parts were to be interpreted in the light of the whole (*analogia fidei*), and the less perspicuous in the light of clearer passages. But to interpret the whole, one must interpret the parts. Thus begins the long and successful career of the so-called hermeneutical spiral. The Reformers took the unity of the canon for granted, but when finally this was surrendered, interpretation could look at the individual books to discern unity on the text's "own" terms, or so it was thought. Books break down into pericopes, increasingly smaller units. Schleiermacher was therefore concerned not only to transcend the medieval hermeneutic of a priori dogmatics, but the Reformers' a priori of canonical unity, in an effort to formulate general hermeneutical rules. Just as Descartes was after a method that could provide certain conclusions for any science, Schleiermacher sought to provide a hermeneutic that could be applied to the Bible or any other text—indeed, to understanding generally. Texts should "speak for themselves," not being predetermined by dogma or canonical unity. Authority is earned, not presupposed. Thus, his own dogmatic prejudices were masked by the pretension to scientific neutrality.

Gadamer's response to all of this is that a text never just "speaks for itself." Schleiermacher starts with his own a priori assumptions, among which is the belief that the process begins with a state of misunderstanding. But Gadamer sees no reason that this should be a legitimate starting point. It is not really the case, says Gadamer, that we seek to understand a *person* in isolation from an *issue*. Understanding is primarily agreement, not empathy. Coming to an understanding consists of coming to agree about *something* (viz., *die Sache*), and that is not arbitrary. So, for Gadamer, the goal of understanding is not to understand the speaker, but to agree with the speaker regarding specific propositional content. Thus, Schleiermacher's a priori necessarily leads to psychologism (e.g., understanding the person), while Gadamer argues that his approach leads to hermeneutics (e.g., understanding the subject matter).

We do not begin with the assumption of misunderstanding. In fact, discourse assumes that we want the other person to say what is true, and when he or she does not, we "fall back" into psychological questions.[21] But this is only the "fall back" measure when the straightforward strategy fails. "Thus the need for a hermeneutics is given precisely with the decline of self-evident understanding," says Gadamer.[22] Romanticism's *usual* method is Gadamer's *exception*.

While Gadamer does not reject Schleiermacher wholesale, he thinks that his original premise (viz., misunderstanding) demands a psychologistic approach. Rather than transposing ourselves into the mind of the author (i.e., psychological interpretation), Gadamer argues that our normal course is not only to assume agreement with what the other person says, but to go one step further: "If we want to understand, we will try to make his arguments even stronger."[23] It is not a mystical communion of souls, but a communion of content, meaning, agreement, that Gadamer says characterizes genuine understanding. In this sense, he prefers premodern hermeneutics, in which, for instance, Augustine tried to underscore the harmony of Old and New Testaments and in an early Protestantism that sought to do the same with the rubric of promise and fulfillment. "It is something qualitatively new when Romanticism and Schleiermacher universalize historical consciousness by denying that the binding form of the tradition from which they come and in which they are situated provides a solid basis for hermeneutical endeavor."[24] It should be noted that these tendencies so marked in Schleiermacher's thought are just as apparent in conservative evangelicalism, with its bent toward an individualistic biblicism.

Modernity, it has been argued, is deeply divided. The Manichean tendency to divide the good god of pure spirit, freedom, the present moment of ecstasy, from the bad god who imprisons the innocent self in physical, causally and historically determined reality has been considerably resuscitated, as the "Jesus of history"/ "Christ of faith" antithesis more than testifies. To the extent that actions, texts, and history are incapable of being regarded as conveyors of meaning and even, in special cases, means of redemption, to that extent we are modern gnostics. Timeless concepts, not historical covenants, guide our contact (such as it is) with "reality" (such as it is). Furthermore, Bultmann was not really engaged in demythologizing, but in allegorizing, an interpretive strategy to which he acknowledged himself an heir.[25]

Francis Watson has shown the striking resemblances of modern theology (concentrating on Schleiermacher, Harnack, and Bultmann) and Gnosticism. One of his chapters is titled, "Erasing the Text: Readings in Neo-Marcionism."[26] Calvin faced a similar challenge in radical sects and defended the unity of the scriptures by means of the unity of God's gracious covenant. "But even though all wicked men, as if conspiring together, have so shamelessly insulted the Jews, no one has ever dared charge them with substituting false books."[27] For the Reformers, the Old Testament was as much the church's canon as the New, and both formed a single play with an intermission, a drama whose leading character was Jesus Christ.[28]

Derrida, Taylor, Milbank, and others are surely right when they insist that the hermeneutical debate is at root a theological debate.[29] The move from a sense of obligation to a God who spoke in and through the scriptures to the explicit project of autonomy (the Sovereign Self/Author) to, finally, the dissolution of the self and the author who could not bear the weight, until finally all meaning is denied: this trajectory makes perfect sense in the light of the Christian critique of human autonomy.

While some Christian scholars are unduly reactionary, others regard post-modern literary trends as an opportunity to cut faith and practice loose of the *sensus literalis* or "plain sense" of scripture. Stanley Hauerwas, for instance, has argued that Stanley Fish and Pope John Paul II are, after all, on the same side of things: in the absence of an authoritative and self-interpreting text, one needs the community (as if any institution were self-interpreting, much less self-authenticating). According to Hauerwas, "the text has no 'real' meaning."[30] Hauerwas sees in radical hermeneutics a moment for reversing the Reformation and retrieving the Bible from the laity.[31] Understandably, Vanhoozer views the parallels between the Reformation and our own day as "particularly striking," and with that observation issues a bold invitation:

> On the one hand, modern "enthusiasts" claim that meaning is new each day, a result of the encounter of text and reader, an encounter governed as much by the spirit of the age as by the Holy Spirit. Modern "papists," on the other hand, claim that the text can be interpreted correctly only in the church. . . . The Reformers, on the other hand, argued that reason, tradition, and experience do not guarantee understanding; yet, at the same time, they claimed that the Bible's meaning was both "perspicuous" (clear) and "simple" (single). . . . As the sixteenth-century Reformers redeemed the text and thus the possibility of literary knowledge, so we have to redeem the text in our time.[32]

We will try to restrict our focus to the hermeneutical implications of the dramatic-covenantal model that we have proposed. We will begin by analyzing the most prominent options whose insights and conceptual schemes we regard as among the closest conversation partners.[33]

INTERPRETING FOR GOD'S SPEECH

While there have been many attempts in recent years to produce theological applications of general hermeneutical theory, this strikes us as an unwise policy. John Webster is correct when he argues that there has been a shift from dogmatics to hermeneutics in theology and that "[s]trict governance by Christian doctrine is largely absent from most contemporary writing in hermeneutics."[34] A general hermeneutical theory, which is normally based on a transcendental anthropology, normally resists the internal theological landscape in favor of universal "understanding." Nor should it be based on ethnographic or sociolinguistic paradigms, "but the electing, reconciling and redemptive activity of God in Christ."[35] That is not to say that we will not be making use of contemporary ways of getting a cognitive grip on this subject, but that "theological appeal to these theories ought only to be ad hoc and pragmatic, a matter of finding a tool to do a job."[36] This ad hoc use of hermeneutical theories has been at least my intention in appealing to communicative theory. Would this project look significantly different without speech-act analysis? I would hope that differences would lie merely in the particular manner in which the phenomena that we call illocutionary acts are described: whether they are taken for granted or are formulated in different terms.

While it would be profitable perhaps to include deconstruction in our "conversation," I have chosen to focus instead on those broad perspectives in which meaning is ascribed, either to the author in some fashion or to the textual product. We begin then with Paul Ricoeur.

A. Textual-Sense Interpretation

According to Mark I. Wallace, Ricoeur's writing is characterized "by a fragile hope that in the borderlands beyond calculative reason there might be a world of transcendent possibilities (mediated through the text) that can refigure and remake the world of the reader."[37] While Marx, Nietzsche, and Freud offered a hermeneutic of suspicion, they failed to realize that "to smash the idols is also to let the symbols speak."[38] Ricoeur's hermeneutic is always moving back and forth between iconoclasm (distanciation) and belief (appropriation).[39] He declares, "It is the text, with its universal power of world disclosure, which gives a self to the ego."[40] And this text is inseparable from a historical existence: "we make history, . . . are immersed in history, . . . are historical beings."[41] For too long, fiction has been associated with untruth, but Ricoeur insists that fiction and history belong together: "The concept of plot—or rather 'emplotment,' as he prefers—is the linking idea that holds together both forms of writing," says Wallace."[42] Certain elements associated with fiction are present in historical writing, just as fiction is never isolated from real life. A human life (ipse-identity) thus "storied" is historical fiction.[43]

At the heart of the hermeneutical problem, the issue of distanciation affects not only writing but even speech, according to Ricoeur.[44] Not only a written work, but oral discourse is already separated not only from the addressee, but from the author herself:

> A work of discourse, as a work of art, is an autonomous object at a distance from the authorial intention, from its initial situation (its *Sitz-im-Leben*), and from its primitive audience. *For this very reason it is open to an infinite range of interpretations.* There is room for interpretation because the recovery of the initial event of discourse takes the form of a reconstruction starting from the structure and the inner organization of the specific modes of discourse. In other words, *if hermeneutics is always an attempt to overcome a distance*, it has to use distanciation as both the obstacle and the instrument in order to reenact the initial event of discourse in a new event of discourse that will claim to be both faithful and creative.[45] (emphasis added)

The italicized sentences indicate assumptions that are highly contested. Ricoeur's emphasis on the autonomy of the text due to distanciation opens the door to multiple sense. After all, completely severed from the author, a text is no longer revelatory of authorial intent or illocutionary stance, but is revelatory of new possibilities for existence. Ricoeur focuses on what revelation *does* for one more than what it *is* in itself. The Bible is *revelatory*, not *revelation*. It opens up a world of possibility, a new being. The influence of Heidegger is made explicit: "Pursuing this line of reasoning to its logical conclusions, must we not say that what is thus opened up in everyday reality is another reality, the reality of the *possible*?"[46] It is possibilities that are true or untrue, authentic or inauthentic. As in Heidegger's thought, truth is not a question of propositions, but of existence—specifically, *my* existence. It is the truth of *Dasein*. But, as we will see, superficial similarities to Bultmann should not be taken too seriously. Ricoeur is convinced that a narrative approach shows the superiority of the biblical writers over classical philosophy: "It is the function of the preaching of the cross and resurrection to give to the word 'God' a *density* that the word 'being' does not possess."[47] Events, and not mere religious feeling, are capable of disclosing new possibilities for one's existence.

> The feeling of absolute dependence would remain a weak and inarticulated sentiment if it were not the response to the proposition of a new being that opens new possibilities of existence for me. Hope, unconditional trust, would be empty if it did not rely on a constantly renewed interpretation of sign-events reported by the writings, such as the exodus in the Old Testament and the resurrection in the New Testament. These are the events of deliverance that open and disclose the utmost possibilities of my own freedom and thus become for me the word of God. Such is the properly hermeneutical constitution of faith.[48]

Given this understanding, how do we as contemporary readers interpret this ancient text? What is the line from the originary community to us?

> There is one act that continues, at least within Christianity, to preserve this double line of delineation, and this is preaching. You preach on canonical texts, but not on profane; the community would be completely changed if you chose a modern poet to do a sermon, or if you took the *Bhagavad Gita* into the church. This is a crisis of the community because its own identity relies on the identity of the text. . . . Preaching is the permanent reinterpretation of the text that is regarded as grounding a community; therefore, for the community to address itself to another text would be to make a decision concerning its social identity. A community that does that becomes another kind of community.[49]

Ricoeur writes, "I wonder whether it does not belong to the nature of proclamation to be always brought back from the written to the oral; and it is the function of preaching to reverse the relation from written to spoken."[50] Despite his warnings against the "secular Christianity" model, Ricoeur's Hebraic sensitivities are still acute: "Revelation is a historical process, but the notion of sacred text is something antihistorical. I am frightened by this word 'sacred.'"[51]

In many respects Ricoeur's analysis marks an advance. First, he does get beyond the "calculative reason" that disembodies thought and his emphasis on emplotment is suggestive for the metaphor of drama to which our proposal is so attached. Furthermore, his broader (and more positive) notion of fiction (viz., that a storied life amounts to historical fiction) does provide conceptual space for pursuing a fuller analysis of narration within the drama that does not depend on a reductive choice between a positivist view of truth and a fanciful view of fiction as entertaining but untrue. His remarks about preaching, which are replete throughout his writings, are also illuminating. Preaching, so long as it is normed by the text, actually mediates the originary community and its self-identity (ipse-identity). As we will see below, Ricoeur combines all of this with an intense interest in the historical event character of revelation, but without demanding a choice between word-revelation and act-revelation. We are also sympathetic to Ricoeur's interest in narrative. We live in an age that shows "ominous symptoms" of a loss of any ability to tell or hear stories, a forgetfulness that can only be healed by a "rebirth of narrative." "In that sense, the fight for a 'rebirth of narrative' . . . is, as such, a specifically Christian task."[52]

But there are some difficulties with Ricoeur's proposal. First, he is still operating within an existentialist framework that is quite close to Tillich's "ultimate concern," "broken myths," and so forth, as well as Bultmann's Heideggerian analysis of *Dasein* as disclosure of new possibilities of being-in-the-world. Thus, despite the laudable interest in the community, Ricoeur's model is largely individualistic. Besides, Christians have wanted to say more than that revelation discloses a new way of being-in-the-world. As important as that is, there has been a central concern (raised by the text itself) with sin and grace within a covenantal context. Ricoeur himself emphasizes this point in a number of places, as we will see below. But if there is no content to revelation—if, in other words, revelation is a new *outlook* and not new *news*—how can the apostle say that the word of God makes known "the mystery that has been hidden throughout the ages and generations but has now been revealed to his saints," identifying the content of that revelation of God's purpose to save the ungodly through the death and resurrection of Jesus Christ (Col. 1:26)? It would seem that, in Ricoeur's proposal, God's word could only extend and improve the existence of the unregenerative self, unveiling possibilities to autonomous reason, instead of crucifying the self and raising it in newness.

Furthermore, Ricoeur's insistence upon the autonomy of the text, with no access to authorial intent or *Sitz-im-Leben*, appears to be based on a particular theory of authorial intent interpretation, namely, a Romantic one in which the reader/hearer is expected to be able to access the inner world of the author/speaker. As we will see below, there is an alternative to the Romantic view that nevertheless retains the possibility of determining the author's intentions *in so far as those intentions are embedded in the text itself.* One might say (but probably shouldn't) that Ricoeur abducts the author and then Derrida does the author in. Our proposal will not seek to eliminate the essential existential component that Ricoeur so deftly puts on view, but will attempt to reinterpret it within a covenantal hermeneutic.

B. Authorial Discourse Interpretation

Probably no one has sought to relate speech-act theory to theological hermeneutics as creatively and profoundly as Nicholas Wolterstorff.[53] Just as Hans Frei charged modern biblical hermeneutics with abandoning the *sensus literalis*, which reigned throughout church history, Wolterstorff claims that, at least in academic circles, the practice of reading the Bible in order to discern what God is saying therein (i.e., "divine discourse interpretation") has been similarly eclipsed. From Romantic authorial-intention interpretation to textual-sense interpretation (Ricoeur), all the way to Derrida's deconstructionism, the landscape appears to leave little room for such an approach. For Ricoeur, writing necessarily prohibits access to authorial discourse, since "the verbal meaning of the text no longer coincides with the mental meaning or intention of the text." Absence of the author renders the text itself mute. "The text is like a musical score and the reader like the orchestra conductor who obeys the instructions of the notation," he says.[54] But Wolterstorff insists that authorial *discourse* interpretation (not authorial *intent* interpretation) is the best way of getting at the designative content.

This process begins by discerning the noematic content of the divinely appropriated discourse. If a sentence has only one meaning, "we take the noematic content of the discourse to be the meaning of the sentence, unless we have good reason for doing otherwise."[55] Further, we assume that people are speaking literally, unless we have good reason to suspect otherwise. When sentences have multiple meanings, we set out the possible meanings and ask ourselves, what is the most likely meaning intended by the author? What was he or she wanting to say by uttering or inscribing this? We expect the speaker to tell us the meaning of the sentence, and this is why we usually blame the speaker if he or she speaks in opaque or ambiguous terms. If we have reason to believe that the speaker is not intending a literal meaning, we consider the possibility that he or she is speaking loosely or indirectly. Only in these unusual cases we must attempt to determine authorial intent. In this, he agrees with Gadamer.

Next, we try to discern the illocutionary stance and designative content. "The main clues to illocutionary stance are carried by the moods of our sentences: declarative, interrogative, optative, and so forth. But literary genre also carries clues."[56] By discerning the noematic content and, then, the illocutionary stance and designative content, we are ready for the second hermeneutic: interpreting for the mediated divine discourse.

To discern divine discourse, we must come to the Bible as one book and interpret according to the so-called *analogia fidei* (although Wolterstorff does not use this phrase, it seems appropriate to his conclusion).[57] The interpreter, he says, must come to the Bible with two sets of convictions: the first concerning the meanings of sentences, the second consisting of convictions "as to what God would and wouldn't have intended to say by appropriating this totality of discourse and locution."[58] As to this latter set of convictions, Wolterstorff paraphrases Augustine's maxim: "If God's saying that would not conduce to our love of God and neighbor, or if its content is incompatible with Christian doctrine, then it follows that God did not say that."[59]

So how do we know when God is appropriating human discourse? First, we must arrive at the correct *rhetorico-conceptual structure*.[60] Second, we must distinguish the main point from the way of making and developing it (the latter possibly containing error). As an example, he cites Psalm 93:

> The Lord is king, he is robed in majesty;
>   the Lord is robed, he is girded with strength.
> He has established the world; *it shall never be moved*;
>   your throne is established from of old;
>   you are from everlasting. (emphasis added)

The main point here is God's steadfastness, but in making the point the human discourser says something that simply is not true: "As a matter of fact the earth is moved, and we all believe that it is; it rotates on its axis, revolves around the sun, and moves with the solar system as a whole through space."[61]

At this point, however, Wolterstorff suggests that we apply the distinction between noematic and designative content in relation to error. "That large elm tree there must be diseased," one says, actually pointing to a sycamore tree. "The point is true enough: the leaves are falling off of it and it is in fact diseased, but it is not an elm tree. Thus, the designative content is true, but the noematic content incorporates a falsehood."[62] Often, when interpreting the Bible for divine discourse, we must realize that that which is predicated of God is the designative content.

Third, we must discern whether the human author spoke literally, while God is speaking metaphorically. While this is infrequent, we see it, for instance, when biblical writers predicate physical parts of God.

Fourth, Wolterstorff says, we need to distinguish between the discourse-generating and discourse-generated discourse, especially of concern in interpreting parables for divine discourse.[63] Fifth, we must distinguish between what God *was* saying to us and what he *is* saying to us.[64] So what do we make of his proposal?

As with speech-act theory more generally, Wolterstorff's proposal circumvents many of the problems associated with more traditional (i.e., Romantic) notions of authorial intent. In fact, Wolterstorff even insists on distinguishing his hermeneutics (authorial discourse interpretation) from authorial intent interpretation. He is even more convinced than Gadamer that the meaning of the text is determined by the author and not by the reader. In fact, Gadamer's "fusion of horizons" is not necessary at all in Wolterstorff's account. And Wolterstorff is also more insistent than Gadamer on the point (first raised by Gadamer) that interpretation usually goes well and that psychological divination is a fallback strategy, not the ordinary direction. Is it possible that Ricoeur's notion of the autonomous text and its distanciation from any author or *Sitz-im-Leben* originates from the breakdown of this Romantic procedure, but instead of turning against the unreasonably high expectations of knowing the author better than she knew herself, he severs all ties with the author? Regardless, Wolterstorff's approach avoids the psychologistic version of authorial intent analysis while affirming access to what the speaker or author intended to do in saying what was said.

But ironically, unlike the traditional understanding of *sensus literalis*, Wolterstorff's method at this point appears to substitute psychological divination of the *divine* author's mind, which at least on the surface seems to be precisely what he eloquently refuted in his analysis of Romantic theories of authorial intention. In the model I am proposing, the analogy of scripture is given this role of figuring out what God might and might not have wanted to say, or rather, what God in fact has and has not said. In this way, God interprets God's own discourse, as difficult passages are interpreted in the light of clearer ones. There are no direct routes to the knowledge of God, even through prayer and devotion. Encounters are always mediated, and one will never know what God meant to say and did or did not mean to do, apart from God's own stated intentions. Wolterstorff seems to accept this sort of position elsewhere,[65] but it is at least qualified by these other statements. We will see a couple of examples of this below.

But Wolterstorff's rather straightforward methodology seems in many respects quite appropriate and fruitful for theological hermeneutics. John Searle takes this line for hermeneutics more generally: "Characteristically, when one speaks one means something by what one says; and what one says, the string of sounds that one emits, is characteristically said to have meaning."[66] A hearer "understands what I am saying as soon as he recognizes my intention in uttering what I utter as an intention to say that thing."[67] One does, however, wonder whether speech-act theorists have sufficiently explained how their strategy is equally applicable to written and oral communication. But if all utterances, whether written or oral, can be regarded as species of speech-action (and I agree that they can), then the *difficulties* arising from written as opposed to oral discourse (such as the absence of the author's commentary, facial expressions, and so forth) actually belong to the category of communicative misfires. In other words, Ricoeur's assumption of the inaccessibility of the author is ironically, like Schleiermacher's psychological divination, based on the exception rather than the rule. The fallback strategy (concluding that one cannot discern the author's intent) becomes the dominant and ordinary strategy.

But meaning is more than intention, as we have already seen. There must be meaningful conventions, so that X counts as Y in context C. Searle holds together "both the intentional and the conventional aspects and especially the relationship between them."[68] We blame people for not being clear in what they are saying, intending, commanding, promising, and so forth, Wolterstorff points out. There are, of course, times when communication misfires, but this is actually not the norm. Therefore, I do not regard distanciation in the case of a written text as problematic for interpretation in general, but only in exceptional cases—that is, when something goes wrong (ambiguity, deceit, contradiction, etc.).

In relation to theological hermeneutics, then, we come to the Bible as a single canon, a unified book. This already assumes a figural (promise-fulfillment) interpretation. At this point Wolterstorff gets specific in facing interpretive challenges. "What God would and wouldn't have intended" is a difficult business, especially when one has insisted that it is not the author's inner thoughts, but stated intentions, that are accessible. Here, it seems, Wolterstorff does think that one can get behind the stated intentions. Hence, "to interpret God's discourse more reliably, we must come to know God better, in both devotion and reflection."[69]

It is true that not all of scripture is appropriated discourse. Obvious examples would include the speeches of Job's friends or, for that matter, much of Job's speech as well. But wouldn't it be simplistic to conclude that appropriated discourse could only come in the form of divine address? In other words, isn't the psalmist's ascription of mercy, steadfastness, justice, and so forth, to God in praise also appropriated discourse? Of course, this is not to deny that the *psalmist* is ascribing this praise to God. But surely a deity who prescribed the minutiae of the temple would have an interest in the community getting God's own attributes and works right in their worship. Is this not an instance, then, of appropriated discourse, although they are directly the speeches of the human author? Through the psalmist's saying, "The Lord is good" or "O Lord, our Lord, your ways are past tracing out," God is fixing an appropriate reference range for descriptive and doxological utterance.

If one does take this aspect of Wolterstorff's proposal, there does seem to be the possibility of a rival hermeneutic here to Wolterstorff's own main line of argument. Surely recent interpreters as diverse as Tillich, Bultmann, Frei, and Henry would affirm the importance of knowing God in an experiential manner and would, moreover, insist that this was essential to their arrival at widely differing views as to what God would have wanted to say. The author insists:

> Appropriation is not license for unbridled play of imagination on the part of interpreters. The human authors of the Bible clearly claimed that God intervenes directly in the course of nature and human affairs; if we choose to depart from that in the course of interpreting for divine discourse, we need good reason for doing so. . . . And let it be added that having good reason to depart is also not license for unbridled play of the imagination. Roughly speaking, we are to stay as close as possible to the mediating discourse, *given our convictions as to what the appropriator would have wanted and not wanted to say by appropriating this discourse thus expressed.* (emphasis added)

While Wolterstorff's proposal may eschew unbridled imagination, does it relieve the wax-nose anxiety—that is, the fear of shaping the text into whatever we wish? Despite his assurances, the examples he himself uses from the Psalms and 2 Timothy do not seem to ameliorate that anxiety. What are the criteria for determining what God said and what God is saying? This seems to be entirely too subjective, as if we could know the ultimate author better than he knows himself. In fact, it seems at odds with Wolterstorff's own approach and speech-act theory more generally. How could one know what the appropriator of any discourse would want to say, apart from his or her discourse somewhere else? The analogy of scripture is an example of what happens in all ordinary interpretation. If, for instance, Jane is known to stretch the truth a bit now and then, her promise will be received in the light of the other things Jane has said and performed (or not, as the case may be).

Will prayer and devotion license us to determine, on the basis of our assumptions about what God would and would not do, what parts of divine discourse are still normative? Here again, a redemptive-historical hermeneutic would provide another solution, an eschatological-historical, not theoretical-conceptual, solution. For exegetical reasons alone (considered below) we could determine, for instance, that God was telling Israel to drive out the Canaanites, but that God is not telling us today to drive out the Canaanites—or anybody else. Anticipating a point to be made below, the polity of God's people changes, depending on the particular economy of God's kingdom. In this age, God does not enter into covenants with nations, and the church is the world's most ethnically diverse society. This is not an assumption imposed on the text by a priori rules or our own judgments about what is right, but arises in the attempt to interpret scripture in the light of scripture, a dialectical process that gives rise gradually to a biblical-theological and systematic-theological program. Even Israel's former oppressors will be her fellow worshipers in that coming day: "The LORD will make himself known to the Egyptians," with "a highway from Egypt to Assyria." "On that day Israel will be the third with Egypt and Assyria, a blessing in the midst of the earth, whom the LORD of hosts has blessed, saying, 'Blessed be Egypt my people, and Assyria the work of my hands, and Israel my heritage'" (Isa. 19:20–25).

Wolterstorff refers to Psalm 93 as an example of the noematic content containing falsehood while the designative content does not. Clearly, Wolterstorff observes, we do not today believe the earth to be unmoved. But surely that was also the case for the psalmist. Was the psalmist asserting the immobility of the earth any more than that our thoughts are actually vapors because they are called "but an empty breath" (Ps. 94:11)? Here Wolterstorff seems to have misfired in his act of interpretation, if we adopt his own rules. We are, he says, to expect a literal interpretation except in those cases where it is obvious that this could not have been the author's intended meaning. Here we have just such a case, it seems. The genre is already trope-laden, so why should we expect the psalmist to be arguing for a pre-Copernican cosmology any more than he is arguing for a divine body to wear the majestic robe to which he also refers in the same passage? In fact, if we were to take the psalmist literally here, we would find him in conflict not only with modern cosmology, but with himself. Compare "[the earth] shall never be moved" with the passage we find only nine psalms later:

> Long ago you laid the foundations of the earth,
>   and the heavens are the work of your hands.
> *They will perish,* but you endure,
>   *they will wear out* like a garment.
> *You change them* like clothing,
>   and *they pass away.*
> but you are the same,
>   and your years have no end.
>   (Ps. 102:25–27, emphasis added)

Is the earth really firm? Shall it *never* be moved? I think that Wolterstorff's distinction between noematic and designative content, in which error is sometimes attributed to the former but not to the latter, is justified.[70] Nevertheless, the example that he has selected indicates a widely shared tendency to read the Bible more literalistically at certain points than its authors ever intended. The result is, on the more conservative side, some not terribly successful attempts at harmonizing and, on the more liberal side, confirmation of the unreliability of scripture. Is the psalmist hedging his bets against two competing cosmologies in his day, cosmologies of which he could not have even been aware? Could he even have been wrong if these modern categories were not in his reference range? It would seem that a simpler explanation is available. Regardless of what modern science tells us, our experience is in many respects quite analogous to that of the ancient Jew. For instance, we return from a long ocean voyage or airline flight and express relief at being "back on *terra firma*." This does not betray a naïveté on our part, any more than an astrophysicist should be held in derision by his peers because he announced to his grandchildren that fishing will be good if they arrive at the pond by *sunrise*.

Different metaphors for different purposes. When, for instance, the psalmist is reaching for analogies to divine immutability, it is normal human experience that is in view, not scientific theories. From the perspective of our daily experience, when we are aware of geological explanation, the earth *is* relatively stable. Even Californians would appreciate the force of the analogy. But this does not mean that the earth is self-existing. Thus, when the psalmist wishes to make another point—this time with regard to divine sovereignty and eternity—the contrast is between the self-existing endurance of God and the very creation whose firmness served as an analogy for divine steadfastness. If analogies break down on their own at some point, then they are certainly even more fragile when enlisted for making different points than those intended by the author.

Michael Polanyi has gone to great pains to collect examples of this from the history of science. For instance, heliocentrism did not triumph because it meshed with normal experience, for it was contrary to the daily "common sense" observation of people. Science may reveal an account of "the way things really are" in terms of physics and astronomy, but this may not be "the way things really are" for ordinary human experience. That is why Calvin had the foresight to say in his commentary on Genesis 1, "Let him who wishes to study astronomy and the secrets of nature, turn elsewhere."[71] This at a time when these very cosmological theories were being hotly debated. To employ Wolterstorff's own approach, we could say that here the noematic content is divine faithfulness and the illocutionary stance is divine assurance rather than scientific assertions. Thus, what God here, by the way of the psalmist, says of his own character is absolutely true in both its noematic and designative content.

I do not take issue here with the method, but with his application in this instance. And if the psalmist did not *intend* to pronounce on the rotation of the earth and related matters, Wolterstorff's own method would caution against an interpretation of his saying something here that was wrong and therefore required us to discard it from the appropriated divine discourse. It is certainly not logically or demonstrably *necessary* to conclude that the psalmist incorporated "a certain amount of error" to make a point, any more than we would impute error in discourse to the astrophysicist referring to "sunrise." This also recalls Wolterstorff's own advice concerning the discernment of "loose" discourse.[72]

Affirming that the writer's intent here is metaphorical, Wolterstorff nevertheless believes that the attribution of emotions to God is literal. Further, the reference to Babylon the "devastator" as having her "little ones" dashed "against the rock" (Ps. 137) is not only taken by Wolterstorff to be metaphorical, but to have been so interpreted *always* by the church. In a similar vein, Francis Watson says of this passage,

> Christian victims of oppression could never legitimately appropriate this psalm in its entirety, however extreme their sufferings; and its use in Christian liturgical contexts can in no circumstances be justified. Although the psalm as a whole belongs to Christian scripture, it is not permitted to enact its total communicative intention: for all communicative actions embodied in holy scripture are subject to the criteria established by the speech-act that lies at the centre of Christian scripture, the life, death and resurrection of Jesus as the enfleshment and the enactment of the divine Word.[73]

These instances makes me anxious about giving oneself such a wide berth for determining what God would and wouldn't have said in scripture. We are not given a clear example of how one might work through these passages in order to be entitled to conclude that God does not have physical parts, but that he does have passions; we have not seen the method applied to the question of the reference, whether literal or metaphorical, in Psalm 137. Where we expect a fruitful demonstration of the method on points that are actually quite contested (especially the last two examples), Wolterstorff and Watson leave us only with assumptions about what God could or couldn't have said. Of course, what God "could" or "couldn't" do (especially in terms of what is loving) differs widely, depending on one's perspective. Wolterstorff himself seems to recognize the liabilities of this move. Many times we say that God could not have said thus and so. "But God did. Our false beliefs prevented us from discerning that God said it; they screened out the divine discourse."[74]

Francis Watson's answer to Psalm 137 is a canon-within-a-canon approach: the scriptures tell us what is central, and that central criterion cancels out things like massacre. But with Wolterstorff's interpretation, there is a potential not only for a canon within a canon, but a canon outside of the canon.

It seems that Wolterstorff's fecund proposal could be enriched by an eschatological, redemptive-historical hermeneutic in which the covenant is placed in prominent view. According to this interpretation, the nation of Israel in the Old Testament is the kingdom of God on earth, an intrusion—if you will, a bit of the consummation in history, typological of the theocracy appearing finally and fully at the end of the age. During these historical moments, God signifies and seals major salvific events by direct intervention. Holy war is just one such convention of this covenant. It is based not on Jewish nationalism, arising from the experience and feeling of the hearers, but on an unrelenting Yahwehism, arising from the speaker and the covenant that this speaker made with their ancestors. Just as God warns the world of the judgment to come, that event is not only anticipated but actually experienced in part by the idolatrous nations that occupy God's land.[75]

One may not find this interpretation attractive or satisfactory for a variety of reasons, particularly if one is presuppositionally committed to the denial of a final reckoning. Nevertheless, if it is the best way of reading this particular text, since it is based on the exegesis of similar passages, then shouldn't one's assumptions about what God would and would not have said be held at bay? After all, given this interpretation, there was no more injustice in these holy wars than there will be at the end of history, since the former are regarded as but a foretaste of the greater judgment to come. Nevertheless, redemptive history is not a flat line of chronology, but is more like a topographical map with peaks and valleys. So, for instance, we know that holy wars are wrong today from the redemptive-historical indicators that scripture itself provides. The end of the identification of the kingdom of God with the nation of Israel was signaled by Jesus in a number of ways, as in the "woes," the cursing of the fig tree, and the parables. But it was also indicated by Jesus' very specific reference to allowing the wheat and weeds growing together until the harvest, his rebuke of James and John for wanting to call down judgment on a Samaritan village for rejecting their preaching, and Paul's command, "Bless those who persecute you; bless and do not curse them" (Rom. 12:14). This phase of redemptive history has its own distinct polity. It is a kingdom of grace, not a kingdom of power, in the present eschatological epoch.

Just as Jesus announced that his kingdom is from another place (John 18:33–38; 6:15), the writer to the Hebrews labors the point that believers dwell in the heavenly city and its temple, while Paul reminds the saints, "For our struggle is not against enemies of blood and flesh, but against the rulers, against the authorities, against the cosmic powers of this present darkness, against the spiritual forces of evil in the heavenly places." Therefore, new covenant believers are to wear "the whole armor of God"—not the gear of an earthly military unit, but that of the gospel, faith, and salvation (Eph. 6:10–17). Without this redemptive-historical hermeneutic, the biblical narrative can easily become a repository for timeless principles. America can become a surrogate Israel, with the blessings and curses of the covenant simply transferred. Driving out the Canaanites is now allegorized for nationalist myths of "manifest destiny" and the like. "Claiming" such promises from the national (Mosaic, in contrast to the strictly Abrahamic) covenant ignores the typological, conditional, and temporary character of the theocracy—the schoolmaster that leads us to Christ. A redemptive-historical hermeneutic forces readers to keep their feet on the ground, with their eyes on the changing applications of the covenant and its sanctions in different periods.

Furthermore, it helps them to understand the justice of divine action in one context (viz., the identification of an earthly people with the kingdom of God), while affirming its nonnormative status for Christians today.[76] This, it seems to me, is far less subjective and far more intratextual than its rivals.

While textual sense and authorial discourse interpretation may provide tremendous methodological insights, they cannot replace the internal strategies of the redemptive-historical drama itself. Eschatology and covenant are not merely important loci within the drama, but are methodological and hermeneutical lenses through which all loci are interpreted. Any account of divine discourse must make sense of *this* discourse generated by or within *this* text, and not merely satisfy a general theory.

C. Narrative Hermeneutics: Revival of the *Sensus Literalist*?

As Hans Frei has carefully reminded us in *The Eclipse of Biblical Narrative*, the *sensus literalis* is hardly an innovation of the Protestant Reformation. This sense may be summarized by several features. First, it describes "the precise or fit enactment of the intention to say what comes to be in the text."[77] Second, it refers to

> the descriptive fit between *verbum* and *res*, sense and reference, signifier and signified, "*Sinn*" and "*Bedeutung*," between grammatical/ syntactical and conceptual sense, between the narrative sequence and what it renders descriptively. . . . Finally, the *sensus literalis* is the way the text has generally been used in the community. It is the sense of the text in its sociolinguistic context—liturgical, pedagogical, polemical, and so on.[78]

Even where medieval exegesis allowed multiple layers of interpretation (viz., allegorical, spiritual, moral, anagogical, typological, tropological), none was allowed to subvert the literal sense. It was clear in theory, if not always in practice, that the literal sense always had priority, at least with respect to the most essential passages.[79] Although the figurative sense may be involved in the intentionality of the divine author (viz., in promise and fulfillment as well as typology), the human author follows a largely literal sense.[80]

The hue and cry for relevance in both conservative and liberal churches, as narrative theology argues, betrays a common commitment to Enlightenment autonomy. And in modernity, on both the left and right in theology, the overriding preoccupation with reconstructing the "real" world above, behind or even in front of the text, has corrupted faithful reading. For the latter to be revived, one must approach the scriptures as one narrative, following its own internal cues the way one learning a new language should follow the grammatical and lexical rules of that particular language and not seek out something beyond, behind, or above it, such as a general, universal "language."

Partly influenced by New Criticism, but especially motivated by a concern for the distinctively Christian hermeneutical practice over the centuries, this brand of postliberalism gives more weight to both the author and the text than to the reader.

In these broad strokes, narrative theology represents a critical step forward in recognizing the priority of an "activistic" *text* over an "activistic" *reader*. Our own proposal depends on that priority. Over and over again, the prophets, Jesus, and the apostles call us to die to self, provoking us by scandalous announcements to see everything in a radically new way. The biblical story does not simply illumine our existence: it throws our whole existence into turmoil. It does not merely answer our questions: it reveals the banality of our questions and gives us new questions that set us on a path to profound discovery. It is not supplemental, but subversive. Thus, the goal is not to relate the Bible to our experience (which is really to say, judge the Bible by our experience), but vice versa. We must set out to make our lives relevant to the biblical story, not the biblical story to our lives. As in Wolterstorff's approach, the priority of the horizon of the text (at least in determining the textual sense) circumvents the "fusion of horizons."

In brief, Frei encourages us to begin to read the Bible once more like Luther and Calvin, a suggestion that is echoed by Brevard Childs and others among the Yale school.[81] But the Achilles heel of narrative theology is the question of reference. So we will develop our analysis of this school more fully by bringing in other conversation partners as we provide our own suggestions on this critical question.

REFERENCE: *SIGNUM* AND *RES SIGNIFICATA*, OR WHERE REDEMPTIVE HISTORY HAPPENS

Many readers are familiar with the Reformation eucharistic debate. As with previous debates, especially in the Middle Ages, controversy swirled around the connection of the "sign" (*signum*) and the "thing signified" (*res significata*). Zwingli, who thought he was simply following Augustine, practically separated *signum* and *res*, the former little more than a representative reminder of what the believer possesses and enjoys quite apart from the sacrament. Luther recoiled at the very idea, and Lutheranism ever since has insisted that in the sacred meal Christ is present "in, with, and under" the bread and wine. Calvin affirmed Zwingli's quite Augustinian point that the ascended Christ is not physically present on the earth again until the end of the age, and also argued that the medieval doctrine of transubstantiation actually abolished the sign, the thing signified simply taking its place. Nevertheless, Calvin strongly denounced Zwingli's memorialism, taking Luther's side with respect to the affirmation of a real presence of Christ in the sacrament, though not in the elements. Of course, there is a lot more that could be said, but I wanted to highlight only the broad outline for its relevance here.

The real question for us, beyond the eucharistic controversies, is whether the relationship between word-tokens and the world is purely mimetic ("Zwingli"), univocal identity ("Rome"), paradoxical interpenetration ("Luther"), or analogical union ("Calvin"). In our model, this relationship is understood as analogical union: words do not mirror reality, but neither are they to be confused with reality. A God's-eye view is never available to creatures, a point that was made by centuries of Christian wisdom long before Richard Rorty's observation. In our estimation, much of historical criticism and fundamentalism fails in the first direction, while much of narrative theology tends to regard the text itself as the real world. In this way, the sign (text) and thing signified (external world, or what Gadamer calls *die Sache*) become somewhat conflated.

Despite its profound critique and constructive program, narrative theology risks becoming a passing fad unless it can get beyond an idealist conception of the word-world relationship. Furthermore, its reticence to make assertions concerning the fit between text and world, while nevertheless insisting upon divine speech and action in history, makes it easy prey to that critique that Gilkey, Barr, and others so successfully prosecuted against the biblical theology movement. Narrative theologians themselves are aware of this criticism and have attempted to address it directly.[82] Michael Goldberg raises the same concerns as a Jewish narrative theologian:

> Although Braithwaite contends that "it is not necessary . . . for the asserter of a religious assertion to believe in the truth of the story involved in the assertions," the Exodus story and the story of Christ carry with them the claim that they are in some basic way essentially true. This truth claim is what partially justifies these stories' putting a claim in turn on those who hear them, for these stories say, "Live your life according to me. Base your life policy—your life story—on this story, for insofar as this story is a true one, it offers a credible basis for the adoption of such a policy and story in your life." Historically, Jews and Christians have adopted certain policies of behavior, certain ways of life, because they have staked their lives on the truth of their respective stories, of their respective stories and no other.[83]

Again, a redemptive-historical and covenantal hermeneutic, with its eschatological orientation, would reject an antithesis between fact and value, *Historie* and *Geschichte*, myth and kerygma. Living "as if" God has acted and spoken in history, and in these ways—that is, treating them as regulative rather than constitutive—leads us back to Kant and to the pendulum of modernity, swinging between various forms of hypertranscendent dualism and hyperimmanent monism. "Salvation history" is not a noumenal history, but a particular (i.e., covenantal) history within world history. As in Shakespeare's *Hamlet*, there is a play within a play that represents a compressed version of the larger plot. The entire creation is involved in one covenant—the so-called covenant of creation (*foedus naturae*) established in the beginning and reestablished in the Noaic covenant. Accordingly, God sustains cultural activity and yet sharply distinguishes cult from culture. The covenant of grace, by contrast, is announced after the fall and develops from Seth and his line, leading to Abraham and the messianic Seed, in whom "all the nations will be blessed." That covenantal line is persecuted from within and without and narrows progressively until it is reduced to a single individual: Jesus Christ. In his wake, it widens again to become even broader than before, embracing people "from every tribe and language and people and nation" (Rev. 5:9). This is but one way of summarizing the plot from the covenantal perspective. But this plot is a mystery that has been revealed, not an eternal truth that has been discovered. The meaning of history—summing up all things in Christ—is, as Moltmann has rightly emphasized in line with the Reformers, hidden under the cross, suffering, and evil. It must be revealed, since it is anything but obvious.

Goldberg is right to suggest that "[f]or both Judaism and Christianity, ordinary, profane time is real, and it is real precisely because it—rather than some other 'Great Time' which transcends it—is the locus (and focus) of redemption and meaning."[84] Goldberg also registers concern that a narrative approach which eschews some sort of correspondence to the world and its history will only lead to "the rather dismal prospect of saying to one another (of *shouting* at one another?), 'I've got my story; you've got yours. That's all there is to it!' If a narrative theology cannot adequately address this kind of problem, then whatever suspicion there may be surrounding the legitimacy of the use of narrative for theology will have been well-founded."[85]

We would concur with narrative theology in its insistence that the biblical narrative itself master our interpretation. But we must also deny the charge that by raising questions of correspondence we are attempting to subvert the text by making an "extratextual" reality normative. In the first place, we should abandon the term "extratextual" when speaking of the ultimate referent. When the Gospels date the nativity "in the time of King Herod," when "a decree went out from Emperor Augustus that all the world should be registered," a census that was taken "while Quirinius was governor of Syria," the reference to world history *is* the narrative's reference.

This does not have to license reduction of the diverse biblical material to historical description any more than to propositional assertions (or, for that matter, to narrative). In contrast to Bultmann, we would insist that the history is kerygma and not myth. But in contrast to some conservatives, we would want to suggest that it is drama, not mere history-writing or statement of facts about reality. It is not merely eternally true propositions, but temporally executed promises, warnings, commands, and assurances. Like their antagonists, many conservative evangelicals do not come to the scriptures assuming a unified christocentric plot, with its corollary emphasis on redemption as a covenantal history. Rather, revelation is often conceived in terms of static, immutable, and eternal principles.[86] Interpreted with these assumptions, the Bible becomes a "handbook" for various human ends, whether therapeutic, ethical, doctrinal, or speculative.[87]

Narrative theology's interest in a developing plot is superior to a static or formulaic model. At the same time, that the biblical narrative "absorbs" other narratives/worlds/texts is an interesting and profitable observation, but it is not exactly an argument or a position. Does this really do justice to the distinction between text and interpretation? Is it not true that, among those who equally insist upon some version of biblical authority, some readings are absorbed more by the text and others display a greater dependence on the contemporary zeitgeist? Apart from the considerably difficult labor of deconstructing rather than either simply accommodating the text to fallen realities or using the text to "absorb" these realities, the life that one actually lives in the world (and not in the text) may be kept separate, leading to a sort of hermeneutical schizophrenia. Church history does not seem to support the notion that the biblical text always absorbs and transforms alien systems of thought. This failure is due not to any weakness in the text, but to the fact that the text never does anything purely *as* text, an *ex opere operato* view of textuality. It is interpretation that is or is not successful in individuals' and communities' being transformed rather than conformed to this age. Structuralist theory must be subjected to the hermeneutical critique, at least in its application to theology.

The question of reference can be postponed only so long. At some point, one must face the matter squarely: To what does the biblical text refer? Do we treat this narrative as world-projection and revelation of possibilities? As mythological or symbolic indicators of limit situations? As correspondence with living history? We would at least agree with Ricoeur's definition of these terms: "Discourse consists of the fact that someone says something to someone about something. 'About something' is the inalienable referential function of discourse."[88] While we cannot reduce divine discourse to propositional content and historical reference, we surely cannot abstract interpretation from these, since they are so obviously present in the text itself.

On this last point, Ricoeur, Gadamer, and Wolterstorff are in agreement.[89] God, Ricoeur maintains, is the ultimate referent of the biblical text. "God is in some manner implied by the 'issue' of these texts, by the world—the biblical world—that these texts unfold."[90] But Ricoeur overemphasizes the difference between oral and written speech, arguing that in writing "there is no longer a common situation between writer and the reader."[91] But Christians have commonly maintained that the common situation is created by (a) the human condition; (b) the divine response, historically enacted; (c) the community created and preserved by the Holy Spirit through the proclamation of the Word and the koinonia of sacramental union. Furthermore, the current eschatological *aeon* is contemporary with the early church; namely, "these last days."[92] Eschewing the romantic effort at getting behind the text to gain access to the author's psyche or ostensibly transporting oneself to the original *Sitz-im-Leben*, Ricoeur nevertheless leaves us wondering what is left to be interpreted.

> My response is that to interpret is to explicate the sort of being-in-
> the-world unfolded in front of the text. Here we rejoin Heidegger's
> suggestion about the meaning of *Verstehen*. . . . I want to take this
> idea of the "projection of our ownmost possibilities" from his analy-
> sis [of understanding] and apply it to the theory of the text. In effect,
> what is to be interpreted in a text is a proposed world, a world that I
> might inhabit and wherein I might project my ownmost possibili-
> ties. This is what I call the world of the text, the world probably
> belonging to this unique text.[93]

David Tracy follows Ricoeur's basic hermeneutic.[94]

But this response betrays an abiding commitment to modernity's inflated individualism and autonomous subjectivity. Although elsewhere Ricoeur emphasizes the importance of fidelity to the scriptures' own message, the subject still reigns, though no longer disembodied. The text merely occasions *Dasein*, the clearing wherein "I might project my ownmost possibilities." This aspect of Ricoeur's hermeneutic is liable to the same devastating criticisms that have been leveled against Bultmann's project. More seriously, it falls prey, along with Bultmann's theory, to Feuerbach's critique of theology as in truth anthropology; projection, not interpretation. Furthermore, it is at this point inimical to any model in which the goal of interpretation is to discern what God said, rather than simply indwelling a proposed world in which one may construct or project new possibilities. Revelation must be a content and not merely a clearing.[95]

Despite Ricoeur's illuminating contrasts between biblical/Hebraic word-centered and pagan vision-centered approaches, one wonders if the "world-projection" in front of the text moves too far toward the latter. At the very least, its analogies are taken from the world of vision, with metaphors such as "displayed," "projected," "unfolded." Locating a middle ground between the extremes of positivism and deconstructionism, Ricoeur wants to retain some form of "revelation."[96] All of this evokes the hermeneutics and aesthetics of Romanticism, but Ricoeur distances himself from modernism. In fact, he distances himself from Gadamer's model of conversation, as a far too benign analogy that can easily mask oppressive moves.[97] Is it not possible that narrative theology could also be as easily liable to such distortions? At this point its greatest strength is also its weakness: Its suspicion of extratextual factors makes the narrative something like an airtight compartment or encased noumenon floating in its own semiotic fluid, disconnected from the ordinary "extratextual" world of power structures.[98] One cannot dismiss the infamous *Sitz-im-Leben* after all.

But one must ask the question that the postliberal himself or herself seems loathe to raise: If the text is judged unreliable in terms of its factual integrity, of what use are the history-like narratives? "If Christ is not raised, then we are still in our sins." We must beware, therefore, of the repeated warnings against being drawn away from narrative hermeneutics because of ostensibly irrelevant questions of historical reference. Only if we are still under the spell of positivistic science and historicist hermeneutics will questions of historical reference be viewed as a threat to faithful interpretation. In fact, the postliberal's alternative is not neutrality or a temporary suspension in judgment on such matters. While they do believe in the historical facticity of the resurrection, for instance, postliberals like Frei and Lindbeck guarantee no safe passage from the contemporary reader to that fact via the text. This is the Gordian knot that must be cut, the Kantian legacy that postliberalism critiques with so much insight and yet cannot itself seem to transcend. Like the earlier biblical theology movement, narrative theology seems divided between (intratextual) faith and (extratextual) doubt, a characteristically modern dilemma.

Yet even David Tracy notes the a prioristic character of the higher-critical enterprise. Were not classical liberals (especially Ritschl), in their "quest" for the historical Jesus in which they simply could not accept the apocalyptic context and the person of Jesus, "hampered by certain narrowly neo-Kantian approaches to the questions of science, morality, and religion and trapped by their ethical fear of anything smacking of 'mysticism' or 'apocalypticism'"?[99] Our plea is for a postliberalism that really is postliberal, post-Kantian, post-Enlightenment, at once classical and contemporary, as indeed all historical study must be. When postliberals chide conservatives for playing by the rules of their liberal nemeses, while both subvert narrative hermeneutics, we take the point, and it is a criticism that has also been made by conservative confessional biblical scholars (particularly of the presuppositionalist school). But sooner or later, postliberals must recognize that they too have made a decision on these questions of fact and reference and in that act have thrown in their lot with the higher-critical school.

Despite his emphasis on the "suppression of the original speech" in order to make room for the unfolding of textual meaning, Ricoeur seems more balanced in his integration of sense and reference. He writes,

> Advocates of a narrative theology try to discard this issue by merely listing biblical narratives among stories for which the question of factual truth is irrelevant. But this apparently merely descriptive stance is a way of begging the question. . . .The suggestion, then, would be to substitute relevance for truth, in the sense of factual truth. And relevance would mean ability to further a certain kind of action, to invite the hearers "to imitate the actions of the story." But the practical use of the biblical stories is not a substitute for an inquiry into the relation between story and history.[100]

Narrative theologians do not believe that Jesus is a legitimate referent merely of the narrative and not of real history. So why would predicating more of his correlation than mere existence be a case of diversion? Why the reluctance to take external, historical reference as seriously as the narrative itself? If, as Lindbeck recognizes, *the whole system* refers (indeed, corresponds) to ontological reality, why not *the parts*? Surely one cannot dismiss this semiotic holism as Hegelian idealism. For Frei, it is probably due to literary (structuralist), cultural-anthropological (Geertz), and theological (neo-orthodox) biases, but is also in considerable debt to what, we will argue below, is a misreading of Wittgenstein's language game analysis. But for Lindbeck there seems to be an additional commitment: an inflexible model in which Christian doctrine is understood *as* and not merely as *analogous to*, a cultural-linguistic system in which the totality is "a gigantic proposition."[101] Has neo-Kantianism simply exchanged the terminology of grammar for that of categories, with both serving essentially the same function, the whole swallowing the parts?

While narrative theology is a far cry from Bultmann's way of expressing his position, I cannot see how postliberals really get beyond the *Historie-Geschichte* divide, after all their efforts. Just as Bultmann surrendered the "Jesus of history" to the critics as an irrelevance to faith, postliberalism's avoidance of reference amounts to the same, despite a theoretical commitment to historical events. If, in this respect, we share with liberalism an undue concern for ostensive reference, we must not, because of that, relinquish our suspicion of fideism. In spite of the remarkable insights and useful chastening at the hands of the postliberal critique, one is still left staring into Lessing's awful chasm.

Reference is not imposed from without, but is part of the warp and woof of the narrative throughout. Nevertheless, narrative theology has directed our attention once more to the sequential, episodic, and emplotted character of divine revelation. Thus, it seems to me, drama is a more comprehensive metaphor than narrative and text, and it shows up at just this point. The relationship between text and world is less of an either-or when viewed as analogous to the relationship between script (textual narrative) and stage (a projected or an empirical world). The play cannot be reduced to either of those, any more than it can be reduced to either speech or action. Each has its own integrity and importance within the drama. While a script performed on stage may be more interesting and perhaps even more meaningful (given the "presence" of the speaker), directors and actors do not normally get uptight over the distanciation of the author when they are reading scripts.

In relation to Wolterstorff's proposal, to which mine is in some measure indebted, authorial discourse interpretation could be enriched not only by a redemptive-historical and covenantal hermeneutic but by this metaphor of drama. What if, for instance, appropriated discourse is more analogous to a playwright who nevertheless—simply by the act of putting the script on stage—leaves lavish space for the actors to interpret and to act it out? Here there is no need to discern which parts are appropriated discourse, any more than to figure out how much of the play is the authorized or appropriated discourse of the playwright. Furthermore, it avoids literalistic approaches that would reduce divine discourse simply to true, timeless propositions, which makes it difficult at times to interpret scripture when it is clear from the text that what an actor/speaker says is not always what God is saying. But the drama is not only *about* the enactment of its characters' identities and a unified plot—it *is* all of this. This drama *is* history, as told from the inside.[102]

Like a good play, scripture possesses a single, unified meaning.[103] But also like a good script, the biblical text does not sacrifice plurality (in terms of genre, implications, applications, complexities and reversals in the plot, surprising twists on prophetic fulfillment, discrepancies in reporting/narrating) to this unity of sense.[104] This single sense is so pregnant with meaning that it must never be confused with a single, much less sufficient, *explanation*. It is to this notion of a unified sense that we now turn.

TEXTUAL SENSE: THE ONE AND MANY PROBLEM AGAIN

As is well known, Alexandria and Antioch represent two distinct tendencies within ancient Christianity: allegorical spiritualizing and literal sense interpretation, respectively. The implications of such hermeneutical distinctives would receive their fullest expression in the christological controversies, which again points up not only the impact of hermeneutics on christology, but of christology on hermeneutics. Antiochene Theodore of Mopsuestia was prolific in his defense of the *sensus literalis* and in opposing any form of docetic spiritualizing of Jesus' true humanity.[105] In the very early Pseudo-Clementine *Recognitions* (ascribed to Clement of Rome and often cited by the church fathers), Greek mythology is scourged not only because it is myth but because it is allegory. In the myth of the supper of the gods, "Clement" then claims that the apostle Peter explained, "They say that the banquet is the world, that the order of the gods sitting at table is the position of the heavenly bodies," down to the dishes which represent reasons and causes in the world.[106] Peter's alleged response is that the scriptures must not be read in this manner.

> For there are many sayings in the divine Scriptures which can be drawn to that sense which every one has preconceived for himself; and this ought not to be done. For you ought not to seek a foreign and extraneous sense, which you have brought from without, which you may confirm from the authority of the Scriptures, but to take the sense of truth from the Scriptures themselves.[107]

It is the *regula fidei*, drawn from the analogy of scripture, that will assist in this interpretation.

Whatever one calls the challenge—the mystical-allegorical sense, demythologized sense, symbolic sense, metaphorical sense—Kevin Vanhoozer is not stretching to conclude that those who defend the perspicuity of scripture (or, for that matter, any text) once again face steep opposition. Contemporary "enthusiasts" and "papists," to appeal to the Scylla and Charybdis of the sixteenth-century context, form a common fortress against the claim that God has spoken clearly (and therefore sufficiently) in scripture. The concern over multiple sense interpretation, however, is hardly modern—even early modern. An early medieval formula based on Augustine was *sensus allegoricus non est argumentivus* (the allegorical meaning is not conclusive). Hardly a minor figure, Nicholas of Lyra (1270–1340) declared,

> One should also understand that the literal sense of the text has been much obscured because of the manner of expounding the text commonly handed down by others. Although they have said much that is good, yet they have been inadequate in their treatment of the literal sense, and have so multiplied the number of mystical senses that the literal sense is in some part cut off and suffocated among so many mystical senses. Moreover, they have chopped the text into so many small parts, and brought forth so many concordant passages to suit their own purpose, that to some degree they confuse both the mind and memory of the reader and distract it from understanding the literal meaning of the text.[108]

According to the *Quadriga* method, each reading could contain the following senses: historical, allegorical, moral, and anagogical (i.e., eschatological). While often appropriated to edifying uses, this method also could be used to underwrite just about any self-serving or fanciful interpretation. As Mickey L. Mattox reminds us, "Pope Innocent III, for example, claimed that the 'greater light' and the 'lesser light' of the creation narrative in Genesis represented, respectively, the papal authority and that of the secular ruler."[109] Calvin used Luke 10:30 (the parable of the good Samaritan) as an example of allegorical exegesis.

> They have nothing more constantly on their lips than Christ's parable of the traveler, whom thieves cast down half alive on the road. I know that almost all writers commonly teach that the calamity of the human race is represented in the person of the traveler. From this our opponents take the argument that man is not so disfigured by the robbery of sin and the devil as not to retain some vestiges of his former good, inasmuch as he is said to have been left "half alive."[110]

But long before the reformers, Aquinas considered it important in his day to defend the priority of the literal sense and to warn against abuse of the subordinate senses:

> The multiplicity of the senses does not produce equivocation or any other kind of multiplicity, seeing that the senses are not multiplied because one word signified several things, but because the things signified by the words can themselves be signs of other things. Thus in Holy Scripture . . . for all the senses are founded on one—the literal—from which alone can any argument be drawn, and not from those intended allegorically, as Augustine says. Nevertheless, nothing of Holy Scripture perishes because of this, since nothing necessary to faith is contained under the spiritual sense which is not elsewhere put forward clearly by the Scripture in its literal sense.[111]

Since so much of the debate over hermeneutics these days lays explicit claim to antecedents either among the mystics and "enthusiasts" or "Rome" on one side (as in comparisons of Derrida and Meister Eckhart or Hauerwas's union of Stanley Fish and Pope John Paul II) or the Reformers (as in the stated goal of Frei and Childs as well as Thiselton, Watson, and Vanhoozer), it might be helpful to indicate some of the key directions of Reformation hermeneutics. First we must understand just how the reformers *did* read, interpret, and use the text. Out of the gate we need to recognize that "literal" does not mean "literalistic." This will become clearer in our development of especially Calvin's emphasis on divine accommodation. The only difference from medieval practice at this point was whether the *sensus literalis* was the *chief* sense, upon which alone conclusions could be based, or whether it was the *only* sense. This did not prejudice the Reformers against nonliteral forms of speech, but against interpretations that are not obvious (or obviously nonintended by the author). This is precisely the advice of Austin, Searle, Wolterstorff, and others: take the utterance or inscription at face value, in its most obvious sense, unless there is very good reason to do otherwise. Thus far, scripture should follow the ordinary rules of general textual interpretation and not be treated as a magical book containing secret codes and hidden meanings.

Adopting Occam's razor as successfully in exegesis as it became for science, in which the simplest explanation for a particular phenomenon is preferred, Luther answered one of his *Schwärmer* critics in 1521:

> The Holy Spirit is the simplest writer and speaker in heaven and on earth. This is why his words can have no more than the one simplest meaning which we call the written one, or the literal meaning of the tongue. But words and language cease to have meaning when the things which have a simple meaning through interpretation by a simple word are given further meanings and thus become different things so that one thing takes on the meaning of another. This is true for all other things not mentioned in Scripture because all God's creatures and works are sheer living signs and words of God, as Augustine and all the teachers say. But one should not therefore say that Scripture or God's word has more than one meaning.[112]

For Luther, when the book of Hebrews, for instance, interprets Christ as the new Aaron, the writer is not employing a sense other than the literal (for instance, the allegorical). Rather, "the Spirit interprets him in a *new* literal sense" (emphasis added).[113]

This becomes a keystone of Protestant hermeneutics, but it was also the method of such church fathers as Ireneaus in their controversy with Gnosticism and the latter's substitution of allegorical flexibility for the perspicuity of an obvious sense. Irenaeus says that they "twist them . . . from a natural to a non-natural sense. In so doing, they act like those who bring forward any kind of hypothesis they fancy," especially by appealing to an allegorical method that they call the "spiritual" interpretation, reserved for the elite who are "in the know."[114]

So Frei is correct in his insistence that figural interpretation is not figurative interpretation; that it is not, in other words, allegorical, but that the plain sense simply *is* the promise-fulfillment pattern of a unified canon. Viewed in this light, it is not that there are no allegories in scripture, but that they are rare and are flagged as such already by the author. For example, in Galatians 4, the apostle says—not of the narrative itself, but of *his particular use* of the Sarah/Hagar narrative in this place—"Now this is an allegory (allēgoroumena): these women are two covenants" (v. 24). It is a self-conscious allegory. Like Jesus' parables, it is already a figure of speech. The *sensus literalis* suggests its figurative character, especially when Paul actually cues us, "Now this is an allegory." Paul does not introduce us to an allegorical *method*, but to his own divinely authorized allegorical *use* of the Old Testament narrative. Both the Old Testament narrative and Paul's allegory are meant to be interpreted according to a single sense (*sensus literalis*), which is to say, as one would normally interpret a narrative in the first case and an allegory in the second. Similarly, there are moral imperatives and moral implications of other forms of speech. But this does not imply an additional "sense."

As we have indicated above, multiple sense interpretation is alive and well in our day. In a narcissistic culture especially, it is easy for interpretation to move from "Thus says the Lord" to "Well, it seems to me." Therapeutic usefulness and well-being become the *norma normans non normata,* or a canon within a canon. This transition is as evident in evangelical Bible studies as in Richard Rorty. Vanhoozer indicates the parallels between allegorical method and deconstruction:

> After all, the primary thrust of the logocentric thinker is to say, "This means that." What of the contemporary penchant for seeing multiple meanings in texts? Is this not a new form of allegorizing? Indeed, does not Derrida's own emphasis on indeterminacy foster the notion that a text has several senses? While there are indeed historical precedents for deconstruction, I believe they are to be found in the rabbinic and gnostic traditions of biblical exegesis, not in Christian allegorizing, much less in figural interpretation. . . . The new element in modern and postmodern allegorizing is, above all, the a/theology that governs its practice. . . . The new allegorism locates textual meaning not in a system of higher truths, but in a sea of indeterminacy.[115]

As we have emphasized in our model, eschatology is not only the topic here and there, but is an interpretive lens. Nevertheless, it is the interpretive lens that the *sensus literalis* gives to us. Noticing that the kingdom of God is a heavenly reality breaking in on "this present evil age" is not the result of interpreting according to an anagogical (i.e., eschatological) sense of a given passage, but is the literal or plain meaning of the passage—or else an implication that may be legitimately made on the basis of correlating it with other passages.

"Calvin's rejection of allegorical and anagogical readings of the biblical texts was, if anything, even more pronounced than Luther's. He was persuaded that the grammatical sense was the genuine sense, except where the writer's intention or the larger context indicated otherwise."[116] Frei is correct here and it is easy to see the close proximity of this position to speech-act theory and, more specifically, authorial discourse interpretation. The most serious flaw in allegorical interpretation is that it marginalizes Christ, allowing the readers in power to manipulate scripture to suit their own purposes. Appealing to the lepers' being sent by Jesus to the priests (to prove Jesus' claims), allegorical exegesis seemed to justify the necessity of auricular confession for the forgiveness of sins. "If they are so fond of chasing after allegories," Calvin writes, "let them set before themselves Christ as their sole priest, and in his judgment seat concentrate unlimited jurisdiction over all things. We shall readily allow that."[117] It is not simply allegory per se, but its tendency to displace *Christ* as the fulfillment of promises that most bothered Calvin. Christ is the fulfillment of the promise made to *Abraham,* not of just any covenant that we are then at liberty to define, he insists. Therefore, Gentiles who in the new covenant seek salvation in Christ must embrace Abraham, Isaac, and Jacob:

> Do you see how, after Christ's resurrection also, [the apostle] thinks that the promise of the covenant is to be fulfilled, not only allegorically

> but literally, for Abraham's physical offspring? . . . But if we listen to
> their trifles, what will become of that promise by which the Lord in
> the Second Commandment of his law pledges to his servants that he
> will be merciful to their offspring even to the thousandth generation
> [Ex. 20:6]? Shall we here take refuge in allegories? That would be too
> frivolous an evasion![118]

On one hand, the Reformers saw Rome as confusing the Mosaic covenant
with the Abrahamic (or, more simply, law and gospel), so that Jesus was a "new
Moses" and the gospel announced in the new covenant was the "new law." On
the other hand, the radical "enthusiasts," to the Reformers, represented a neo-
Marcionism. "Christ the Lord promises to his followers today no other 'King-
dom of Heaven,'" said Calvin, "than that in which they may 'sit at table with
Abraham, Isaac, and Jacob' [Matt. 8:11]."[119] Defending the unity of the canon
Old Testament revelation is accommodated to the era of the church's infancy, as
God's people were led by shadows to Christ.[120]

While it is true that he equates the literal or obvious sense with the authorial
intention, it would be gross anachronism to identify this position with psychological interpretation. For Calvin and Luther, figuring out what the author
intended has nothing to do with divining the author's inner thoughts, but merely
with discerning the intentions that were stated in the discourse itself. Contemporary linguistic theory might suggest that this is to engage in *discourse* analysis.

While Hans Frei has directed our attention once more to the *sensus literalis*,
almost merging sense and reference, narrative theology continues to accept the
separation of the *sensus historicus* from the *sensus literalis*. It does not do this consciously, but in its suspicion of "external reference" it renders the historical sense
somewhat problematic or at the least redundant. As the author has been separated from the text by textual-sense interpretation and deconstruction, sense has
now been severed from reference and the literal sense from the historical. As with
reference, however, the historical sense cannot be so separated, precisely because
of the inherently historical character of this particular text. The classic categories
of historical and literal sense, which were integrated in traditional figural exegesis, have now drifted apart under the categories of the universal-historical and the
hermeneutical. We can see the line from Troeltsch to Tracy in the former, and
from Barth to Frei in the latter. Pannenberg is right to insist that the textual-sense
theologian simply cannot ignore the historian:

> For us, the historical sense [*sensus historicus*] and the literal sense
> [*sensus literalis*], which were considered identical in the Middle Ages
> and even in the Reformation, have moved apart as belonging to two
> different dimensions of the interrogation of a text. Therefore, the
> dogmatician has not only to deal with exegetical statements that
> bring out the original meaning of the different writings, but also,
> beyond this and above all, with historical statements (in the broad-
> est sense of the term) about the history of Jesus himself and the
> process of its transmission in tradition and interpretation in primi-
> tive Christianity.[121]

Pannenberg noted that the divorce between sense and reference is largely motivated by the suspicion that the biblical reports are not in fact historically reliable. Pannenberg himself does not insist upon a uniform reliability, but his point is suggestive even for those who do. Often, one wonders whether the recurring postliberal lament concerning the propositionalist's obsession with facticity betrays a prejudice, not against historical-critical studies, but against the conservative's refusal to *accept* those "conclusions."[122] Francis Watson states the matter directly: "The programme of reconstructing an original *Sitz im Leben* as an interpretative matrix for a text may stem from the sense that the verbal meaning alone is too 'obvious' to be interesting. It is in extracting non-obvious meanings out of apparently straightforward texts that interpreters can best demonstrate their own virtuosity."[123] Instead, we have to ask what the speech is trying to *do*. In the Gospel of Mark, "What Mark is *doing* is not simply telling a story but *proclaiming the gospel*."[124] This already places limits on interpretive possibilities.

To conclude this section we will briefly touch on the question of canon, since this is inseparable from a unified sense or meaning of the text. While it is not our purpose in this work to provide a defense of the canon, it is necessary at least to indicate that this very notion implies some notion of divine authorship. The sources are simply too diverse in terms of background, style, date, and circumstances of composition to possess an inherent unity without some sort of "omniscient narrator" or "playwright." And in the process of reading, Christians have traditionally found just that kind of unity from Genesis to the Apocalypse. God must not only authorize this "collected writings" as divine speech, but must directly guide the process from inscription to canon. Furthermore, the Spirit's *inspiration* in this process is matched by the Spirit's *illumination* for the believing reader. The Spirit's illumination does not complete the meaning of the *text*, but exposes *us*—or better yet, disposes us—*to* the active text. We will touch on this topic more directly below.

By being confused with Enlightenment and American individualism, the Reformation's idea of scripture's perspicuity—the text's essential clarity and unity—has often been caricatured as an invitation to a naive hermeneutical realism.[125] But in Reformation and post-Reformation hermeneutics, the "obvious sense" may not be so obvious in every place. As the Westminster Confession acknowledges,

> All things in Scripture are not alike plain in themselves, nor alike clear unto all; yet those things which are necessary to be known, believed, and observed, for salvation, are so clearly propounded and opened in some place of Scripture or other, that not only the learned, but the unlearned, in due use of the ordinary means, may attain unto a sufficient understanding of them.[126]

According to Francis Watson, the literal sense comprises "(i) verbal meaning, (ii) illocutionary and perlocutionary force, and (iii) the relation to the center."[127] It is "from the centre of holy scripture" that we interpret the whole. This perspective has the merit of being christocentric, but in our estimation it reverses the proper relation. Luther's definition of the canon as "that which preaches Christ" has been taken by many such as H. Faber and Kümmel as an invitation to reduce "scripture" to a few essential elements in the name of christocentric exegesis. Pannenberg also follows this canon-within-a-canon perspective (in this case, the deity of God).[128]

But at least for Reformed theology, the rationale for the canon is frankly circular: "The divine character of the Bible itself gives it its authority."[129] Bavinck adds, "The canonicity of the books of the Bible is rooted in their existence. They have authority in and of themselves, *iure suo*, simply because they exist."[130] As Barth put it, "The Bible makes itself to be canon."[131] This is hardly biblicism, since the scriptures, according to Jesus' own testimony, are "they that testify concerning me" (John 5:39). This christocentricity is determined not by picking out the central figure and taking it upon ourselves to determine what is in keeping with his centrality (as if the whole of scripture did *not* witness to him), but is already the content of the canon. It is precisely because the canon is normative apart from any central motifs that its central motifs can be regarded as organically arising from its soil and not as a result of imposing an already-constructed interpretation. The whole of scripture is therefore canon not because Christ is preached throughout, but because it is the product of divine discourse. Having said that, we can assert with Jesus himself that the whole of the self-authenticating canon testifies concerning him (cf. Luke 24:27).

Nevertheless, there is a danger of emphasizing canon and the self-authenticating nature of scripture *apart from* the *res* of scripture itself, namely, God's promise in Christ through the covenant of grace. As we have argued above, it is the covenant that constitutes the biblical canon as canon. It is not an ontological principle or primal *Urgeschichte*, but a constitution or charter, that ties the diverse elements together as historical prologue (which justifies that which follows), stipulations and sanctions, and then the covenantal hymnal (the Psalter), the new covenant treaty with its continuities and discontinuities in administration, but altogether the fulfillment of one covenant of grace as the seed of Abraham appears in history "in the fullness of time." The Gospels and Acts announce a new—or better yet, redrawn—historical prologue, while the epistles are the new covenant prophetic and wisdom literature, the Apocalypse serving as a "summing up of all things in Christ." This unity is therefore not imposed from without, nor even constructed from a central dogma, but is organic, eschatological, and redemptive-historical, from its Alpha-point to its Omega-point.

When the undoubtedly central figure, Christ, is abstracted from the drama or is moved to the periphery, he is easily transformed into a cipher for all sorts of things (transcendence, immanence, essence, existence, universals, particulars, truth, goodness, beauty, love, and service, etc.). In other cases, one runs roughshod over the parts in favor of the whole, which does justice to neither. But what we actually have with this text is a script of the drama of redemption. Rather than an ahistorical "center" radiating from a textual core to its edges, there is a time line running through history—not just one moment or central figure or event pulsating outwards, but a plot moving forward, served by diverse characters, sub-plots, reversals, and, above all, promise and fulfillment.

This figural interpretation assumes, of course, the *sensus plenior*, or the fuller sense. In the interaction between divine and human authorship, the representatives of the covenant could only prophesy, rather than know, the future. From their horizon, defined not by a general hermeneutic but by the redemptive drama up to that point, biblical writers could not foresee the precise details of what they themselves were committing to the history of prophetic announcement.[132] "Long ago God spoke to our ancestors in many and various ways by the prophets, but in these last days he has spoken to us by a Son, whom he appointed heir of all things, through whom he also created the worlds" (Heb. 1:1–2). This is what makes this messianic era of redemptive history, "the last days," a fulfillment that could not be totally comprehended in the prophetic anticipation. So while Israel quite correctly read Isaiah's prophecies as referring penultimately to Cyrus, king of Persia, she was led to look further over the horizon. After all, it is clear from the text itself that much was left in the prophecies that simply did not and could not have fit Cyrus, and this realization of the nonfulfillment of Old Testament prophecy more generally seems to have fueled Israel's expectations of Messiah within Second-Temple Judaism.[133]

An excellent example of this *sensus plenior* occurs when the Sanhedren meets to determine what to do with Jesus:

> But one of them, Caiaphas, who was high priest that year, said to them, "You know nothing at all! You do not understand that it is better for you to have one man die for the people than to have the whole nation destroyed." He did not say this on his own, but being high priest that year he prophesied that Jesus was about to die for the nation, and not for the nation only, but to gather into one the dispersed children of God. So from that day on they planned to put him to death. (John 11:49–53)

First, Caiaphas was an authorized carrier of divine discourse, the last high priest of the Mosaic covenant. Ironically, he sat in judgment over the one whose servant he was deputized to be. But, despite himself, he prophesied Jesus' death, and not only for Israel, but for the world. If any of Israel's prophets said more than the prophet could have been aware of, it was surely Caiaphas. He was not forced to say it, but he also "did not say this on his own." Note the centrality of the covenant again: it is not the individual—his person, his character, his spiritual sensitivity or piety—but his office as the representative of the covenant, that determines the status and reliability of his discourse.

To reverse a phrase of Polanyi's, prophets *tell* more than they can *know*, just like the apostles themselves in relation to the still future eschaton. Quoting Isaiah, Paul writes, "But, as it is written, 'What no eye has seen, nor ear heard, nor the human heart conceived, what God has prepared for those who love him'" (1 Cor. 2:9). This is not to embrace equivocity, however, as Paul says in the next sentence: "[T]hese things God has revealed to us through his Spirit" (v. 10). As in all analogical description, the dissimilarities are greater than the similarities, but efforts to reduce all of scripture to equivocal discourse ignore the genre codes explicit in the text itself.

Watson is correct in his objection to attempts to convert rather straightforward Gospel narratives into "parabolic" or "metaphorical" interpretation. Of course, there are parables in the Gospels, but we know where they are. "Why should the Gospel of Mark not be read as a multiple, opaque text, as recommended by postmodern homiletics?" he asks. "The answer is that, if it is indeed *gospel*, it cannot be multiple or opaque. . . . The Gospel of Mark is gospel, not parable."[134] Whether one chooses to accept the unity and perspicuity of scripture's message is one thing. Nevertheless, to read the scriptures as a covenant is to treat it as consisting of sections that belonged to every ancient Near Eastern treaty: historical prologue, stipulations, and sanctions. A covenantal, redemptive-historical, and eschatological approach accounts for both unity (because of the "promise made to Abraham and to his seed") and diversity (because of the distinct administrations and polities of God's kingdom in different "acts" of the drama).

Single meaning does not entail either uniformity or a uniformly simple meaning. Nor does it require, but in fact resists, the possibility of exhaustive meaning. No interpreter or interpretive community could ever so fully and faithfully interpret the scriptures that there would be nothing left to exegete. Ironically, it is its fecundity that opens itself up to multiple interpretations, but this largesse will limit interpretive options, once we as readers touch ground again. The covenant in its concrete canonical unfolding constitutes that terra firma. Perspicuity and *sensus literalis* do not entail complete explanations but do indicate the potential for being able to sufficiently summarize the work as a whole.[135]

Having joined the conversation, indicating general lines of agreement and overlap with certain trends in hermeneutics, we turn next to some of the distinctives of our own proposal.

Chapter Seven

Implications of a
Covenantal Hermeneutic

Understanding begins . . . when something addresses us.[1]

To be sure, there are pure acts of recording what other people say. Court reporters do this sort of thing. But most of the time, we are listening for what we want (or are expecting) to hear. Print and broadcast reporters do this sort of thing. If we are to be taken seriously as agents of reporting or interpretation, we have to develop a habit of sympathetic listening, but we do nevertheless listen especially for some things and ignore others. The only cases in which our own personal involvement does not affect the relation of the spoken or written material is when it does not matter quite as much. While the text of a witness's testimony in a criminal trial may be of interest (especially if the accused is well-known), in most cases it is not. Vitally important for those involved in a particular trial, these texts are rarely consulted in public libraries or made the topic of conversation at dinner tables.

When, however, we make the claim that God, who transcends history and eludes our own daily individual observation, has nevertheless spoken and acted in history—and in such a way that God's discourse and acts have been observed and related by eyewitnesses—suddenly the interest widens and deepens. This interest is compounded if the action and speech involved happen to address the ultimate crisis of human existence. If it should perhaps be true, it concerns everyone. But the really interesting events of discourse have to be interpreted and have been so interpreted by experts and the public since their utterance or inscription. In those acts in which we are interpreting a piece of discourse that really matters, it is especially the case that our dispositions, beliefs, expectations, and the like form tacit hypotheses that in some sense have already set perimeters as to what the discourse *can* say or is *supposed* to say, even before we have read it. While the object is not submerged into the subject, it can never be separated from its reader/interpreter. It is what Polanyi has termed *personal knowledge*. This is one important ingredient of the covenantal relationship. Neither party is wholly passive, and understanding is not just a matter of receiving information but involves a covenantal response in the very act of interpretation.

In scriptural discourse the original human author may never have intended his or her words to be put to use in later, often quite distanciated, contexts, but the divine speaker is doing just that. Thus, the story of deliverance from Egypt through the Red Sea becomes not only a metaphorical, but a living, present reality for Israel crossing the Jordan River into Canaan and, just as appropriately, for the ministry of Jesus of Nazareth. And it is still figural (but not metaphorical) of a yet future migration through the waters of death into the heavenly Jerusalem and not just for individual salvation, but for the redemption of a people and indeed of the whole creation. By repeating these themes (a general biblical phenomenon) and in certain circumstances repeating words or sentences (a specific biblical phenomenon), the expectation is that Israel, already assured that Yahweh alone is her shepherd, will finally "indwell" the story he bequeathed to her by divine grace. In turn, therefore, parents are to imitate this covenant-keeping God in repeating these things to their children.

It has to be said that this is not only pedagogical, but epistemological. By using this form of address and the style of repetition, God is reinforcing this point that he is the speaking actor, more than the scrutinized object. And unlike objects of contemplation, perception, or observation, speakers are not waiting to be discovered but are themselves the active agents in dialogue. As a free speaker, God says what God wishes to make known, and what God hides is hidden indeed. As Gadamer puts it above, "Understanding begins when something addresses us." And by addressing us within the context of a *covenant*, God breaches the yawning chasm between the past and the present in understanding. This is accomplished not by a general hermeneutical theory, but by the Spirit who baptizes Jews and Gentiles into Christ and thus into the new creation. This does not obliterate distance, but it does issue in an *eschatological* rather than generally *hermeneutical* account of the believer's contemporaneity with Christ (and the "cloud of witnesses" in both testaments), participating in the age to come. At the same time, Gadamer's general hermeneutical theory comports better than historicism with the Christian reading of scripture:

> Time is no longer primarily a gulf to be bridged because it separates; it is actually the supportive ground of the course of events in which the present is rooted. Hence temporal distance is not something to be overcome. This was, rather, the naïve assumption of historicism, namely that we must transpose ourselves into the spirit of the age, think with its ideas and its thoughts, not with our own, and thus advance toward historical objectivity. In fact the important thing is to recognize temporal distance as a positive and productive condition enabling understanding. It is not a yawning abyss but is filled

with the continuity of custom and tradition, in the light of which everything handed down presents itself to us.[2]

Our proposal has exploited Gadamer's critique of historicism, but has introduced the covenantal motif and the eschatological work of the Spirit as a thicker description of distance as a prerequisite, not problem, for understanding. Separated perhaps by unfamiliar customs, worldviews, and even different locations in redemptive history, believers throughout the ages are united by their belonging to the same covenant. In this way, those who were not a people become children of Abraham. It is not only time, but the biblical structure of covenant, that provides the continuity between our tensed existence. Redemption is not merely a timeless doctrine (although it may be legitimately exposited systematically in its logical and not just historical relations); it is a living history. And the biblical text is not merely a record of past and future events of redemption, but the medium of our own incorporation into that history.

R. Stephen Humphreys titled his interesting analysis of the modern Middle East *Between Memory and Desire*, but this could as easily designate the substance of this chapter, since in this age believers live between the "already" and "not yet." Our proposal has all along emphasized the importance of eschatology, not merely as a locus but as a lens. Having analyzed the nearest options, in many cases appropriating their insights, we turn now to the distinctives of our proposal for a theological hermeneutic. We will first take up the analogical emphasis. We will then turn to the priority and prevenience of the divine speaker over the human reader/community in the covenant and conclude by drawing together the threads of this section under Kant's essentially eschatological question, "For what can I hope?"

We have seen that the contrast between a theology of glory (God considered in himself) and a theology of the cross (God disclosed through prophets and apostles, though supremely and univocally in Christ) generates a considerably more restrained approach to metaphysics. Archetypal theology (*theologia archetypa*) is God's own self-knowledge, which is never accessible to creatures, and even ectypal theology (*theologia ectypa*) is further distinguished in terms of a theology of pilgrims on the way (*theologia viatorum*) and a theology of glorified saints (*theologia beatorum*). In this way, God's hiddenness is guarded and reason is held within the bounds of revelation alone.

This approach seems quite appropriate, especially in an age that is becoming increasingly aware of human weakness and finitude, as well as being disillusioned with modernity's broken promises and unrequited triumphalism. Furthermore, the space being given these days to particularity as opposed to pseudoscientific appeals to universal foundations, together with a renewed openness to the past, suggests that a real conversation could begin between erstwhile unlikely partners, namely, post-Reformation scholasticism and contemporary philosophy, hermeneutics and science.

In this chapter we collect the various strands of our thesis and in the next chapter apply the proposal to the challenge of reintegrating theology.

THE DIVINE "LISP":
ACCOMMODATION AND ANALOGY

As we have seen in our definition of analogy, assertions are made concerning the being of God, and not just concerning our concept or experience of God, and yet God is in every respect *sui generis*, such that analogies will always break down and will never make the inner life of God accessible to creatures, either as pilgrims or as glorified saints. For this archetypal self-knowledge belongs to the Trinity alone.

But Kant's notion of analogy is different from that of classical theology, as John Milbank observes:

> This is why Kant only allows analogous talk of God as a "regulative" discourse concerning his relationship to the world; he does not, like Aquinas, analogously "attribute" notions like necessity to God "in himself"—insofar as created effects resemble their formal-final causes—although our practical insight into freedom gives us, for Kant, a univocal grasp of the essence of transcendence, which Aquinas could not have allowed.[3]

Even the "critique of metaphysics" has turned out to be a new metaphysics. Kant and others could know the limits of reason only because "they believe of course that they can see beyond these," Wittgenstein observed.[4] But the doctrine of analogy that emerged within the Reformed tradition added an element that was missing in the formal Thomist version, though not in Thomistic thought entirely: the theme of divine accommodation. Unlike either Thomas or Kant, Calvin attributed to God predicates like necessity on the basis of God's self-revelation, which is accommodated to human capacity, and not to God *in se*. Seventeenth-century Reformed theologian Francis Turretin formulates it as follows:

> But when God is set forth as the object of theology, he is not to be regarded simply as God in himself (for thus he is incomprehensible [*akataleptos*] to us), but as revealed and as he has been pleased to manifest himself to us in his word, so that divine revelation is the formal relation which comes to be considered in this object. Nor is he to be considered exclusively under the relation of deity (according to the opinion of Thomas Aquinas and many Scholastics after him, for *in this manner the knowledge of him could not be saving but deadly to sinners*), but as he is *our* God (i.e., *covenanted in Christ . . .*). (emphasis added)[5]

So how does this notion of accommodation shape a distinctive analogical account? While one might quibble over some applications of his thesis, Ford Lewis Battles was on target when he saw the importance of the notion of divine accommodation as a component of Calvin's theological hermeneutic.[6] In the eucharistic debate, Calvin strenuously objected to the Zwinglian position that faith was so strong that it did not need any props. In fact, he objected so strenuously that this role of the sacraments as props was placed front and center in his discussion.

But it is not only due to the eucharistic controversy that Calvin developed this major emphasis on divine accommodation to human weakness. It is a guiding, though not necessarily explicit, hermeneutic for nearly every locus. Scripture itself is a form of divine accommodation to human weakness:

> Three Evangelists recount their history in a humble and lowly style; for many proud folk this simplicity arouses contempt. This is because they do not pay attention to the chief divisions of doctrine from which it would be easy to infer that the Evangelists are discussing heavenly mysteries above human capacity. . . . Here, indeed, if anywhere in the secret mysteries of Scripture, we ought to play the philosopher soberly and with great moderation; let us use great caution that neither our thoughts nor our speech go beyond the limits to which the Word of God itself extends. For how can the human mind measure the measureless essence of God according to its own little measure, a mind as yet unable to establish for certain the nature of the sun's body, though men's eyes daily gaze upon it? Indeed, how can the mind by its own leading come to search out God's essence when it cannot even get to its own? Let us then willingly leave to God the knowledge of himself . . . [lest we] enter into a labyrinth.[7]

The emphasis on making scripture relevant or "translating" its message, so important in modernity (on both the left and the right), stands in marked contrast to the premodern assumption that scripture is *already* the product of divine accommodation to human weakness.[8] Through Moses' speech, God was "accommodating himself to the rudeness of the common folk."[9] For instance, "When God repents of having made Saul king, the change of mind is to be taken figuratively." Is this arbitrary? Not in Calvin's view: "A little later there is added: 'The Strength of Israel will not lie, nor be turned aside by repentance; for he is not a man, that he may repent.' By these words openly and unfiguratively God's unchangeableness is declared."[10]

To take a different example, scripture often represents our redemption as if we were under God's wrath until the atonement. But does this not contradict the teaching that God was already moved by love for sinners to send the Son? What are we to make of such statements as, "you who were once estranged . . . [God] has now reconciled in his fleshly body" (Col. 1:21–22)? With the notion of accommodation one is not trapped between the choice of either univocal literalism or equivocal symbolism: "Expressions of this sort," says Calvin, "have been accommodated to our capacity that we may better understand how miserable and ruinous our condition is apart from Christ." The whole point of such expressions is to drive home the force of the point that apart from Christ there is no favor with God.[11] In both of these cases we see the *analogia fidei* at work: scripture interpreting scripture. And we see a willing acceptance of an *accommodated* form of divine discourse. "Better to limp along this path than to dash with all speed outside it."[12] But this accommodationist hermeneutic requires a constant dialectic of whole and parts, systematic and biblical theology on one hand and particular items of exegesis on the other, trying not to allow any resting place, any final synthesis in which dogmatism, biblicism, or skepticism could get the upper hand.

Closely related to accommodation, then, is analogy. In fact, the latter could be regarded as a species of the former. According to Platonism's hierarchy of being (or at least the version of it found in the *Cratylus*), the eternal forms correspond to thought in the mind (or concepts, to be Kantian about it); then there are the things in the realm of appearance, which poorly reflect thought. Finally, there is speech, which corresponds to presence. At least the speaker's mind is somewhat present to another mind, so that thoughts may be transferred from one mind and deposited into another's. But writing is yet another step removed, since presence is exchanged for absence. Although what we know of Plato's ideas come to us from his writings, writings that he seems to have thought capable of effectively communicating, his view of writing is similar to his view of painting and other arts: It's bad enough that everything we sense around us is an imperfect copy of the eternal ideas; why make copies of copies? Vanhoozer rightly sees that Socrates was faced with a dilemma here: "If one rejects the imitation theory, the only alternatives are to appeal to the '*Deus ex machina*' (e.g., the gods gave the first names) or to the 'veil of antiquity' (i.e., we do not know how things got their names). Plato is unhappy with either alternative, for each would force him to acknowledge that he has no reason to believe that he can speak truly, that is, according to a thing's nature."[13]

Socrates' dilemma is precisely that of postmodern literary theory, especially of French poststructuralism. What anchors not only *parole*, but *langue* itself? After the answers offered by modernity, it is no wonder that postmodernism has simply lumped the very idea with wood fairies and gnomes. But our model proposes that God is the basis for existing and knowing. If God has spoken, then human speech has a foundation but not an *autonomous* foundation. Truth is established as both a goal and a possibility of communicative acts—it has its archetype in the communicative action of the creator of the human race. Although our knowledge doesn't penetrate the archetypal self-knowledge of the Trinity, it is ectypal of it. Our knowledge does have ultimate reality as its foundation even if the former has an analogical relation to the latter. The old theologians spoke of God as the *principium essendi* (foundation for existing) and the *principium cognoscendi* (foundation for knowing), but this should be extended to include the claim that God is the *principium loquendi* (foundation of saying). Language is a divine construction, just as the reality that language both apprehends and is apprehended by. Conceptual antirealists are correct in rejecting a self-existing and self-interpreting reality, but realists are correct in insisting on the independent existence of that which is known. These two aspects are united in the Christian understanding of reality as a divinely constructed gift.

In the case of scripture itself, the truthful fit between *signum* (sign) and *res significata* (thing signified) is neither mimetic nor devoid of ultimate referential grounding. But rather than finding this anchor in human *ascent* (deconstruction correctly identifying the search for ultimate meaning with the search for "God" as the transcendental signified), it is located in divine *condescension*. As with Jesus Christ the living Word, the divine kerygma appears in swaddling clothes lying in a manger.[14] In this preached word we also discover, or are discovered by, Emmanuel, God-within-Reach (Rom. 10:8).

Unlike Platonic "speech," which is an imitation or mirror of eternal ideas, biblical "speech" is in the analogical mode and is, therefore, distinguishable from Platonic "speech" in at least the following ways: (1) it refers to writing as well as speech; (2) it has nothing in common with absolute presence or access to the consciousness of the author (denied by archetypal-ectypal distinctions and by the theology of the cross); (3) it doesn't promise a "picture" of reality or univocal knowledge of reality. Rorty's intriguing analysis of the dominance of vision as the metaphor for grasping reality is on the mark at this juncture. "The notion of 'contemplation,' of knowledge of universal concepts or truths as theoria, makes the Eye of the Mind the inescapable model for the better sort of knowledge."[15] It is interesting to note in passing that theoria (theory) meant "sight" in classical Greek. Colin Gunton points out that Coleridge was critical of reigning views of perception that owed so much to the "despotism of the eye."[16] "Coleridge says that it means that 'we are restless because invisible things are not the objects of vision.' . . . That is to say, not only God but all the other features of thought by which the mind attempts to penetrate the structure of reality are hidden from the mind. . . . Coleridge believed that an overemphasis on the place of sight encourages us to believe that what cannot be pictured cannot be held to exist."[17] In truth, seeing is believing.

But analogical thinking cuts this picture theory off at the pass, by denying access to the ultimate "fit" between word and reality. Unlike the Living Word, the written word offers no icons of the invisible God. Even the theophanies cannot be designated sites of full presence, but of sacramental union between the sign and thing signified: as with all analogies, the temple is and is not God's house; the ark of the covenant is and is not God's presence. Only in Jesus is God fully present.[18] Yet even here, God is partially veiled: although we often identify the life of Jesus with miracles, the Gospels indicate that miracles were the exception; the rule was that his true identity was largely missed.

Idolatry tends to reify, to worship, its own interpretations of God (cf. Rom. 1, 2), while in scripture God constantly destabilizes the drift toward univocity (immediate/full presence, direct, intuitive vision) by dramatically new (though not contradictory) disclosures. Resting on any other univocal core than Jesus of Nazareth—including our attempts to reduce biblical analogies to univocal predicates—represents the temptation to idolatry across the theological spectrum.

Long before Wittgenstein, Calvin argued in his own way, and in connection with scripture particularly, that language was suited to a form of life. Language was not a static and immutable code to which the speaker had to submit, a type of calculative reasoning; it was a dynamic tool of human existence and divine communication. In other words, it is not merely what the words mean in themselves, but what the speaker *does* and *intends* in using them. God wished to make a particular point, to promise, to warn, to persuade. As in the instance of apparent conflict over whether God loved humanity before the cross, Calvin not only engages in appropriate analysis of grammar and syntax, but interprets the *intention* of the discourse. God was intending to say something then and there that would make a point in a particular context and for a particular illocutionary purpose, not to establish eternal ideas.

Unlike pictures, which capture an image and, because of their identical representation, are inflexible to interpretation, analogies belong to the linguistic world in which people do things by saying things. Thus, the question of contradiction recedes into the background in the context of personal language, and the question now becomes, What is God doing here in saying this, in this way? The goal is not only to interpret words *about* God, but words *of* God. It is this designative content that is taken as reliable communication from God.

Unless we recognize the analogical character of all language about God, religious language cannot help but become hopelessly problematic. Philosophers of language are right when they demand to know whether we are really referring to anything or whether we are really making assertions at all. Asserting that "the cat is on the mat" is hardly the same as saying "'God' is the symbol of our ultimate concern."[19]

Let us remember, too, that the appeal to analogical categories is not a modern apologetic move, as if to equivocate about the status of religious language that was supposedly taken for granted by our forebears. Rather, its importance in premodern theology was already determined on explicitly theological grounds. The Cappadocians, Augustine, Anselm, Aquinas, and their scholastic successors were agreed that the divine essence was impenetrable. Luther's claim that the medievals nonetheless set out to scale heaven and find the *Deus nudus* lay behind his concern to distinguish God's hidden essence (*Deus absconditus*) from God's self-revelation, insisting that even in revelation God hides himself. It finds expression in Calvin's replete warnings against probing the "secret will" and "hidden essence" of God, and the need for satisfying ourselves with God's mediated presence in the living and written Word and sacraments.

This impulse forged the Protestant scholastics' appropriation of the distinction between the *theologia archetypa* and the *theologia ectypa*, the former being God's self-knowledge and the latter being the knowledge of which creatures are capable. Even under this latter category, there is the *theologia viatorum* (the theology of pilgrims) and the *theologia beatorum* (the theology of glorified saints). All attempts to discover God in divine hiddenness—that is, all attempts to make God an object (in the strictest sense) who is known by abstraction or mystical encounter—is a theology of glory, an overrealized eschatology unbecoming pilgrims and always on its way to idolatry. This is why theologians like Turretin avoided a general or abstract doctrine of God and insisted upon the knowledge of God that is (a) given by God and on God's terms; (b) accommodated to the needs and weakness of the audience; (c) focused on God's covenant in Christ.[20]

Thus, the Reformation's systematization was calculated to obstruct the path of the very "ontotheological" speculative pursuits that came to dominate modern philosophy and theology, especially in absolute idealism. Before the assault of the Enlightenment and higher criticism, the tradition itself, with entirely intrasystematic, theological motives, turned to analogy as a safeguard against idolatry. Just as God can speak to us only in terms that we can understand (and therefore engages in analogical speech himself), we answer God's revelation by appealing to the linguistic patterns that are available to finite creatures who are "pilgrims on the way." While for some analogy can only be regarded as weakness, it is in this very weakness of accommodation that God acts in strength, as Paul reminds.[21]

So analogy is not an extratextual invention, but forms the very pattern of divine speech-accommodation. In this way, both divine utterances and human response (divinely authorized in scripture and witnessed to in the church) are united by analogical patterns of discourse.[22] So Calvin, using the example of "hypostasis," affirms Augustine's reply; namely, that

> on account of the poverty of human speech in so great a matter, the word "hypostasis" had been forced upon us by necessity, *not to express what it is, but only not to be silent on how Father, Son and Spirit are three.* And this modesty of saintly men ought to warn us against forthwith so severely taking to task, like censors, those who do not wish to swear to the words conceived by us, provided they are not doing it out of either arrogance or frowardness or malicious craft. (emphasis added)[23]

The goal is to find "a useful manner of speaking," not a perfect language. And the "object" is God's action (including speech), not God in himself (*visio Dei*).

This analogical method faces objections from proponents of both univocity and equivocity. After judging that analogy has lost favor in Roman Catholic theology, Carl Henry remarks, "The main logical difficulty with the doctrine of analogy lies in its failure to recognize that only univocal assertions protect us from equivocation; the very possibility of analogy founders unless something is truly known about both analogates."[24] In the next sentence, Henry cites his mentor Gordon Clark in support of this criticism of analogy.[25] Many conservatives like Carl Henry apparently share with liberal theology the assumption that language must be either univocal or equivocal, setting the bar for "truth" so high that at some point a crisis must inevitably arrive in interpretation. "The key question is: are human concepts and words capable of conveying the literal truth about God?"[26] If so, these words and concepts must directly mirror the divine being, or they represent *untruth*. In terms remarkably similar to the sort of reply that A. J. Ayer might make, Henry criticizes Robert Blaikie for regarding as analogical the statement "that God acts, God is agent." "But must not even this claim be disallowed as unintelligible if the term has different meanings throughout the universe of human discourse?"[27] Would Henry really want to say that such isolated predicates (or any predicates) have only one meaning, regardless of reference or context?

In his laudable interest to safeguard the reliability of scripture, Henry conflates the *sensus literalis* and his somewhat idiosyncratic understanding of univocity. Thus, the "literal sense" seems practically identical to literalism. "The evangelical rule," he says in this connection, "has been to opt for the literal sense of the Bible where the language does not preclude it."[28] But that is not the Reformers' view. The *sensus literalis* asks, What is the text saying up front? What is its most obvious sense? The rule was never to treat figurative language as untrue or somehow less true than nonfigurative language. Figurative descriptions may be the *sensus literalis* of a passage, but Henry seems to think that interpretation must extract from the ore of literature the pure essence of propositional assertion. Is this not to "demythologize" in a different way? "Truth-content," it seems to me, is tied too closely to a reductionistic view of language in this account.

The problem often with liberalism's appeal to figures of speech is that it interpreted, used, or applied scripture by converting the "truth-content" into allegorical or otherwise tropological content. But this is not what the analogical model does. It affirms that there are divinely authorized conclusions at which we are *entitled* to arrive, but without knowing how *exactly* our truth statements (and other forms of speech) match the divine essence. In analogical discourse, to say that "God is good" is to really *affirm* something about God, but does not claim to know the essence of this goodness in God. Apparently not appreciating this essential affirmation of analogy, Henry only sees two options: "If none of our statements about God is literally true, is God truly known at all?"[29] This problem only arises because "literally true" is confused with "univocal."

In the inspiration of scripture and its preservation, we would argue, God directs the "reference range." And the covenant as context of canon anchors that range considerably. Not all "certainties" are alike. There are a certainty of axioms and mathematical conclusions, a certainty of one's own existence, and a certainty of a promise—and countless other kinds of certainty, no doubt. In other words, certainty is not a one-size-fits-all notion, but is context-specific. "Appropriate enough" may not be a justified conclusion until one becomes convinced that this text is somehow "God's book"—with dual authorship understood in ways similar to theories of double agency. After all, if God has somehow (for now leaving aside theories of inspiration) caused the production of the Bible as the medium of divine discourse, then the analogies are sufficient to each context and for each purpose. Pressed too far or rendered in univocal or equivocal terms, these analogies undergo semantic breakdown. But God has entered into the fragility of human existence, including linguistic existence, in order to command, promise, and so forth. As Bavinck put it, God's word, in becoming scripture, "as writing subjected itself to the fate of all writing."[30] "Accommodation" opposes both "docetic" and "Arian" theories of inspiration. Or, since we are playing off of the christological controversy, we might say that it opposes both the Eutychian tendency to lose the humanity of scripture in divinity, and the Nestorian tendency to separate the human and divine authorship.[31]

Opposite to univocity stands Rudolf Bultmann. "According to mythological thinking," he writes, "God has his domicile in heaven. What is the meaning of this statement? The meaning is quite clear. In a crude manner it expresses the idea that God is beyond the world, that He is transcendent."[32] But this is not mythological thinking, however much it may draw self-confidently upon pagan myths in its own demythologizing.[33] Remarkably, Bultmann seems trapped within a positivism in relation to the Jesus of history and an idealism/existentialism in relation to the

Christ of faith: naive objectivity in the first, anthropocentric subjectivity in the latter. It is Bultmann's own literalism (i.e., his view of descriptive language) and his apparent attribution of univocity to the biblical writers that forces a demythologizing move. Like so many modern theologians, Bultmann entertains a caricature of the tradition, as if Basil, Augustine, Aquinas, Luther, and Calvin really took as univocal a reference to God's heavenly abode, which would imply a denial of divine omnipresence and spirituality. Both Henry and Bultmann seem to misunderstand premodern hermeneutics and the potential of analogy for reinvigorating theology.

The alternative to symbolic reductionism is not to reduce all Christian language to univocal discourse (which is impossible to do in any field, including the natural sciences in which models play such a significant role). Nor is it to give up talking about God simply because of anxiety over the different uses to which language is put. We are not left to choose between relativism and literalism. "For although we do not regard the divine love as identical in kind with human love, divine creation as identical with human making," writes Crombie, "none the less the words which are chosen for use in theological predicates are chosen for some kind of appropriateness."[34] We look not for univocal identity, but for "reference-range."[35] Guided by a covenantal hermeneutic, that range is determined by the *analogia fidei*. Everything in the decision between Kant and Christian theology turns on whether we are convinced that scripture has God as its ultimate author—whether God has crossed the divide to act and speak in our history. This seems to be reflected in the common ways in which the Christian believers actually live out their faith, knowing that faith is "the substance of things hoped for, evidence of things not seen" (Heb. 11:1 KJV). Notice the eschatological rather than mimetic and ocular way of putting this: that which is hoped for in the age to come is in some sense already present, though not fully present, in this present age. Neither full presence (hyperimmanence) nor full transcendence (hypertranscendence) is allowed in this life or the next, according to both the theology of pilgrims and the theology of the glorified saints in heaven.

The relationship between our language about God (especially the language that God has authorized and appropriated in scripture and preaching) and God's being is neither identical nor entirely equivocal. We do not know God as God *is* in the divine hiddenness, but we do know God in his condescension, in his willingness incompletely yet truthfully to reveal himself. "Some kind of appropriateness," as Crombie puts it: this is what we are aiming at in our view of Christian language. But it is an appropriateness that after all *God* has determined, guarding against equivocity.

THE SUMMONS OF THE OTHER

"Struck blind in such a dazzling theater" is Calvin's description of humanity's situation before God.[36] What humans know, even apart from scripture, should evoke gratitude, wonder, awe, and delight in God; but instead, like Adam, rebel sons and

daughters flee the one who made them. "It is therefore in vain that so many burning lamps shine for us in the workmanship of the universe to show forth the glory
of its Author. Although they bathe us wholly in their radiance, yet they can of themselves in no way lead us into the right path. Surely they strike some sparks, but before
their fuller light shines forth these are smothered."[37] "Like Adam," Ricoeur writes,
we are all "responsible and captive, or rather . . . responsible for being captive."[38]

Epistemology and hermeneutics are inextricably bound up with the ethics of
what Paul called "the suppression of truth in unrighteousness," where the goal is
to eradicate any trace of the Other to whom one is accountable, even if that means
erasing the self with its *imago* of the abandoned God. In this section I want to
flesh out the hermeneutical implication of our model with specific focus on the
turning of the tables of interpretation. We have observed the direction of modern hermeneutics under the tutelage of modern theology: from the most remarkable sense of being addressed by God (in the Reformation) to the reversal, where
the interpreter knows the author better than he or she knows himself or herself
(Schleiermacher). As John Searle has reminded us, the intent of authorial discourse does not complete textual "meaning." For Schleiermacher, however,
hermeneutics became the study of *thoughts,* not *things* (i.e., *die Sache*). The result
is Schleiermacher's twofold definition of hermeneutics as involving both grammatical and psychological interpretation.

> This is, in fact, Schleiermacher's presupposition, namely that all
> individuality is a manifestation of universal life and hence "everyone
> carries a tiny bit of everyone else within him, so that divination is
> stimulated by *comparison with oneself.*" Thus he can say that the indi-
> viduality of the author can be directly grasped "by, as it were, *trans-
> forming oneself into the other.*" (emphasis added)[39]

At the end of the day, genuine understanding comes about only by overcoming this distance "by *feeling,* by an immediate, sympathetic, and congenial understanding."[40] "The result of this process is that the interpreter comes to understand
the author better than he understood himself."[41] By reconstructing the original,
even the unintended meanings appear.

Already, the author becomes distanciated from his or her own work: the
painter, for instance, is no longer sovereign interpreter of his or her production.
To pick up a point we will elaborate below, the self takes the other hostage and
refuses to listen, refuses to be called up short or to be in debt or grateful to the
other. Already with Schleiermacher, the sovereign self exercises dominion and
oppresses the author, marginalizes the speaker, and from his God's-eye perch pre-
sumes to know the author/speaker better than she knows herself. This recipe for
oppression and violence is not subverted by postmodern literary theory but, especially in poststructuralism and neopragmatism, is the radicalization of this trajectory. So, Richard Rorty advocates, "The pragmatist thus exalts spontaneity at
the cost of receptivity, as his realist opponent did the reverse. In doing so, he
shows his indebtedness to Romanticism and Absolute Idealism."[42]

The violence that will be deepened rather than ameliorated by postmodern theory is already apparent in Dilthey's insistence that

> Understanding is a rediscovery of the I in the Thou. . . . This identity of mind in the I, in the Thou, in every subject within a community, in every system of culture . . . and of world history, makes possible the joint result of the various operations performed in the human studies. *The subject is here one with its object.* (emphasis added)[43]

One is reminded of a frequent white, middle-class response to racism, when one says to a coworker or neighbor, "I don't even notice that you're black."[44] Modernity erases the other by beginning with the erasure of the divine Other. Understanding means sympathy, which means appropriating another to and for oneself, and this understanding is successful to the extent that the other is assimilated to oneself. From romantic hermeneutics the project arrives at the distancing of the author completely from the text (Ricoeur) until finally the autonomous *cogito* resurfaces as the sovereign Reader who has taken the place of the deceased Author.[45] David Tracy notes, "Pure subjectivity can account for an inability to play, a refusal to act, an impossibility of ever entering any game other than one's own self-designated role, the narcissist game where one is sole actor and sole spectator."[46] It is this "pure subjectivity," still implicit in many leading forms of theology today, that is illustrated in the title of Neal Gabler's recent book, *Life: The Movie, Starring Everyone* (Knopf, 1999). As in our entertainment-driven culture, theology has given far more attention to the psychology of religious experience than to the traditional loci. In the divine drama, however, the subject is no longer sovereign. Again quoting Tracy, "In playing, I lose myself in the play. I do not passively lose myself. In fact, I actively gain another self by allowing myself fully to enter the game."[47]

But if scripture is essentially a covenantal document, the suit that the prophets brought against Israel is brought against us.[48] It is a summons to appear before the one to whom we are accountable. It is a moment to listen and to hear. As Serene Jones observes in relation to Calvin's view of God as the Great Orator, using as her metaphor "the rhetoric of piety," this is a persuasive power that overcomes the audience's suspicions. We therefore become "God's captive audience."[49] So we will examine this covenantal summons first in relation to the individual and then the covenant community.

A. The Summoned Self

"In the beginning, humankind projected a god": that could serve as the prologue to the covenant of modernity, at least according to Feuerbach, Marx, Nietzsche, and Freud. Modern theology, in a host of ways, has seemed to adopt this posture, or adapt to it, in its assumption that religion, including Christianity, is the product of a culture's reflective self-consciousness. Its narratives illustrate universal longings of the soul, the feeling of absolute dependence, unity (identity) with

Absolute Spirit, the triumph of spirit over nature, ultimate concern, or new possibilities. But whatever general account of religion one might provide, the biblical text is not so easily summoned by the reader in this manner. As Austin Farrer
strikingly puts it, "The recipients of revelation see themselves to be addressed by
God. . . . And this is nothing like poetical experience, anyhow on the face of it;
it is like personal encounter."[50] Elsewhere he observes that part of our mind bends
to "the inexorable truth that we are rebellious creatures under the eye of our Creator, and that our Creator has come upon us in Christ. Credulity, here, is the
crime of pretending to believe that there is any way out of this situation but one—
to reconcile ourselves to the truth of our nature, which demands our submission
to the God who made us."[51]

All of this fits, of course, with the image of liberated slaves called to assemble
before the throne of Yahweh on Mount Sinai and then on Mount Zion, and then
summoned to assemble once more after returning from the Babylonian captivity
centuries later when the scroll of the covenant was rediscovered and read aloud
to the weeping crowd. It is this call to assembly that one finds in the prophets
when the covenant servant assembles Yahweh's people and then reads out the suit,
"Hear ye, hear ye, the Lord brings a charge against his people." It also fits with
the image of the servant of the Lord assembling his own twelve servants, corresponding to Israel's twelve tribes. The calling of the disciples, as related by the
evangelists, has that ring of summons to it: Jesus calls and they leave all to follow. Jesus speaks not as the religious leaders, but as one having authority. He reads
the hearts of his auditors, like the Samaritan woman, and summons them to sit
with Abraham, Isaac, and Jacob at his table in his kingdom. Barbara Brown Taylor makes a similar point from this story. At first, the Samaritan woman whose
secret is exposed to this Jew who knows how many husbands she has had wants
to take a few steps back. So she diverts attention to the question over who is right
in the Jewish-Samaritan debate.

> But it does not work. When she steps back, he steps toward her.
> When she steps out of the light, he steps into it. He will not let her
> retreat. If she is determined to show him less of herself, then he will
> show her more of himself. "I know that Messiah is coming," she says,
> and he says, "I am he." It is the first time he has said that to another
> living soul. It is a moment of full disclosure, in which the triple out-
> sider and the Messiah of God stand face to face with no pretense
> about who they are. . . . By telling the woman who she is, Jesus shows
> her who he is. By confirming her true identity, he reveals his own,
> and that is how it still happens. The Messiah is the one in whose pres-
> ence you know who you really are—the good and bad of it, the all of
> it, the hope in it.[52]

After three and a half centuries of being especially intoxicated with the sovereign self and subjectivity, the other (divine and human others) has been marginalized and, as we will note below, postmodern theory has served only to intensify
Nietzsche's "man of azure isolation" (Barth's memorable description). The later

Heidegger's emphasis on being opened up, exposed, interrogated in interpretation represents a welcome interlude from the theater of cruelty, in which the other is exegeted but never the exegete. Like Gadamer, Ricoeur shares Heidegger's preference for hermeneutics as a matter of being interpreted as well as interpreting, and he applies it to biblical faith.[53]

We know enough about Luther's own experience to recognize how it was that a whole epoch seemed to feel itself exposed to God, both in wrath and grace. Preaching became that summons, identical in its illocutionary force and its eschatological power to the great assemblies of Israel at the foot of God's mountain. Bultmann and dialectical theology, generally correctly, saw in scripture and the Reformers the inseparability of encounter from interpretation, even if their account of revelation tended to isolate individual existence in the eternal moment from covenantal existence across time.[54]

By the *analogia fidei* (and this is true for Calvin also) Luther does not mean merely that the clear passages interpret the obscure, but that scripture interprets us, and that this is dominant even over our own interpretation, though not exclusive of it. It is this that forms Luther's concept of *sola scriptura,* according to Bruns.[55] It is not simply scripture as a sacred book or sacred announcement, but its illocutionary force (command and promise) that provokes this encounter in which one ends up being interpreted by the text. The categories of "law" and "gospel" are not merely exegetical, but existential; they make sense only in relation to us. We must not confuse the Reformers' *pro me* (or more often, *pro nobis*) orientation with Bultmann's reduction of theology to anthropology or existence. Their point is that the scriptures are not merely a collection of true statements about God, humanity, salvation, and ethics, but that when they are preached the Spirit actually performs what is threatened in the law and what was promised in the gospel. Such instances of performative utterances Calvin, for example, found in Ezekiel 37, in the light of which Christ "taught that the voice of the gospel gives life."[56] Scripture was essential first of all for existential reasons: not only *to learn* how one is set right with God (although that is a component), but *to be set right* with God. This was the crisis. "Law" is God's speech in whose presence all stand as offenders, while "Gospel" is God's speech in whose presence believers stand as justified.

Thus, interpretation cannot be divorced from one's existential relationship to that which is said. So Bultmann did have a point when he said that genuine understanding is self-understanding. For that reason Calvin opened the *Institutes* with that famous affirmation of the dialectical relationship between knowledge of God and knowledge of self. The same phrase "the righteousness of God" can be interpreted as either law or gospel, depending on one's eschatological location ("in Adam"/"in Christ").[57]

This is not just a matter of application, for although the noematic and designative content of the address is textually fixed and its meaning identifiable according to the *sensus literalis, understanding* does depend in part on the hearers and their situation. Their *Sitz-im-Leben* or "horizon" is not neutral or merely passive, even when the speaker has priority. But that's understanding, not meaning, and here I would differ with Gadamer's widely influential notion that meaning is actually constituted by the horizon of the interpreter as well as that of the text.[58]

Gadamer's theory of "fusion of horizons" arises because of the *problem* of distanciation between the original situation and our own. But this shows why a general hermeneutical theory cannot provide a sufficient account of *Christian* reading/hearing of *this* text. While there is no divine promise to heal this breach in general reading or hearing, there is the promise that wherever God speaks through the word, the Spirit of God is present with the people of God. For Christians, who take the specific character of biblical hermeneutics seriously, the real divide is not ultimately ontological or epistemological/hermeneutical, but eschatological and ethical. While thought and interpretation cannot be reduced to the latter pair, there can be no adequate account of the former without it. The problem is not whether two thousand years or two hours have passed, but whether we are located in "the age to come" that is present eschatologically in Christ's presence among his people by his Spirit or in "this present evil age"—that is, whether one is a slave of sin, repressing the truth in unrighteousness, or a child of God. "And because you are children, God has sent the Spirit of his Son into our hearts, crying 'Abba! Father!' So you are no longer a slave but a son, and if a son then also an heir, through God" (Gal. 4:6–7). (It is important theologically that we follow the distinct Greek word for "son" here; the inclusion of both females and males as "sons" in the New Testament is a radical break with traditional cultures in which only males [especially the firstborn] could ordinarily hold title to the inheritance.)

A theology of proclamation will appreciate in this respect a hermeneutics of suspicion in relation to this aeon and its promises, convinced that all human attempts to understand are attended by the desire to master, distort, justify oneself, and use the other for one's own purposes. One thinks of Barth's vivid picture of the autonomous self waving its finger in self-assertiveness, like a child playing the part of a king. Proclamation and the decentering of self-identity are correlates. David Tracy captures this aspect:

> For those theologies whose major focus for understanding the self is proclamation, the emphasis shifts radically. The seeming impossibility of authentic existence in the confrontational light of the actuality of radical sinfulness disclosed by the actuality of grace now haunts the shaken conscience of the faithful self. The terror of existence in all its forms is now felt with power: especially the terror of the self vainly, despairingly attempting to flee from its unwelcome recognition of its own twisted reality, attempting to justify itself before itself, others, God. This frightening self-recognition releases the dialectic of the self who has heard a Word of proclamation, this self *simul iustus et peccator* who has experienced the defamiliarizing force of a judging and liberating word from God.[59]

Critical of what he perceives as the one-sidedness of this approach, Tracy nevertheless captures its essential ambitions (albeit exaggerating the dilemma):

Driven by the real power of the not-yet in our graced state, the theologians of the word will force their negations upon the consciousness of all selves: Reason may become a "whore"; images may become "idolatry"; a Christianity focussed on the manifesting giftedness of all creation will begin to seem "pagan"; agape will have nothing to do with eros; sins will become sin; teleological orientations will be dismantled and replaced with deontological commands; grace will be justifying and that justification forensic; what was once seen as cooperative grace now seems self-justifying "works."[60]

To be sure, we have not attempted a thorough treatment of political theology or ethics, and there is a lot to fill out in such an account. One should not conclude that this model encounters no difficulties or that its implications would not require further interaction with those who have suffered in this world far more than this author. Still, the hermeneutical implications of saying that God speaks, within this covenantal situation, requires that something be said about the summons of the Other and the theology of the cross. A hermeneutic of suspicion has an important role to play in our general hermeneutics, but a hermeneutic of *hesed* (covenant trust: "Here I am") norms our reading, preaching, and hearing of this particular text.

As we have seen, this violence against the other and the claims of the other has its roots finally not in the technical issues of interpretation, not even in the criticism of the text. Rather, this fundamental suspicion of scripture has its roots in the rejection of the particular claims made by this text. If the matter is as theological as even postmodern theorists insist, it is perhaps not going too far to suggest that a secularized hermeneutic of suspicion derives ultimately from the will to power, to control the other and to attain freedom from the other. This tyranny of the self is, at bottom, theological. Spinoza, for instance, suggested that one should interpret the Bible rather directly and simply, until arriving at the miracles and other parts that distance us from the text. Then we turn to history for some explanation.[61] In this scheme, the self is distanced from the text simply by the latter's otherness, *its claim on us.* History "saves" us from a God who really acts and speaks. Hence, the emerging antithesis of faith and history at least in part receives its clearer theological underpinning, despite the attempts to render hermeneutics a strictly secular affair. Derrida and his circle know better, of course, and are only too happy to recognize its theological character.

This dilemma stalks contemporary hermeneutics. It also marks the battle lines between stereotypical "modern" and "postmodern" zones. But what if, rather than some rational principle, idealist structure, romantic feeling, existentialist Moment, or deconstructionist play, God is the *principium essendi* (foundation of existence) and scripture the *principium cognoscendi* (foundation of knowing)? Since both foundationalism and antifoundationalism have the same foundation, viz., the autonomous self, whether author or reader, should one be surprised that alterity has been eclipsed by and reduced to self?

Post-Marxian analysis is correct to expose the reality of power regimes, a component too often neglected or suppressed in the study of history, culture, and religion. But Marx and Nietzsche were wrong in their insistence that Christianity represents apathy or surrender to powerlessness. In his profound analysis of this point, Miroslav Volf not only concedes but celebrates the distinctly Christian power regime.[62]

Is it not the case, in the first chapters of Romans, that Paul displays, front and center, the power regimes at work? He says there, and elsewhere, that "powers in heavenly places" are at work in the interpretation and response of those who hear the message of Christ. The power of the gospel is not powerlessness, but the power of cruciform weakness. If "god" has been used to legitimate oppression and violence as the archetypical Author/ity of a destructive will to power, it would seem that some good, old-fashioned iconoclasm is in order, not a/theology. The power of the God who raised Jesus from the dead can dethrone the authority of the *Übermensch* who is nothing more than the projection of human rebellion at its apex. The death of the Tyrannical Author has only substituted the Tyrannical Reader, consigning all texts and readers to "aimless wandering."[63]

What post-Marxian criticism has yet to criticize is this new hierarchy of being, this new sovereignty of the Reader. With apparently too much to risk, such analysis has resisted observation of the remarkable "other side" of Christian history in which God as the *principium essendi* has authorized sacrifice of oneself for the good of the other. This is not weakness, but the greatest strength: "For this reason the Father loves me, because I lay down my life in order to take it up again. No one *takes* it from me, but *I lay it down* of my own accord. *I have power* to lay it down, and *I have power* to take it up again. I have received this command from my Father" (John 10:17–18, emphasis added). This assertion transforms our ordinary notions both of "victim" and of "power." While according to scripture God is most powerfully present and effective in this self-giving, empirical reality seems flatly to contradict that this is in fact the site of such enormous power and presence. There is nothing inherently contradictory, except that our notions of power and its effective use are, in our fallen condition, dominated by analogies of manipulation, exploitation, and coercion. "I lay it down" is not just an insight into the humanity of Jesus—an example of authentic existence—but is an insight into the deity of God. Unlike the way in which "power" is normally used in modern, Western societies, here the One who exercises his power to the fullest does so as servant and victim: "[he] was handed over to death for our trespasses and was raised for our justification" (Rom. 4:24).

It is *this* Other who says, "All authority in heaven and earth has been given to me." It is *this* Other who becomes the founder not of the absence of hierarchy or power, but of a new hierarchy in opposition to "the powers [oppressive hierarchies] of this age." The sole reign of Christ over his kingdom constantly summons the church to look at power differently: "Truly I tell you, whoever does not receive the kingdom of God as a little child will never enter it" (Luke 18:17). Here is the Other who legitimizes a regime of respect, listening, hearing, attentiveness; who brings to the center of his regime those who are marginalized. To play off of Philippians 2, we could say that he who possessed all authority became weak so that the weak could be made strong. He legitimizes the illegitimate, first of all because he "justifies the wicked."

But there is a further implication. Some have encouraged this sort of interpretation, seeing in Jesus Christ the weakness and poverty of God on behalf of others. But this is only the view from the cross. Important as that is, the resurrection opened up a new destiny both for Jesus Christ and for those who are organically related to him as "harvest" to "firstfruits." Here one no longer accepts the identity of victim, but embraces a "new creation" of freedom and adoption that has already dawned in the resurrection (cf. 1 Cor. 15:23). Now Jesus is no longer only the victim who was slain, but is also the triumphant lamb who judges with equity at the last day. In contrast to an ideology that would leave the victim, the oppressed, the marginalized wandering aimlessly (what could better represent "opium for the masses"?), this judge of sovereign selves neither winks at tyrants nor leaves the lonely and violated to the free play of drifters.

The kingdom that Christ announces is then truly a power regime, the power of divine weakness that has triumphed over worldly strength, the power of "the age to come" interrupting, upsetting, and in the end finally unseating the powers of "this present evil age." That "we struggle not against flesh and blood, but against principalities and powers in spiritual places" is ominously illustrated in Nietzsche's boast, "We immoralists are today the strongest power: the other great powers need us—we construe the world in our image."[64]

This clash of powers is why, for instance, Calvin was convinced that in scripture "God . . . opens his own most hallowed lips,"[65] that through oracles and visions God "put into their [the writers'] minds what they should then hand down to their posterity. At any rate, there is no doubt that firm certainty of doctrine was engraved in their hearts, so that they were convinced and understood that what they had learned proceeded from God. For by his Word, God rendered faith unambiguous forever, a faith that should be *superior to all opinion*" (emphasis added).[66]

The Reformers were not interested in certainty as an epistemological concept, but as an existential reality. Uncertainty about whether God had really spoken here in this word entailed uncertainty about God's covenantal *promises*. One did not need a special discourse from God concerning God's majesty, power, justice, and wrath. All of this could be discerned through God's creation and providence. But to the unreconciled sinner this could only be "law" and lead one to despair.[67] What is needed is good news, with the firmness and clarity that only divine authorship could secure. If God is mute and passive, then he is an unknowable noumenon or, more likely, a projection of human longing. This is why Calvin stresses the unambiguous certainty of scripture's authorship when in it one is summoned by God. "If we desire to provide in the best way *for our consciences*," he says, "—that they may not be perpetually beset by the instability of doubt or vacillation, and that they may not also boggle at the smallest quibbles—we ought to seek our conviction in a higher place than all reasons, judgments, or conjectures, that is, in the secret testimony of the Spirit" (emphasis added).[68] In the very next sentence, Calvin the nonfoundationalist grants, "True, if we wished to proceed by arguments, we might advance many things that would easily prove—if there is any god in heaven—that the law, the prophets, and the gospel come from

him. . . . Yet they who strive to build up firm faith in Scripture through disputa-
tion are doing things backwards."[69]

While Plato and philosophy generally had placed religion in the realm of opinion (*doxa*) and reason in the realm of genuine knowledge (*noesis*), the Reformers
were gripped by the "manifest signs of God speaking in scripture."[70] Their
emphasis on certainty in the concrete struggle of finding a gracious God is even
echoed perhaps in Wittgenstein's remark in his lectures on ethics:

> What inclines even me to believe in Christ's Resurrection? It is as
> though I play with the thought.—If he did not rise from the dead,
> then he decomposed in the grave like any other man. *He is dead and
> decomposed.* In that case he is a teacher like any other and can no
> longer *help*; and once more we are orphaned and alone. So we have
> to content ourselves with wisdom and speculation. We are in a sort
> of hell where we can do nothing but dream, roofed in, as it were, and
> cut off from heaven. But if I am to be *really* saved,—what I need is
> *certainty*—not wisdom, dreams or speculation—and this certainty is
> faith. . . . What combats doubt is, as it were, *redemption.* Holding fast
> to this must be holding fast to that belief. (emphasis in original)[71]

The testimony of the Spirit, which "is more excellent than reason," is not
something added to scripture but is the evidence of scripture itself. "For as God
alone is a fit witness of himself in his Word, so also the Word will not find acceptance in men's hearts before it is sealed by the inward testimony of the Spirit. The
same Spirit who has spoken through the mouths of the prophets must penetrate
into our hearts to persuade us that they faithfully proclaimed what had been
divinely commanded."[72] To be sure, Calvin admits (having been trained in
Renaissance literature, with a preference for Cicero), the rhetoric of scripture is
weak, often clumsy, and lacking in eloquence. But this is so that faith would be
founded "upon God's power, not upon human wisdom" (1 Cor. 2:5).

The power of divine rhetoric is not in its style, for the poverty of its style, like
Bethlehem's manger, hides the power of God from human pride. From the beginning, Christians have known what Calvin describes when he writes,

> Read Demosthenes or Cicero; read Plato, Aristotle, and others of that
> tribe. They will, I admit, allure you, delight you, move you, enrap-
> ture you in wonderful measure. But betake yourself from them to this
> sacred reading. Then, in spite of yourself, so deeply will it affect you,
> so penetrate your heart, so fix itself in your very marrow, that, com-
> pared with its deep impression, such vigor as the orators and philoso-
> phers have will nearly vanish. . . . As far as Sacred Scripture is
> concerned, however much froward men try to gnaw at it, neverthe-
> less it clearly is crammed with thoughts that could not be humanly
> conceived.[73]

One would miss Calvin's point entirely by dismissing this as fideism. Nor is
he a proto-romantic at heart, impressed with the poetic force of scripture as his
"classic." Rather, when one reads this text, one encounters God speaking so

clearly by the Spirit's work both in inspiration and in the illumination of the reader, that having to justify that God has spoken here and now is equivalent to having to justify that one has heard one's spouse this morning at breakfast. It is not merely the quality of the text itself (which is admittedly weak), but what one encounters in that text (namely, God acting and speaking) that sets this apart from any other act of interpretation. It is drama. In it, one not only encounters events of divine activity and discourse, but one actually becomes an addressed and responding character in the drama. Much of contemporary hermeneutics, as John Webster remarks, "eclipses what in fact is most interesting, about what happens when Christians read the Bible: that the Bible as text is the *viva vox Dei* addressing the people of God and generating faith and obedience."[74] It is this emphasis on God's acting and speaking, rather than the subject's interpreting, that is missing from hermeneutical or methodological schemes drawn largely from general theories. The meaning of the text does not depend on human receptivity or resistance, conversation or contempt, sympathy or suspicion. But its perlocutionary force does. One can resist the general summons of scripture, both law and gospel. But one's resistance cannot make an utterance untrue any more than one's acceptance can render it true.

We can see how this approach would differ at various points from George Lindbeck's "cultural-linguistic" model. His example of the crusader's cleaving the skull of an infidel while crying, "*Christus est Dominus*," provides a good illustration of the differences in the light of the preceding discussion. This cry is "false when used to authorize cleaving the skull of the infidel (even though the same words in other contexts may be a true utterance)."[75] But why does the textual *sense* have to be false because of the context? Why can't it be that the *speaker* is false in uttering it? It is not a false statement just because it is uttered in this context. As speech-act theory points out, one of the prerequisites for a "happy" utterance is that "the particular persons and circumstances in a given case must be appropriate for the invocation of the particular procedure invoked."[76] "Thus," Austin writes, "when I say 'I promise' and have no intention of keeping it, I have promised but . . ." He calls these infelicities "abuses." In these cases, "we speak of our infelicitous act as 'professed' or 'hollow' rather than 'purported' or 'empty.'"[77] In such a context, the speaker is not *authorized* to issue this ascription of praise. Gottlob Frege's distinction between "true" and "taking-to-be-true" is helpful on this point.[78] This is not the same as fact and value, but rather refers to the inherent quality of the utterance itself distinct from reflexive acts of evaluation.

The person who is authorized to say, "*Christus est Dominus*," is one who has been made a servant of the one named. One of the classic statements of this biblical emphasis is found in Luther's *The Freedom of a Christian* (1520). In it we read, "A Christian is free and independent in every respect, a bondservant to none. A Christian is a dutiful servant in respect, owing a duty to everyone. These two axioms are clearly found in 1 Corinthians 9, where St. Paul says: 'Though I am free from all men, I have made myself a servant to all."[79] This follows the pattern that we have observed in Jesus Christ, "the pioneer" of this route. Not only by his example, as still autonomous individuals seeking to justify themselves, but by being baptized into his life, death, and resurrection, believers who were once slaves to unrighteousness are willing servants. The irony is that while they are now free for the first time, they *choose* to be servants.

This is hardly the "resignation" that Nietzsche and his heirs have imputed to Christianity. In Christ, believers are also given the power to lay down their lives in order to take them back again—or rather, to have them given back to them new. Trying to remain the autonomous self, ruling and attaining eternal life or ultimate satisfaction by one's own efforts, leads to disaster. "But I advise you if you wish to pray, or fast, or make an endowment," says Luther, "let it not be with the idea that you will benefit yourself. Rather do it freely in order that others may benefit; do it for their advantage—then you will be a real Christian."[80] This is the way of the cross and resurrection. Out of this gospel of the covenant truly emerges a new way of being-in-the-world. Instead of focusing on saving one's own soul, the freedom of the Christian in grace frees one to become a servant. Iris Murdoch aims at something like this when she observes that "Freedom . . . is not an inconsequential chucking of one's might about, it is the disciplined overcoming of self."[81] But the Reformers would insist on an important caveat: It is not the disciplined overcoming of self, which in any case could be closer to stoicism, but rather the dramatic rescripting of self that occurs when one is confronted by the word of God.

Calvin experienced this when he wrote sympathetically to Cardinal Sadoleto that "it certainly is the part of a Christian to ascend higher than merely to seek and secure the salvation of his own soul. I am persuaded, therefore, that there is no man imbued with true piety, who will not consider as insipid that long and labored exhortation to zeal for heavenly life, a zeal which keeps a man entirely devoted to himself, and does not, even by one expression, arouse him to sanctify the name of God."[82] Only by giving up one's own claim to sovereignty can one actually become free and in that discover that true freedom is service to God and neighbor, the *telos* for which humanity was created.

In this light, we could concur with Kevin Vanhoozer, who has posed an intriguing reversal of postmodern theory in which the Reader as Lord (Overstanding) is displaced by the Reader as Servant (Understanding).[83] For the hermeneutical and ontological realist, it is precisely because there is a "there" there that one must not absolutize one's own interpretation.[84] The real world or text resists assimilation and precisely for that reason opposes violence. On the other hand, antirealism invites it. Reducing "other" to "self" in interpretation underwrites the cycle of violence. When the reader is no longer accountable to authors, texts, meanings, purposes, and a final reckoning, to what author/ity can the silent (or silenced) appeal? Derrida's, Rorty's, and Barthes's "Reader" represents Descartes's "Ego" in a different form. The death of the Author is the death of the Other. "One should respect fatality—that fatality that says to the weak: perish!"[85]

We have noted how the dethroning of this *res cogitans* or *res legens* is the aim of preaching and the prerequisite for faithful hearing and reading. This has not been built on a general hermeneutical theory, but we have underscored the covenantal structure of this encounter. One more word should be said of this.

As Levinas and other critics have pointed out so thoroughly, the Enlightenment model of "conversation" often serves only to obliterate or dominate the Other. It is part of that assimilation that Schleiermacher and Dilthey initiate. Our challenge then is to sacrifice everything for the sake of preserving the "otherness" of the other, whether divine or human. What is remarkably different about scripture, however, at least as we have seen in the biblical text and its interpretation by the Reformers, is that God's power (clearly acknowledged *as* power) is cast in a rhetorical rather than coercive mold. In other words, the word of God converts and restores—not by eviscerating or erasing the other, but by persuasive discourse. In this case, discourse is not alone (a "dead letter"), but is accompanied by the Spirit, who is God. Persuasion is an intrinsically concursive enterprise. In oppression, the weaker party acquiesces, but in liberation, the weaker party rejoices and joins the ranks of "the persuaded."

We see this persuasive crisis/encounter in the stories of Adam and Eve, Abraham and Sarah, Jacob wrestling with the angel of the Lord, Israel in the wilderness, Jesus in his own temptation and in his conversation with the Samaritan woman; Peter in his vision of the unclean animals, and Paul in his Damascus road experience. In all of these instances, God overwhelms not by force (although he could), but by respecting the alterity of the creature—even the rebellious creature. Perhaps no better example of this exists than Mary's encounter with the angel. After the angel's announcement that she would bear "the Son of the Most High," she replies, "Here am I, the servant of the Lord; let it be with me according to your word" (Luke 1:38). This is covenantal epistemology, where mastery is exchanged for a relationship of listening and being heard. Mary did not bend under superior pressure, but rather freely accepted the role that God had prepared for her in the drama of redemption.

This course contrasts markedly with Nietzsche's reductionistic choice between Christianity's putative acquiescence to weakness or celebration of the will to power and mastery over others. Not only is God the archetypal Other; this Other is all-powerful. But—and this is where tyranny gets written out of the script— having ultimate power, God does not use it capriciously or arbitrarily.[86] Still, God does nothing from necessity, but *covenantally*. In a covenant, neither party is absorbed or manipulated. Yet, in this arrangement God not only obligates the servant, but places himself under obligation (in this case, even greater obligation) to the covenant's success for the future. There is therefore no wild, arbitrary God of capricious will, but a free God who condescends to bind himself in a legal relationship to creatures. Even Heidegger still says that "what the hermeneutical philosopher must explicate and understand is not external and alien to him,"[87] but the covenantal model of understanding God's commands and promises preserves the space, the proper distance, between self and other, so that God really is Other (*pace* hyperimmanence), though not "*Wholly* Other" (e.g., hypertranscendence). Nor is the self practically obliterated by the other's presence, as one might conclude from some of the lines of Levinas's thought.[88]

The model we have been proposing no longer accepts the presuppositions of unbelief to establish belief or variations on that theme. Even Pannenberg's almost visceral reaction to any notion of heteronomy on the question of biblical authority tends to mask the fact that without the authority of this particular covenant-making God above all "authorities," we are left not to no-authority but to false ones.[89] Pannenberg himself must substitute his own somewhat authoritative demands that the reasonable person *must* accept the resurrection of Jesus, and thus a new kind of power is introduced than the one we have considered, the sinister power that has characterized the seductions of modernity.

Scripture as the word of God not only proposes a new world or opens up new possibilities. It is neither a mere *occasion* for God to work (a "Zwinglian" separation of the sign from the thing signified in favor of God's freedom, perhaps an influence on Barth's view of revelation), nor a *communicatio idiomatum* that would lose the sense of the genuine human authorship in all of its weakness as a sign. Rather, scripture as the word of God is "covenant," which requires accommodation on God's part, weakness, rhetorical simplicity, to persuade us to be reconciled in Christ by means of it. Walter Brueggemann expresses similar sentiments and is worth quoting at length:

> In that diseased present tense, the church utters its word about an alternative. It *speaks of a self* that is open to obedience (Psalm 119), satisfied with goodness and mercy (Ps. 23:6), and reclothed in holiness and righteousness (Col. 3:5–17). *It asserts a world* that stands safely under God's good promise (Gen. 9:8–16). *It imagines a church* fully cared for and not orphaned (Isa. 54:7–10; Jn. 14:1, 18). That is, it offers a present-tense self, world, and church that are held safely in the fidelity of a covenant that is not disrupted by our fearfulness, a covenant that decisively reshapes and redefines. The present construed as covenant fidelity is not an easy, romantic word about intimacy and "relationships." It bespeaks rather a readiness to receive life from the other, from God and neighbor, rather than from self. Whereas commoditization presents the self as the sufficient and principal actor, covenant hosts the other as the focus of well-being. That trust in the other opens the way for a very different psychology of self, a very different public possibility, a very different ecclesiology. At the heart of the matter, the contrast of *commodity* and *covenant* hinges upon the reliability of the other.[90]

Seen in this light, every event of Word and sacrament—the covenantal meeting with God—represents a crisis of powers in which hearers are constituted a people, a new nation of servants who listen and hear, rather than belonging to the old nation of lords who, "having ears, they cannot hear." Particularly interesting is Brueggemann's contrast between covenant and commodity. We might even suggest that the former is agapic attentiveness to the other, while the latter is erotic acquisitiveness.[91] Long after Nietzsche's proclamation of the death of God and the end of "meaning," as theology acquiesced to its own interminable Babylonian captivity, the clash of empires can still be heard:

> When the church conducts its liturgy, when the church reads the
> Bible, when the church declares the gospel, it engages in a counter-
> act, counteracting the world so long dominant among us. The most
> importance resistance to this evangelical counter-imagination does
> not come from militant secularists. It comes from well-intentioned
> believers who are infected with modernity. It comes from the pastor's
> own sinking sense that none of this is true. So we worship and pro-
> claim: a memory in a community that aggressively forgets, a covenant
> in a community deeply enmeshed in commodity, and a hope in a
> community that believes very little is promised or possible.[92]

"Readers can only *receive* meaning, they cannot *create* it," Francis Watson rightly notes.[93]

And yet, a covenant involves two parties, although in this covenant the divine partner even gives the other what is needed in order to respond and act out his or her part. In the drama of redemption, the hearers of the covenant are neither wholly passive spectators in the audience nor aggressive improvisationalists. Rather, they are cast in supporting roles together with Abraham, Isaac, and Jacob around the central character. And only the Spirit can create this reality in history: there is no inner, immanent, self-determining *telos* within history itself that would lead to this result. In fact, it happens contrary to all appearances.

When the reality came, even the grandest promises could be seen as falling short of the fulfillment itself. This certainly fits with the redemptive-historical pattern of seeing Christ as the center of all Scripture, formally as well as inter-pretively, as in parables the central character of the overarching narrative himself recounts the meaning of the play in that form.[94] While semiotic analysis is not the end of interpretation, it certainly represents a good beginning, especially after the critical enterprise. "We are accompanying *the interpretive dynamism of the text itself,*" Ricoeur points out. "The text interprets before having been interpreted" (emphasis added).[95] In this revitalization of the *analogia fidei*, the static picture of dissecting a text as one might a laboratory specimen is exchanged for a richer, dynamic image of being euphorically grasped by the text's hand and escorted into its storied world:

> In effect, what progressively happens in the Gospel is the *recognition*
> of Jesus as being the Christ. We can say in this regard that the Gospel
> is not a simple account of the life, teaching, work, death, and resur-
> rection of Jesus, but the communicating of an act of confession, a com-
> munication by means of which the reader in turn is rendered capable
> of performing the same recognition that occurs inside the text.[96]

The apostles' story becomes the habitat of the contemporary reader, not by reconstructing a past, nor by its mere textuality, but by the Spirit's work with the word in effecting its command and promise, so that the world that is opened up by the text-drama becomes contemporary with the reader today. But this is not the reader's projection, an occasion for envisioning new autonomous possibilities. Rather, it is a divine summons that surprises and disturbs. One is brought to those moments in which he or she must answer, with Peter, the question, "Who do *you* say that I am?" Thus, to return to the dramatic image we have been employing, the contemporary reader or hearer is not an aloof spectator who merely grasps, but an actor in the drama itself who is grasped. "The narrative of the life and death of Jesus is organized in such a way that the knowledge unveiled right at the beginning should be appropriated by the actors themselves and, beyond them, by the reader. It is the work of the text to do this."[97] Ricoeur has effectively turned the tables here on the critique of Feuerbach, Marx, Nietzsche, and Freud: true religion is *not* the autonomous projection of the self upon the world (including textual "others"), but the self's disorientation and reorientation in the direction of a textual projection.

Thus, even within the Old Testament itself, the anticipation is that the identity of the people of Yahweh, from its text to its worship, its faith and practice, will be redrawn around the incarnate Word rather than Torah. The gravitational center will shift from Moses to Christ, from Exodus-Sinai to Cross-Resurrection. The new redemptive-historical event—not only new, but the definitive fulfillment of which all others were but steps along the way—will alter the identity of individuals, the community, and indeed all of human history. By thus extrapolating Ricoeur's point concerning the unity of law and narrative in the Old Testament, we could extend it. We can then say that the resurrection of Christ "qualifies not just the event of its giving but all the narratives in which this giving is encased."

> The new is not anticipated as radically different but as a sort of creative repetition of the old. Very concretely, the prophets of the exile and the postexile anticipated the return as a restoration, and they described this restoration in advance as a new exodus, a new desert, a new Sinai, a new Zion, a new Davidic descendance, and so on. . . . A few centuries later, the early church will turn this procedure into a hermeneutic and find in it the basic structures of its typological reading of the Old Testament. This development authorizes us to speak, with a certain prudence to be sure, because of the retrospective use of the term, of an interpretation of the New in terms of the Old already at work in the Old Testament.[98]

And yet, the *newness* of the novum bursts the wineskins of anticipation to the extent that even the Old Testament must be reread now in the light of the New in order to be properly understood. Prophecy and eschatology, then, keep tradition from becoming sterile and, in fact, false. This is why the prophets are always cast in an adversarial role with respect to traditionalism, and yet why the apostles are forever warning against the first-century "enthusiasts" whose propheticism exceeded the limits of redemptive revelation.

B. The Summoned Community

Over the last two chapters, we have alluded to the striking similarities between the Reformation in the sixteenth century and our own situation in theology. And we have noted how thoughtfully these interesting analogies have been pursued by, for instance, Stanley Hauerwas and Kevin Vanhoozer.

In this section, we will flesh out the implications of the reading/hearing event as a divine summons—this time not only for individuals, but for a community that God is forming "from every tribe and language and people and nation . . . to be a kingdom and priests serving our God" (Rev. 5:9). We hope this approach will not simply repristinate Reformation positions, but reformulate them in the light of our proposal. To do this, we must begin with the relation of Word and Spirit and then the relation of these to the church. We will then compare and contrast our account with those of the *enthusiast* and *dogmatist*. These are not meant to be pejorative of any individual or group, but as general typologies that cut across the ecclesiastical fabric.

In outlining our approach to this relationship, we must refer again to the connection between canon and covenant. As we have seen, the scriptures do not simply contain a covenant or covenants, but as a whole can be said to constitute the covenant document itself. Just as tablet copies of Hittite treaties would be archived by both partners, the copies of the Decalogue were placed in the ark of the covenant, and God's presence among Israel was thereby identified with this treaty chest. As with the Hittite suzerainty treaties in which the judgment of the gods was invoked in the case that the covenant would in any way be altered, in the Yahweh covenant warnings are posted against adding to or taking from the word of the Great King.[99]

Furthermore, even to suggest that the covenant document was somehow less authoritative than the suzerain himself was to enter into the treaty without good faith from the start. If a fellow human being is only as good as his or her word, that was more emphatically true in the treaty structure of the ancient Near East, where international diplomacy rested on the correspondence between the integrity of the covenant-maker and the covenant itself.

A second point to be made in this connection has to do with the prevenience of the divine partner in this covenant.[100] According to suzerainty treaties, a great king annexes a lesser people. This could be an act of aggression or of establishing a client-state relationship in which the lesser king could secure his subjects' continued existence in the face of mounting threats. In other words, it is imposed unilaterally. "You will be my people, and I will be your God" is the formula of the divine treaty, and when it is renewed in the midst of exilic suffering, that same divine initiative is present: "I will take away the heart of stone and give them a heart of flesh," "I will forgive their iniquities," "I will bring them from all the nations where they have been driven," "I will make them one flock with one shepherd," "I will cause the nations to come to Zion with thanksgiving," and so forth.[101] In the new covenant, as an administration of the Abrahamic covenant, God is the partner bearing ultimate responsibility for this treaty.

Bringing together the soteriological criterion raised by Thiemann and others, as well as this covenantal structure, it should be beyond doubt that the people of God are constituted such by the covenant, not vice versa. To say that the community creates the canon is tantamount to saying that it also creates the covenant. Such a view would seem to approach the height of institutional hubris and represent yet another version of modern Pelagianism.[102] After recounting the divine prevenience and initiative in election, redemption, and renewal, Paul writes, "So then you are no longer strangers and aliens, but you are citizens with the saints and also members of the household of God, built upon the foundation of the apostles and prophets, with Christ Jesus himself as the cornerstone" (Eph. 2:19–20). Gentiles are no longer outsiders, but insiders—not because they are Gentiles, but because they are united to Christ through faith. They belong to "the household of God." And Jews are related on the same basis (Gal. 3:29).

So belonging is not a matter of being individuals having an encounter or experience with God, apart from belonging to that visible household. Nevertheless, the house itself is "built upon the foundation of the apostles and prophets, with Christ Jesus himself as the cornerstone." What is that foundation of apostles and prophets, centering on Christ, but the entire word of God written? In fact, Paul invoked the slogan "Nothing beyond what is written," even while the apostolic era had not yet been drawn to a close (1 Cor. 4:6). As in the old covenant, God founds the redeemed community not only on divine events that are then dependent on the covenant community for their meaning, but on divine events that are divinely interpreted by divine speech. The church is built on the foundation of the scripture-covenant.

We have already observed the inextricable link between canon and covenant. Drawing on parallels in ancient Near Eastern politics, M. G. Kline takes this a step further, arguing that scripture functions in both testaments as a "house-building instrument" for God. He writes,

> As word of power, Scripture finds a prototype in the original, creation house-building of God. The divine creative fiats were God's effectual architectural utterances by which he actually produced and actively manipulated ultimate materials—light, life, and spirit—so fashioning his creation house. Similarly, the Scriptural word of God effectually wielded by the Spirit is the fiat of God's new creation. . . . So employed by the Spirit, Scripture is architectural fiat. . . . Inasmuch, then, as canonical Scripture is God's house-building word, the community rule for his covenant people, the Reformation insistence is confirmed that the Scriptures form the church, and not vice versa.[103]

While it is true, of course, that in human relations such instruments emerge out of communal initiative and a sense of a particular people's experience—their fears, longings, and assumptions about what constitutes "life, liberty and the pursuit of happiness," for example—this covenant is delivered to the community by the *divine* partner in the arrangement. It is not a social contract or a covenant "of the people, by the people, and for the people." Paul emphasizes that Abraham received justification and partnership in the covenant, not that he generated it. He, after all, had been an idolater in Ur. Furthermore, Israel was reminded that it was "a chosen people" not because of its righteousness, but because of God's covenantal promise to Abraham (Deut. 7:7–11). If this is true of Abraham, then it is certainly true of the community founded on God's covenant with him and his messianic seed. The church never ceases being a *sum-*

moned community, founded and funded by another. It can never become its own foundation.

But if it is true that scripture (as covenant treaty) gives rise to the church (as covenant people) and not vice versa, it is just as true that scripture is prior to the individual. While the community did not create its own canon, the canon was received by the community and was produced within it, and apart from this community there could not even be something called a canon, since "canon" is a context-dependent entity. Kline adds to his point above that "traditional formulations of the canon doctrine have not done full justice to the role of the community":

> The community is inextricably bound up in the reality of canonical Scripture. The concept of covenant-canon requires a covenant community. Though the community does not confer canonical authority on the Scriptures, Scripture in the form of constitutional treaty implies the community constituted by it and existing under its authority. Canonical authority is not derived from community, but covenant canon connotes covenantal community.[104]

From this standpoint, one does not have to choose between the one and the many. With the Trinity as an apt analogy, the church's existence is plurality in unity and unity in plurality. Further, it is neither the individual (radicalized in Kierkegaard) nor the community (radicalized in Hegel) that founds this monarchy, but Yahweh. There can be no legitimate use of the canon (treaty) in isolation from the visible community founded by Christ as Covenant Lord (Suzerain), just as there can be no legitimate use of scripture when the community supplements the treaty or by its response ignores or silences any part of it. After the closing of the canon, the community is never more than a witness to divine speech and action.

The covenant motif must not only show its relationship to canon and community; it must indicate the connection, so fragmented again in our day, between Word and Spirit.

Calvin's well-known appeal to the *testimonium Spiritus Sancti* underscores the necessity of illumination, and on this point the reformer is simply echoing Augustine's notion of the "inner teacher." Without the Spirit's activity, the meaning or sense of a biblical text may be grasped but not generate the genuine understanding that comes with faith. At the same time, the Spirit is not a secondary source for divine revelation in addition to scripture, but the latter's author as well as illuminator. The canon is revelation regardless of a given person's response, but it can only be recognized as such through the event of illumination. This classical distinction circumvents many of the inner contradictions often involved in, for instance, dialectical theology's reduction of revelation to an immediate encounter. Thus, as we will see, the inner testimony of the Spirit is hardly something alongside the Word, but is effected from within the Word. "Therefore," Calvin notes, "the Spirit promised to us has not the task of inventing new and unheard-of revelations, or of forging a new kind of doctrine, to lead us away from the received doctrine of the gospel, but of sealing our minds with that very doctrine which is commended by the gospel."[105] The Spirit's speaking is always the speaking of scripture.

Reformation emphasis on this important role of the Holy Spirit emerges despite the Reformers' sharp criticism of the so-called *Schwärmerei* ("enthusiasts"). It was not the case that the Spirit grants a certitude that the scriptures are the very word of God apart from the message. Rather, their conviction was that the work of the Spirit unites us to Christ, the *res* of scripture, so that we inevitably hear the voice of mere mortals *as* the voice of the Shepherd himself. Scripture is not self-authenticating prior to faith or the Christian life, but is such only within that context. It is therefore not an abstract theory that would guarantee, a priori, the certainty of scripture, but simply underscores the fact that the Spirit and the Word are united in delivering Christ, since "faith comes by hearing."[106] The witness of the Spirit and the witness of scripture agree in their source (the Trinity) and in their substance (Christ and all his benefits). The former is the internal, the latter the external, source of certainty in God's promise. Herman Bavinck observes that "our belief in Scripture decreases and increases together with our trust in Christ."[107] A doctrine of scripture that can be articulated or formulated apart from the content or message of scripture shares uncomfortable affinities with Jesus' critics who "search the scriptures because [they] think that in them [they] have eternal life; yet it is they that testify on my behalf. Yet you refuse to come to me to have life" (John 5:39). The so-called formal principle (*sola scriptura*) cannot be established apart from the material principle (*solus Christus*).

Berkouwer emphasizes that this certainty derived from the testimony of the Spirit is inseparable from Christ as the message and faith. "The Spirit's witness begins by binding us to the center of Scripture, namely, Jesus Christ."[108] It is the faith-generating promise of God in scripture (especially in preaching) that the Spirit makes effective. "When one is in contact with Holy Scripture, the testimony of the Spirit shows him as the sinner and shows the marvelous way of deliverance."[109] A number of New Testament passages support this view, keeping together the letter and the Spirit, so that the church does not have to choose between enthusiasm and dead orthodoxy.[110]

So we must not formalize this notion into a theory for establishing the certainty of scripture that is abstracted from the concrete reality of being confronted with the speaking God in judgment and justification. Berkouwer is correct: "The powerful operation of the testimony of the Spirit centers in the salvation that has appeared in Christ."[111] In this connection Calvin writes, "This, then, is the true knowledge of Christ, if we receive him as he is offered by the Father: namely, clothed with his gospel. For just as he has been appointed as the goal of our faith, so we cannot take the right road to him unless the gospel goes before us."[112] Calvin's view of this testimony as more certain than all reason is hardly mystical. It is not a higher *gnosis* that he advocates, since the Spirit is adding nothing formally to the content. Rather, he is contrasting personal knowledge with mere speculation or observation. Knowing one's spouse is a more certain species of knowing than, for instance, knowing the genetic and chemical composition of that person's body.

We could also compare the relation of Word and Spirit to sacrament and Spirit. The sacrament, whether baptism or the Supper, retains its essence regardless of faith. One is truly baptized even where genuine faith never receives that which is promised in that divine act. Apart from the Spirit, one still receives the *signum*, though not the *res significata*. The Spirit's role is not to confer some content apart from Christ or the written and preached word, but to give the thing signified along with the sign. So too, apart from the Spirit's work, the Word remains the Word: its meaning is already determined. The Spirit's role is to give hearers the *res* through the *signum*—not to supplement the Word of God, but to render that word effective.

Faced with a new era in which there is a widespread suspicion that texts in general are opaque, wholly undetermined, and susceptible to an infinite range of interpretations, many contemporary theologians and other scholars have been attracted to either the Holy Spirit or the church as alternative sources or safeguards for certainty that God has spoken and certainty concerning that which God has said. How do we navigate then between "enthusiasm" and "dogmatism"? That is the question to which we now turn.

1. Enthusiasm

Paul says that he and his fellow apostles are "ministers of a new covenant, not of letter but of spirit; for the letter kills, but the Spirit gives life" (2 Cor. 3:6). This contrast between the deadly letter and the vivifying Spirit has often been interpreted to mean that scripture belongs to a category of law, rationality, final truths, dogmatism, and other ostensibly horrible things, while "spirit" (not even necessarily the Holy Spirit, but "spirit" as an ontological universal) represents freedom, flexibility, spontaneity, and love. Such an antithesis between written scripture and "spirit" or "the Spirit" is prominent in Gnosticism ancient and modern (and postmodern) and its peculiarly domestic variety that Harold Bloom summarizes in his book *The American Religion*.[113] Due in part to a reaction against higher criticism and a growing appreciation for reader-response theory, there has arisen a fresh insistence on "pneumatic" exegesis that bears at least superficial similarities to those revolutionary groups of the so-called Radical Reformation.

Regardless of the pedigree of this new excitement surrounding the spiritual over literal meaning of scripture, the radically historical, covenantal, nonspeculative, and soteriological orientation of biblical theology cannot be assimilated. But, as we have noted, much of historical criticism has been built on a foundation of ontological dualism. If theology posits a *principium essendi* that is the basis for its *principium cognoscendi*, there is a direct ontological refutation for any and every epistemological dualism. "The *Logos* became flesh" is the astonishing announcement that the noumenal became phenomenal. Here is the *principium essendi* for the view that the words of scripture (flesh) are not merely the occasional instrument or medium of pure ideas (spirit), but that God's words are themselves lifegiving. While its failures, when settling down in the Platonic chasm, are serious and deep, orthodox Christianity has nevertheless been battling such ontological dualism repeatedly, especially against the medieval sects, Renaissance Neoplatonists, radical Anabaptist "enthusiasts," some extreme pietists, American revivalists, and Pentecostals. This gnostic tendency has been evident not only on the extreme margins, but within much of modern theology.

Ireneaus faced precisely this issue with the gnostics, as the Jesus of history was identified with "the letter [that] kills" and the Christ of faith was identified with "the Spirit [that] gives life."[114] One example of this will suffice from the Reformation period, especially as it is related to the debate over the use of Paul's declaration that "the letter kills, but the Spirit gives life" (2 Cor. 3:6).

This debate between the Reformers and the "enthusiasts" or "fanatics" (obviously, epithets selected by the Reformers themselves) revolved around this very ontological dualism that we have traced to the Platonist trajectory. Luther warned against those in his day who were "swarming everywhere, . . . regarding Scripture as a dead letter, extolling nothing but the Spirit and yet keeping neither the Word nor the Spirit."

> But Scripture is not pure spirit, as they sputter that the Spirit alone must do it, that Scripture is a dead letter and can give no life. But it is like this: Although the letter does not in and of itself give life, yet it must be there, must be heard and received, and the Holy Spirit must work through it in the heart, . . . for if it were to let the Word go, it would soon entirely lose Christ and the Spirit. Therefore you had better not boast much about the Spirit if you do not have the visible, external Word.

Ironically, the medieval magisterium and the radical sects shared a common presupposition: namely, that scripture is opaque. From that point, they of course took entirely different directions, the former strengthening its confidence in the perspicuity and authority of the Spirit working through the magisterium, while the latter tended to rely on the perspicuity and authority of the Spirit working in the ecstatic community, often through prophets. In both cases, postcanonical *revelation*—and not just *illumination*—was possible and in fact expected. "For of late," Calvin complained, "certain giddy men have arisen who, with great haughtiness exalting the teaching office of the Spirit, despise all reading and laugh at the simplicity of those who, as they express it, still follow the dead and killing letter." As the body is to the soul, so the word of God is to the Spirit, says Calvin. "Hence we conclude that by a heinous sacrilege these rascals tear apart those things which the prophet joined together with an inviolable bond."[115]

What then did Paul mean by the letter that kills versus the life-giving Spirit? It is certainly not an ontological antithesis. Rather, the apostle is criticizing those who, relying on their own obedience to the law rather than on Christ, refuse to enjoy the fulfillment of Jeremiah's prophecy, namely, that in the new covenant, the Spirit would engrave God's word on the hearts of believers.[116] "The letter, therefore, is dead, and the law of the Lord slays its readers where it is cut off from

Christ's grace and, leaving the heart untouched, sounds in the ears alone. But if through the Spirit it is really branded on our hearts, if it shows forth Christ, it is the word of life."[117] Thus, "letter" is not equivalent to the text itself, but to the law without the gospel and the command without Christ and the Holy Spirit. These attempts to correct misunderstandings were carried forward into the confessional writings.[118]

A redemptive-historical, rather than philosophical, exegesis of "letter" and "Spirit" is required. "Letter" and "Spirit" are no more static ontological categories than are "flesh" and "Spirit" ("this present evil age" as it is dominated by human striving, in contrast to the age of the Spirit as the in-breaking of "the age to come" in this age, one day to be consummated).[119] Thus, one cannot legitimately set up from this passage an antithesis between scripture and a spiritual kernel of some sort hidden within the husk.

Word and Spirit are divided in contemporary theology at least as often as was the case in early modern "enthusiasm." More in its popular piety than in its works of theology, many varieties of contemporary American evangelicalism and Pentecostalism represent this type as much as many liberal Protestants who have leaned heavily on the Spirit's leading over the "letter" of scripture concerning specific beliefs and practices. Gabriel Fackre points to the secularity of this kind of conservative Protestantism: "'Born-again' evangelical piety regularly succumbs to reductionism and is a showcase of the allurements of interiority. Thus the preoccupation with 'my story' can obscure the other chapters of the Great Story. Pietist and revivalist traditions, stressing the centrality of personal decision, are tempted to reduce the revelatory narrative to the moment of conversion." Fackre cites examples from "gospel songs." The "Grand Narrative of both reconciliation and revelation" can easily become submerged in subjective piety. "But the understanding of God as the Giver of enriching soteric and noetic experiences—therapeutic, 'enthusiastic' and even financial—needs to be held accountable to the biblical Grand Narrative."[120]

Across the conservative-liberal spectrum, then, the Spirit's activity in one's interior experience often takes precedence over the preached word; some evangelical church growth leaders even suggest, simply on the basis of demographical analysis, that the message and even the medium of preaching itself may need to be set aside in favor of more attractive features. The Spirit's work is viewed as independent of formal means prescribed in the covenant canon. Like the revivalists of the recent past, marketing executives tend to shape evangelical identity today more than theologians or denominations. Probably without intending to sound like a reader-response theorist, evangelical George Barna nevertheless insists, "It is critical that we keep in mind a fundamental principle of Christian communication: the audience, not the message, is sovereign."[121] Yet few evangelical theologians seem to regard the transformation of the church from a covenant community into a commodity community (Brueggeman's insightful contrast) as a serious threat, despite the fact that this direction is more radical, for instance, than Paul Tillich's method of correlation. The role of later pietism in the evolution of the old liberal theology should remind us that concentration on the inner self and divine immanence in personal experience is not a temptation of only theologians of the left.

While hardly fitting that description, even Pannenberg appeals to the Pauline "letter"/"Spirit" contrast in an effort to distinguish, or rather to separate, the *res* of scripture from scripture itself (the *signum*). Even the Old Testament scriptures "were considered by the church to be divinely inspired, because they witnessed to the gospel of Jesus Christ, not in their function as 'letter of the law' but in their function as prophetic Scripture (*graphe*)."[122]

But more extreme examples abound. For instance, Edgar V. McKnight has recently defended reader-oriented hermeneutics as a retrieval of his heritage in the Radical Reformation.[123] Kevin Vanhoozer has pointed out the tendency not only among radical theorists to regard the Spirit as "some kind of Derridean supplement that adds to or improves upon the written Word."[124] For Richard Hays and Stanley Hauerwas, for instance, "Only a prayerful reading that invokes the Spirit can perceive the true meaning in what is otherwise a dead letter."[125] Responding to Hauerwas's claim that there is no "real meaning" in the text, but only, as Hauerwas puts it, "that use to which I put these texts for the upbuilding of the Church," Vanhoozer states, "The question that such an approach raises is both important and troubling: How can the church know what God is saying through Scripture if what God is saying fails to coincide with the verbal meaning of the text?"[126] So the locus of authority moves from the text to the community of interpretation and therefore from the treaty itself to the pragmatic preferences of the people. Divine sovereignty and initiative are then easily, if unwittingly, undermined. But aside from theological questions, is this not to simply multiply hermeneutical difficulties? After all, if a single canon cannot yield a coherent message, is it any more likely that one will discover "meaning" in myriad ecclesiastical interpretations that are, after all, just other texts? Whose community, which interpretation?[127]

Interestingly, just as Calvin observed an ironic similarity between the Radical Reformers' "enthusiasm" and the medieval church's appeal to charismatic authority resident in the magisterium, many today who embrace reader-response criticism avoid the sovereign *self* to which such theory tends by turning to a sovereign *community*. Just as both sixteenth-century groups appealed to allegorical interpretation,[128] multiple-sense interpretation dominates much of poststructuralist theory. Both "enthusiasts" and "traditionalists" in the Reformation debate tended to regard the Spirit as an alternative source, a "word" above the word. And in the same way, much of modern theology (*especially* Protestant theology) has turned repeatedly to "what the Spirit is saying to us today" while neglecting or in many cases rejecting rather significant sections of scripture. This done, one can either turn to his or her own inner light or to an authoritative magisterium.

But here the ironies recede, as the "enthusiast" eschewed tradition and dogma, while the medieval church emphasized both. The Reformers were hardly critical of tradition and dogma per se. A cursory perusal of the source index to the Battles/McNeill edition of the *Institutes* is one of many evidences of the dependence of

Calvin on patristic and medieval exegesis. Further, Calvin criticizes the Anabaptists for this reason repeatedly. As Willem Balke points out,

> Behind the Anabaptist concentration on purity of life and their
> determination to live close to Scripture there lay an aversion to dog-
> matism. Calvin insisted that anyone who wanted to go back to the
> Bible while rejecting dogmatic theology should not be so naïve as to
> ignore the record of history. Calvin therefore charged that the
> Anabaptists broke the *consensus interpretationis* with the Church
> Fathers. Their biblicism and lack of doctrinal concern was therefore
> the trapdoor that opened upon purity of doctrine.[129]

As we have noted, Hauerwas and many others have turned to the church/
community as normative by making a straw man of *sola scriptura*. Robert Louis
Wilken is correct to insist that this Reformation notion is "an ecclesiastical principle." "The reformers assumed that the Bible was a Christian book, that it was
divinely inspired, and that it ought to be understood and interpreted in relation
to the Church's creeds, worship, sacraments, and moral codes."[130] It was largely
pietism and rationalism that reacted against this communally oriented reading,
hearing, and living of the scriptures that was practiced by the Reformers and their
scholastic successors. They would have had almost no frame of reference for the
suggestion that individual Christians could (much less should) interpret the Bible
by themselves "in a corner." That which writers such as Hauerwas attribute to
the Reformation is more accurately attributed to enthusiasm.

The problem with the "enthusiast" position then is (a) its tendency to separate Word and Spirit; (b) its use of allegorical interpretations in the passion for
personal/individual application and exhortation; (c) a biblicism that is motivated
by a Donatist ecclesiology in which the ecclesiola (or even the individual) is considered a pure remnant of an apostate whole. Much of this was exacerbated by
political factors, particularly the terrible persecution Anabaptists experienced at
the hands of Roman Catholic and Protestant alike.

2. Dogmatism

The hermeneutical spiral, interpreting the parts in the light of the whole and vice
versa, is at the heart of Reformation exegesis; as it is practiced, it necessarily results
in a synthesis (i.e., system), parsed in biblical-theological and systematic-theological
conclusions. To emphasize the parts at the expense of the whole inevitably leads
to biblicism; to emphasize the whole at the expense of the parts leads to dogmatism. The Reformers were convinced that the radicals were guilty of the former,
Rome of the latter. While "dogmatism" is often in the eyes of the beholder (even
a little dogma is too much for some), it was at least the stated aim of the Reformers to restrain curiosity and speculation, content to stop theologizing when they
ran out of textual ground beneath them. According to Calvin, Christians should
not be interested in "that knowledge which, content with empty speculation,
merely flits in the brain, but that which will be sound and fruitful if we duly perceive it, and if it takes root in the heart."

> Consequently, we know the most perfect way of seeking God, and
> the most suitable order, is not for us to attempt with bold curiosity
> to penetrate to the investigation of his essence, which we ought more
> to adore than meticulously to search out, but for us to contemplate
> him in his works whereby he renders himself near and familiar to us,
> and in some manner communicates himself.[131]

Thus *sola scriptura* was not *scriptura solum*. While scripture was regarded as the only norm without any norms, the Reformers and their successors were not under any illusion about freeing themselves of communal interpretations. They recognized the difference between text and interpretation. Not only were the ecumenical creeds integrally related to the catechetical and liturgical existence of these churches; through the enormous rise of lay familiarity with the creeds and the new evangelical confessions and catechisms, the Counter-Reformation itself called for renewed attention to communal forms of life.

While it would be hermeneutically naive to think that depending on scripture means that one is no longer accountable to tradition (since it is an ineluctable reality in any case), it is also true, at least according to the covenantal model we are proposing, that the *sensus communis* arises out of the *sensus literalis* rather than vice versa. We are, as a Christian community, clear, plain, and united in our confession to the degree that we have together perceived the clarity, particularity, and unity of what we have heard. While interpreters such as Stanley Hauerwas deny to scripture this sort of clarity, unity, and sense, they seem to regard "the church" or "tradition" with as much hermeneutical naïveté as they impute to biblicists.[132] Though beyond the scope of this work, it would be interesting to compare and contrast the biblical canon on this point with centuries of ecclesiastical decisions, not only in the Roman Catholic communion, but in Orthodoxy and Protestantism as well. For some communions, as in rabbinical midrash, the sacred tradition "closes" the gap between text and interpreter. But does it? Or does it just create *more* texts to be interpreted?

Finally, there is the eschatological critique of "dogmatism." Viewed from this perspective, the notion of a living tradition that bears charismatic authority is both an underrealized and an overrealized eschatology. It is underrealized because it does not sufficiently recognize the definitive and epochal nature of the apostolic era and it is overrealized to the extent that it erases any distinction between text and interpretation. Ironically, this happens frequently (though less formally) in conservative Protestant circles as well as in "high church" bodies, when one's own exegesis is taken to be identical with scripture while that of others is regarded as mere interpretation. And this erasure is commended in radical literary theory also. Borrowing on the latter, Hauerwas declares, "When *sola scriptura* is used to underwrite the distinction between text and interpretation, then it seems clear to me that *sola scriptura* is a heresy rather than a help in the Church."[133]

This perspective has obviously had considerable support outside of Western Christianity. For instance, Orthodox theologian Georges Florovsky writes that the church's interpretations are endowed with "charismatic authority, grounded in the assistance of the Spirit: *for it seemed good to the Holy Spirit and to us.*"[134] But what does the apostle mean when he justifies this particular action on the basis that "it seemed good to the Holy Spirit and to us"? Who is "us," and is this a contextually defined group (viz., apostles), or is it broader (viz., Orthodox patriarchs)? As with the question of holy wars and holy nations, interpretation must take account here of the place of this passage within redemptive history. Florovsky uses this text as a timeless truth, a formula that can be invoked in all times and places, as others have used land-promises specifically given to Israel within a particular historical context as timeless and universal offers for one's own nation to be a privileged society. Such hermeneutical generalizing ignores just what it is in a given instance that God is commanding or promising and to whom. In other words, it ignores the redemptive-historical location of the covenant and its administration. It is at least interesting that in the Old Testament, "tradition" is generally viewed positively, referring to the faith and practice handed down to the children from their parents, while in the Gospels, Jesus refers to tradition pejoratively in every context. In fact, it is by the rabbinical traditions that scripture itself is silenced (cf. Matt. 15:6).

Only when we come to the epistles do we pick up again on the positive reference to "tradition." Paul warns believers not to be led astray by those who do not follow "the tradition which they received from us" (2 Thess. 3:6). "Therefore," Paul exhorts, "stand firm and hold fast to the traditions that you were taught by us, either by word of mouth or by our letter" (2 Thess. 2:15). These are the two chief passages on "tradition" in the New Testament and, again, the only two positive examples. But these two examples certainly are positive. What is important about them both is that neither is open to a timeless interpretation. In other words, there is no abstract principle here for building the notion of a charismatic authority that is being exercised today, when there are in fact no apostles. As we have argued, the church is founded on the prophets and apostles. Elsewhere, Paul says that it is Jesus who is the foundation laid by the apostles. Regardless, the point is the same, since the apostolic foundation is the apostolic message. There is no other foundation that *can* be laid, Paul emphasizes (1 Cor. 3:11).

In other words, "the tradition" is not something in addition to the written word of the apostles, but is precisely that word before its inscripturization. Paul clearly limits his reference to "the traditions that you were taught by us, either by *word of mouth* or by *our letter.*" There is no suggestion of a general, evolving, living tradition to be observed after the apostles, but of an epochal ministry of apostles who, like prophets, have their words confirmed as divinely authorized by accompanying signs. Once the foundation of the prophets and apostles is laid, the charismatic ministry ends, and the ordinary ministry of Word and sacrament is built on this foundation. By virtue of its apostolic preaching, the church is then itself endowed with charismatic authority.

As with the hermeneutical spiral, there is another dialectic that must never rest in any synthesis prior to the eschaton: the dialectic between what we might call founding and funding. The church is the interpretive context only to the extent that it is formed by the Word. The Word charters, founds, and refounds the church. The church must constantly renew that charter and reassess its fidelity to it. It is a lease, not an ownership. "Not all who are of Israel are Israel." The covenant bars all jingoism and smug confidence in belonging to the right group. In fact, each legitimate gathering of the summoned community is a divinely constituted covenant renewal ceremony.

In some groups, there is a tendency to think that the community owns the Word and Spirit, or at least that the material principle of scripture itself is the church: *Interpretations* as well as *texts* are divinely inspired and are rightly done and understood by our group.[135] The distinction between text and interpretation becomes blurred indeed. It is not only individual readers, but communal readers who are capable of violence to the other, of presuming to know the author of scripture better than that author has in fact revealed, of claiming interpretive superiority not only because of rigorous skill in exegesis, philology, dogmatics, and the like, but because of a supernatural gift of the Spirit that renders its exegesis infallible.[136] If a church succumbs to the temptation of reducing the other to itself, this violence is destructive of its very identity and legitimacy. The "summons" element is retained only if the word-canon is external not only to the individual but to the church, that is, if the church, instead of finding her decisions and actions "rubber-stamped," finds herself scrutinized, unsettled, disturbed—that is to say, *addressed*. This is why Reformed theology has generally resisted formalistic theories of the canon.[137]

The principle that the Spirit works through the Word, and not outside of it, is axiomatic for a model that is covenantally determined and eschatologically sensitive to the decisive conclusion of the apostolic era. By recognizing its eschatological horizon, such a model should be tempted neither by arrogance nor paralyzing ambiguity. In response to both modern "enthusiasm" and "dogmatism," we would insist upon that opening announcement of the writer to the Hebrews: "Long ago God spoke to our ancestors in many and various ways by the prophets, but in these last days he has spoken to us by a Son." The testimony of the prophets and the apostles is sufficient to place the floodlights of revelation on this other who both speaks God's words and is God's speech.

What is the Word but law and gospel; command and promise? And given the link between covenant and canon, is it possible to say that the unfaithful human partner determines what God did and did not say? Or is it rather the case that, with clear criteria for determining authorship and authenticity, the church recognized which writings were generated by the Holy Spirit through the apostles? At the end of the day, however, the most important criticism one could offer in response to the idea that the community creates the meaning of scripture (if not scripture itself in terms of canonical formation) is that it threatens the prevenience of divine grace. Again Calvin turns our attention to the question of certainty—not general epistemological certitude, nor merely a doctrine of biblical authority, but certainty of God's promise: "[W]hat will happen to miserable consciences seeking firm assurance of eternal life if all promises of it consist in and depend solely upon the judgment of men? Will they cease to vacillate and tremble when they receive such an answer?"[138]

To summarize thus far, then, our account of the canon as covenantal treaty affirms the priority of God, the character of the canon as divine summons, and the inseparable unity of Word and Spirit in founding and forming a faithful community around the substance of the covenant, Jesus Christ and all his benefits. We have offered this as an alternative to models that would reverse the priority of canon and community, as well as to those that would imply a retreat from the communal reading and hearing of scripture into interiority and individualism. Furthermore, we have rejected the canon-within-a-canon approach, which we believe to be inherently schismatic and sectarian, in favor of the ecumenical perspective, witnessed to by the scriptures themselves, that there is a meaning in the text external to an individual's or community's religious consciousness, that can be discerned by careful reading and hearing together in patient discipleship. But this assumption rests on the *eschatological* horizon that scripture projects, a horizon of hope, of trust in the Promise.

Chapter Eight

Reintegrating the Rhetoric of Redemption

For a variety of reasons, theology has become increasingly fragmented, as everyone now knows. Overspecialization may be one way of describing it, but the fragmentation of biblical and theological studies in the academy has had far-reaching implications for the people in the pew. Furthermore, there seems to be a conflict, not only between scholars of various stripes, but within each theologian, over doing theology when one really doubts its intrasystematic foundations. As part of a growing chorus, Francis Watson has registered his anxiety about this increasing polarization and atomization within disciplines related to theology:

> First, the situation exactly mirrors the enforced privatization of religious commitment in modern western societies. Religious commitment is tolerated only in so far as it accepts its exclusion from the realm of properly public discourse. . . . Second, it is believed that theological concerns have an inevitable tendency to distort the autonomous processes of biblical exegesis—a prejudice so strong that to identify a theological motivation underlying an exegetical position is often held to be sufficient refutation. Third, there is an unwillingness to accept the existence and the significance of theology as a discipline in its own right.[1]

In this situation, biblical scholars may tend to think of themselves as working with primary texts, while theologians may fancy themselves too philosophically sophisticated to create their own system with direct dependence on explicit exegesis. Systematic theologians are (or at least used to be) accused of proof-texting, while biblical scholars are accused of naïveté. G. E. Wright expresses the general sentiment of biblical theologians and biblical scholars when he judges that traditional "propositional" dogmatics "lacks the colour, the flexibility, the movement of the Bible" and "attempts to freeze into definite, prosaic, rationality that which was never intended by the Bible to be so frozen." He cites his own Westminster Confession in its chapter on God. "By its cold, abstract and tight nature such a definition of God somehow separates us from his living, active and warm Presence which we come to know by contemplation of what he has done and by seeing ourselves as the recipients of his gracious work."[2] Furthermore, "theology must always beware of the scholastic tendency to become unhistorical."[3]

On one level, Wright's point is well-taken. To the extent that system building has replaced other essential disciplines in theology (biblical, exegetical, ethical, historical), the entire enterprise has been impoverished, and the credibility of systematics has suffered for unsuccessfully bearing an impossible weight. It is certainly true that the method of systematic theology is largely discursive—more like a street map than a topographical map. The goal here is to see logical relations more than to exhibit the dynamic instances in which their definitive events come to the historical stage. But Wright's criticism, which is widely held across the theological spectrum in our day, fails to appreciate the distinct operations of biblical and systematic theology, the former unfolding redemptive revelation sequentially, underscoring its organic development in history, the latter seeking to recognize the coherence of Christian assertions that arise in the course of this development. Beyond this failure to appreciate the distinctive contributions of each subdiscipline and its concomitant method, contemporary biblical scholarship is often influenced by a biblicism that undervalues the systematic, philosophical, and historical aspects. Watson points to a certain (frequently evangelical) interpretation of *sola scriptura* that sunders biblical interpretation from wider fields of input upon which theology has traditionally depended to aid in exegesis. This popular interpretation is quite unlike the classical Protestant doctrine of *sola scriptura*; nevertheless, it is pervasive in biblical studies:

> When one has the Bible, what need is there for subtleties and sophistries of theology? In evangelical Christianity, the Bible is typically read with scant regard for the long and intricate dialogue with the Bible that is the history of Christian theology. Many (most?) Protestant biblical scholars are attracted to the field in the first place by an evangelical piety of this kind, and—whatever else is abandoned under the notoriously destructive impact of the so-called "historical-critical method"—the abstraction of the biblical texts from their theological *Wirkungsgeschichte* is tenaciously maintained.[4]

Whatever the causes, it is quite possible these days for a biblical theologian or Old Testament/New Testament scholar to remain ignorant of the history and substance of dogmatics, while systematicians often get away with paying scant attention to exegesis, sometimes turning to the deliverances of a particular philosophical school as the new method of proof-texting ("The Theology of . . ."). Whatever one makes of the great systems of the ancient, medieval, and early modern eras, they display a rigorous attention to integrating those threads that in our day seem hopelessly tangled or separated.

As we have argued earlier, biblicism tends to miss the forest for the trees, while dogmatism misses the trees for the forest. In this chapter we want to make a case for reintegrating the fragmented discipline of theology. The reintegration of exegesis and systematics itself requires subordinate moves: under the exegetical side, reintegration of history and eschatology, word and act, and Old and New Testaments; under the systematics side, the reintegration of biblical and systematic theology, the *fides qua creditur* and the *fides quae creditur*, and faith and practice. So it is to this task that we now turn in the application of our model.

EXEGESIS

1. Eschatological–Historical

As Carl Braaten pointed out, much of modern theology demands that one choose between the historical and the eschatological.[5] Even when both are affirmed, they are often treated as if they lie side by side, as if fully integrating them might lead to a combustible mixture.

In the model we are proposing, eschatology provides the vertical corollary for the horizontal line of history. In other words, redemptive history not only moves forward, that is, through history, but advances by being acted upon "from above." This is not due, as Pannenberg and Moltmann imply, to the antitheses of gnostic intrusion and apocalyptic progress synthesized in Christian eschatology. That is to draw on alien categories when the historical-eschatological structure is already intrinsic to the narrative and even when borrowing on such categories subversively reinterprets them. Nor, given our penchant for analogical hermeneutics, do we ignore that fact that such references to "above" and "below," which so occupied Bultmann, are self-conscious anthropomorphisms of the biblical writers. These biblical authors clearly affirm that God is omnipresent spirit, so they can hardly be interested in confining God to an ostensibly geographical precinct. They recognized, as we should, that these terms refer analogically to God's holiness—that is, to the creator-creature distinction and to the ethical "proximity" of a holy God to unholy people. Demythologization would only be necessary if we were to take these statements more univocally or literalistically than the authors did themselves.

It is in that sense that eschatology is "vertical" in its dimension. It is similarly analogical to say that such divine action is an "irruption" or "intrusion."[6] While such terms have their own problems, they serve to contrast biblical eschatology with a Hegelian (immanentistic) teleology. The ordinary course of history would not yield a redemptive interpretation. As Moltmann correctly reminds us, "The mysteries of the 'End-time' and of God's future new world are veiled and impenetrable under our present conditions of knowledge, because the present world of sin and violence cannot sustain the new world of God's justice and righteousness." He adds:

If we look at Christ's resurrection from the standpoint of this modern paradigm "history," using the categories of the modern historical mind, then—in spite of all the disputes—it makes no great
difference whether we see the resurrection as a product of the disciples' imagination, or view it as a historical fact; for as a past event that
is becoming ever more past and ever more remote, Christ's resurrection can neither determine the present nor have any relevance for the
future. The modern category "history" has already turned the happening into something past and gone; for anything historical is something that comes to pass, and then passes away.[7]

Christian theology cannot simply correlate its message to the interests of "history" apart from recognizing the presuppositions of modern historical method,
according to which redemptive events or divine actions are either irrelevant or
impossible. History would be a sufficient category if reality were merely the
unfolding of an immanent telos. Yet, as Moltmann emphasizes, the reality of the
presence of "the age to come" here and now is contradicted by our experience "in
this present age." We proclaim as a present reality the "new creation" of which
Jesus Christ is the firstfruits, and yet we cannot point to the present state of the
world or any part of it (including the church) and indicate univocally what this
means. This fuels the now–not yet dialectic in our own Christian experience and
activity. Capable neither of resting nor of waiting, we are driven by the historical
fulfillment and the eschatological hope to act in the liminal space in which faith,
hope, and love are simultaneously inflamed and threatened.

To render this language univocal is precisely what was accomplished in
Enlightenment deism. The assumption was that this phenomenal world is not
the product of God's constant providence, so that any divine action in history
was regarded as "miraculous." "God" became the answer to the gaps in the ever-
increasing data until finally the conclusion became obvious in Laplace's famous
declaration, "We have no need of that hypothesis."

Nevertheless, we should not be afraid of—in fact, we should now recover—
the analogical perspective of eschatology as a divine irruption into history. It is
not the intrusion of a foreign agent that is in view here, as if God were trespass-
ing on his own property. Rather, it is God acting in one way in the world (viz.,
miraculously), rather than in another, more common manner (viz., providentially). It is the former sort that is picked out by the terms, "eschatology" and
"irruption." It is the interruption of God's ordinary way of preserving the world
by his common grace, in specific cases, during specific times and among a specific people.[8]

It is this penetration of history from "above" that creates the three-dimensional
topography that would otherwise be flattened into a one-dimensional time line.
It is not the Future that is coming toward us, the past that we are reliving or reconstructing, or the Eternal Moment that meets us as a tangent in a uniquely individual address, but the New Jerusalem that is coming down out of heaven. It is
"the age that is to come" already dawning in Christus Victor and casting
its bright rays wherever the Word, the sacraments, and the Spirit conspire to

reconcile hostile enemies to God and to each other. Here, the spatial analogies "above" and "heavenly" indicate God's transcendence and "the age to come." In such events as public worship, eschatological inbreaking (though identified with the extraordinary or miraculous order belonging to heaven) is not only frequent but is promised by God as the ordinary expectation. This is how we are to understand the nature of the ministry and the keys: this is the meeting place of heaven and earth, the individual and the corporate body of Christ, the ordo salutis (systematic theology) and the historia salutis (biblical theology), this age and the age that is to come. Those within this sphere of the Spirit "have tasted the heavenly gift, and have shared in the Holy Spirit, and have tasted the goodness of the word of God and the powers of the age to come" (Heb. 6:4–5).

Thus, in Word and sacrament, through the power of the Holy Spirit, the eschaton breaks through into the present, in judgment and life. The Last Judgment is past, present, and future: one event in three "stages." The first (at the cross) is finished; the second is in process (in the proclamation that "the wrath of God is being revealed from heaven"); the third is future (second advent). In subjective justification, the past and future aspects of this one event are declared once and for all in the moment in which faith is first exercised. Furthermore, in the logic of Romans 6, the past of Christ's death is the present of our death, our Good Friday that is already being overcome by Easter. This unity is not allegorical but organic: Christ is "the firstfruits," and his past resurrection not merely ensures but initiates the present "harvest" that will make this single resurrection event complete only at the last day in the general resurrection. The resurrection of Jesus as "the firstfruits" of the whole harvest inaugurates the latter's resurrection in three stages: the inner person (new birth), the outer person (bodily resurrection), and the whole creation (consummation).[9] We proclaim this reality, says Paul, "because we know that the one who raised the Lord Jesus will raise us also with Jesus, and will bring us with you into his presence. . . . So we do not lose heart. Even though our outer nature is wasting away, our inward nature is being renewed day by day. For this slight momentary affliction is preparing us an eternal weight of glory beyond all measure" (2 Cor. 4:13–17).

The Pauline system cannot be adequately understood apart from this "trialectic," shifting attention back and forth among the three tenses of the eschatological horizon. Thus, the present activity of the Spirit involves the application not only of the work of Christ in the past, but the work of Christ in the future. Together, these points of origin define the work of Christ in the present, in the power of the Holy Spirit, to the glory of the Father. Otherwise, our soteriological topography will be utterly flat: that happened; this is happening, and one day that will happen. The familiar pattern, "I have been saved; I am being saved; I will be saved," is true enough as it stands, but fails to appreciate Paul's eschatological dynamism. God is doing in history and in our redemption right now what he has done and will do: both justification and sanctification derive their energy from this common source. Justification is the future verdict rendered in the present, sanctification the future reality of glorification begun in the present; the church the future kingdom experienced embryonically in this age.

Finally, we may say that this redemptive-historical model not only places soteriology (and therefore, Christology) front and center, but requires a monergistic principle. That is to say, while modern prolegomena tended to regard methodological questions as distinct from the content, our model maintains that all methodologies are determined already by theological assumptions. Just as one cannot develop a doctrine of scriptural authority, revelation, or canon that is abstracted from the content, Christ, one must necessarily be circular when one finally reaches one's final vocabulary.

So, for instance, rather than debating divine sovereignty and human freedom abstractly and philosophically, we would do better to observe the eschatological triumph of God's electing and redeeming purpose in the face of human rebellion, allowing the anxiety to lose itself (without fully resolving itself) in the action of the dramatic narrative. In this understanding, the "self" is the *imago Dei*. Rather than being in the position to construct our "selves," the redemptive-historical eschatology faces us with the selves that we are, in creation (made in God's image), the fall (the image defaced but not effaced), and in redemption (the image restored—"conformed to the likeness of Christ"). "Just as we have borne the image of the man of dust, we will also bear the image of the man of heaven" (1 Cor. 15:49). Selfhood viewed in terms of an eschatological ontology points us also to "the age to come" and the final redemption of the embodied self. In this "new age" into which we are baptized, the guilty self is justified, is being restored, and will be glorified. And this is guaranteed by Christ's resurrection and the active indwelling of the Spirit as the "pledge of our inheritance toward redemption as God's own people, to the praise of his glory" (Eph. 1:14). Modernity has taught us to construct our selves and, in protean fashion, continually refashion our selves, or depend on others to make and remake us. But in Christ we can escape this determinism and receive our self as his gift. "It does not yet appear what we shall be."

This model, then, guards against the tendency both to *identify* revelation with history in general (hyperimmanence) and to *separate* revelation from history (hypertranscendence). It is not the case that history and eschatology lie side by side, much less that they are antithetical poles determined, respectively, by Jewish apocalyptic and gnostic trajectories. Rather, both testaments show evidence of a unified understanding in which history is viewed eschatologically, while remaining history. History is not related to eschatology as fact is to value. Rather, history is the forward development of divine and human interaction, while eschatology is identified by vertical intrusions or irruptions of both word and deed. In the case of both history and eschatology, the parts must be interpreted in the light of the whole, and vice versa.

One implication is that the concept of revelation must not be allowed to be dehistoricized. For instance, revelation did not even belong to Israel as an ordinary phenomenon. It was not a "revelational community." While in the history of revelation some periods were more marked by revelatory events and speech, this should not be viewed simplistically, as if one were to cordon off a particularly active period as "revelational." But neither is historical development revelational. We must abandon any notion that locates the miraculous or revelational ontologically within historical categories as vigorously as we eschew the tendency to relocate these events to an unapproachable noumenal realm.

Revelation is subservient to redemption, involving specific divine acts. It is the authorized discourse itself that is "God-breathed" (theopneustos), not the personalities, the community or the age that produced them.[10] Even the apostolic age was not a period of revelation in general, but a period in which a greater density of specific acts of divine discourse occurred, for the purpose of unveiling the mystery of Christ. In fact, once again the centrality of the covenant motif appears, since fresh periods of signs and wonders are always heralds of new events in divine covenant making. That is why these signs cluster around particular redemptive-historical events. They are not chiefly intended to serve as general apologetics for divine existence, nor primarily to improve the lives of individuals, but are preeminently flares announcing an event or series of events that bear divine authority and significance for an unfolding drama. Church theology is therefore concerned with "the proclamation of Jesus Christ, according to the revelation of the mystery hidden for long ages past, but now revealed and made known through the prophetic writings by the command of the eternal God, so that all nations might believe and obey him—to the only wise God be glory forever through Jesus Christ" (Rom. 16:25–27).

It was certainly not as if everything Luke did or said in his *person* was divinely inspired or, for that matter, attributable to God. In fact, some of it may well have been erroneous. The disputes between apostles apparently settled by the Council of Jerusalem (Acts 15) frankly displays this fact. We have no greater stake in the certainty or indubitable reliability of the apostles themselves than the New Testament record itself attributes to them. It is not in their persons but in their covenantal office that they become agents of divine discourse. In the Synoptics, they appear as "slow to understand," prone to misunderstanding, and occasionally insightful, only to commit themselves to blunders later in the story. Even after the forty days of study in which Christ showed them how everything in the scriptures pointed to him, Luke does not hesitate to record both good and ill together as part of the apostles' ministry. And yet, it is this very text that claims divine authority for what came to be recognized as the canonical New Testament.

By attributing divine inspiration to the text and not to the authors themselves, we are less likely to see a great metaphysical chasm between ourselves and the authors, although the historical distanciation that would be present with any classical work remains. And, as Gadamer reminds us, it is precisely by embracing rather than attempting to circumvent that distance that we are actually able to understand. Just as we are too overwhelmed by prejudices that we ourselves do not recognize to be able to make judgments about our age—as well as those who will come after us many years hence—we are actually in a better position to read the texts than were the Christians of the first few centuries. We must avoid an Enlightenment model of progress that assumes our knowledge is better than theirs simply because "the education of the human race" has advanced so far. But we must also avoid Romanticism's inversion of that view of progress, as if the earlier we go, the more pristine the doctrine and church life. As the New Testament churches addressed by Paul clearly demonstrate, a primitivistic hermeneutic does not come to terms with the historicity, not to mention ecclesiastical embarrassments, of all periods.

One of the tendencies that unites diverse modern theologies is anthropocentrism, which projects autonomous existence. This undoubtedly contributes to the aporia of historical understanding. Related to theology, it assumes that the only basis for certainty is to relate (or absorb) the strange into one's own horizon, however many ways that might be construed. Classical liberalism attempted to locate in the "life of Jesus": examples, universal principles, ethical ideals for individual and corporate flourishing. Romanticism sought in the inner life of Jesus a connection with unsurpassed God-consciousness through feeling and inwardness. Bultmann could locate the meaning of Jesus only in his (Bultmann's) own present experience. Günther Bornkamm has rejected Bultmann's anthropocentrism by arguing "that Paul is not concerned only with a new self-understanding but with 'a new history and existence,' in which I am taken up into the history of Christ.'"[11] This is the idea behind the redemptive-historical model that we have been exploring.

In many ways, a contemporary recovery of the Pauline eschatology in the face of modern dualisms parallels two periods from which so much of this fund is drawn. The first is the apostolic and early postapostolic era, in which the theology of the cross was set against "the wisdom of this age" and incarnation and resurrection were opposed to gnostic hostility to nature, history, and the world. The second is the Reformation of the sixteenth century. Perhaps as revolutionary as his exegetical insights into justification is Luther's repudiation of the centuries-old preoccupation with being and essence. "While the accustomed philosophy occupies itself with the being of things, this appears to the 'apostolic philosophy' as a foolish approach. For the true being of things does not lie in their existence and condition, but in their final purpose. Therefore, the apostolic philosophy is thoroughly eschatological," writes von Loewenich, citing several statements from Luther in this vein.[12] Although perhaps carried away at points by the trends in biblical theology, Loewenich demonstrates Luther's position in the debate: "For eschatology has moved into the center of theology."[13] One should add as a supplement that the Reformation moved Christology into the center of eschatology and thus, into the center of theology.

As we have seen, there are also parallels between this redemptive-historical method and the narrative theology of Hans Frei. And yet, the eschatological is not well-developed in narrative theology, allusions to it usually serving merely as a warning against epistemic or hermeneutical arrogance.[14] (This recognition fits quite well with the dogmatic tradition's at least theoretical adherence to a *theologia viatorum*, rather than an overrealized eschatology.)

Despite the lack of attention to eschatology, criticism that this version of narrative theology lacks any interest in history is an overstatement. *Eclipse of*

Biblical Narrative is nothing if not a manifesto for recovering a figural (i.e., promise-fulfillment) hermeneutic, a suggestion that is quite inconceivable if one were not interested in the historical horizon. Frei writes of Kant,

> For him, every person that he discovered in the Bible was a mark or stage along a single-storied succession, none of which took place in time; instead, each is a stage in the self-understanding and self-improvement of the moral reasoner. The biblical story as a whole, and every part of it, is an allegory. There is Adam, who is really the moral reasoner as freely disobedient to his own rational freedom. There is the incarnate Christ, who is the archetype of humanity well-pleasing to God, ineradicable in the moral reasoner's mind.[15]

While he applauds Barth's consistency, Frei even observes that Barth "cannot specify the manner or mode in which the textual statements are historical, while nonetheless asserting that they are," adding the following:

> He will often and rightly say that textually the resurrection happened to, is a predicate of, Jesus, not to the disciples, and he will go on to say that there is no reason to think something nonhistorical just because it is in principle not accessible to scientific historical inquiry. In what sense, then, is the resurrection, unlike the crucifixion, historical? To consign the resurrection to the category of myth is a typical species of modern laziness or a typically lazy modernism.[16]

And yet, I am not quite certain how the narrative approach escapes its own criticism unscathed. Lindbeck refers to a phrase often employed by Frei:

> The Bible is often "history-like" even when it is not "likely history." It can therefore be taken seriously in the first respect as a delineator of the character of divine and human agents, even when its history or science is challenged. As parables such as that of the prodigal son remind us, the rendering of God's character is not in every instance logically dependent on the facticity of the story.[17]

But historical narratives are not parables. C. Stephen Evans puts it quite simply: "If the narrative is 'history-like,' maybe it is because it is historical."[18] Here is where once more the dramatic analogy seems far more comprehensive of both word/narrative (script) and event/history (dramatic action). Perhaps the structuralist limitations are too intrinsic to a merely narrative approach.

But more important than the root analogy we employ is the significance of the redemptive-historical model for overcoming ontological dualism. On the one hand, then, this redemptive-historical model avoids the Platonic-Kantian antinomies. Instead of an ontological dualism, it locates in the New Testament, especially in Jesus' explicit two-age references, the dualism between "this present age" and "the age that is to come," an epoch set against God's person and reign, and one in which he is universally acknowledged and worshiped. It is not a dualism of nature and grace, the phenomenal and the noumenal, *Historie* and

Geschichte. Proponents would therefore be more inclined to speak of creation, fall, redemption, and consummation rather than static and ontologically laden categories of nature and grace or modern equivalents. As Gaffin describes it,

> It is a cosmic "dualism" resulting from the repatriation of (the incarnate) Christ into heaven through his resurrection and ascension. So his personal movement from humiliation to exaltation takes on cosmic dimensions, as he acts not only in his own person but as the organic and federal head of his new humanity. Redemptive history moves from the cross to the resurrection, from humiliation to glorification.[19]

Nevertheless, we live in the already and not-yet of this movement. It is both a reality and a hope, in one sense a present possession and yet (in its fullness) a future anticipation. Justified in Christ's justification (through his resurrection), believers nevertheless await their bodily resurrection and their glorification. Eschatology does not have reference merely to this future aspect (resurrection and glorification), as one might think from traditional systematic theologies; rather, it is the shape of theology as a whole.

Like the biblical theology movement represented by such towering figures as Oscar Cullmann, the Dutch (redemptive-historical) school emphasized the importance of "salvation history." Also like Cullmann, they sharply criticized dialectical theology for pitting myth against history, rendering the "eschatological drama" timeless. (Recall H. R. Niebuhr's criticism of Brunner's insistence that the resurrection "cannot be called a fact," but "is a super-historical or eschatological happening and 'no longer history at all.'")[20] But unlike Cullmann, they repudiated entirely the Kantian dualism of *Historie* and *Geschichte*. As Cornelius Van Til expressed this criticism that he shared, Cullmann still "does not want this mid-point [the Christ-event] to be the invasion of the eternal into the temporal," but wants to render all of revelation a matter of history. The death and resurrection of Christ, for Cullmann, serves as a beacon to illumine all of history, rather than being an eschatological invasion from another realm. So anxious is Cullmann to reverse the dialectical flight from history."[21] Cullmann correctly identified dualism even in Kierkegaard's thought, for whom the "idea of contemporaneity with Christ still assumed that time came to a stand-still with Jesus Christ," ignoring the fact that redemptive history is even now moving toward its fulfillment in time. But, Van Til insists, Cullmann has not really avoided this impasse himself: "All of them have followed Kant's effort to escape the dualism inherent in the position of Descartes, but all of them have only fallen into a new and deeper dualism . . . by a leap into the unknown. They have projected a God and a Christ into the realm of the unknown."[22] Mutatis mutandis, Pannenberg's version of the theology of history seems particularly vulnerable to this criticism. And it would appear that until neo-Kantianism (in which even neo-Hegelian thought remains trapped) is overcome, Feuerbach's analysis of theology as anthropology will hit its mark.

So, in Kantian fashion, one speaks of Christ *as if* we had knowledge of him, conceptual knowledge of Christ representing a transgression of religion's limits. Despite these differences (especially that of collapsing eschatology into history while maintaining the *historische-geschichtliche* dichotomy), the redemptive-historical school shared Cullmann's passion for a defense of history as the field of divine revelation. Cullmann was surely correct, for instance, when he asserted that the *skandalon* of Christianity (viz., its historical claims) is actually the irreplaceable "essence and centre of the New Testament proclamation." It has nothing to do with a new worldview, as Bultmann claimed, "but was felt to be just as offensive in the ancient world," in which the metaphysical biases also screened out that which individuals were unprepared to entertain.[23] We have seen how Pannenberg has especially emphasized the historical dimensions of redemption. Yet, like Cullmann (and *unlike* the so-called "Dutch" redemptive-historical school), Pannenberg seems too much under the spell of Hegel's synthesizing magic. Eschatology is reduced to a completed future that proleptically illumines the present, leaving the history of redemption flattened, a horizon in which the quite central events of Christ's passion and resurrection swallow up all other events of redemptive history instead of being their climax. The unknowable noumenon is just as evident, although now it is a tense (the future) rather than an essence, open rather than determined, and its nature is therefore equivocally articulated by believers.

Reintegration does not mean absorption: history remains the stage upon which double agency is played out, with secret providence as the story behind the story. Here common grace is God's normal way with creatures. But in this same history that God rules by providence, through common grace, there are those episodic irruptions of eternity *within* (not against) time, where God acts by miracle and through redemptive grace. Thus, while the contemporary believer does not look for a restoration of an earthly Jerusalem, but joins "the Jerusalem that is above," he or she does so in anticipation of the day when the heavenly city descends consummately to fill the earth. The historical and eschatological aspects are dialectically, not antithetically, related. The consummation in the future is the present reality "above," where believers are already "seated with Christ in heavenly places," but this does not extinguish the hope that when this future eschatological inbreaking occurs "on the last day," the body and the whole creation will be restored as a world-historical event of judgment and redemption. Revelation is therefore not reduced to a past, present, or future, but to the unfolding drama of redemption in all three tenses.

Anticipating Moltmann's plea, Vos wrote in the early twentieth century, "Biblical religion is thoroughly eschatological in its outlook." This lens could be valuable, for instance, in observing the element of change and diversity as well as constancy and unity. "Nature-religion revolves around the thought of what the deity is for all men and under all circumstances. It presents to the worship of its devotees a face the same yesterday, today, and for ever. There is no action of the deity here, no history, no progress."[24] This essentially Parmenidean theology characterizes the Platonic orientation of one extreme of modern theology, as we have seen—so much so that it is increasingly popular to attack the divine attribute of immutability. Given this Stoic alternative, it is no wonder.[25] Nevertheless, is it not possible that the restoration of the distinction between the immanent and economic Trinity—the former referring to God's hidden essence while the latter is revealed by God in word and action—could restore our balance on this point? In our approach, then, change is everywhere to be seen. The revelation of God is inherently dynamic. In contrast to Plato, biblical religion looks for true knowledge of God in the realm of history, particulars, and flux, rather than in an ostensibly higher realm of rational certitude based on transcending these factors. God may not change in his essence, but he certainly changes in his relation to us, our world, our history, and our destiny. Similarly, the covenant is administered differently in externals, though immutable in its eternal decree and promissory content.[26]

At the center of this eschatological motif is the resurrection of Jesus Christ, which, Gaffin argues, "is not simply a guarantee; it is pledge in the sense that it is the actual beginning of the general event."[27] Based on the Pauline analogy of "firstfruits," Gaffin emphasizes the eschatological implications of the resurrection. At this point, the contrast with the notion of "timeless truths" is most evident: "Only as he himself is one 'from the dead' is Christ 'firstborn.' Only as he is part of that group which is (to be) raised does he enjoy this exalted status."[28] Jesus Christ is not eternally "firstborn from the dead," but became so at a datable moment in history. Ridderbos put it this way: "With him the great Resurrection became reality. . . . He ushers in the world of the resurrection."[29] So it is not only a historical event in which the future is proleptically projected (Pannenberg), much less the future leveling the present and rendering the importance of the past questionable (Moltmann). It is "the age that is to come" actually brought into "this present evil age" by the first stage in the "new creation." The Holy Spirit establishes this link by baptizing into Christ those who "were dead through the trespasses and sins" (Eph. 2:1), raising them together with Christ in newness of life, awaiting the resurrection of their physical bodies in which the whole creation will participate (Rom. 8:18–25).

The source of this New Creation does not lie immanently within the past (old liberalism), the present (existential theologies), or the future (neo-Hegelian theologies), but is "coming down out of heaven from God" (Rev. 21:2). It is not that the new creation does not admit an individual and subjective aspect, but that the foreground belongs to the fact that the New Creation has objectively dawned (eschatologically) in the resurrection of Christ and the subsequent descent of the Spirit, this time not to confuse and to scatter—as at Babel, when humanity sought autonomy—but to enlighten and to gather all things together in Christ, who is in truth already the New Creation, the firstfruits of the harvest, the pioneer of the new world.

We really are, then, moving toward the future; it is not merely moving toward us. It is on this basis that we can boldly affirm, with Julius Schniewind in his debate with Bultmann:

> The chronological future may hold in store for us temptations which may assault even the very elect. Even the apostle awaits this future, which is the day of judgement, with fear and trembling (2 Cor. 5.10, 11), lest he be found reprobate (1 Cor. 9.27). Yet God's future is stronger than any of these things to come—God's future is his age to come, his ages of ages, his last things, his future period of time, which by virtue of the incarnation and resurrection paradoxically juts out as it were into this present age of ours. Christ alone is the clue to the meaning of past and future, the past wiped out, our rebellion against God, and the future of the new age of God opened up for us.[30]

This model that we have explored offers a fresh opportunity to reintegrate history and eschatology.

2. Word–Act

Since the Enlightenment, theology has encountered various ways of finding substitutes for "propositional theology": ethics, feelings, decision, existence, history, and now narrative. Can we conceive of an approach that takes account of objections to theological positivism without abandoning propositions? From a purely empirical standpoint, is there such a thing as a nonpropositional theology?

At the same time, conservatives have sometimes impoverished the understanding of this enterprise by tending to reduce scripture to a catalogue of true propositions. Narrative theology has reminded us that narrative is the most basic character of scripture, and we would only add drama as a more comprehensive analogy. Our psalms and hymns are narrative, as are our dominant liturgies—even our prayers often take a narrative approach to petition. *Lex orandi, lex credendi.* Propositions are generally derivative, but derivative is not equivalent to secondary, much less somehow less than normative (e.g., contextually relative wrapping in which the absolute "story" appears). Torah is "narrativized" by the Exodus: this redemptive narrative not only reveals the context in which God delivers the law and makes a covenant at Sinai, but serves as the prologue of the charter *legitimizing* Torah. Yet, some narrative theologians, confusing derivative with secondary, fail to recognize that the propositions of scripture itself and those that may be deduced by good and necessary consequence from scripture are precisely that which keeps this narrative from being some other story.

Reacting against the quasi-gnostic theologies of "word-revelation," the biblical theology movement broadly and the Heidelberg circle particularly (including especially von Rad and Pannenberg) understandably emphasized ordinary history as the place where revelation happens. Beyond that, it is divine actions or events that constitute revelation, rather than divine speech. This allows Pannenberg, for instance, to accept the higher-critical approach to scripture while upholding the centrality and truthfulness of the resurrection of Jesus. After all, the latter may be read off of the surface of history *as* history.

We have already provided a brief criticism of this perspective. Suffice it to say here that Pannenberg himself acknowledges the dependence of the resurrection as

The Resurrection on the narrative structure of Israel's history. This concession (which was, after all, at the heart of von Rad's own approach) should make one wary of adopting a naively realist posture that would make everything depend on the event without linguistic interpretation. It would be like watching a play without words. Yet even the events reported in scripture are linguistically mediated. If traditional theories of divine inspiration do not compel Pannenberg, then at least his theory should be modified by the realization that all experience of reality is linguistically mediated. And one should not be surprised, since the creator of that reality is presented in scripture as the one who acts by speaking. Fiat-words become carriers of creative and redemptive efficacy. In addition to such obvious illustrations as the creation narrative, other biblical examples might be the covenant-making ceremony with Abraham in Genesis 17, where fiat-words are intertwined with sacramental acts. There is also the familiar pattern in the prophets, where God announces what will happen, brings it to pass, and then explains why it occurred and what will come next in redemptive history. Word-Act-Word, not word or act alone, represents the Bible's own way of answering this question.

In defining biblical theology, Vos argues for this integration of word-revelation and act-revelation, both in subservience to redemption. First, he says, it is "the historic progressiveness of the revelation-process. It has not completed itself in one exhaustive act, but unfolded itself in a long series of successive acts." Thus, "revelation does not stand alone by itself," but is "inseparably attached to another activity of God, which we call Redemption."[31] Here again we are reminded of the point emphasized by Bavinck and Berkouwer, that one cannot develop abstract theories of scripture or hermeneutics, but must always develop them from the content itself (viz., the unfolding plan of redemption). Revelation is not *gnosis*, a way of salvation by discovering God's hidden essence or will, nor is it in any way an end in itself. Redemption cannot be reduced to revelation (*pace* neo-orthodoxy). It is not an act of downloading eternal ideas or principles onto our noetic desktop or revealing that which has always been true. Rather, says Vos (in line with the Reformed scholastics), "Revelation is the interpretation of redemption." This is what interests us in terms of revelation.[32] So revelation unfolds in exact proportion to the unfolding of redemption, announcing and interpreting the acts of God in history. In redemptive history, there are objective-central and subjective-individual events, the former referring to unrepeatable founding events such as the exodus and the incarnation, death, and resurrection of Christ. There are no second or third crucifixions or Pentecosts, and yet every new believer is crucified and raised with Christ, sealed with the Holy Spirit, and empowered as his witness by being baptized into these realities. This is what Vos means by "subjective-individual" redemptive events.

Second, this approach is concerned with "the actual embodiment of revelation in history":

> The process of revelation is not only concomitant with history, but it becomes incarnate in history. The facts of history themselves acquire a revealing significance. The crucifixion and resurrection of

Christ are examples of this. We must place act-revelation by the side of word-revelation. . . . Two points, however, should be remembered in this connection: first, that these two-sided acts did not take place primarily for the purpose of revelation; their revelatory character is secondary; primarily they possess a purpose that transcends revelation, having a God-ward reference in their effect, and only in dependence on this a man-ward reference for instruction. In the second place, such act-revelations are never entirely left to speak for themselves; they are preceded and followed by word-revelation. The usual order is: first word, then the fact, then again the interpretive word.[33]

So this view challenges, on the one hand, the obsession with revelation in modern theology, both conservative and liberal varieties. While it is understandable that the assault of higher criticism has elicited a little over two centuries of apologetics, evangelicalism and neo-orthodoxy have, in different ways, reflected an unhealthy preoccupation with revelation, sometimes even reducing the material principle to the formal principle. Reading scripture in a nonchristocentric manner is a peril of theology across the spectrum, but it is the goal of the redemptive-historical model to regard the text (including preaching, teaching, and theological reflection) as instrumental toward the goal of proclaiming, confessing, obeying, and embracing Jesus Christ. So Richard Gaffin writes,

Revelation never stands by itself, but is always concerned either explicitly or implicitly with redemptive accomplishment. God's speech is invariably related to his actions. It is not going too far to say that redemption is the *raison d'être* of revelation. An unbiblical, quasi-gnostic notion of revelation inevitably results when it is considered by itself or as providing self-evident general truths. Consequently, revelation is either authentication or interpretation of God's redemptive action.[34]

This emphasis on the relationship of divine speech to action (and, consequently, of the dependence of revelation upon redemption) stands in some contrast to the way evangelical theology has often understood the doctrine of revelation. Richard Lints correctly observes,

Evangelicals have traditionally emphasized the speech of God by encapsulating it in doctrinal formulations. In doing so, they have neglected the acts of God. They have ably defended the historicity of these acts, but they have virtually ignored their theological character. It is one of the fundamental principles of biblical interpretation in any standard evangelical text that "didactic material interprets historical material." This is simply another way of saying that the speech of God is more important than the acts of God.[35]

Word and deed come together, however, in a redemptive-historical approach, Lints argues.[36] This also gives full weight to particulars as well as to the general plot. Only a God of infinite wisdom could bring such a plot to its appointed resolution without in any way extinguishing the individuality and freedom of human agents. So neither redemption nor revelation serves to simply manifest or describe God as an illustration (in the realm of appearances) of a universal and eternal truth. Apart from these new events and interpretations in each period of redemptive history, we know nothing of God that is useful for reconciliation and worship. "For religion," Abraham Joshua Heschel notes, "is more than a creed or an ideology and cannot be understood when detached from acts and events."[37] In the light of their respective interests, narrative theology and the redemptive-historical school have much in common and every reason to engage in conversation for the edification of the church. Some time ago David Cairns observed the promise of biblical theology in the contemporary setting when he gathered that the future of theology was "some form of the school" associated with biblical theology, "where faith is seen, not only as encounter, but also as incorporation into a history, and where there is a place for an unrepeatable, unique event."[38]

The dramatic, redemptive-historical approach eschews the basically Platonic (mimetic) account of the relation of reality and representation. By recognizing the already fully integrated nature of word and act in revelation, neither God's eternal being (which believers will want to say something about, though analogically) nor God's temporal and ever-changing interaction in the world is sacrificed to the other. In fact, revelation is incarnated in history, quite literally in the case of God's supreme self-revelation in Christ.

3. Old Testament–New Testament

Not only is the theologian these days often bereft of the company of the biblical scholar; overspecialization and fragmentation have also separated the Old Testament scholars from New. As Watson and others have recently pointed out, this has contributed to much of the "neo-Marcionite" tendency of New Testament scholarship, and since some New Testament scholars have also contributed a great deal to the larger enterprise, this has had no small effect.

Schleiermacher thought of the Old Testament as "but the husk or wrapping" of pure religion and maintained that "whatever is most definitely Jewish has least value."[39] Barr points out,

> For instance, Schleiermacher's *The Christian Faith* contained only a very brief section on the Old Testament at the very end, in which he advised that the Old Testament should really be printed after the New as a sort of appendix. . . . In general the Old Testament as an ethnic and local production cannot be put on the same level as the Christian spirit, which is universal.[40]

Harnack exuded that Marcion "has been my first love in church history. . . . He is the only thinker in Christian history to take quite seriously the conviction that the God who redeems us *from the world* has absolutely nothing to do with cosmology or cosmic teleology."[41] Openly embracing this approach, Harnack concludes, "to preserve [the Old Testament] in the nineteenth century and beyond as a canonical document for protestantism is the result of religious and churchly paralysis."[42] Thus, it is only God's universal love and fatherhood, experienced in the inwardness of religious experience, that counts; and "the question of the Old Testament, first posed and decided by Marcion, remains urgent today for evangelical Christianity," Harnack urges.[43] As we have seen, Bultmann fused his neo-Kantianism with this "neo-Marcionism," concluding that the history of Israel is "[n]ot our history," since "the events which meant something for Israel mean nothing more to us."[44] Bultmann listened well to Harnack when the former wrote that "to the Christian faith the Old Testament is no longer revelation as it has been, and still is, for the Jews." After all, "to us the history of Israel is not history of revelation. The events which meant something for Israel, which were God's Word, mean nothing more to us."[45] Watson has made a compelling case for the idea that modern theology's general tendency to place the written text (disparaged "for its deadness, its fixity, its purely legal authority") in opposition to speech, abusing Paul's "letter" and "Spirit" contrast as ciphers for Old and New Testament, respectively, constitutes a new Marcionism.[46]

But as with other issues, the "neo-Marcionite" temptation is not limited to liberal and existential theologies, but has been quite evident in evangelical theologies, particularly those influenced by the dispensationalism of C. I. Scofield.[47] Having been reared in these circles, I commonly heard, "But that is the Old Testament," as a sufficient and self-evident condition for rejecting certain arguments. Consequently, the Old Testament often served more as a resource for character studies and moral examples than as the first act of a christocentric drama of redemption. Happily, there are signs of revision afoot in such circles.[48]

Whether from the liberal or conservative quarters of contemporary theology, the role of the Old Testament and the hermeneutical approach to it have been ambiguous, to say the least. As Christopher Seitz indicates, the New Testament itself requires familiarity with God's history with Israel. Otherwise Jesus Christ loses all his narrative coordinates.

> Instead of being a correlative expression, "He is risen" replaces "the God of Israel raised him from the dead." Jesus relates not to the God of the Scriptures, with an identity provided there, but to a private God, known somehow else. And so Christians struggle at present to give this God a name: Godself, Creator, Mother/Father, Mother. . . . Christians are only issued library cards to read the Old Testament in the first place by Jesus; else they would always remain outsiders to this privileged discourse between God and God's people.[49]

Seitz suggests that the theological curriculum include "some course in Christian scripture or biblical theology in which a natural movement from Old Testament to New, and from New to Old, is the focus of scholarly theological attention."[50]

Just as Irenaeus in his controversies with the gnostics, Calvin felt obliged to spend much of his time in the *Institutes* demonstrating the unity of the testaments in one covenant of grace, against radicals who set the New Testament against the

Old. To be sure, there are discontinuities, as one might expect of a multiple-act play. But, as with any good drama, unity perseveres amid diversity. Gadamer's point is utterly consistent with what we have been arguing when he writes that we cannot "conceive of the unity of truth as a timeless identity of a given essential content. It can be conceived only as the whole of a historical career."[51]

Rather than the model of an eternal realm impressing its forms into the clay of the temporal realm of appearances, it is the model of a seed growing into a mature tree. With each new "twist" and "turn" in the road effected by divine activity, the history of redemption really does advance. It is always changing, always different from what it had been—although the central purpose (redemption through the "seed of the woman") ensures its continuity. Nor is it a calm progress toward fulfillment, but a series of cycles and reversals: divine blessing, human rebellion, divine judgment, divine promise/redemption, human failure, and so forth. As Vos adds, "It does not proceed with uniform motion, but rather is 'epochal' in its onward stride."[52] The conjunction "But God . . ." is the only thing that saves the history of redemption in the face of human disloyalty. It is not at all like a predictable movie, with a transparent plot that can be figured out at the beginning. It is a mystery now made known, not an eternal principle now discovered.

As we have seen previously, the biblical story does not simply move in one obvious straight line, say, from law to gospel, or from a "God of wrath" to a "God of love." There are law and gospel, wrath and love, in both testaments. To further complicate (or enrich) matters, intrigue revolves around two cities, both of which undergo different relations to the covenant throughout the drama. These elements are themselves related to the differences between the covenant treaty made with Abraham, which is identified in scripture as irrevocable and based on pure promise, and the Mosaic covenant, with its strictly conditional promises and sanctions relating to the land and Israel's national election. Furthermore, there are different administrations of the Abrahamic covenant, old and new. So not only do law and gospel, as well as wrath and love (though distinct), run continuously through this unfolding mystery; the two covenants (represented in the Hagar-Sarah allegory of Gal. 4:21–31) and their distinct administrations add layers of interest and depth to the continuity.

Simplistic and reductionistic approaches to the two testaments have resulted not only in an alleged "neo-Marcionism," but have been demonstrably linked to anti-Semitism in nineteenth- and twentieth-century theology. Much of modern criticism of the unity of the canon, which has motivated the atomism of form-criticism, rests, ironically, on the assumption of uniformity. But multiformity is precisely what one expects from an organic process. This assumption that biblical reliability rests on a "dull uniformity" (viz., How can there be canonical unity if Peter and Paul have different views?) is, at bottom, a type of deism, Vos contends.

> It conceives of God as standing outside of His own creation and therefore having to put up for the instrumentation of His revealing speech with such imperfect forms and organs as it offers Him. The didactic, dialectic mentality of Paul would thus become a hindrance

for the ideal communication of the message, no less than the simple, practical, untutored mind of Peter. From the standpoint of Theism the matter shapes itself quite differently. The truth having inherently many sides, and God having access to and control of all intended organs of revelation, shaped each one of these for the precise purpose to be served.[53]

This conclusion raises the stakes considerably. While certainly not all formulations of canonical disunity proceed from precisely the same foundations, Vos's point seems more than an intuition. If one presupposes the God who is actually revealed in scripture by word and deed, many of the arguments that have seemed compelling to the majority of biblical scholars and theologians over the last two centuries will lose their force.

A final point on this topic is in order, relating to our discussion of covenant and canon. We have argued that the canon is a covenant charter, a treaty. While normativity is determined by redemptive-historical factors, such as the inapplicability of the theocratic polity, aspects of the Old Testament administration of both the Abrahamic and Mosaic covenants are intertwined with aspects of the New Testament economy. Figural interpretation alone will not reveal this, but attention to the covenantal structure(s) of scripture itself will indicate how impossible it would be to read the Bible faithfully without integrating the testaments. If it is true, as the saying goes, that the Old is in the New revealed, it is just as true that the New is in the Old concealed. A "big picture" analysis, which biblical theology is supposed to provide, will pay close attention to this interdependence without losing the distinctiveness of the parts. However, walking into the play in the middle will leave individuals and communities with little context for the plot.

SYSTEM

1. Biblical–Systematic

Our discussion so far has focused on reintegrating a fragmented biblical theology. But more is needed. Not only must the different aspects of exegesis be put together again; once done, *exegesis* itself must be reunited to *systematics*. Unfortunately we cannot engage in a profitable discussion of the challenges to the "dogmatics" enterprise as a whole after the apparent death of "the System." I must therefore assume an audience that is already convinced that studying doctrine is a worthwhile affair for the people of God.

Across the theological spectrum, from evangelicalism to radical theologies, one observes a sometimes visceral reaction against doctrine and especially against systems. Both pious laypeople and biblical scholars seem to assume that the very suggestion of a system does violence to the text, an act regarded as both impious and unscholarly, respectively. While some of George Lindbeck's "cognitive-propositionalists" may still haunt the halls of evangelical scholarship, the evangelical movement itself, to the extent that its revivalist impulse has triumphed over its dependence on formal theology, increasingly reflects the "experiential-expressivist" approach. Watson surmises that there is also a bias among many academic theologians against relating their scholarship to a particular confessional stance to which they are themselves committed: "The lines of demarcation between systematic theology and Old and New Testament scholarship represent more than a mere division of labour; they are ideologically motivated. They represent the collective decision of biblical scholarship that the biblical texts are to be construed as something other than Christian scripture."[54]

Is it advisable, much less possible, to still maintain, as the dominant "church theologies" have always done, that a particular confession of faith "contains the system of doctrine taught in the holy scriptures"? And is it then still possible to articulate the essential features of such a system?

On one hand, I think that it is salutary that we have to ask ourselves that question. For too long, this was taken for granted, and in that environment it became increasingly easy for systematicians to lord it over the text and to engage in (sometimes dubious) exegesis only to endorse a position that may not arise organically, either directly or by good and necessary consequence from clear passages. In some cases, especially among the manuals of the eighteenth and nineteenth centuries, there appeared derivative systems, imitations of imitations, summaries of summaries. Protestants, as well as anyone else, can forfeit the surprise of wrestling with a text and rely on textbook formulations. Just as the Reformers complained that if one wanted to investigate the scriptures it was almost always done by digging through several layers of commentaries, too much theology has been received (and even done) secondhand in the circles of orthodoxy.

Many of the paragons of systematic and dogmatic theology were also exegetes, masters of philology, antiquity, and textual criticism, in addition to being as competent in Old and New Testament studies as many specialists. Many Roman Catholic, Lutheran, and Reformed scholastics, despite what one might think of the style and method of their dogmatics (and even there a wide diversity exists), were adept in writing tomes on preaching, biblical commentary, liturgy, and pastoral care. They recognized that different tasks called for different methods, but their diverse corpus was united by their ecclesiastical *vocatio* and accountability. Beza, Calvin's successor in Geneva and a formative scholastic, is perhaps more widely known today for his contributions to New Testament scholarship than for his *Tabula*. The Heidelberg Catechism, unparalleled in its warmth and simple profundity, had as its chief author one of the most precise of the federal theologians, Zacharias Ursinus. Abraham Kuyper, along with Herman Bavinck and others, sought also to reintegrate exegesis and system, biblical theology and systematic theology, after decades of languishing in liberalism. Long before it was fashionable to emphasize the eschatological and historical shape of theology, a growing ad hoc circle of biblical theologians was developing in the Netherlands and in the United States.[55]

Some of the Reformed scholastics were also founders of the discipline of biblical theology, a fact that has been underscored by such contemporary theologians as Moltmann and Pannenberg and represents a challenge to the caricature of post-Reformation theology as engaged in mere ahistorical abstraction.[56]

None of this is to be slavishly imitated or merely repristinated. This cannot be done, even if it should. For instance, advances in biblical studies—including the prominence of biblical theology as a distinct subdiscipline—necessarily reconfigure the process of discovery and refinement. It is in biblical eschatology that dogmatics jumps out of mere propositional stasis and theology is caught in the act, in the history of redemption. The massive achievement of the older systems was integrating exegesis and system in a never-ending dialectic that yielded considerable fruit, not only for the academy, but for the church, and not only for faith, but for practice as well. Post-Reformation orthodox systems may be less animated than the preaching and popular polemics of the Reformers themselves, just as the sermons and popular pamphlets of these scholastics differed in style from their theological writings. Nevertheless, in its growing appreciation for the federal model of Christ the Mediator, the "second Adam" in a history of redemption, these systems turned away from the dualisms that preoccupied the medieval synthesis and have haunted modern criticism and apologetics. In so doing, they turned away from the model of timeless ideas, approaching theology as one might approach another person, rather than an experiment or an instrument. Because they drew on the covenant theology that they were convinced rose organically from the sweep of biblical exegesis, their theology had a structural commitment to a historical-eschatological hermeneutic centering on Christ.

"Covenant" could be elaborated in a biblical-theological manner, by tracing the specific arrangements throughout redemptive history, and it could be developed systematically by organizing the material in their thematic relations. Thus, for instance, this federal union with Christ could become the paradigm within which one could relate election, justification, sanctification, adoption, and glorification. In both biblical theology and systematic theology, the dialectic of whole and parts, never resting on one or the other, is always generating greater refinement as well as scope. In light of the more recent work that has been done on the covenant, within both biblical and systematic theology, a reinvigorated and enriched covenant theology could provide not only an exemplary exercise, but a rich paradigm for the reintegration of these subdisciplines and their implications for praxis.

As Richard Muller has argued with laborious citations, all of the major sixteenth- and seventeenth-century Protestant systems engaged in this double movement of analysis and synthesis, exegesis and system. One may criticize a given system or tradition for its results, but one cannot fairly conclude that the most representative efforts were arbitrary in their exegesis or that they simply imposed a ready-made system on the text.[57]

Not only do we find fruitful exemplars among the magisterial systems of our various traditions; the contemporary redemptive-historical school with which we have identified in this project does not, for its part, reject or downplay the importance of systematics, but only with certain approaches to the task that pay scant attention to the historical-eschatological aspect. Vos, for instance, distinguished the two tasks without setting them in opposition: "Biblical theology draws a line of development," he says. "Systematic Theology draws a circle."[58] Similarly, Gaffin writes, "biblical theology and systematic theology may not be arbitrarily and artificially separated."[59] Nor is this redemptive-historical model imposed on the biblical text. "The Bible is, as it were, conscious of its own organism; it feels, what we cannot always say of ourselves, its own anatomy. The principle of successive *Berith* [covenant]-makings, as marking the introduction of new periods, plays a large role in this, and should be carefully heeded."[60]

This approach exchanges the one-dimensional map for a relief map, with raised peaks and indented valleys. It is theology not from a "God's-eye" perspective, but from down on the ground, where one is never quite sure what looms over the horizon of the next mountain range until one arrives there. To be sure, there are directions, prophetic anticipations of what one will find, but the fulfillment always surpasses expectations. Thus, redemptive history cannot be reduced to a single picture, a unity without diversity. "A leaf is not of the same importance as a twig, nor a twig as a branch, nor a branch as the trunk of the tree."[61] Revelation itself will indicate which is which here, and it will all be in proportion to its chief concern: redemption.

But while relief maps are helpful for some tasks, one-dimensional freeway and street maps are helpful for others. Biblical and systematic theology keep each other in check, in the all-important effort to avoid both enthusiasm and dogmatism. Far, then, from the model which Professor Lindbeck has identified as "cognitive-propositionalist," Vos argues, "The Bible is not a dogmatic handbook but a historical book full of dramatic interest." At the same time, "[b]iblical Theology can counteract the anti-doctrinal tendency of the present time. Too much stress proportionately is being laid on the voluntary and emotional sides of religion. Biblical Theology bears witness to the indispensability of the doctrinal groundwork of our religious fabric."

> Biblical Theology is of the greatest importance and value for the study of Systematic Theology. . . . For anything pretending to supplant Dogmatics there is no place in the circle of Christian Theology. . . . Dogmatic Theology is, when rightly cultivated, as truly Biblical and as truly an inductive science as its younger sister. And the latter needs a constructive principle for arranging her facts as well as the former. The only difference is, that in the one case this constructive principle is systematic and logical, whereas in the other case it is purely historical.[62]

Finally, Vos reckons that this approach is superior to the cul-de-sac of isolated proof-texting. "There exists a higher ground on which conflicting religious views can measure themselves as to their Scriptural legitimacy. In the long run that system will hold the field which can be proven to have grown organically from the main stem of revelation, and to be interwoven with the very fibre of Biblical religion."[63] This tendency to view scripture chiefly as a doctrinal handbook or as a collection of proof texts is frequently associated also with a soteriological individualism that ignores the organic and eschatological character of biblical theology.

Gaffin is not at all opposed to systematic theology, but he does argue that Paul's marvelously synthetic mind had already woven together a system. While further synthesis is necessary, why should we start from scratch, assuming that the Bible is merely a source *for* theology rather than a substantially biblical-theological and systematic-theological text in its own right?

In a discussion of God as the object of theology, for instance, we may observe an example of this sort of approach. While it would have been just as appropriate to synthesize or systematize the various texts related to God's attributes, it seems even more fruitful at least to begin with the narrative of redemption. Is this not recommended in the Reformed scholastics' emphasis on knowing God in his works rather than in his essence? How better to take notice of God in his works than by surveying the field of history where he has acted most concretely for our redemption? As we survey that landscape, we begin to observe certain identifiable traits that may be parsed out as items for systematization and categorization. We see from the story itself that the details of redemptive revelation, with all of its variety, "can all be subsumed under the categories of justice and grace as the two poles around which henceforth the redeeming self-disclosure of God revolves."[64] This fact, which Vos discerns from the narrative or biblical-theological, organic development of redemptive revelation, was (as we have seen) observed from the more systematic-theological vantage point in the Reformed insistence that all of scripture could be subsumed under the categories of law and gospel, command and promise. "All the new processes and experiences which the redeemed man undergoes can be brought back to the one or the other of these two," says Vos.[65]

At the risk of special pleading, we suggest that the dramatic analogy also could have a role to play in this reintegration. The metaphor of "text," as we have argued, is too confining. It already prejudices us toward theology as an "indoor sport," where individual readers are transformed, albeit in communities, in a process that is essentially static and hermeneutically sealed. Instead of the text being the world that we are to inhabit, we suggest that the world is a stage on which we are to act out the part assigned to us. As in the narrative analogy, one can be absorbed into the play and can be rescripted as a participant in the victory of the hero instead of a villain. A new world is indeed intruding through the enactment of this performance: "Once you were not a people, but now you are God's people; once you had not received mercy, but now you have received mercy" (1 Pet. 2:10). Jesus and Paul speak of outsiders being grafted onto a vine, an analogy that seems congenial to the notion that those who do not belong in the drama, at least as heroes and insiders, are nevertheless being written into the script as just that. If the primary actors will not show up for the climactic scene, the director will send out casting agents to bring in people off the street for the vacant parts. But unlike the narrative metaphor, the dramatic one provides an evocative analogy for reintegrating the script and the action outside of the script.

Already in Calvin, the theater/drama analogy was prominent.[66] These models may be heuristic devices, but they exercise an enormous, though often tacit, methodological force. As we learned from Geertz, "game" analogists concentrate on play and strategy, "drama" analogists on ritual and rhetoric, "text" analogists on "against-interpretation" (deconstruction) and "symbolic-domination" (neo-Marxists).[67] Inasmuch as the redemptive-historical model works more like a drama than a game or a text, it may be expected to concentrate, as Geertz suggests, on ritual and rhetoric, which is precisely what is captured in the dictum "Wherever the Word is correctly preached and the sacraments are correctly administered, there is no doubt a true church there." Rhetoric and ritual, dramatic movement within history—not only then and there, but also here and now, real characters and a genuine plot, all orchestrated by an all-wise and omnipotent God who has made himself known to those who were without hope in the world.

Our model offers a more comprehensive and textually defined paradigm within which biblical and systematic theology could be reintegrated.

2. Personal Encounter–Metaphysics

Perhaps the most sensitive of all, this question has to do with the relationship between the dynamic, personal, historical context that is especially emphasized in biblical theology and the susceptibility of that I-Thou relationship to such important systematic tasks as making assertions about divine attributes and the relationship between God and the world.

First, our proposal has focused a great deal of attention on this personal aspect. God addresses individuals and communities and acts in the world in covenantal contexts. "Personal" is the key in which "covenant" is played. We have emphasized the dynamic quality of redemptive history. The "new creation" really is a *novum*, just as the "old covenant" was at one time contemporary for a particular people, place and time. In the redemptive-historical model, doctrine is a creature of time, not a denizen of the disembodied *res cogitans*. Doctrinal or ethical formulations ignore the discontinuities and new, specific situations in redemptive history at their own peril.

Furthermore, unlike the calculative rationality of mathematical certitude, analogical discourse requires imagination. David Tracy's title *The Analogical Imagination* is richly suggestive of a necessary but often undervalued relationship. Although his work seems to be doing something different (viz., metaphorical theology), the role of imagination in analogical discourse requires comment. In a recent chapter, Kevin Vanhoozer, citing Bernard Ramm, has underscored this undervalued element in theological hermeneutics: "There is appeal to imagination in Scripture as well as to mind, and we certainly know that imagination far more powerfully affects the self than conceptual thinking."[68] Vanhoozer maintains that "drama reinvigorates the anemic imagination of our contemporary culture," adding:

Instrumental reason results in the atrophy of the cultural imagination and a loss of contact with ultimate reality. Our modern and postmodern lives are suffering from spiritual malnutrition. We need more
imagination, not less, for the best imaginative literature does not
remove us from the real but allows it to take residence in it: "The
play's the thing." Dorothy Sayers laments the amount of "slipshod
thinking and trashy sentiment" that has taken the place of the divine
drama and calls the church to "set it on an open stage to startle the
world into some sort of vigorous reaction."[69]

Instrumentalism is a good word for this cultural habit, which we detect in the
pragmatic tendencies of evangelicals as much as any other group. Whether the
Bible is reduced to a handbook of doctrine or a handbook of moral wisdom, therapy, managerial principles, or ideology, there is little need of imagination. As a
pure object, "God" is used rather than worshiped. Calculative reason, working
in terms of timeless abstractions, hardly befits a revelation that has come in the
dramatic form in which we have it. Imagination has suffered at the hands of conservatism and liberalism for much the same reason: both have tended to regard
it as a species of "make-believe." Even Hans Frei's characterization of biblical narrative as "history-like" seems to fill in the gap for a missing category of analogical imagination. Imagination has suffered a fate similar to that of analogy; at both
ends of the theological spectrum many understand them as "non-literal," which
is equivalent to "not really true."

When God accommodates by speaking "baby talk," he is presupposing imaginative powers in the creature that he himself gave in the first place. Just as he has
the archetypal ability to create imaginative analogies, human beings have the
ectypal ability to understand and interpret them—and reflexively generate a few
of their own. Precisely because analogies are not univocal (but not necessarily
nonliteral), imagination is required. Univocal description simply mirrors reality:
one can recognize the "fit" between subject and predicate. The flip side of univocal description, equivocity, is agnostic about that fit. In the case of analogical
revelation, however, God calls us to imagine his ways with us in a manner that
communicates literal truth without knowing exactly what that fit looks like from
the only purely objective perspective, namely God's.

It is important to observe that nobody can escape imaginative constructions.
Regarding descriptions of God univocally, in fact, involves a more dangerous
imaginative effort—the tendency to reify or objectivize in such a way that one
mistakenly believes herself to be staring at God (or at least a mirror of God) face
to face. This is the recipe for idolatry. Evangelicals and liberals, with their common inheritance from pietism, have often absolutized their experience, as if direct
knowledge of God is impossible in terms of true propositions, but is attainable
through subjective encounter. It is equally possible, however, for us to absolutize
our formulations as if they were the object, rather than the description of the
object of faith. In John 5, Jesus even alluded to the danger of treating scripture
as an end in itself, rather than as the hand leading us to himself. Equivocal

accounts of Christian description, however, are liable to agnosticism, yet allow liberty to imaginative possibilities that may also lead to idolatrous fascination. The persistent rivalry between univocity and equivocity, whether in terms of experience, propositions, or communal interpretation, is the lingering legacy of doing theology in a post-Kantian milieu. Idolatry is an ethical condition and cannot be alleviated by recourse to a method; however, the intentionally imaginative mode of analogical discourse and reflection warns us against both rationalism and relativism in its exercise.

The moment we point up the role of imagination, biblical examples flood our thoughts. It is more than pretending that we are there with the Israelites walking on dry land through the exodus from Egypt. This would hardly get us beyond a Romantic hermeneutic that leads to sentimentalism and naive efforts at reconstruction. Rather, it is a matter of imagining the *fact* that we have been brought into the reality that the exodus event foreshadowed. That we have "passed from death unto life" is meant to be received as a literal truth about us, and yet it can be received by us only as an imaginative construction—an analogy—of the truth about us.

But the strictures we have indicated for our understanding of analogy prohibit a free range of imaginative construction. As we have argued, the analogical imagination is restrained by the scriptural form in which it is given. Here the notion of divine authorization is once again required. To avoid idolatry, we must recognize that (a) the imaginative constructions that govern our theology are the effects of divine *poiesis*, not self-created productions and (b) the imaginative range of our analogies must therefore be constrained by the discourse that we find in scripture. Or, to state it in terms of our root metaphor, imagination is constrained and evoked by a specific plot and its scripted codes. A stage production is not threatened by, but requires, the imaginative participation of the audience—and, even more so, of its players.

Imagination, therefore, must not be surrendered to either rationalism or relativism. We are called to regard ourselves as "dead to sin but alive to God in Christ," "no longer strangers and aliens," but "children of Abraham," "living stones being built into the temple" of God's dwelling, as those who are "elect in Christ," "called," "justified," and "glorified." What is it to "regard" ourselves as such if not by imaginative reconfiguration of our identity? To conclude that "imagine" and "regard" cannot be equated in this way is an indication of a faulty notion of imagination as falsehood and make-believe. We are not called to imagine ourselves with the Israelites in the exodus, but we are called to imagine ourselves as those who have been written into that same script by being swept into the culminating action to which the exodus itself only pointed.

This analogical account differs from both pure propositionalism and a strictly cultural-linguistic approach, and is in quite radical antithesis to the experiential-expressivist view of theological language. In our model, doctrines as truth claims (second order) *are* often, *pace* Lindbeck, direct statements about reality, although their meaning is context-dependent and that context may well be described as the "grammar" (i.e., theological system). Theology involves both extrasystematic and intrasystematic truth claims, and this cannot be neatly organized into first order and second order, respectively. The person making a dogmatic assertion is engaging in an act of confession/worship just as surely as when he or she is engaged in an act of formal worship. Some doctrinal claims are directly extrasystematic, while others are intrasystematic. Not all formulations are equal: the Nicene utterance, "very God of very God; begotten, not made; of one substance with the Father, by whom all things were made" is simultaneously a first-order confession and a second-order claim. On the other hand, the precise formulation of the *communicatio idiomatum*, though both intra- and extrasystematic in its reference, is second-order reflection on the church's first-order claim. At the same time, the assertion, "Jesus rose from the dead," is first-order (correspondence) and second-order (coherence). It is both a claim about extrasystematic reality and its irreplaceable position within the system. Apart from the history of Israel and the theology arising from both testaments, the resurrection of Jesus can be regarded as, at best, a historical curiosity.

While Lindbeck is anxious to identify ironic similarities between David Tracy and Carl Henry, there may also be some similarities between Lindbeck and Henry: both seem to reduce theological statements to hard and fast epistemological and ontological categories. Thus, Lindbeck criticizes Henry for rationalism ("cognitive-propositionalism"), while Henry charges Lindbeck with relativism ("cultural-linguistic" solipsism). Wouldn't it be better to suggest that at least a great many theological statements (like all statements in general) are themselves neither extrareferential nor intrareferential, but are whatever they are because of what a speaker/writer is doing with them in a given instance? Here, once more, speech act theory would encourage us to attend to the action being performed and, in particular, the illocutionary stance being taken, rather than to a predetermined status of a particular sentence. At this point, Lindbeck is not cultural-linguistic enough, it seems to me.

The following story may help us contrast the dominant biblical approach and that of excessive abstraction. Early in the twelfth century, the famous Jewish philosopher Jehuda Halevi engaged in a fascinating dialogue with the Moslem scholar and the king of Khazars. Jehuda Halevi is represented in the dialogue as the rabbi. Upon being asked by the Khazari the basis of Jewish belief, the rabbi replied,

> I believe in the God of Abraham, Isaac and Israel, who led the Israelites out of Egypt with signs and miracles; who fed them in the desert and gave them the (Holy) Land, after having made them traverse the sea and the Jordan in a miraculous way; who sent Moses with his Law, and subsequently thousands of prophets, who confirmed his Law by promise to those who observed and threats to those who were disobedient. We believe what is contained in the Torah— a very large domain.[70]

The Khazari, however, is interested in more metaphysical questions and is not sure how this account satisfies the quest for genuine wisdom. "That which thou dost express," the rabbi replies, "is speculative and political religion, to which inquiry leads; but this is open to many doubts." The philosophers cannot agree among themselves: everything is a theory. The rabbi continues, "If thou wert told that the King of India was an excellent man, commanding admiration, and deserving reputation, only because his actions were reflected in the justice which rules his country and the virtuous ways of his subjects, would this compel you to revere him?" "How could this compel me," the king replied, "whilst I am not sure if the justice of the Indian people is natural and not dependent on their king, or due to the king, or both?" But, says the rabbi, if the king of India brought this king of the Khazars gifts known to be available only in India, with an official royal letter, and medicines that actually preserved the Khazars' health and defeated their enemies, "would this make thee beholden to him?" The king of the Khazars could only reply affirmatively. "How wouldst thou then, if asked, describe him?" the rabbi asks.

> In this way I answered thy question. In the same strain Moses spoke to Pharaoh, when he told him "The God of the Hebrews sent me to thee"—viz. the God of Abraham, Isaac and Jacob. For the story of their life was well known to the nations, who also knew that the Divine power was in contact with the Patriarchs, caring for them and performing miracles for them. He did not say: "The God of heaven and earth" nor "my Creator and thine sent me." In the same way God commenced His speech to the assembled people of Israel: "I am the God whom you worship, who hath led you out of the land of Egypt"; He did not say "I am the Creator of the world and your Creator." In the same style I spoke to thee, O Prince of the Khazars, when thou didst ask me about my creed. I made mention to thee of what is convincing for me and for the whole of Israel, who knew these things, first through personal experience, and afterward through an uninterrupted tradition, which is equal to experience.[71]

This approach is expressed in Christian terms by S. Greijdanus, whom Gaffin cites: "The gospel as such is not simply that He became man, has two natures, and reigns in glory, but that He came from David's seed *kata sarka*, bearing the punishment of our sins and for our redemption, and in connection with this was clothed with divine majesty and given supreme authority—that is the message of salvation."[72] But notice that it is not an either/or: "The gospel as such is not *simply*" the doctrinal affirmation—but it involves that. Whether in narrative or in praise, both testaments place the accent on things that have happened or will happen: good news or bad, it comes as *news*, and not merely (or even chiefly) as information or instruction.

But some theologies have so emphasized this important aspect that they have rejected what our model affirms: namely, that while the dominant form is news and not information, the former is inconceivable apart from the latter. This is where we have sharp disagreements with encounter-theology. Even within the Old Testament itself, there is Law and Wisdom literature. In the New Testament as well, especially in the epistles, the parallel to Law and Wisdom literature is the largely didactic and pastoral material. Romans is a classic example of integrating biblical and systematic theology, as well as organizing this material in a refined synthesis that is, for the most part, assertory rather than descriptive, propositional rather than narrative, formulaic rather than dynamic. These are never isolated or abstracted from their narrative context, like a jewel pried from its setting. Nevertheless, they represent examples within the text itself of being able to state specific doctrines or principles that can be legitimately deduced from God's action and speech in redemptive history. This provides us with both a model and justification for making the sort of doctrinal statements that generally fall into the metaphysical category. If this analysis of the diversity within the biblical literature is accurate, Harnack's highly speculative but influential account of the rise of orthodox dogma over the Jesus movement as the triumph of hellenization falls wide of the mark.

Beginning with the revelation of the divine name (in each case a lodestar of metaphysical predication), leading to the *Shema* and other confessional statements, God authorized Israel to ascribe distinct attributes and to form succinct propositions concerning the divine being and God's relation to the world. Inasmuch as it is a fuller revelation, especially given the decisive revelation of God in Christ, it is not surprising that the New Testament would add exponentially to this repertoire. While this is not the place to make the case, the consensus of the first five centuries concerning the two natures of Christ, for example, is inconceivable apart from the already systematized and significantly articulated formulations that one finds in the Gospels and epistles, as well as in the sermons in Acts. The Bible may certainly not be a handbook of doctrine, but its remarkably coherent structure resists reductionism in the other direction.

We have referred to Francis Turretin's representative criticism of medieval scholasticism when he, echoing the Reformers, demands that theology "treats of God not after the manner of metaphysics inasmuch as he is Being (*Ens*)," adding that "theology deals with creatures not as they are things of nature (*res naturae*) but as they are things of God (*res Dei*)."[73] In fact, Richard Muller directs us to the similarities of Calvin and Turretin on this point. Calvin writes,

> When faith is discussed in the schools, they call God simply the object of faith, and by fleeting speculations, as we have elsewhere stated, lead miserable souls astray rather than direct them to a definite goal. For since "God dwells in inaccessible light" (1 Tim. 6:16), Christ must become our intermediary. . . . Indeed, it is true that faith looks to one God. But this must also be added, "to know Jesus Christ whom he has sent" (Jn. 17:3).[74]

Now Turretin:

> But when God is set forth as the object of theology, he is not to be regarded simply as God in himself (for thus he is incomprehensible [*akataleptos*] to us), but as revealed and as he has been pleased to manifest himself to us in his word. . . . Nor is he to be considered exclu-

sively under the relation of deity (according to the opinion of Thomas Aquinas and many Scholastics after him, for in this manner the knowledge of him could not be saving but deadly to sinners), but *as he is our God (i.e., covenanted in Christ as he has revealed himself to us in his word not only as the object of knowledge, but also of worship).* (emphasis added)[75]

In fact, Turretin goes on to elaborate the differences between various medieval approaches and his own approach, as well as that of his colleagues:

> Thus although theology treats of the same things with metaphysics, physics and ethics, yet the mode of considering is far different. It treats of God not like metaphysics as a being or as he can be known from the light of nature, but as the Creator and Redeemer made known by revelation. . . . This mode of considering, the other sciences either do not know or do not assume. . . . For theology treats of God and his infinite perfections, not as knowing them in an infinite but in a finite manner; nor absolutely as much as they can be known in themselves, but as much as he has been pleased to reveal them.[76]

These theologians insisted that theological prolegomena are related to the doctrinal system itself in an a posteriori rather than a priori fashion.[77] By following the Reformers in turning away from "the god of the philosophers" to "the God of Abraham, Isaac, and Jacob," and from the knowledge of God's essence to the knowledge of God's self-revelation in covenantal, historical relatedness to the people chosen, redeemed, and called by God, we can recover a distinctly biblical narrative from its Platonizing distortions, medieval and modern. Christ as the mediator of the covenant of redemption is the *fundamentum* of all fundamentals, including prolegomena. The formula of "God, not as he is in himself, but as he has covenanted in Christ," is more than pious platitude for these systematicians. Conscious of their departure from medieval system, they were inscribing a new method with a distinct aim: metaphysics was to take its cue from redemptive action and revelation. This fits well with Hans Urs von Balthasar's claim that Jesus Christ is the center of revelation and redemption "not only in and through his teaching, through the particular or universal truths which he stands for, but essentially and above all by his existence."

> We cannot separate his word from his existence: it possesses his truth only in the context of his life, that is of his giving himself for the truth and love of the Father even unto death on the Cross. Without the Cross, which means equally without the Eucharist, his word would not be true. . . . Hence when we are attempting to grasp him, there is no place for abstraction, for disregarding particular cases, for bracketing off in essential accidentals at the historical level of his life, because it is precisely in this uniqueness that his essential, normative character lies.[78]

At the same time, even approaching the theological task in this manner, one must engage in metaphysical propositions. Even to say that "God is one" or to assert divine immutability on the basis of God's self-testimony, "For I the LORD I do not change" (Mal. 3:6), is to practice metaphysics. Diffidence to any kind of such assertion suggests that we cannot even attribute love to God. At stake, of course, is not only the possibility of theology, but the possibility of faith and piety. Prayer would be meaningless or at least arbitrary, and worship would be denied a referent beyond individual or communal experience, constructing a god on the basis of our projected needs or transcendent deductions.

As with the other false dilemmas, what is required here is a distinctively Christian metaphysics that is suspicious of speculation. If all of theology is analogical, the alternative to rationalism need not be agnosticism. By reintegrating exegesis and system along the lines we have suggested, Christian theology can not only cease being intimidated by the assault on metaphysics (which is inevitably pursued by engaging in it), but can begin to wean itself from the false metaphysics (caught between Heraclitus and Parmenides) that critics have every reason to deconstruct.

There is a time for every purpose under heaven and different methods as well. Systematic theology is not merely edifying literature, as important as that is. Nor is it evangelistic or practical, although the same systematician may also engage in writing those sorts of books. I think that we are quite right to explain the Christian kerygma in terms of the history of redemption (i.e., chiefly biblical theology). Nevertheless, at some point, challenges to even the simplest assertions naturally arising from the narrative itself will call for comparison of particular passages with others. Each time this occurs, greater refinement will result and, we hope, a greater sense of the connectedness not only of canon and covenant, but of Christology and ecclesiology, our understanding of relation of the kingdom of God to election and of the sacraments to faith will emerge.

Further, clashes between interpretations will, depending on their magnitude, continue to excite this refinement. This is why biblical-theological critics of systematics must beware of ignoring their colleagues who have taken account of these clashes. Rather than being the product of steady exegetical refinement, much theological advance has been due to the crisis in which exegetes confronted extratextual challenges (philosophy, science, history, etc.) and had to rethink their exegetical formulations. The doctrine of the Trinity, for instance, is hardly the product of hellenization, but is rather largely the result of being forced by non-Trinitarian groups who were motivated by Hellenistic a prioris to formulate a cumulative body of exegesis and reflection with greater consistency. James Barr was quite correct to criticize the oversimplifying tendency of the biblical theology movement, especially its obsession with categorizing whatever it did not appreciate as "Hellenistic" as opposed to "Hebraic."[79] Characteristically, the former becomes the umbrella for metaphysics and systematic reflection, while the latter encompasses biblical theology. Often, genuine contrasts of this nature are undermined out of fear of the tendency to oversimplify.

Modern theology's apparent fear of the *fides quae creditur* (which encounter theology largely rejects as objectifying God—I-It rather than I-Thou) rests on an

Enlightenment suspicion of referential religious assertions, authority, and assent—and even more basically, on a false dilemma posed by a nonbiblical understanding of transcendence and immanence. But the environment today is more open to a greater range of possibilities. For instance, Ricoeur's distinction between referential inquiry (He/She) and reflexive inquiry (I-You) better serves all pursuits of inquiry.[80] As Polanyi and Kuhn have shown regarding scientific revolutions, periods of "prophetic" and revolutionary insight are followed by systematization. It is simply wrong-headed to pit the Cappadocian Fathers and Augustine against the simple-minded fishermen at Jesus' side, or the Protestant scholastics against the Reformers. Nevertheless, to every method there is a time and place. Our time seems to parallel those impoverished periods in which authentic evangelical proclamation is threatened by "powers and principalities." It may be chiefly a time requiring fresh witness and confession of Christ, not a time chiefly of systematization and new scholastic enterprises. Closer to the periods of the apostolic church and the magisterial Reformation than to the remarkable ages of medieval and Protestant scholasticism, our own moment calls for a new commitment to kerygmatic tasks. Thus, a doctrine of God in our day will be best presented not only by repeating or reformulating classical formulae, but by announcing and explicating the sense of God's relation to history as "the God of Abraham, Isaac, and Jacob," which is to say, "The God and Father of our Lord Jesus Christ, in the face of late modernity and its collapse." It is catechetical, confessional, pastoral in its method, and concerned to rehearse God's story. Although it will not shrink from apologetics, its greatest apologetic strategy will be to announce God's saving activity in history.

Whether they followed their own rule as well as one might have hoped, the Protestant scholastics distinguished between a magisterial and ministerial use of reason. Today we would want to add, under the "ministerial" resources, experience and tradition. While reason, experience, and tradition are not allowed to be foundational in Reformed systematics, as they are, for instance, in the Wesleyan Quadrangle, they are indispensable as servants of exegesis and system. Philosophical theology, the natural sciences, history, the arts, politics, sociology, and cultural studies are all crucial as ministers but become tyrannical as masters. Kept in dialectical tension, with scripture treated as the final court of appeals, each of these disciplines in service to theology keeps its watch on the other and is allowed to critique theological formulations without determining them. This helps to keep evangelical faith from becoming the slave of a particular secular tradition ("Western civilization," "modern," "postmodern," "existential," "Kantian") or even ecclesial tradition, while attentive to both. Drawing its confidence from its constituting Word, church theology is free to appreciate secular insights and the wisdom of its own reflection. But it would be an act of apostasy in the one case and an act of solipsism in the latter if church theology should adopt these as foundational. God, not in the hiddenness of the divine essence (archetypal theology), but God as God has covenanted with us in Christ (ectypal theology of pilgrims), is the path toward reintegration of metaphysics and personal encounter.

3. Faith–Praxis

As we have already observed, the redemptive-historical model underscores that theology is chiefly practical—not in the sense that it is chiefly ethics, but in the sense that it is primarily concerned with the concrete issues of life and death, on an individual and global scale. This, of course, is consistent with our analysis of the Reformation tradition. Even here our sources suggest contours of reintegration. Vos fleshes this point out a bit:

> It is true, the Gospel teaches that to know God is life eternal. But the concept of 'knowledge' here is not to be understood in its Hellenic sense, but in the Shemitic [Semitic] sense. According to the former, 'to know' means to mirror the reality of a thing in one's consciousness. The Shemitic and Biblical idea is to have the reality of something practically interwoven with the inner experience of life. Hence 'to know' can stand in the Biblical idiom for 'to love', 'to single out in love.' Because God desires to be known after this fashion, He has caused His revelation to take place in the milieu of the historical life of a people. The circle of revelation is not a school, but a 'covenant'. To speak of revelation as an 'education' of humanity is a rationalistic and utterly un-scriptural way of speaking. All that God disclosed of Himself has come in response to the practical religious needs of His people as these emerged in the course of history.[81]

Compare this with Abraham Joshua Heschel's observation:

> Greek philosophy began in a world without God. It could not accept the gods or the example of their conduct. Plato had to break with the gods and to ask: What is good? Thus the problem of values was born. And it was the idea of values that took the place of God. Plato lets Socrates ask: What is good? But Moses' question was: What does God require of thee?[82]

Heschel here points up the ethical implication of metaphysical and epistemological autonomy. It is an ethics that must necessarily lead to abstract speculation and anxiety over whether one has really, after all that work, found the *Ding-an-sich*. It is an ethics without covenant, duty without a personal Other who acts and speaks, taking the illocutionary stance of command and promise that renders me a responsible "I." But the emphasis on the word, which parallels the Reformation's emphasis on the *fides ex auditu* (not to mention the Hebraic suspicion of images), signals a way forward for a biblical theology. The Platonic paradigm of vision is based on the notion that this realm of appearance is a mirror or copy of the eternal ideas. In modern idealism, that ideal realm may have been located in the mind of the empirical or universal "I," but speculative reason retains its medieval centrality. It is idols of the mind which mirror universal truth. But the linguistic turn represents a long overdue protest against the idols of the inner eye. The priority of language to thought is a necessary presupposition for the model we are proposing.

The Platonizing tendency also created a dichotomy between *theoria* and *praxis*, the former linked to the contemplation of the eternal forms, the latter to action in the real world. And just as the word-based liturgy of the Reformation unleashed an unprecedented period of faithful and sometimes unfaithful action on the part of laypeople in the world, so too the renewed emphasis on language in general and the text in particular may prove to heal the rift between faith and action that is so alien to the biblical world. Paul Ricoeur writes,

> Saying and doing, signifying and making are intermingled to such an extent that it is impossible to set up a lasting and deep opposition between "theoria" and "praxis." The word is my kingdom and I am not ashamed of it. . . . As a listener to the Christian message, I believe that words may change the "heart," that is, the refulgent core of our preferences and the positions which we embrace.[83]

This changing of the heart of individual hearers to which Ricoeur refers is an indispensable dimension of praxis, and the prerequisite of any general corporate witness against the powers that would oppress others and ignore the divine summons. A familiar word in Calvin's vocabulary is "piety." Reduced to caricature in our day, this term was actually used to encompass the whole of Christian belief, worship, and service. Without confusing faith with works, justification with sanctification, or law with gospel, it nevertheless served as a bond that united them. As has been often observed, Calvin's discussion of predestination in the *Institutes* follows his discourse on prayer, which is of comparable length. It is the singular privilege of God's children to be able to cry, "Abba! Father!" and to receive gifts from his hand by virtue of union with Christ. "So true it is that we dig up by prayer the treasures that were pointed out by the Lord's gospel, and which our faith has gazed upon."[84]

Theology, as heavenly *sapientia* (wisdom), is borne out of prayer as much as study. It is a devotional as well as intellectual exercise, and while doctrine shapes piety, the reverse is also true. The experience of being damned, Luther said, makes a theologian one who stands *coram Deo* and not merely *coram hominibus*. So the theologian is a penitent who must stand with the other publicans crying out, "Lord, be merciful to me, a sinner!" It is first and foremost before God and the church, rather than the world (or the academy), that the theologian stands. Not only does sound piety require sound theology; sound theology requires sound piety.[85]

Our first two criteria referred to the two principal marks of the church; Reformed dogmaticians have often added a third: discipline. Far from unleashing individualism and anarchy, the Reformers emphasized communal interpretation of scripture. One still could not interpret the Bible "for herself," but had to do this together with others under the authority of Christ in his church. The royal office of Christ was still just as surely mediated through the officers of the visible church for the Reformers as it had ever been for Rome. The difference, of course, was that "the church" meant not the magisterium, but the whole community of faith. It is baptism, not ordination, that makes a priest. And yet, the

Reformed (and Lutheran) symbols are amply clear, against the "enthusiasts," that the office of the keys was entrusted after the apostles to their successors, as the age of an extraordinary ministry paved the way for the ordinary ministry.

Despite its one-sidedly punitive connotations today, "discipline" simply refers to the regulation of church life in such a way that both tyranny and anarchy will be less likely to upset the ministry of the means of grace. This meant that there was always to be an internal judicial process that included the pastors and other officers as well as those under their charge. Of course, this system cannot operate by itself, but requires faithfulness to truth and godliness. One of the consequences of modernity is that we no longer take this mark very seriously: "heresy" is rarely mentioned apart from a pejorative context, and even more rarely prosecuted. And yet, this is precisely the chief responsibility of the *presbuteroi* in the epistles. The church does not—cannot—determine the truth. Its role is interpretive rather than formal, ministerial rather than magisterial. But there is a teaching office in the church to which the faith and life of the covenant community must be held accountable, and it is as essential for the visible church to mediate the royal office of Christ as his priestly and prophetic offices.

Just as sound piety cannot be separated from its source in justification and adoption, personal piety cannot be separated from public activity. An evangelically shaped piety will inevitably turn one away from "forever gazing within" (Calvin), to look out onto a world in need. Medieval piety had not only emphasized merit; it pointed the energetic saint to a life of isolation from the world in meditation upon the eternal Good by transcending the world of appearances. But Reformation piety could not stand in greater contrast. First, it emphasized God's redemptive activity in history and in the hearing of the gospel, sharply criticizing the Platonized elements of the medieval synthesis, shifting the emphasis from contemplation to action. Second, it emphasized free justification, which freed one from at least the theological motive for serving oneself by serving God and others. If justification before God is already accomplished, God and neighbor are not instrumental to one's own salvation. This point was made by Calvin in his debate with Cardinal Sadoleto.[86] Although not without excesses and failures, Reformed scholasticism produced some of the greatest works of biblical commentary, devotion, and pastoral care, in addition to contributing some of the first works in early modern political theory (especially resistance to tyrants, rights and responsibilities, and church-state relations) and actually established models of diaconal service to society that continue to shape attitudes even where the underlying theology has been attenuated or lost. It was this body of pastor-scholars that participated more directly in the shaping of evolving political and social institutions of Western democracies than perhaps at any time since. In fact, numerous studies in recent decades have examined the critical contribution of federal theology (i.e., the covenant motif) in its application to political and social theory.[87] And it was on these shoulders that Abraham Kuyper stood in his formative role in both theology and Christian social theory (which he acted on even before he was prime minister).

Reformed churches—and Reformed Christians—have much of which to repent. Many examples could be found of complicity with unjust regimes that plundered natural resources and instituted oppressive structures of economic and social existence: South African apartheid, violence in northern Ireland, and an all too mixed legacy in the face of American genocide on the frontier, slavery in the South, urbanization in the North, suburban anonymity, and so on. Both mainline and evangelical energies often seem so spent on politics and protest that the ministry of Word and sacrament, which transforms individuals and communities, has become secularized. Piety is surrendered to ideology. In other cases, the American obsession with therapeutic well-being has substituted narcissism for sacrifice. In a myriad of forms across the theological spectrum, the theology of glory appears to be more pervasive than the theology of the cross and resurrection. And in the meantime, genuine day-to-day participation in building strong communities, in our roles not only as fellow believers but as fellow neighbors, is often made difficult by the fatigue of church activities and self-assured social and moral causes beyond the scope, authority, mission, and expertise of the institutional church. Our bourgeois, liberal, commercial existence labors to demoralize our visions for our immediate future in the light of the eschatological consummation. The more our churches eschew proclamation for "practical" mission, the more irrelevant they become; "prophetic" has become a euphemism for the most banal reaffirmations of secular solutions.

There are, however, theological reasons that this should not be so—especially a theology that takes God's redemptive purpose and sovereign activity in this world so seriously and offers ample historical precedents to give us some pause for self-criticism. In providing the background for the rise of liberation theology in Latin America, José Miguez Bonino points to the strengths of this theological tradition. Sarmiento, a social reformer and president of Argentina, observed the practical consequences of a religious life centered around the word, public proclamation and consequent activity in the world rather than around a chiefly interior and private piety.[88] While many Latin American thinkers and activists were not particularly interested in becoming Protestants themselves, they admired the connection that they often saw among Protestants between faith and life in the real world. Verging on a Weberian analysis, Bonino writes,

> Protestantism (they referred mostly to Puritanism) had helped to shape the virtues needed for the modern world: freedom of judgment, reliability, a pioneering and enterprising spirit, moral seriousness. It was the religion of activity, culture, and life as opposed to ritualism, idle speculation, and the next world. Under the auspices of these men, conditions were created for the introduction of Protestant missions in Latin America. Religious freedom was insured—not without resistance—and, in some cases, missions or Protestant immigration were sought and invited.[89]

Bonino cites a respected Colombian writer during the 1950s: "It seems to me that one merchandise that is urgently needed in this land is that of ideas. . . . It is time that the breezes of the Reformation . . . should blow this way."[90] In Bonino's narrative, the all-too-familiar story is told of how genuine religious concerns that brought liberation were followed by a period of secularization in which capital-hungry Westerners were willing to forge partnerships with Latin American oppressors in order to line their own pockets. The purpose of relating this is not an exercise in self-congratulation, but as evidence that theology does shape praxis when it is allowed to thrive in a community of faith, where the preached Word, administered sacraments, and discipline of the church is maintained.

But in our day, many would rather participate on the margins of remote causes with a great deal of popular support among the elites at home than belong to communities, social and ecclesiastical, in which they stand in obligation to the face of the other who stands before them. If preaching is preoccupied with relevance, worship is reduced to entertainment, teaching is exchanged for technique, and mutual obligation is eclipsed by individualism and globalism, there is hardly sufficient reason to be identified as a Christian body. This concern spans the theological spectrum, from liberal to conservative and Quaker to Roman Catholic, including our own Reformed communion. While liberation theology tends to identify Christ with culture with just as disastrous spiritual results as conservatism, it does make the point that theology is not *simply* discovered in the classroom and then applied in praxis. Rather, as Gutiérrez puts it, theology is "critical reflection on praxis."[91] In a more balanced definition, he describes theology as "critical reflection on the presence and action of the church in the world in the light of faith," and has more recently added, "critical reflection on historical praxis in the light of the Word."[92] Despite the criticisms that we have noted elsewhere, there is much in Gutiérrez's theology of liberation that may help to correct the mind-body Gnosticism of so much of modern theology. While he risks losing the faith-praxis dialectic to the subjection of theology to action, his emphasis warns against the opposite reduction:

> By preaching the gospel message, by its sacraments, and by the charity of its members, the church proclaims and welcomes the gift of the kingdom of God at the heart of human history. The Christian community professes a "faith which works through charity." It is—at least it ought to be—efficacious love, action, and commitment to the service of others. Theology is reflection, a critical attitude. The commitment of love, of service, comes first. Theology follows; it is the second step. . . . The pastoral activity of the church does not flow as a conclusion from theological premises. Theology does not generate a pastoral approach; rather it reflects upon it. . . . The life, preaching, and historical commitment of the church will be a privileged *locus theologicus* for understanding the faith.[93]

"Reformed theology," writes anti-apartheid theologian John de Gruchy, "as an evangelical and prophetic theology, has, as it were, been in the field much longer than liberation theology. Moreover, it has certain insights into the nature of

Christian faith and obedience that it rightly treasures and brings to the dialogue."[94] In *Black and Reformed*, Alan Boesak observed that the period of orthodoxy occasioned the greatest racial unity in the early days of the South African
colony and that only when pietism and revivalism undermined theological clarity did apartheid emerge as a missionary strategy of growth.[95] Throughout the
period of apartheid, both Boesak and de Gruchy inform us, there were few
appeals to scripture and the confession. Arguably, the triumph of the struggle
against apartheid was in some measure due to the admission of the Dutch
Reformed Church that apartheid, which it had supported, was *heresy.* Here is an
obvious illustration of the covenantal character of preaching as divine summons,
judgment, and justification. This is what good theology does—or must do. In
such experiences, one's theology changes. After a period of taking its theology for
granted, and then finally surrendering it to ungodly ideologies, the church was
faced with a condition that tested its faith and practice, and in the light of that
its rediscovered theological resources were able to reshape the praxis. The dialectical nature of this relationship is unmistakable, a point that is somewhat at odds
with both traditional and liberationist tendencies to reductionism.

The reforming impulse of Calvinism can easily devolve into triumphalism,
but it has also led to social, political, economic, and cultural effects that are amply
acknowledged across the theological spectrum. This impulse, theologically
shaped and not merely productive of theology, must be recovered in the church's
diaconal responsibility to the world today. "So then, whenever we have an opportunity, let us work for the good of all, especially for those of the family of faith"
(Gal. 6:10). As Walter Brueggemann observes,

> This new covenant now claimed for Christianity has become an
> intensely theological-christological claim, as in 1 Corinthians 11:25.
> It is also the case, however, that the category of covenant and new
> covenant entered into the political vocabulary and political theory of
> the West, largely through the Calvinist tradition and more especially
> the work of Theodore Beza. . . . Seen as a source of new polity, the
> new covenant is not a proposal for individualism, as Jeremiah 31:33
> is often taken to be. Rather, it is a powerful protest against the indi-
> vidualist autonomy of modernity and an insistence that we are
> indeed members one of another.[96]

However, Brueggemann surmises, "It is not at all clear how a covenantal polity
will reemerge amid the widespread and uncritical commoditization of Western
culture."[97] While that is undoubtedly true of the wider culture, the Christian cul-
tus, as the foretaste of the age to come, has a burden to eschew such rivals and
not only think but organize itself according to the covenantal pattern of its canonical scriptures.

Despite the enormous contributions, liberation theology, generally speaking,
still seems trapped in the turn to the subject, too anthropocentric, too instru-
mentalist in its understanding of theology (indeed, of "God," "Christ," and
"church"), too dependent on radical Hegelian teleologies, which are largely

secularized eschatologies with immanent progress rather than divine irruption. Without maintaining a robust understanding of divine alterity, the eschatological not-yet, and the creature-creator distinction, these theologies even risk losing the important ingredient of final justice: namely, that one who stands outside of the web of violence alone is capable of judging fairly and conclusively.

The imperative (ethics) set over against the indicative (theology), and its obverse, have had disastrous consequences in the modern era. There is the further tendency not only to get the Bible to answer our questions (as in Tillich's method of correlation), but to determine what in the scriptures is and is not useful to that end. Liberationists are surely correct to remind us of the importance of reading the scriptures with the poor and the marginalized—that does make a difference in faithful interpretation. Nevertheless, in many instances there is a blatant and explicit disregard for the text. With Marx, the goal is not to understand, but to change things. But is this not a secular form of works righteousness, an autonomy that is always speaking and never listening, the very violence that underlies the injustice that liberationists frequently critique with such convicting power? Are the "liberators" ever implicated in the judgment they announce? Or, for that matter, are the oppressed also regarded as sinners as well as sinned-against? This is a question that "Christian" politics of the left and the right may be fairly asked.

There is the constant danger in immanence-oriented theologies to exploit scripture and theology for the ends of a particular group, and this is evident in right-wing as well as left-wing ideologies. In both cases, the labor of exegesis and systematization is often treated as a diversion from the real business of practical existence, but this is to leave communities trapped within the narrative of "this present evil age." The difficult task, it seems to me, is to reintegrate justification and justice without surrendering either to the other. In contrast to the Reformers and the post-Reformation era (on both the Roman Catholic and Protestant sides), modern Protestantism has been all too eager to choose either justification or justice, and even when it has engaged in the latter, it has often been without much reflection on the theological indicatives that drive the imperatives. By contrast, scripture moves easily from the indicative ("I am the God who brought you out of Egypt") to the imperative ("Therefore, you shall have no other gods before me"). For example, in Paul's letters the doctrinal analysis is not conflated with ethics, but a conspicuous "therefore" marks the transition, not away from doctrine or separate from it, but toward the application of Christian distinctives to an active life in the world. Pietism marks the break in this balance, at least for Protestant theology. With its rise, theology increasingly came to be regarded as a diversion from piety (and in later orthodoxy, it probably was). After the triumph of modern rationalism, these sibling enterprises tended to go their separate ways in the pursuit of a universal ethics that could transcend confessional strife.

Despite its conspicuous and often profound appeals to biblical narrative, many versions of liberation theology reflect this foundationalist temptation, using such stories as the exodus as ciphers for universal principles of justice. Even when it appeals to the history of Israel, one often gets the impression that the biblical narrative is chiefly an allegory for political struggle in much the same way that Old Testament narratives were used to underwrite imperialism (the many versions of "manifest destiny"), rather than simply being the narrative that incorporates the church in every age. One frequently observes the same hermeneutical tendencies, but with different versions of who gets cast as "Israel" and "Egypt." While liberationists are generally more sensitive to the biblical identification of God with the poor and oppressed, this allegorical use of scripture needs to be criticized if a genuinely Christian theology is to be allowed to shape communal praxis once more.

Without a serious eschatology of present in-breaking (and not merely a movement of the future toward the present), there is every danger of regarding the kingdom of God as not only in the world, but of it. Furthermore, the church is not merely the anthropological *summum bonum*, the highest expression of human being whose existence serves chiefly secular ends. Rather, it is God's chosen race, "from every tribe and language and people and nation" (Rev. 5:9).

Given such qualifications, we can still learn from liberation theologians something about the relationship of faith and praxis. If traditional theologies ordinarily regard praxis as theology applied, liberationists regard theology as praxis defined. Both approaches fail to recognize the dialectical relationship from which Christian piety emerges. For instance, Vedantic Buddhist convictions will generate a kind of life and service different from that generated by Shiite Islam. If Bonino was correct in his analysis, the same is true of Protestant and Roman Catholic theological emphases. Practice inevitably flows from theology. And yet, it is not a one-way street. As in the case of Paul, Augustine, Luther, Pascal, Kierkegaard, Bonhoeffer, and Barth, life experience in a particular time and place often affects one's theology. It is too one-sided to say merely that the way things are said—their conceptual scheme, their linguistic form—is culturally and historically conditioned. This is too gnostic and a too typically modern separation of thought from language and existence. As our own horizon changes, we see things differently, even in the Bible. While "those things" may have been there all along in scripture, we were not. Our horizon may always be judged, but it cannot be eliminated, nor should we desire this any more than the amputation of a limb. We cannot help but see things from our perspective; the alternative is not objectivity, but blindness.

But our proposal touches directly on this severed connection. It does not claim that a sound theology will inevitably lead to sound discipleship; rather, it insists that doctrine is already practical and directed toward aims, while praxis is already theological. Notice that praxis is not merely reflective of a particular theology, but is in its execution already a theology. Here again the covenant motif is a major integrative catalyst. *Hesed* in Hebrew is much richer and comprehensive than its typical translations, "love" and "faithfulness." It is a word that belongs to the covenant; in fact, it has been appropriately translated in some versions as "covenant faithfulness" or "covenant loyalty." One is not faithful to the covenant by assenting to the history of God's redemptive acts and its doctrinal explanation, but by responding faithfully in community. It is not a matter of choosing between doctrine or life, but of actively participating in a particular form of life shaped by a particular form of teaching. Only by indwelling this covenant community faithfully can this unity of faith and praxis be formed.

We have seen how the paradigmatic doctrine of the covenant animated the integration not only of exegesis and system, but of theology and praxis, contributing significantly to the development of a model for conceptualizing the one and the many problem in terms of the body politic. It would be worthwhile, for instance, to pursue the implications of the "common grace" covenant, a pact that God has made with Cain, renewed in Noah, and then renewed again in Jesus' ministry.[98] The "secular city," east of Eden, though never identified with the Kingdom of Christ in this age, is guarded and tended by providence until the last day.

The eschatological orientation that has been emphasized here deserves greater attention in connecting faith and practice. As the age to come dawns in a semi-realized eschatology here and now, genuine transformation of individuals and communities is not only possible but is an empirical reality. The influence of one's eschatological orientation on ethics cannot be overestimated. One eschatology has led to the construction of "Christendom," or at least the expectation of history gradually progressing toward such a golden age, while another type of eschatology has led to paralysis and ambivalence in terms of one's responsibilities in a world that is, according to its proponents, getting worse and will likely not survive this generation. Overrealized eschatologies have given rise to enormous energy in the advancement both of mission and culture, as well as often leading to triumphalism and suppression of rival eschata. Underrealized eschatologies have often led to greater restraint of ecclesiastical ambition, but have also tended to create a quasi-gnostic alienation from the God of creation, history, ordinary providence, and stewardship in the world.

Too much of Protestant theology has been formed in the womb of a type of pietism with an antitheological bias and a fascination with praxis merely as an interior experience of God and grace. Precisely its lack of concern for doctrine contributes to an individualistic and dualistic practice that is often shared by conservative evangelicals and liberals. Could a renewed covenant theology contribute to a reintegration of faith and practice that is communal, connected, and theocentric rather than anthropocentric? While there are no national covenants in this era of redemptive history, there is a covenant of grace in which, as Paul said, "From now on, therefore, we regard no one from a human point of view," but as those who are "in Christ," "a new creation" (2 Cor. 5:16–17). Rescripted, racists become agents of reconciliation. A greedy tax collector, judged and justified, is not content to start today with his new role, but insists—out of gratitude, not guilt—to repair his injustices of the past. Only a biblical theology of grace and of covenant can produce this inner ambition that is far more powerful than guilt or sentimentalism. The church is called, like Athanasius, to be *against* the world *for* the world.

As our old theologians remind us, a covenant has two sides. Although even the human side rests on the foundation of divine gift (faith, repentance, perseverance), it calls for a response. The summons is not merely delivered into the air, but accomplishes its intended purpose. We realize that we are not, after all, the objective masters of the world—or of the way it should be—but that there is someone else to whom we are accountable and who can see the self-righteousness and pride clinging to our best attitudes and performances. In the context of a gracious covenant, in which one's ultimate destiny is already settled in Christ, service to one's neighbor out of self-interest loses at least its theoretical basis.

In contrast to the Greek conception of knowledge as *noesis* (Lat., *scientia*) transcending concrete, historical existence (a disparaged "realm of appearances"), underwritten by the analogy of vision, we have defended the Hebraic understanding of what our older theologians called the *habitus credendi* (a disposition to believe) in terms of an obedient, covenantal response to a personal redeemer in history, underwritten by the analogy of word. In this latter view, the biblical way of knowing is already practical in the sense that it meets the human need for reconciliation with and worship of God, with corresponding action in the world in response to the human other who addresses us as the bearer of God's image. In outlining a philosophy of Judaism, Abraham Joshua Heschel observes the unity of three aspects of the biblical "way of knowing": Worship ("Lift up your eyes on high and see: Who created these?"[Isa. 40:26]), Learning ("I am the LORD your God" [Ex. 20:2]), and Action ("We will do, and we will be obedient" [Ex. 24:7]). "The three are one, and we must go all three ways to reach the one destination. For this is what Israel discovered: the God of nature is the God of history, and the way to know Him is to do His will."[99] And, we might add, the way to know God as redeemer is as God offers himself in the Son, within a covenant of grace, through Word and sacrament.

The antignostic thrust of liberation theology contributes to this discussion of a fully historical drama in which revelation is subservient to redemption and theology is chiefly practical rather than theoretical. However, practical is not equivalent to pragmatic, nor can we rebound from dualism, only to embrace a confusion of God and creation or grace and works, much less mistake the effects of eschatological in-breaking within the covenantal context for the arrival of the consummation itself. To announce prematurely the union of the kingdoms of this world with the kingdom of Christ is to secularize the covenant and thereby to undermine that very authority and counter-cultural efficacy of the kingdom of grace in an age dominated by injustice. A theology that is genuinely eschatological (upholding the character of divine action from above as in-breaking) and historical has a potential for reintegrating the convictional and activist aspects of Christian, covenantal discipleship, without merely imitating secular alternatives.

Instead of simply moving on, forgetting what is past, Reformed Christians who want to remain faithful to the apostolic faith renewed in the Reformation must enter a period of soul-searching in order to identify infidelities to that witness in this time and place. Learning the lessons from the past, we may be more likely at least to make different mistakes in the future. For too long, conservative Reformed churches have tended to divorce their theology from worship and life, rendering the former irrelevant and the latter like a body without an animating soul. In ecclesiastical terms, it separates the ministry of the elders (spiritual) from that of the deacons (physical), a disjunction that is not only harmful in the present but out of sync with our own tradition. Genuine reintegration of theology and ethics, belief and action, cannot live by theory alone, just as it cannot live without it. For this to work, there must be a concrete covenantal existence, definitively (though never fully) determined on the practical level by the reintegration of the pastoral and diaconal ministries of the churches.

In summary, then, theology is not only an exegetical enterprise but a systematic one, not only redemptive-historical but doctrinal, not only interior but exterior, not only individual but covenantal, and not only theoretical but practical.

CHURCH–ACADEMY

French postmodernist thinker Michel de Certeau now offers a criticism of liberal religion that might have been dismissed only a couple of decades ago:

> Today a Christian group protects itself often by hiding its particularity, by speaking as the testimony of all good wills, by identifying itself with positions held in common, by announcing only the insignificant truths of every man. This poor universalism is a mask; it is a compensation against the fact of the Christian particularity.[100]

Systematic theology has often, in the modern age, turned to exegeting texts in philosophy, literary studies, hermeneutics, politics, social studies, and psychology. In this setting, it is no wonder that biblical scholars feel more remote than ever from systematics. If reintegration is to be more than a slogan, exegetes will have to become more familiar with the history of dogma and at least a key representative system of their own ecclesial tradition. George Lindbeck and others have reminded us, as Barth did, that theology is not comparative religion, but an exercise in clarifying the rules of a distinctively Christian grammar. Watson is correct: "To practise theology is always to practise a particular theology. . . . The discipline of theological hermeneutics is not mere prolegomena; it exists only within the sphere of biblical theology."[101]

At the same time, the laudable reticence to reduce theology to comparative religion must not be allowed to degenerate into an easy dismissal of what David Tracy calls "publicness." It is not only those identified by Lindbeck as "cognitive-propositionalists" who make truth claims. "Every theologian, therefore, should render those claims explicit by rendering disciplinary criteria as explicit as possible."[102] Even those, like Barth, Frei, and Lindbeck, who have insisted on "church theology" have been employed by university faculties. To what extent can theologians bite the *wissenschaftlich* hand that feeds them? What is the entrance fee at this table, and is it too high in terms of covenantal faithfulness? Tracy insists that Christianity's own inner commitment to publicness already renders acceptance of the rules of the academic game. "To ask the question of the truth of religious claims is not a luxury for theology," he says, but a necessary aspect of its own internal integrity. "Even theologians who 'will not stay for an answer' to that question soon find that the drive to speak a truth about religious meaning—and thereby about the most fundamental, existential questions of our common humanity—will not [have a hearing]. . . . Without that demand for publicness—for criteria, evidence, warrants, disciplinary status—serious academic theology is dead."[103]

This stark challenge no doubt rings true for many readers. Those questions of criteria, disciplinary status, and related issues are yet to pursued in a future work. Could the "program" that has been sketched here answer those questions in a way that could satisfy both Lindbeck and Tracy? Perhaps not, but surely theology should attempt to remain faithful to the internally coherent confessional theology of the church and to the externally corresponding claims concerning the truth of that confession. Theology is both confessional and public, and whatever we make of that in terms of specific answers to those criteriological questions, finding satisfying resolution to that conundrum is an urgent challenge. It is not an either-or, we are often told, and yet it seems that many of the available proposals are precisely that. Theological faculties, it would seem, have to defend their usefulness to actual, living ecclesial communities and to the university disciplines. No other discipline has such a double burden or is tempted by such divided loyalties.

But this responsibility for theological formation must not be placed ultimately at the door of divinity schools, much less universities. It is chiefly a domestic and ecclesial responsibility to inculcate a literate laity, and in a period in which catechesis has been traded in for therapeutic "sharing," the church must reassess its mission and methods as well. William Willimon troubles the waters of both expressions of the establishment in our day:

> Left to our own devices, seminary teachers attempt to mask the depressing sameness of our almost universally ill-informed students with talk of "diversity." We speak proudly of "openness" and "freedom" while rigidly policing ourselves for deviation from the conventional norms, as we anxiously await the world to tell us which "issues of the day" we may address in our "variety of ways." . . . Our difficulty is that we have students who have been formed in no specific ecclesial tradition—other than the tradition which has taught them that they ought to honor no tradition. . . . Too many of us theologians have left our students to wallow in their own subjectivity rather than challenging them with a perspective not of their own devising. . . . What the church needs from leaders today requires more than merely experientially based theology.[104]

If "covenant" is to be more than a leitmotif of airy theory, our entire approach to ministry will have to change, reconnecting the children to their fathers and mothers, as well as to their own descendants yet in the future, in dynasties of faith. As in pietism, in its earlier and more recent expressions, biblical scholars sometimes evidence an arrogant disdain for these tasks, as if they are the only ones working with the primary sources and the theologians are experts merely on what others have said about those sources. But in fact, the biblical scholar is also engaging in interpretation, just as those who have labored together (and sometimes fruitfully against each other's interpretations) to understand. On the other hand, systematicians are inevitably forced with a decision as to whether they will do theology both from the church and for the church, a charge with which Barth left our craft. This will entail, especially for systematicians, a personal commitment to the scriptures as the source for conclusions, rather than depending on speculative and imaginative constructions that simply mirror trends in other disciplines. Would it make a difference if those engaged in academic theology recognized themselves to be among those addressed by God as fellow actors in the divine drama, across time as well as within it, within the context of a covenant that established the possibilities and limits of such discourse? It would seem that the integrity and value of theology as a distinct discipline depends on it.

Chapter Nine

Community Theater
Local Performances of the Divine Drama

We conclude this work with an application of our model to the concrete life of the people of God in their ordinary cultic environment: the liturgy of word in sacrament, which, in local situations, enacts the drama we have been describing, exhibiting the dialogical life of the covenant principle. We attempt this in the light of the counterdrama that was set up in the first two chapters by Derrida's "Theater of Cruelty" and Mark C. Taylor's a/theological metanarrative of the wanderer.

THE PLOTLESS PLOT

Nietzsche was particularly insightful when he observed that modernity wanted Christian morality without Christian theology—the fruit without the tree itself—and that this was an impossible project. In fact, we have seen its effects played out in the extreme in our own day. Despite notable exceptions, theology has fallen on hard times in both evangelical and mainline Protestantism. Surely Richard Lints is correct when he says that "the epistemology of the typical modern person is essentially schizophrenic." "Theology," he says, "ought to possess a pride of place in evangelicalism, but, like serious biblical study, it has on the whole been relegated to the backwaters of a few theological seminaries. . . . Like their archenemy Rudolf Bultmann, evangelicals have begun to embrace 'relevance' as a fundamental criterion of truth."[1] But we contend that in the divine liturgy theology and praxis, the individual and communal solidarity, history and eschatology, transcendence and immanence, come together dramatically. This is not to replace Christ with liturgy but to suggest that in this covenantal context

Christ's prophetic, priestly, and royal ministry among us takes concrete expression here and now. But before we explain how this works, we must remind ourselves of the counterdrama of our time, whether we identify it as "modern" or "postmodern."

We recall Nietzsche's claim: "That my life has no aim is evident from the accidental nature of its origin; that *I can posit an aim for myself* is another matter."[2] This assertion of absolute and autonomous selfhood represents the climax of modernity's turn to the subject; yet it is the foundation of allegedly postmodern selfhood. Whatever ironies are involved here, the condition of our time presents in the starkest possible terms the counterdrama to the biblical one we have outlined here. As such, it provides the ideal foil for the divine drama. Mark C. Taylor writes, "Postmodernism opens with the sense of *irrevocable* loss and *incurable* fault. This wound is inflicted by the overwhelming awareness of death—a death that 'begins' with the death of God and 'ends' with the death of our selves. We are in a time between times and a place which is no place."[3]

Living parasitically off of the vanishing memory of the divine drama, the a/theological play presents sin and guilt as not only normal but heroic, for it opens the way to "endless wandering," "straying," "transgressing." "The death of the Alpha and Omega, the disappearance of the self, and the overcoming of unhappy consciousness combine to fray the fabric of history," according to Taylor. "When it is impossible to locate a definite beginning and a decisive end, the narrative line is lost and the story seems pointless. *Endgame* now appears to be a play about ending endgames." Citing Stanley Cavell, Taylor adds, "The 'end' of the endgame, however, is at the same time the beginning of an unending game. From the perspective of the end of history, the 'final' plot seems to be 'that there is no plot.'"[4] It is precisely this realization of a plotless plot that finally leads us to a conclusion that is, says Taylor, simultaneously alienating and liberating:

> Such homelessness underscores the anonymity of the saunterer. Attached to no home and *always* separated from father and mother, the wanderer is nameless. . . . In this case, lawlessness proves to be inseparable from grace—grace that arrives only when God and self are dead and history is over. The lawless land of erring, which is forever beyond good and evil, is the liminal world of Dionysus, the Anti-Christ, who calls every wandering mark to carnival, comedy, and carnality.[5]

With this script in mind, we turn to our brief outline of the liturgical enactment of the divine drama.

WORD: PERFORMATIVE SPEECH

Our proposal has argued that the covenant that God has established with his people is distinguished from theologies of manifestation in which symbol, myth, metaphors and other forms of projection. The latter we regard as having been substantially defeated by Feuerbach's critique. In contrast, the history of the covenant develops as a theology of proclamation. We are not left speechless in making constitutive assertions about God, because God is not left speechless. The One who spoke the world into existence, upholds creation by this same word, and will speak the consummation into full realization still speaks new worlds out of darkness and void: "For God, who *said*, 'Let light shine out of darkness, made his light shine in our hearts to give us the light of the knowledge of the glory of God in the face of Christ" (2 Cor. 4:6, NIV, emphasis added). Notice the performative—indeed, perlocutionary—activity of God's speaking.

Throughout scripture, God's speech is represented as not only descriptive (i.e., true propositions), but as performative (action). Examples of this performative utterance include Ezekiel's familiar vision of the valley of the dry bones (Ezek. 37:1–14). Here the Holy Spirit was "upon me," says the prophet, while God spoke in a vision, asking Ezekiel whether he thought these bones—representing Israel in its exile and, ultimately, the world in its sin—could live. Wisely, the prophet answers, "O Lord GOD, you know." God commands Ezekiel to preach to the bones: "Then he said to me, 'Prophesy to these bones, and say to them: O dry bones, hear the word of the LORD'" (v. 4). But Ezekiel's words are not merely his own. He is to speak as God to the bones: "Thus says the Lord GOD to these bones: I will cause breath to enter you, and you shall live . . . and you shall know that I am the LORD" (vv. 5–6). As Ezekiel preaches, the bones grow flesh and the breath of life enters them, until they are standing as "a vast multitude" (vv. 7–10). As interpreted by the New Testament, this was not fulfilled in any subsequent era of Israel's history until Pentecost. After that postresurrection event, however, the apostles, deputized by the Son and empowered by the Spirit, became witnesses whose preaching did exactly what was prophesied by Ezekiel. By preaching—and not just by preaching anything, but by the preaching of the gospel—the dead were raised. This resurrection of the "inner person" became the first event in the self's incorporation into "the age to come."

So Paul writes that "the righteousness of faith" contrasts with "the righteousness of works" in that the latter strives to enter through self-effort (rising to the heights to bring God down or to the depths as if to bring Jesus up from the grave), while the former receives "the word of faith that we proclaim" (Rom. 10:6–8). The righteousness of works assumes that God's secrets must be penetrated by human *poiesis*, while the righteousness of faith recognizes that the transcendent God makes himself immanent through this performative utterance. Christ is made the hearer's Savior by hearing, as this operation of Word and Spirit itself creates faith in the hearer. The apostle goes on then to correlate this strange method with God's additional foolishness in calling and sending ministers from his court to effect the same revolution to the ends of the earth (vv. 14–15). As with Ezekiel and Paul, God's word in the mouth of God's deputies will conduct God's promises to their appointed destination.

In view of this, Reformation theology has ordinarily understood the ministry of the Word to include not only the sermon, but all of the actions in which God addresses the covenant people. This begins with the *votum* or salutation ("God's greeting," as it has come to be called in contemporary Reformed circles) and includes the reading of the law. Turning from his covenantal role of representing God to representing the people, the minister leads the assembly in public confession and then represents God again in pronouncing the absolution. This back-and-forth movement (the dialogical principle) between God and his people involves not only the minister, of course, but the people. God acts in greeting, commanding, and assuring his people of their forgiveness, while the people respond in praise and adoration. Reflecting the priesthood of all believers, the people not only sing in responsive praise, but in their singing also participate in the mutual teaching and proclamation of God's word. They too are "filled with the Spirit, as [they] sing psalms and hymns and spiritual songs among [themselves], singing and making melody to the Lord with [their] hearts" (Eph. 5:18–19). "Let the word of Christ dwell in you richly; *teach and admonish one another* in all wisdom; and with gratitude in your hearts sing psalms and hymns and spiritual songs to God" (Col. 3:16–17, emphasis added).

Far from being a "dead letter" waiting to be brought to life through the ingenuity of the minister or other performances, "the word of God is living and active" and through it "before him no creature is hidden, but all are naked and laid bare to the eyes of him to whom we must render an account" (Heb. 4:12–13). As we have argued, this view of preaching represents a classic example of a perlocutionary act. The word itself effects what is threatened and promised in it, through the operation of the Spirit. So when Jesus attributes this new birth to the Spirit and not to the flesh, he is not separating the Spirit from the word, as his next sentence indicates: "the *words* that I have spoken to you are spirit and life" (John 6:63, emphasis added).

Representing God once more, the minister intercedes on behalf of the covenant people who have thus experienced the drama of the exodus again for themselves. They too have passed from death to life in this liturgical drama, from alienation and despair to the assurance of reconciliation and the response of praise from their side of the covenant—and on that basis they enter the Holy of Holies in this semirealized eschatology. With their covenant mediator and advocate representing their case in heaven, the community's intercession is effective, and the people are prepared to hear God's word in the sermon. While Protestant liturgies often reduce the ministry of the word to the sermon, the sermon is the climax of the word event, as is easily discerned from its dominance in prophetic and apostolic ministry. Furthermore, the sermons in Acts (like so many of the Psalms) cannot get away from a retelling of the divine drama; once again, the play-within-a-play analogy seems appropriate here.[6] The story of divine creation and faithfulness is followed by the unfaithfulness of the covenant partner, which in turn is met with divine solidarity to overcome the sin and unbelief of his people through his messiah. When we allow Christian preaching to drift from this plot, it easily becomes a pretense for other dramas, whether that takes the form of moralism, pragmatism, consumerism, or therapy.

Even the human "parts" of this play are scripted by God, as represented by the Psalter. In this section of scripture God provides the appropriate analogies of ascription to be used faithfully in praise. Even here, then, the covenant servant is not left on her own to determine what to ascribe. And yet, there is a genuine "free play" to interpret one's lines in the script with distinct nuance, just as the sermon is inevitably a paraphrase of scripture and is nevertheless designated the word of God. God takes up the speech of his covenant partners as his own and is thereby not only the one who serves, but condescends to be served by them. The offering is gratefully received by the God who needs nothing—except inasmuch as he represents himself in Christ as hungry, thirsty, a stranger, naked, sick, and in prison (Matt. 25:35–36). Thus, covenant solidarity demands inclusion of those excluded by the drama of "this passing evil age." More than that, those on the margins are moved to the center. As in the larger drama itself, the "needy" (spiritual and physical) are given the prominent roles in the local performance.

As a covenant involves two parties, the indicative and the imperative are necessarily related dialectically: "I am the LORD your God, who brought you . . . out of the house of slavery; you shall have no other gods before me" (Ex. 20:2–3). Yet the human side of the covenant is not allowed the last word. This is reserved for God, and his parting word is once more the word of gospel, as God's blessing is laid upon the covenant people in the benediction.

As the sermon accomplishes this reenactment in miniature, the liturgy as a whole (including the Supper, as we will see below) recounts the cycle of sin and redemption, law and gospel, moving from creation to fall to redemption to grateful obedience and consummation. Failing to view the liturgy of the word as a local performance of the divine drama often leads to the impoverishment of worship. In practical terms, how often have we heard the criticism that the service seems to "go nowhere"? In other words, it fails to follow the plot line of the drama that is indicated by the script. It is no wonder that churches replace the liturgy of the word with dramas patterned on TV sitcoms. At least the culture of consumerism and entertainment evokes response. However, the covenant renewal ceremony offers the only service in which God promises to make the new creation a reality among his people.

SACRAMENT: PERFORMATIVE SIGN AND SEAL

Illustrating the ecumenical purchase of a covenantal approach, Luther describes baptism as "a covenant" repeatedly throughout his treatise. "This blessed sacrament of baptism helps you because in it God allies himself with you and becomes one with you in a gracious covenant of comfort."[7] "We must humbly admit, 'I know fully well that I cannot do a single thing that is pure. But I am baptized, and through my baptism God, who cannot lie, has bound himself in a covenant with me. He will not count my sin against me, but will slay it and blot it out.'"[8] Faith "establishes a covenant between us and God to the effect that we will fight against sin and slay it, even to our dying breath, while he for his part will be merciful to us, deal graciously with us." So baptism is "a sign and covenant" of grace. Melanchthon's treatment, which Calvin translated into French, is along the same lines. More than anything else, the sacraments are "signs of God's goodwill toward us, that is, added testimonies of the promises of grace"—first and foremost, God's action. But the rite also calls for response in repentance and faith. "For he understands a mutual obligation and a mutual covenant."[9]

It is hardly any wonder that when one separates divine action from earthly means, God's activity in the world can only appear arbitrary. Predestinarianism without the covenant becomes precisely what Calvin warned against: the labyrinth from which we can never safely emerge. To the extent that the ministry of Word and sacrament is treated as merely talk about God and about divine action (instruction), rather than as also constituting divine speech and action here and now, these earthly instruments will lose their importance and meaningfulness. Furthermore, to the extent that the sacraments are regarded chiefly as testimonies or pledges from humans to God, rather than vice versa, the covenant itself comes to be seen primarily in terms of imperatives rather than indicatives.

In contrast to the traditional Roman Catholic emphasis on the sacraments as human achievements, the Reformers and their theological heirs have underscored their utterly gracious character. Within the local performance of this play, the sacraments serve alongside the word as means of grace—not in terms of the analogy of infusion, but in terms of the analogy of declaration. While Augustine (and the Reformers) certainly had more in mind, they called the sacraments God's "visible word." Like the word, they are performative utterances. "Baptism is the means in God's hand," says Ridderbos, "the place where he speaks and acts."[10] Through them, God strengthens the faith that he creates through the preaching of the gospel. Not even these visible signs and seals get beyond a proclamatory function. Never are they the back door to a theology of vision and manifestation: "For as often as you eat this bread and drink the cup, you *proclaim* the Lord's death until he comes" (1 Cor. 11:26, emphasis added). And yet, as visible word and means of grace, the sacraments promise the same content as the gospel and, together with the preached word, confirm it for the believer's wavering faith.

This leads to the second analogy for the sacraments: sign and seal. Circumcision is not supplanted by baptism in terms of the content of that which was promised, since the covenant of grace cannot be altered. However, this one covenant is administered with different signs and seals in each of its two "acts." Through baptism, believers and their children are incorporated into the divine drama, rescripted from "strangers and aliens" into "the people of God," grafted onto Jesus Christ as their life-giving vine. Similarly, the apostle says of the Supper, ". . . is it not a sharing in the body/blood of Christ?" (1 Cor. 10:16). Along with the word—in fact, by word and Spirit—baptism and the Communion become means of personal incorporation into the drama in progress.

Calvin often appealed to sacraments as props, against the Zurich reformer Ulrich Zwingli, who insisted against Luther that the believer's faith was sufficient to itself and required no "external props." In making his argument, Calvin added to his larger analogy of the "theater" that of "props." This encourages us to see, as he did, the importance of the liturgy of Communion for the ordinary assembly of God's people. Just as God performed signs and wonders throughout redemptive history that either pointed to or confirmed his verbal promise, so here and now in the local performance God joins his preached word with these indisputable assurances of unconditional mercy in Christ. There is a difference between the perlocutionary acts involved in saying, "With this ring I thee wed," and "With this ring I represent to thee this union." Despite the virtual elimination of Zwinglian strains in the confessional symbols, the Reformed and Presbyterian tradition has been frequently dogged by the Platonic *contrast* of sign and thing signified rather than Calvin's emphasis on the *union* of sign and thing signified.

Of course, this can become a "performance" in the pejorative sense, but when we participate in faith, it is the concrete means of "putting on Christ," taking up our new role in the play. While the action of the divine player in the covenant is primary in the sacraments, this divine initiative is not without its effects. The human partner in the covenant is enjoined to faithfulness by his or her participation. In time, the baptized will profess faith for themselves and take their first Communion. They will respond individually, confessing the faith and acknowledging their responsibilities. The Strasbourg reformer Martin Bucer particularly emphasized the role of the sacraments as objective means of grace and the "ratification" of the covenant, "since by these sacraments remission of sins and the holy communion of Christ are imparted, and the covenant of eternal salvation is sealed and confirmed."[11] And yet, it was also a means of creating covenantal solidarity between the rich and the poor, as well as with those in other places and times. In his *De regno Christi*, Bucer argued that the poor not only needed the wealthy, but that the latter needed the former as well.[12] Bucer related this directly to the sacramental life of the covenant community, as did Calvin. The remarkable social effects of this approach have been fruitfully explored in recent years.[13]

Equipped with a set, a script, performers, and props, the divine drama takes on concrete form not only as a redramatization, but as the enactment of that redemptive-historical reality. Unlike the performers of *King Lear*, contemporary actors in the covenant renewal ceremony actually participate in the reality that is indicated by the performance. But there is one final aspect of this local performance that, though often overlooked, greatly enriches the integrity of this performance before a secular audience.

CHURCH ORDER AND DISCIPLINE: KEEPING TO THE SCRIPT

While one can hardly deny the abuses of church authority throughout history, the last few centuries have surely supplied sufficient evidence that tyranny can take many forms. At its best, order and discipline in the church serve to reign in special interests and hold all performers (including its officers) accountable to the common script. The point here is not to defend Presbyterian polity, but to provide an account of the political dimensions of the kingdom of God in its ecclesial expression "between the times."

As we have seen with respect to the liturgy, church officers "stand in" for God. Here again we encounter the principle of authorization and deputization in the covenant. Their role (office) is neither to take God's place on the stage nor merely to represent themselves in their person, but to represent Christ in their office. They are to do and say what they see God saying and doing through them, as they are directed by the script in the power of the Spirit. Practically, this means that the performance of each part is communally accountable. There are no virtuoso performances or one-man plays. A church or an individual refusing to keep to this particular play writes itself or himself/herself out of it. It is not *bad* performances, but the refusal to *participate* in the performance of this drama, that effects this "disconnect." Church discipline more generally attempts to correct bad performances through good coaching. It is those who participate in this drama who are "in Christ" and are thus assured of all his benefits, but the script must be institutionally normative for every performance. Scripture's sufficiency comprehends not only teaching, but is given "for reproof, for correction, and for training in righteousness" (2 Tim. 3:16). The Christian life cannot be merely a means of taking what each performer wants for one's own life movie, but must involve sometimes even painful submission to the rigor of learning the role and performing it within a creative tension of form and freedom. All of this leads to performers who are "equipped for every good work" (v. 17).

The eschatological dimension makes its appearance here also. Just as God's future "intrudes" on the present through Word and sacrament (the inauguration, sign, and seal of the new creation and the wedding feast), excommunication is an eschatological sign of the last judgment in the present. As a sign, however, it is declarative and not definitive: absolution is always held out as the end goal. The public absolution, given in the name of Christ generally to the congregation in the ordinary worship, is here given particularly to repentant individuals in the covenant of grace. And once more, it is a performative utterance: "I absolve you in the name of Jesus Christ of all your sins."[14]

This practice, at sharp variance with the autonomy and individualism of this age, enables the drama to continue without disintegrating into scattered performances. The church's ability to discipline itself (i.e., to remain faithful to the covenant) in large measure determines whether the only form of the divine drama that many passersby see is in fact the transformative-performative production that *God* has performed in history. In other words, it changes individual and corporate practice to bring it in closer harmony with the covenant charter. A classic example in our own recent history, to which I alluded in the previous chapter, is the dismissal of the Dutch Reformed Church in South Africa (NGK) from its international Reformed fellowship, which contributed in no small measure to the former's repentance of the heresy of apartheid. Refusing Communion to slaveholders often had the same effect in local churches within the Anglo-American context, just as the failure of nerve in the exercise of discipline served to entrench sinful theologies and practices. The wider social effects in both cases were significant. While these examples are hardly representative of the wide range of consistency to which God summons his covenant people, they indicate the lines along which such renewed church practice could liberate and nourish church theology. This issue challenges the church and individuals in the churches to re-evaluate their contemporary compromises in concrete ways.

CONCLUSION: A TALE OF TWO CITIES

The category of performance unites God's action (word and deed) and that of the covenant people, but it also unites our own often divided realms of understanding and action. There are, of course, dangers of this analogy leading to a synergistic soteriology, but it all depends on how one interprets the performance itself. In typical Reformed and Presbyterian liturgies, for instance, the unconditional divine side of the covenant is emphasized: "I will be your God and you will be my people." But though they are passive in their incorporation into Christ and his covenant (even faith in this sense is a passive reception), they are active in faith and obedience. Hence, such liturgies often continue, "A covenant has two sides." Although God alone saves, the covenant partner is also a responsible agent who is obligated to the covenant Lord. Performance, therefore, incorporates the divine and human sides, but does so (at least in our account) in a way that clearly distinguishes the perfect divine performance (grace) from the imperfect human performance (gratitude).

The covenantal model indicates lines along which such reintegration might take place, not only at the theoretical level discussed above, but even where theory meets practice on the streets. Faith and praxis obviously need to be reconciled not merely in theory, but in concrete and lived contexts. We have argued that the covenant fixes the context, but, more specifically, it is the covenant in its enacted form (the church) that constitutes the theater of grace. While there is a danger of becoming unduly introverted in such an account, this reconciliation occurs in this in-between time chiefly in the church, and only secondarily in the culture. By its reasonably accurate performance the cast actually grows, but by accommodating it to other plays, the cast leaves the world without a witness. Through vertical (synchronic) intrusions (on God's own terms through fixed covenantal actions), God preserves the church's horizontal (diachronic) continuity with "the cloud of witnesses" in the past, present, and future. This continuity is solidarity, as we see in the prophets: "Why do you come to church and praise me and then oppress your neighbor during the week?" The connection between liturgy and life is anchored, however, not in the solidarity of the people with each other or with God, but in the solidarity of the redeeming God of the exodus, who, dwelling among his covenant people, creates their solidarity with him and each other over time. "Forgive us our debts, as we forgive our debtors." The service of worship is the place where the drama is not only remembered and recounted, but is enacted as its ongoing work.

In his essay "Modernist Painting" (1965), Clement Greenberg observed concerning the arts, "Having been denied by the Enlightenment of all tasks they could take seriously, they looked as though they were going to be assimilated to entertainment, pure and simple, and entertainment looked as though it was going to be assimilated, like religion, to therapy."[15] As an expanding range of human thought and endeavor becomes enslaved by the supposedly neutral and perhaps even benevolent marketplace, Christian theology has a remarkable opportunity to resist this urge in its own domain and from there to claim the whole of creaturely reality for its counterdrama of genuine human existence and community. In his field architectural theorist Kenneth Frampton calls for "an architecture of resistance"—an approach that respects regionalism and resists the bland homogeneity of modernity and its obsession with the myth of progress.

> Architecture can only be sustained today as a critical practice if it assumes an *arriere-garde* position, that is to say, one which distances itself equally from the Enlightenment myth of progress and from a reactionary, unrealistic impulse to return to the architectonic forms of the preindustrial past. A critical *arriere-garde* has to remove itself from both the optimization of advanced technology and the ever-present tendency to regress into nostalgic historicism or the glibly decorative.[16]

Might this serve as a parallel for the theological task today? A merely nostalgic antimodernism is as irrelevant in its despair as aimless progressivism is irrelevant in its false relevance. What we need most is a critical *arriere-garde* theological praxis, a drama of resistance. As Ricoeur pointed up in a fascinating passage of *History and Truth*, "Everywhere throughout the world, one finds the same bad movie, the same slot machines, the same plastic or aluminum atrocities, the same twisting of language by propaganda, etc. It seems as if mankind, by approaching *en masse* a basic consumer culture, were also stopped *en masse* at a subcultural level. . . . There is the paradox: how to become modern and to return to sources."[17]

This is true for theology not only in the sense of recovering once-treasured resources buried in the archives of modernity. It certainly does mean the retrieval of the "Great Tradition" now underway in various circles and across theological divides.[18] It also involves a renewed attention to distinct confessional theologies that have been surrendered to totalizing Enlightenment and anti-Enlightenment programs. But if the cry *Ad fontes!* is going to really mean a rebirth of theological activity in, for, and by the church, it must be principally concerned with the fountain of all fountains: the covenantal canon and its unfolding drama. Like the returning exiles who stood all day to hear the rediscovered Torah read by Ezra, we too will confess our unfaithfulness and weep under the overwhelming reversal that God has accomplished in history for his straying people. Then we will understand justification and reconciliation not merely as dogmas, but as the encounter here and now with the God who judges and justifies us in our own personal histories.

Where Nietzsche, Derrida, Taylor, and other advocates of a/theology are wrong is in their quite modern claim to have risen above metanarrative. There is a plot after all—just a different one, perhaps one more sequel to *Waiting for Godot*. Ironically, the biblical drama confirms their counternarrative as descriptive of human existence apart from God's covenant blessings. "Under the sun," the Preacher tells us, we are all, in the words of the Beatles song, the "nowhere man" without any clear sense of origin or destiny. It is not just epistemic humility, but a tragic loss of meaning. With no vertical intrusion, history had become "one damned thing after another"—otherwise known as "vanity"—and the Preacher's only conclusion was to give himself to a life of worldly wisdom, food and drink, professional achievement, wealth, and sex. After all, he reasoned, no matter how one tries to live virtuously or make sense of life, injustice and violence underscore the pointlessness of it all. The righteous fare no better than the unrighteous. Like Nebuchadnezzar, the Preacher's sanity is restored only by raising his eyes to heaven, opening himself up to God as the transcendent source of meaning in a world that in its present condition offers no immanent hope.

The denial of hope—and not hope in general, but the concrete hope that is held out in Christ as he is proffered in the covenant of grace—is not unique to *la condition postmoderne*, but marks the path of "endless erring" that is part and parcel of the unfolding plotless plot that we may title "Under the Sun" or "This Passing Age." Peter faced the same opposition to the apostolic witness that Schweitzer and Weiss represented along with Nietzsche and Taylor. Calling his readers to remember the prophets and their announcement of the time that is now being fulfilled, Peter warned,

> First of all you must understand this, that in the last days scoffers will come, scoffing and indulging their own lusts and saying, "Where is the promise of his coming? For ever since our ancestors died, all things continue as they were from the beginning of creation!" They deliberately ignore this fact, that by the word of God heavens existed long ago and an earth was formed out of water and by means of water, through which the world of that time was deluged with water and perished. But by the same word the present heavens and earth have been reserved for fire, being kept until the day of judgment and destruction of the godless.
>
> But do not ignore this one fact, beloved, that with the Lord one day is like a thousand years, and a thousand years are like one day. The Lord is not slow about his promise, as some think of slowness, but is patient with you, not wanting any to perish, but all to come to repentance.[19]

Because God has created and upheld the world—even a world under judgment—by his performative word and has fulfilled his promises to the patriarchs and prophets by that same word, God's word for the future is reliable. The apparent absence of God in the present is due to the contradiction between the promise and visible reality, Peter argues. But aimless wanderers and drifters will once again miss God's great reversal by failing to recognize the "last days" as the era in which God's saving work is hidden under the form of its opposite. Only those who are looking for a theology of glory will be disappointed. According to the theology of the cross and resurrection, it is not God's slowness, but God's patience, says the apostle, that is providing so much lag time between this last stage of promise and fulfillment, since in the in-between time God is showing mercy. His revealed desire is for the salvation of the entire human race.

Among other things, this mercy-showing time is the extension of the Christocracy to the Gentiles as well as the Jews. As wild and dead branches grafted onto a living vine, "strangers" are radically redefined as "children of God." Scattered rocks—from which Jesus prophesied he would make children of Abraham—are now "living stones . . . [that are being] built into a spiritual house, to be a holy priesthood, to offer up spiritual sacrifices acceptable to God through Jesus Christ" (1 Pet. 2:5). This rescripting draws "nowhere" people into a new plot: "But you are a chosen race, a royal priesthood, a holy nation, God's own people, in order that you may proclaim the mighty acts of him who called you out of darkness into his marvelous light. Once you were not a people, but now you are God's people; once you had not received mercy, but now you have received mercy" (vv. 9–10).

This is no abstract, general role, but a concrete, covenantal existence. "Nowhere" people receive a new part: "the people of God." Paul adds, "[R]emember that you were at that time without Christ, being aliens from the commonwealth of Israel, and strangers to the covenants of promise, having no hope and without God in the world. But now in Christ Jesus you who once were far off [wandering, straying, erring, transgressing] have been brought near by the blood of Christ" (Eph. 2:12–13). Having been strangers and aliens to the covenant, the ungodly are now being made "aliens and exiles" in this world (1 Pet. 2:11). This is the greatest role reversal in theatrical history. Here outsiders become insiders while insiders become outsiders—and all because of the central character, the "Rock of offense," the "living stone, though rejected by mortals yet chosen and precious in God's sight" (1 Pet. 2:4). Joining the cast of Abraham, Isaac, and Jacob, believers take their place in the divine drama in their new role of pilgrims living toward the future by promise. This role is easily distinguished from either endless drifters or final possessors, and this is why our older theologians distinguished their *theologia viatorum* (theology of pilgrims) from the *theologia beatorum* (theology of glorified saints). Reigning in univocal theologies of glory that downplayed the "not-yet," they were equally suspicious of equivocal theologies that underestimated the "already" of God's redemptive action and revelation.

With our eschatological bearings somewhat in place, our epistemological bearings are reset by the pattern of promise and fulfillment in the covenant of grace. As a result of these reflections, we can finally summarize the definition of the theological task with which we began this study: Theology is the church's reflection on God's performative action in word and deed and its own participation in the drama of redemption.

Notes

Introduction

1. Hans Frei, introduction to *Types of Modern Theology*, ed. George Hunsinger and William Placher (New Haven: Yale University Press, 1992).
2. For an interesting analysis of this development from the Catholic side, see David Tracy, *The Analogical Imagination* (New York: Crossroad, 1987), chapter 10. Yet Tracy himself still reflects the commitment to prolegomenon as predogmatic: "Where the fundamental [i.e., 'prolegomenist'] theologian will relate the reality of God to our fundamental trust in existence (our common faith), the confessional systematic theologian will relate that reality to their arguments for a distinctively Christian understanding of faith" (65).
3. In *Post-Reformation Reformed Dogmatics*, vol. 1: *Prolegomena to Theology* (Grand Rapids: Baker, 1987), Richard Muller observes the reversal from the human search for God to the divine search for humans: "The distinction between *theologia gloriae* and *theologia crucis*, thus, not only partakes of a distinction between *theologia in se* and *theologia in subiecto* but also adds, together with its soteriological thrust, a re-evaluation of the language of the object of theology. We cannot discuss God as such, but God according to the form of his revelation" (65). Furthermore, theological certainty was distinct from mathematical certainty, a point that "was crucial" for post-Reformation protestant dogmatics (67). They also moved increasingly from the Thomistic manner of viewing theology as *scientia* (knowledge), toward seeing it as *sapientia* (wisdom), although the two were somewhat interdependent (77). In all of the major systems surveyed by Muller, "theological prolegomena are never *vordogmatisch* [predogmatic]: they are an integral part of dogmatic system that develops in dialogue with basic dogmatic conclusions after the system as a whole has been set forth" (81).
4. Karl Barth carried forward the modern antipathy toward Protestant orthodoxy, but this attitude is pervasive beyond neo-orthodox circles. Historical theologian Richard Muller has led a reassessment on the basis of the primary sources themselves. See especially his *Post-Reformation Reformed Dogmatics*, 3 vol. (Grand Rapids: Baker, 1978–); *Christ and the Decree: Christology and Predestination in Reformed Theology from Calvin to Perkins* (Durham, N.C.: Labyrinth, 1986); and his two seminal articles, "'Calvin and the Calvinists': Assessing Continuities and Discontinuities between the Reformation and Orthodoxy," *Calvin Theological Journal* 30 (1995): 345–75, and 31 (1996): 125–26. Muller indicates the scholastic influences on Calvin's method also in *The Unaccommodated Calvin* (New York: Oxford University Press, 2000), chapter 3.
5. Paul Tillich, *A History of Christian Thought*, ed. Carl Braaten (New York: Simon & Schuster, 1968), 276–77.

6. Ibid., 306.
7. Michael Polanyi, "Faith and Reason," *Journal of Religion* 41 (Oct. 1961): 247.
8. Robert T. Osborn, "The Possibility of Theology Today," *Theology Today* 55, no. 4 (Jan. 1999): 562–63.
9. David Tracy, *Analogical Imagination*, 65–66.
10. I am referring here to Geerhardus Vos, Herman Ridderbos, and others in that vein. However, the interest in eschatology has hardly been limited to these confessional writers. For an interesting tour of eschatology's career in modern theology, see particularly Gerhard Sauter, *What Dare We Hope? Reconsidering Eschatology* (Harrisburg, Pa.: Trinity Press International, 1999).
11. David Tracy, *On Naming the Present* (Maryknoll, N.Y.: Orbis, 1994), 32–33.
12. Illustrating the secular "eschatologies" (often of the overrealized variety) that have dominated modernity is a letter from John Adams to Thomas Jefferson in 1813: "Our pure, virtuous, public spirited, federative republic will last forever, govern the globe, and introduce the perfection of man."
13. For more detail on this concern, see Richard Gaffin, *Resurrection and Redemption: A Study in Paul's Soteriology* (Phillipsburg, N.J.: Presbyterian & Reformed, 1978), especially chap. 2.
14. Referring to an ancient christological debate, Eutycheanism was charged with teaching a confusion of Christ's human and divine natures, while the Nestorians were accused of separating the two natures too sharply. Without naming these views, the Creed of Chalcedon (A.D. 451) steered a course between these shoals.
15. Clifford Geertz, *Local Knowledge: Further Essays in Interpretive Anthropology* (New York: Basic Books, 1983), 27.
16. Ibid., 27–28.
17. Ibid., 30.
18. Richard Rorty, *Philosophy and the Mirror of Nature* (Princeton: Princeton University Press, 1979), 12.
19. Nancey Murphy, *Beyond Liberalism and Fundamentalism: How Modern and Postmodern Philosophy Set the Theological Agenda* (Valley Forge, Pa.: Trinity Press International), 117.
20. For instance, there is Hans Urs von Balthasar's *Theo-Drama: Theological Dramatic Theory*, vol. 1, *Prolegomena*, trans. Graham Harrison (San Francisco: Ignatius Press, 1988), which, to my shame, I have not yet read. There is also Rene Girard's *Jesus im Heilsdrama: Entwurf einer biblischen Erlösungslehre* (Innsbruck: Tyrolia-Verlag, 1990). This is a recurring metaphor in Geerhardus Vos's work as well. I have also quite recently come into possession of a fascinating article by Kevin Vanhoozer titled "The Voice and the Actor: A Dramatic Proposal about the Ministry and Minstrelsy of Theology," in *Evangelical Futures: A Conversation on Theological Method*, ed. John G. Stackhouse Jr. (Grand Rapids: Baker, 2000), 61–106.
21. Susan Schreiner, *The Theater of His Glory: Nature and the Natural Order in the Thought of John Calvin* (Grand Rapids: Baker, 1995).
22. Dorothy Sayers, *Creed or Chaos* (New York: Harcourt, Brace, 1949); *The Man Born to Be King* (New York: Harper & Brothers, 1943).
23. Derrida, "The Theater of Cruelty," in *Writing and Difference*, trans. Alan Bass (Chicago: University of Chicago, 1978), 235, 239.
24. See especially Walter Brueggemann's excellent essay, "Preaching as Reimagination," *Theology Today* 52, no. 3 (Oct. 1995): 313–29; Raymund Schwager, *Jesus in the Drama of Salvation*, trans. James G. Williams and Paul Haddon (New York: Crossroad, 1999); Kevin Vanhoozer, "The Voice of the Actor: A Dramatic Proposal about the Ministry and Minstrelsy of Theology," *Evangelical Futures*, ed. John G. Stackhouse Jr. (Grand Rapids: Baker, 2000).

25. Alasdair MacIntyre, *After Virtue: A Study in Moral Theory*, 2d ed. (Notre Dame, Ind.: University of Notre Dame Press, 1984), esp. chap. 15.

26. Richard Gaffin Jr., ed., *Redemptive History and Biblical Interpretation: The Shorter Writings of Geerhardus Vos* (Phillipsburg, N.J.: Presbyterian and Reformed Publishing Co., 1980). Gaffin's introduction on xviii cites Vos's original comment from *Biblical Theology* (Grand Rapids: Eerdmans, 1948), 17.

27. David Tracy, *Blessed Rage for Order: The New Pluralism in Theology* (New York: Seabury, 1975), esp. chap. 4.

28. Peter Berger, *The Noise of Solemn Assemblies: Christian Commitment and the Religious Establishment in America* (Garden City, N.Y.: Doubleday, 1961), 125–26.

29. Ibid.

30. Miroslav Volf, "Theology, Meaning, and Power," in *The Future of Theology: Essays in Honor of Jürgen Moltmann*, ed. Miroslav Volf, Carmen Krieg, and Thomas Kucharz (Grand Rapids: Eerdmans, 1996), 103–4.

31. H. Richard Niebuhr, *The Meaning of Revelation* (New York: Macmillan, 1941), 44 ff.

32. Ibid., 45.

33. Ibid.

34. Ibid., 53.

35. Karl Barth, *Evangelical Theology: An Introduction*, trans. Grover Foley (Grand Rapids: Eerdmans, 1963), 205.

36. Ibid., 205–6.

37. See esp. John 5:39–40 and Luke 24:13–27.

Chapter One

1. Mark C. Taylor, *Erring: A Postmodern A/Theology* (Chicago: University of Chicago Press, 1984), 157.

2. Friedrich Nietzsche, *Twilight of the Idols*, trans. Duncan Large (Oxford: Oxford University Press, 1998), 20.

3. Nietzsche, *The Birth of Tragedy*, in *The Philosophy of Nietzsche* (New York: Random House, n.d.), 947 ff. My "typological" use of this text is admittedly reductionistic if its intention is to provide an analysis of the work as a whole.

4. Plato, Meno, from *The Great Dialogues of Plato* (New York: Mentor, 1956, 1984), 42.

5. Ibid., 7:315.

6. Ibid., 317.

7. "The Jesus of history is not kerygma any more than my book was. . . . So far, then, from running away from *Historie* and taking refuge in *Geschichte*, I am deliberately renouncing any form of encounter with the Christ after the flesh, in order to encounter the Christ proclaimed in the kerygma, which confronts me in my historic [not historical] situation," *Kerygma and Myth: A Theological Debate*, ed. Hans Werner Bartsch, trans. R. H. Fuller (London: SPCK, 1953), 117.

8. Cf. Hans Jonas, *The Gnostic Religion* (Boston: Beacon, 1958); Kurt Rudolph, *Gnosis: The Nature and History of Gnosticism* (San Francisco: Harper & Row, 1983); Dan Merkur, *Gnosis: An Esoteric Tradition of Mystical Visions and Unions* (Albany, N.Y.: SUNY, 1993).

9. Rudolf Bultmann, *Theology of the New Testament*, trans. Kendrick Grobel (New York: Scribner's, 1951), 1:166. Cf. Frederick Copleston, S.J., *A History of Philosophy*, 1 (New York: Doubleday, 1965): "According to Irenaeus the Gnostics borrowed most of their notions from Greek philosophers," especially Plato (1:22).

10. Moving beyond Strauss's 1835 *Leben Jesu*, which had argued that the Gospels were folk myths that projected the Jewish hopes, Feuerbach turns from history to psychology. Religion arises out of the fears and aspirations of human beings. "I, by reducing theology to anthropology," he writes, "raise anthropology to theology, just as Christianity, by lowering God into man, made Man into god. Religion is the dream of the human mind." Ludwig Feuerbach, *The Essence of Christianity* (New York: Ungar, 1957), 3, 49. "To live in projected dreamimages is the essence of religion," he says.

"Religion sacrifices reality to the projected dream: the 'Beyond' is merely the 'Here' reflected in the mirror of imagination. Our essential task is now fulfilled. We have reduced the otherworldly, supernatural, and superhuman nature of God to the elements of human nature. We have arrived in the end to where we started from the beginning. The beginning, the center, and the final goal of religion is—Man." Ibid., 49. Belief in a hereafter is "an escape mechanism," Feuerbach insists, adding (in anticipation of Marx), "Religion is as bad as opium," ibid., 46–47. All of this, of course, sets the stage for Nietzsche's (not to mention, Marx's) criticism.

11. Brian Ingraffia, *Postmodern Theory and Biblical Theology* (Cambridge: Cambridge University Press, 1995), 7.

12. Ibid., 2.

13. There are many issues involved in this critique that do not touch directly upon eschatology. For instance, there is the rise of the nominalist conception of God as an arbitrary and capricious Will, *potentia absoluta,* so "wholly other" that it cannot be expected to operate through secondary causes or in patterns of regularity and order. Unable to cope with this deity, Descartes sought to create space for the self that could not be threatened by this unpredictable deity. But already even in Descartes, God ends up, like nature, a captive to human mastery. It is significant, given the misconceptions of his thought, that John Calvin explicitly denies the notion of the *Dei potentia absoluta* in *De aeterna Dei praedestinatione.* Also, in his sermons on Job (Job 23:1–10), "What the Sorbonne doctors say, that God has an absolute power, is a diabolical blasphemy which has been invented in hell." To sever God's will or power from his justice, love, wisdom, order, etc., would be "to treat men like balls in the air," and would render God nothing more than a tyrant. In this, Calvin's warning anticipates the darkening clouds of early modern skepticism on the horizon. Cf. Susan E. Schreiner, *The Theater of His Glory: Nature and the Natural Order in the Thought of John Calvin* (Grand Rapids: Baker, 1995, from Labyrinth Press, 1991), 14; Heiko Oberman, "Some Notes on the Theology of Nominalism with Attention to its Relation to the Renaissance," *Harvard Theological Review* 53 (1960): 46–76.

14. Louis Dupre, *Passage to Modernity* (New Haven: Yale University Press, 1995); Michael Allen Gillespie, *Nihilism before Nietzsche* (Chicago: University of Chicago Press, 1995); Henry Ruf, ed., *Religion, Ontotheology, and Deconstruction* (New York: Paragon House, 1989); Brian Ingraffia, *Postmodern Theory and Biblical Theology: Vanquishing God's Shadow* (Cambridge: Cambridge University Press, 1995). "The new thing in Nietzsche," said Barth, "was the man of 'azure isolation,' six thousand feet above time and man; . . . the man who is utterly inaccessible to others; . . . the man beyond good and evil, who can only exist as a consuming fire" [hereafter *CD*] (*Church Dogmatics*, III/2:232, 240).

15. Jacques Derrida, *Writing and Difference* (Chicago: University of Chicago Press, 1978), 271.

16. Mark C. Taylor, *Erring,* 155.

17. Ibid., 53.

18. Ibid., 66. But this criticism is limited to the sort of argument employed by Pannenberg; viz., that the resurrection (as other miraculous events) may be read off of the surface of historical phenomena. We would argue that, while such events leave historical traces and evidences, they are constituted as significant events of a particular type only because of their place in the narrative tapestry.

19. Ibid., cited 66.

20. Immanuel Kant, *Political Writings*, ed. by Hans Reiss, trans. H. B. Nisbet (Cambridge: Cambridge University Press, 1970), 43.

21. With Kant, the *Ding-an-sich* is unknowable; with deconstruction, it is a construction of the self.

22. Taylor, *Erring*, 13.

23. Ibid., 20–30.

24. Ibid., 97.

25. Ibid., cited 156.

26. Ibid.

27. Ibid., 157.

28. Ibid., 108.

29. Ibid., 110. Though it is beyond our scope here, it would be interesting to interact with this point on the basis of the Christian dialectic of the hidden and revealed God. In the person of Jesus Christ, "the fullness of the Godhead dwells bodily," and yet *finitum non capax infiniti*. In the incarnation, the attributes of omnipresence, transcendence, immutability, and eternal self-existence are in no way diminished or altered but are united in one person whose human nature is local, immanent, growing, and utterly dependent upon the same Creator who made all things through him. Chalcedonian Christology's resistance to perennial temptations to err on one side of the Greek antithesis or the other represents the most enduring challenge to pagan dualism. It is not surprising that the great modern philosophers were unitarian rather than Trinitarian—and Arian, Apollinarian, or Docetic, rather than Chalcedonian.

30. Ibid., 112.

31. Jacques Derrida, *Positions*, trans. Alan Bass (Chicago: University of Chicago Press, 1981), 77.

32. Derrida, in *Deconstruction in a Nutshell*, ed. John D. Caputo (New York: Fordham University Press, 1997), 22.

33. Immanuel Kant, "Religion within the Bounds of Mere Reason," in *Immanuel Kant: Religion and Rational Theology*, trans. and ed., Allen W. Wood and George Di Giovanni (Cambridge: Cambridge University Press, 1996): "So too the so-called religious struggles, which have so often shaken the world and spattered it with blood, have never been anything but squabbles over ecclesiastical faiths. . . . Now whenever, as usually happens, a church passes itself off as the only universal one (even though it is based on faith in a particular revelation which, since it is historical, can never be demanded of everyone), whoever does not acknowledge its (particular) ecclesiastical faith is called an unbeliever, and is wholeheartedly hated" (140–41). If it comes down to a contest between the right doctrine ("salvation by grace") and right moral conduct, "then the pure moral faith must take precedence over the ecclesiastical" (148).

34. Derrida, in *Deconstruction*, 22.

35. Ibid., 23–24.

36. Ibid., 162.

37. Ibid., 163.

38. Ibid., 167.

39. Ibid., 173.

40. Ibid., 15–19; cf. Derrida, *Totality and Infinity*, 89 ff.

41. Ibid., 177; cf. on this theme in general, David Wood, ed., *Of Derrida, Heidegger, and Spirit* (Evanston, Ill.: Northwestern University Press, 1993).

42. Gregory Bruce Smith, *Nietzsche, Heidegger, and the Transition to Postmodernity* (Chicago: University of Chicago Press, 1996), 336.

43. John Caputo, in *Deconstruction in a Nutshell*, 162.

44. John Milbank, *Theology and Social Theory* (Oxford: Blackwell, 1991, 1993), 310–11. It seems to me that a worthwhile question, which I am not competent to address, is the extent to which Derrida's "trace" is still a modern (even autonomous?) subject. In fact, in reading Derrida, one might, *mutatis mutandis*, gain the impression that the trace is a cipher for the *res cogitans*. Is it not the case that "meaning" is "discovered" in *differance*? This spacing (not unlike Heidegger's *Dasein*, although Derrida objects) may strike some as more than a little like an ironic twist on the Neoplatonic privation of Being/Good as the "origin" of "meaning." *Differance*, spacing, alterity, absence: these do not appear to be mere signifiers in an infinite web of intersignifications. Rather, the same, presence, and selfhood are swallowed whole in a system that does perhaps involve a synthesis after all. For an example of this, see particularly Jacques Derrida, *Positions*, trans. and annotated by Alan Bass (Chicago: University of Chicago Press, 1981), 91–92.

45. Milbank, *Theology, and Social Theory*, 311. Commenting on the post-Nietzschean view of history, Moltmann writes, "In this sense scientific historicism stands in the service of the mystico-messianic idea of the 'end of history' and is itself a factor in the 'ending of history,'" *Theology of Hope, On the Ground and Implications of a Christian Eschatology* (Minneapolis: Fortress, 1993), 237.

46. I am, of course, assuming the unity of the canon rather than demonstrating it. See, for instance, Brevard S. Childs, *The New Testament as Canon: An Introduction* (London: SCM, 1984) and *Old Testament Theology in Canonical Context* (London: SCM, 1985).

47. For Barth's version of the ontic antithesis between *Chronos*-time and *Kairos*-time (or *Historie* and *Geschichte*), see his contrast between "our time" and "God's time" in *CD* I/2 (1994): 66–121.

48. Geerhardus Vos, *The Pauline Eschatology*, reprinted (Grand Rapids: Baker, 1979, from the Princeton University Press edition, 1930), 33–34.

49. Rudolf Bultmann recognized this New Testament contrast with gnostic uses of "spirit" and "flesh." For instance, see his excellent analysis of Paul's terminology and contrasts on these points in *Theology of the New Testament*, trans. K. Grobel (New York: Charles Scribner's Sons, 1951), 1: esp. 227–58. It is difficult to understand how Bultmann could have really understood as he did the Pauline categories in their opposition to Platonism and Gnosticism while embracing, via the Marburg neo-Kantians, a modern form of this same ontological dualism.

50. Especially Geerhardus Vos, Herman Ridderbos, Meredith Kline, and Richard Gaffin, all of whom find their roots in classical Reformed (covenant) theology.

51. Moltmann, *Theology of Hope*, 70. Strictly speaking, though, this represented a renewed interest in eschatology as the unfolding of God's redemptive plan within a federal scheme, not a revival of millenarianism. The latter is not necessary for a future orientation, as Professor Moltmann's comments often seem to imply.

52. See especially his *Summa doctrinae de foedere et testamento Dei* (1648).

53. Wolfhart Pannenberg, *Systematic Theology* (Grand Rapids: Eerdmans, 1998), 3:530.

54. Karl Barth noted the importance of this federal theology in shaping even certain forms of Lutheran theology in "the earlier form of the 'redemption-history'

school of Erlangen," especially with its attempt "to understand the work and Word of God attested in Holy Scripture dynamically and not statically, as an event and not as a system of objective and self-contained truths." At the end of the day, however, Barth rejected federalism as "a theological historicism," "Can we historicise the activity and revelation of God? The Federal theologians were the first really to try to do this in principle," *CD* IV/1: 57–66.

55. Moltmann, *Theology of Hope*, 16.

56. Geerhardus Vos, *Biblical Theology* (Grand Rapids: Eerdmans, 1948), 26, 24. Nevertheless, these writers insisted (as do their successors) that the events and their narrative interpretation have the same source, viz., the God of the covenant. Hence, it is not only the events that constitute divine revelation, but scripture itself. Furthermore, their insistence upon the pattern of doctrine-shaped-by-drama (i.e., redemptive-history narrated) should not be confused with a generic antidogmatism. It is an attempt to discover the unity of the eternal and the temporal, decree and covenant, dynamic "intrusion" and linear "progress," an eternal Trinity and this God's temporal self-revelation in successive stages as deemed appropriate for redemption and covenantal obedience. This approach seems to hold together, in a genuine dialectic, the exegetical-concrete-temporal grounding of dogmatics with the systematic and more deductive development. It is, among other things, an attempt to allow the biblical stress on divine condescension to human capacity (a much-noted emphasis of Calvin's)—an incarnational model—to redeem "our time" in the temporality of divine revelation. This revelation, which culminates in Christ, including the consummation, does not save one from ordinary time but transforms ordinary time. Thus, "the fullness of time" is always an eschatological, not an ontological, designation. As with Calvin's criticisms of the radical "enthusiasm" that he regarded as a new Manicheanism, it is not surprising that our approach here has a decidedly Irenaean ring to it.

57. Herman Ridderbos, *When the Time Had Fully Come: Studies in NT Theology* (Grand Rapids: Eerdmans, 1957), 48.

58. Ridderbos, *Paul: An Outline of His Theology*, trans. John R. W. De Witt (Grand Rapids: Eerdmans, 1975), 21.

59. Moltmann, *Theology of Hope*, 165–66: "Christianity stands or falls with the reality of the raising of Jesus from the dead by God. In the New Testament there is no faith that does not start a priori with the resurrection of Jesus. . . . A Christian faith that is not a resurrection faith can therefore be called neither Christian nor faith."

60. Vos, *The Pauline Eschatology* (Princeton: Princeton University Press, 1930; Phillipsburg, N.J.: Presbyterian & Reformed, 1994), 39

61. Richard Gaffin, introduction to *Redemptive History and Biblical Interpretation: The Shorter Writings of Geerhardus Vos* (Phillipsburg, N.J.: Presbyterian & Reformed, 1980).

62. Those who forsake all for the kingdom will "receive a hundredfold now in this age [αἰών] . . . and in the age [αἰών] to come eternal life" (Mark 10:30). Jesus speaks of the judgment "at the end of the age" (Matt. 13:40) and refers to those who will not be forgiven "either in this age or in the age to come" (Matt. 12:32). He distinguishes between "those who belong to this age" and those who have "a place in that age and in the resurrection from the dead" (Luke 20:34–35). In fact, the latter are "the children of the resurrection" who can never again die (v. 36). "The harvest is the end of the age. . . . Just as the weeds are collected and burned up with fire, so will it be at the end of the age" (Matt. 13:39–40). The disciples themselves asked Jesus to reveal "the sign of your coming and of the end of the age," which Jesus identifies with the arrival of false messiahs

(Matt. 24:3–5). The writer to the Hebrews reminds readers that through the ministry of Word and sacrament, they have "been enlightened, and have tasted the heavenly gift, and have shared in the Holy Spirit, and have tasted the goodness of the word of God and *the powers of the age to come*" (Heb. 6:4–5, emphasis added). For intertestimental evidence of this two-age apocalyptic model, see Vos, *Pauline Eschatology,* 15 ff.; cf. Herman Ridderbos, *The Coming of the Kingdom,* trans. H. de Jongste (Philadelphia: Presbyterian & Reformed Publishing Co., 1969).

63. Calvin, *Institutes,* 1.14.3: "The Manichees have only one foundation: that it is wrong to ascribe to the good God the creation of any evil thing. This does not in the slightest degree harm the orthodox faith, which does not admit that any evil nature exists in the whole universe. For the depravity and malice both of man and of the devil, or the sins that arise therefrom, do not spring from nature, but rather from the corruption of nature."

Later, he writes in a similar vein, "We deny that [evil] has flowed from nature in order to indicate that it is an adventitious quality which comes upon man rather than a substantial property which has been implanted from the beginning. Yet we call it 'natural' in order that no man may think that anyone obtains it through bad conduct, since it holds all men fast by hereditary right. . . . Thus vanishes the foolish trifling of the Manichees, who, when they imagined wickedness of substance in man, dared fashion another creator for him in order that they might not seem to assign the cause and beginning of evil to the righteous God" (2.2.11).

64. Ridderbos, *When the Time Had Fully Come,* 52.

65. Moltmann, *Theology of Hope,* 27.

66. Ibid.

67. Ibid., 29. Kierkegaard: "The moment characterizes the present as a thing that has no past and no future. The moment is an atom of eternity" (cited, 29).

68. Ibid., 30.

69. Ibid., 16.

70. Ibid., 31.

71. M. Douglas Meeks, *Origins of the Theology of Hope* (Philadelphia: Fortress, 1974), 60.

72. Moltmann, *Theology of Hope,* 46.

73. Karl Barth, *The Epistle to the Romans,* trans. Edwyn C. Hoskyns, 6th ed. (Oxford: Oxford University Press, 1968), 498.

74. Moltmann, *Theology of Hope,* 56–57. Taking issue especially with W. Kreck's exposition of Barth's rejection of the *analogia entis,* Moltmann objects strongly: "This well-known position, however, is not one of Christian theology, but has its source in Neoplatonic gnosticism, appears in the reflections of mediaeval mysticism, and is found also in Hegel's philosophy of religion. . . . It [the question of revelation and knowledge of God] is not applicable to that bundle of historic reports from which Christian faith lives, but rather to an esoteric gnosis."

75. Barth, *Dogmatics in Outline,* trans. G. T. Thomson (London: SCM, 1949), 135. But in 2 Thess. 2:3–9, the "lawless one" is also spoken of as hidden, to be "revealed" eventually. Surely this is not "revelation" or "manifestation" in Barth's usage. Against proto-gnostic sects, a running polemic of the epistles insists that the appearance of Jesus "in the fullness of time" is an eschatological-historical irruption rather than an existential-gnostic encounter.

76. Meeks, *Origins,* 72.

77. Moltmann, *Theology of Hope,* 229.

78. Pannenberg criticizes Moltmann on this point: "Moltmann sees in the resurrection of Jesus a validating rather than a fulfilling of the promise. He is critical of the primitive Christian enthusiasm of fulfillment, thinking he perceives in the supposed fulfillment of all expectations the basis of the Hellenizing of Christianity (*Theology of Hope*, 154 ff.). The resurrection was present to believers as promise (154 ff.). In this way Moltmann could evade the historical question raised by the resurrection (167 ff.). The cross is provisionally taken up into the promise and the hope of a new eschaton that is yet to come (161). We may call the resurrection of Jesus from the dead 'historical' only in the light of faith in the promise, namely, as we define the history of Jesus in terms of the eschaton (172 ff.)," *Systematic Theology*, 3:538.
79. Ridderbos, *When the Time Had Fully Come*, 48.
80. Ibid., 50.
81. Ibid., 59.
82. As Meredith Kline points out, the objective of the creation narrative in Genesis is to clearly represent God as both Alpha-Creator and Omega-Consummator. "God sets for this creative acts within the pictorial framework of a Sabbath-crowned week and by this sabbatical pattern he identifies himself as Omega, the One for whom all things are and were created. . . . It is the seventh day of the creation week, the climactic Sabbath to which the course of creative events moves, that gives to the pattern of the week of days as a whole its distinctive sabbatical character. . . . He who can speak in an effective 'Let there be' must inevitably arrive at his Sabbath and say, 'It is finished,'" *Kingdom Prologue* (self-published class notes), 1:26–27. Not surprisingly, then, the identification of Jesus Christ with the Sabbath rest, in the Gospels, Colossians, Hebrews, and elsewhere, together with his designation as the Creator-Word, is the identification of Jesus as "the Alpha" by whom and for whom all things exist and "the Omega" (Rev. 1:8) who brings the weary and the guilty into the Seventh Day, which is "the age to come."
83. Cf. Ephesians 1:19–2:2.
84. Cf. Richard Gaffin, *Resurrection and Redemption: A Study in Paul's Soteriology* (Phillipsburg, N.J.: Presbyterian & Reformed, 1978), 41 ff.
85. Ibid., 61.
86. Cf. Romans 6:12–14.
87. Ridderbos, *Paul: An Outline of His Theology*, 215.
88. See his fascinating comparison/contrast of Aquinas and Joachim of Fiore on this point, in "The Trinitarian View of History: Christian Hope—Messianic or Transcendent? A Theological Conversation with Joachim of Fiore and Thomas Aquinas," in *History and the Triune God: Contributions to Trinitarian Theology* (New York: Crossroad, 1992).
89. The use of this typology here is heuristic rather than making any stand on the exegetical possibility of such a distinction in the Greek of the NT period. Cf. James Barr, *The Semantics of Biblical Language* (Oxford: Oxford University Press, 1961); *Biblical Words for Time* (London: SCM, 1962); Oscar Cullmann, *Christ and Time* (London: SCM, 1951).
90. This is not, however, to be understood in either a positivist or existentialist manner. Whether the active "principle" is reason, imagination, feeling/sympathy, or will/decision, it is the autonomous self projecting its mastery. For Paul, "contemporaneity" with Jesus and the apostles is determined by the eschatological rift between the two ages and the fact that the redemptive-historical events which defined the first community continue to shape the hermeneutical horizon of the believer today. Thus, "these last days" include the events between the two

advents. The time of Christ is the common era for all believers. Vos: "Still we know full well that we ourselves live just as much in the New Testament as did Peter and Paul and John" (*Biblical Theology*, 325). This raises issues of historical hermeneutics that we cannot address here.

91.   G. Vos, *The Pauline Eschatology* (Princeton University Press, 1930), 40. In one of his typical idiosyncratic (and difficult) expressions, Vos observes concerning the "new thing" present in the resurrection, "As soon as the direction of the actual spiritual life-contact becomes involved, the horizontal movement of thought on the time-plan must give way immediately to a vertical projection of the eschatological interest into the supernal region, because there, even more than in the historical development below, the center of all religious values and forces has come to lie. . . . Thus the other world, hitherto future, has become present. . . . Consequently the idea of 'heaven' and such metaphorical locally-oriented phrases as 'things above' had to take the place of the older technical terms. 'Heaven' offered moreover the advantage of expressing the provisionally-realized final state lies on a higher plane than the preceding world-development. Thus we find the Apostle declaring that the Christian is blessed in Christ with every spiritual blessing 'in the heavenly regions,' Eph.i.3, a way of expression, clearly indicating the Christological basis of the transfer of the believer's domicile and possessions to heaven: it is 'in Christ,' i.e., because of his being in heaven, that the affirmation is to be made."

92.   Ibid., 41.

93.   Ibid., 41, 290.

94.   We can illustrate the intratextual coherence of Paul's thought with the following example. The petition, "Your will be done on earth as it is in heaven," involves asking God to bring the "vertical" and "horizontal" dimensions of the kingdom into a unity. Although God had taken the kingdom back up into heaven in the Babylonian exile (when the glory-cloud left the temple), the locus of heaven on earth became Jesus Christ, and in his incarnation the kingdom was present among the Jews. But the prayer for heaven to come to earth (vertical) is simultaneously the commission of Jesus to go into all the world with the gospel, beginning in Jerusalem, and reaching out in ever-widening circles to the ends of the earth. This anticipates the day when the whole earth will be filled with the glory of YHWH. The New Jerusalem comes down out of heaven (Rev. 21:2) as it reaches the ends of the earth: these are not two distinct, much less antithetical, realities, but are two ways of indicating the same reality. This sort of exegesis, weaving the threads of eschatological parts with the whole, is typical of the scriptures even beyond the obvious messianic texts and the promise-fulfillment pattern of the *sensus literalis*. For Jesus' own insistence on this eschatological (and therefore christocentric) hermeneutic, see especially John 5:39–40 and Luke 24:25–35.

95.   Ibid., 14.

96.   Ibid., 21.

97.   Note the prominence of the certain and objective knower, alone eternal and unchanging, reducing the other to historicism and relativism: "It is impossible to use electric light and the wireless and to avail ourselves of modern medical and surgical discoveries, and at the same time to believe in the New Testament world of daemons and spirits. . . . The mythical eschatology is untenable for the simple reason that the parousia of Christ never took place as the New Testament expected. History did not come to an end, and, as every schoolboy knows, it will continue to run its course" (*Kerygma and Myth: A Theological Debate*, ed. H. W. Bartsch, trans. R. H. Fuller [London: SPCK, 1953], 5). Interestingly, as Bultmann's interlocutors in that work argued and recent NT scholarship has

underscored, the NT writers knew exactly what they were doing by employing metaphors. It is part of divine accommodation to human capacity to use figures of speech. As for the "delayed" Parousia, the well-known work of E. Käsemann, Martin Hengel, and others seem to have rendered Bultmann's thesis obsolete. Further, Bultmann's thesis rests on a denial of the assumption that the first and second advent constitute for the NT writers an "already" and a "not yet" aspect to a single resurrection event. The organic texture of Pauline concepts (i.e., Jesus as the "firstfruits," "firstborn from the dead," the Holy Spirit as "the deposit guaranteeing the final redemption," etc.) certainly point in this direction, as do Jesus' parables about the wheat and the weeds growing together until the harvest (as a corollary, sharply rebuking James and John when they seek to realize—in fact, exercise—eschatological judgment (glory) in this period of eschatological humiliation and kerygma (cross). Finally, it is not as if Bultmann's thesis is new. Regardless of one's dating of the epistle, 2 Pet. 3:1–13 already confronts this challenge in more general terms.

98. Moltmann, *The Coming of God: Christian Eschatology*, trans. Margaret Kohl (Minneapolis: Fortress, 1996), 135.

99. Ibid., 13.

100. Vos, *Pauline Eschatology*, 7.

101. Ibid., 24.

102. Ibid., 25.

103. Colin Gunton, *The One, the Three, and the Many: God, Creation, and the Culture of Modernity* (Cambridge: Cambridge University Press, 1993), 93.

104. Ibid., 90, 92.

105. As we have seen, Derrida, for instance, continues to insist upon "justice" as if it were an absolute and transparent good. Hardly willing to abandon humanism when it comes to politics, they blink in the face of Nietzsche's challenge to become supermen "beyond good and evil." But they can provide no rationale for their humanism, which might lead to disastrous practical consequences if nothing but the sheer, arbitrary will of "the just" (any more than the "genius") is sovereign. Another possibility is that it will lead to that very resignation and apathy toward power regimes that Nietzsche attributed to an exhausted Christian (i.e., Kantian) morality.

106. Miroslav Volf, "Theology, Meaning, and Power," in *The Future of Theology: Essays in Honor of Jürgen Moltmann*, ed. Volf, Carmen Krieg, and Thomas Kucharz (Grand Rapids: Eerdmans, 1996), 109.

107. Isa. 59. In a courtroom scene, the covenant prosecutor proves that YHWH is not the problem, nor his creation: neither his goodness nor his power is questionable. "Rather, your iniquities have been barriers between you and your God, and your sins have hidden his face from you so that he does not hear." Seeing no one righteous and no one capable of interceding on behalf of the people, YHWH himself will descend and gain salvation for the people. "[T]hey cannot cover themselves with what they make" (v. 6), and they are engaged in voluntary rebellion. Here we have a microcosm of the sin-and-grace dualism which, against all philosophical decoys, dominates the field of Paul's eschatological vision.

108. Moltmann correctly remarks that although the emphasis on history and eschatology received a rebirth in Johannes Cocceius and federal theology, pietism (especially J. A. Bengel) emphasized one progressive line unfolding in dispensations or "economies." So it sought its eschatological bearings "not from the cross and the resurrection, but from other 'signs of the times'—from an apocalyptic view of the corruption of the Church and the decay of the world, or from an optimistic view of the progress of culture and knowledge—so that revelation became a predicate of history, and 'history' was turned deistically into a

substitute for God" (*Theology of Hope*, 71). The synchronic irruption (which Bultmann attributes to a mythological worldview) is precisely what keeps Christian eschatology from becoming a mere illustration for Lessing's *The Education of the Human Race*. But it also keeps it from the wild speculations of millennialists who displace the eschatological and thus christological center for preoccupation with the developments that arise from portentous but not particularly redemptive events.

Part One

1. Introduction to *Divine Action: Studies Inspired by the Philosophical Theology of Austin Farrer*, ed. Brian Hebblethwaite and Edward Henderson (Edinburgh: T. & T. Clark, 1990), 1.

Chapter Two

1. Langdon Gilkey, "Cosmology, Ontology, and the Travail of Biblical Language," *Journal of Religion* 41 (July 1961): 200.
2. Johann Baptist Metz, "A Short Apology of Narrative," in *Why Narrative*, ed. Stanley Hauerwas and L. Gregory Jones (Eugene, Ore.: Wipf & Stock, 1997), 256.
3. Gilkey, "Cosmology," 194–205.
4. Wright's title, *God Who Acts: Biblical Theology as Recital* (London: SCM Press, 1952), comes readily to mind.
5. Rudolf Bultmann, *Jesus Christ and Mythology* (New York: Charles Scribner's Sons, 1958), 61. Of course, his classic statement of the problem and the need for demythologizing is found at the beginning of his essay "New Testament and Mythology," in *Kerygma and Myth: A Theological Debate*, ed. Hans Werner Bartsch, and trans. Reginald H. Fuller (London: SPCK, 1953), 1.
6. Gilkey, "Cosmology," 194–205.
7. Ibid., 195.
8. Ibid., 196.
9. Ibid., 200.
10. Ibid.
11. Ibid., 197.
12. Ibid., 198.
13. Ibid., 199.
14. Ibid., 203.
15. Representative works include Schubert M. Ogden, "What Sense Does It Make to Say, 'God Acts in History'?" in *The Reality of God and Other Essays* (New York: Harper & Row, 1963); Gordon Kaufman, "On the Meaning of 'Act of God,'" in *God the Problem* (Cambridge: Harvard University Press, 1972); Maurice Wiles, *God's Action in the World: The Bampton Lectures for 1986* (London: SCM Press, 1986); Thomas F. Tracy, *God, Action, and Embodiment* (Grand Rapids: Eerdmans, 1984); Ronald Thiemann, *Revelation and Theology: The Gospel as Narrated Promise* (South Bend, Ind.: University of Notre Dame Press, 1985); Grace Jantzen, *God's World, God's Body* (Philadelphia: Westminster Press, 1984); Vernon White, *The Fall of a Sparrow: A Concept of Special Divine Action* (Exeter: Paternoster Press, 1985); William P. Alston, "God's Action in the World," in Ernan McMullin, ed., *Evolution and Creation* (South Bend, Ind.: University of Notre Dame Press, 1985), 197–220. Owen Thomas, to whom I owe much of this bibliography, has collected some of the earlier important essays in one volume, *God's Activity in the World: The Contemporary Problem*

(Chico, Calif.: Scholars Press, 1983). His chapter, "Recent Thought on Divine Agency," in Hebblethwaite and Henderson, eds., *Divine Action,* is a good update to the earlier collection.

16. See, for instance, David C. Steinmetz, "The Superiority of Pre-Critical Exegesis," *Theology Today* 27 (1980): 27–38; *The Interpretation of the Bible in the Sixteenth Century,* ed. (Durham, N.C.: Duke University Press, 1990).

17. Cited by Wolfhart Pannenberg, *Basic Questions in Theology* (Philadelphia, Westminster Press, 1970), 1:221, n. 14. "The original intention of this formula," Pannenberg relates, "consists in the denial of the attempt of Gilbert of La Poree to understand the trinitarian unity according to the analogy of the union of believers with Christ" (ibid.).

18. Gilkey, "Cosmology," 197.

19. Ibid.

20. Wolfhart Pannenberg, *Basic Questions in Theology* (Philadelphia: Westminster Press, 1970), 1: chap. 7.

21. Bultmann in *Kerygma and Myth: A Theological Debate,* 5.

22. Peter Berger, *A Rumor of Angels: Modern Society and the Rediscovery of the Supernatural* (New York: Doubleday, 1960, 1990), 46–47.

23. For an excellent, though now somewhat dated, summary of the literature on this topic, see Owen C. Thomas, "Chaos, Complexity, and God: A Review Essay," *Theology Today* (April 1997), 54, no. 1: 66–80.

24. William P. Alston, "How to Think About Divine Action," in *Divine Action: Studies Inspired by the Philosophical Theology of Austin Farrer,* 54. Gordon Kaufman shares the confusion of Bultmann and Gilkey on this point: "Our experience is of a unified and orderly world; in such a world acts of God (in the traditional sense) are not merely improbable or difficult to believe: they are literally inconceivable. It is not a question of whether talk about such acts is true or false; it is, in the literal sense, meaningless; one cannot make the concept hang together consistently," *God the Problem* (Cambridge: Harvard University Press, 1972), 134–35. F. Michael McLain writes, "Kaufman's point may boil down to little more than this, then: those imbued with the scientific mind look for an explanation in terms of a natural, not divine, force. That may be true, but it gives us no *reason* to rule out the latter. . . . I do not mean to suggest in all of this that I do not share the bias of our scientific culture. I do. It is just that when I reflect on the matter, I do not find that my bias is rationally warranted. I do not, however, for a variety of reasons, wish to drift back in the direction of an uncritical acceptance of Biblical narrative" (Hebblethwaite and Henderson, eds., *Divine Action,* 158).

25. Henry Chadwick, ed., *Lessing's Theological Writings* (Palo Alto, Calif.: Stanford University Press, 1967), 53.

26. Ibid., 51–56.

27. Ibid., 55.

28. Ibid., introduction, 32.

29. Ibid., 106.

30. Ibid., 105.

31. Bultmann, "Reply to Theses of J. Schniewind," in *Kerygma and Myth,* 117.

32. Bultmann, *Jesus Christ and Mythology,* 14–15.

33. It is difficult to resist the admittedly ad hominem observation that Professor Kaufman's reconfigured Kantianism is just the sort of thing that has emptied mainline churches while those churches that most self-consciously emphasize God's personal intrusion into this world are bursting their seams. This is true not only of those of modest educational and economic resources, as the evangelical movement transcends demographic stereotypes. As with beauty, the

question concerning "dead metaphors" appears to lie in the eye of the beholder. Bultmann and Kaufman should not have confused the consensus of their friends and colleagues with an argument, a consensus that is being challenged today more in the human and physical sciences than in theology. Thus, what was "unintelligible" to Bultmann is no longer so for a growing circle of educated people.

34. Max Müller "The Philosophy of Mythology," in *Introduction to the Science of Religion* (London, 1873), 353–55.

35. Ernst Cassirer, *Language and Myth,* trans. Susanne K. Langer (New York: Dover, 1946), 6.

36. Ibid., 8.

37. Ibid., 9.

38. Ibid., 45.

39. Ibid., 50–53.

40. One thinks immediately of Peter's insistence, "For we did not follow cleverly devised myths (mythois) when we made known to you the power and coming of our Lord Jesus Christ, but we had been eyewitnesses of his majesty" (2 Pet. 1:16).

41. Cassirer, *Language and Myth,* 61.

42. Ibid., 63 ff.

43. Ibid., 61.

44. Bultmann, in *Kerygma and Myth,* ed. H. W. Bartsch, 10 and 10, n.2.

45. A. C. Thiselton, *The Two Horizons: New Testament Hermeneutics and Philosophical Description* (Grand Rapids: Eerdmans, 1980), 253. Cf. Schubert Ogden in Owen Thomas, ed., *God's Activity in the World.* Ogden seeks to supplement Bultmann's underdeveloped references to analogy with Hartshorne's thought, seeing in the latter a model for speaking of God (di-polar) as analogous to Heidegger's conception of self-understanding in persons (83–84). See also Ogden's critique of Bultmann on 85.

46. Ibid., 11.

47. Ibid., 62.

48. For an excellent analysis of this dependence, see A. C. Thiselton, "Ingredients of Bultmann's Hermeneutical Concerns," in *The Two Horizons: New Testament Hermeneutics and Philosophical Description* (Grand Rapids: Eerdmans, 1980), 205–52. See also R. A. Johnson, *The Origins of Demythologizing: Philosophy and Historiography in the Theology of Rudolf Bultmann* (Leiden: Brill, 1974).

49. Ibid., 65.

50. Ibid., 68.

51. Ibid.

52. Schubert Ogden, "Myth and Truth," a paper for the colloquium on "Myth and Modern Man," held at McCormick Theological Seminary, Chicago, Ill., Oct. 22, 1964.

53. Paul Tillich, *Dynamics of Faith* (New York: Harper & Row, 1957), 41–54.

54. Ibid., 137.

55. Ibid., 138–40.

56. Ibid., 141.

57. Ibid., 142.

58. Ibid., 143.

59. Ibid., 144.

60. Paul Edwards, "Professor Tillich's Confusions," *Mind,* 74, no. 294 (April 1965): 197–206.

61. Ibid.

62. Ibid.

63. Ibid. Edwards cites Berkeley's *Principles of Human Knowledge,* sections 16–17.
64. Ibid.
65. Paul Edwards, "Professor Tillich's Confusions."
66. Ibid.
67. Ibid.
68. Ibid.
69. Sallie McFague, *Metaphorical Theology: Models of God in Religious Language* (Philadelphia: Fortress, 1982), 2.
70. Ibid., viii.
71. Ibid., 10.
72. Ibid., 13.
73. Ibid., 16.
74. Ibid., 19.
75. Ibid., 16.
76. Ibid., 40.
77. Ibid., 41.
78. Ibid., 26.
79. Psalm 18:8–10.
80. Papers of the Meeting of the Aristotelian Society at 5/7 Tavistock Place, London, W.C.1, Monday, February 6, 1978, paper number 8, p. 125.
81. Bartsch, ed., *Kerygma and Myth,* 215.
82. There is a great deal of literature on this topic, but for representative discussions see Ford Lewis Battles's essay, "God Was Accomodating Himself to Human Capacity," *Interpretation* 31 (1977): 19–38; also published in Ford Lewis Battles, *Interpreting John Calvin,* ed. Robert Benedetto (Grand Rapids: Baker, 1996), 117–37.
83. Wright, *God Who Acts,* 117.
84. Ibid., 119.
85. Ibid., 126.
86. Ibid., 126–27.
87. Ibid., 38–39.
88. Ibid., 127.
89. Ibid.
90. Ibid., 128.
91. Ibid.
92. Frank B. Dilley, "Does the 'God Who Acts' Really Act?" *Anglican Theological Review* 47 (1965): 66–80, reprinted with permission in Owen C. Thomas, ed., *God's Activity in the World,* 45–60.
93. Ibid., 47.
94. Ibid., 50–51.
95. Ibid., 51.
96. Werner Lemke, "Revelation through History in Recent Biblical Theology," *Interpretation* 36, no. 1 (Jan. 1982): 34–46.
97. Ibid., 45–46.
98. F. Michael McLain, "Narrative Interpretation and the Problem of Double Agency," in Hebblethwaite and Henderson, eds., *Divine Action,* 143.
99. Ibid., 150.
100. Ibid., 151.
101. Ibid., 152.
102. Ibid., 166.
103. George Lindbeck, *The Nature of Doctrine: Religion and Theology in a Postliberal Age* (Philadelphia: Westminster Press, 1984), 80.
104. Ibid., 123.

105. Thomas F. Tracy, "Narrative Theology and the Acts of God," in Hebble-thwaite and Henderson, eds., *Divine Action*, 176. See also Tracy, *God, Action, and Embodiment* (Grand Rapids: Eerdmans, 1984).
106. Ibid., 181.
107. Ibid., 193.
108. Ronald Thiemann, *Revelation and Theology: The Gospel as Narrated Promise* (Notre Dame: University of Notre Dame Press, 1987).
109. Thomas F. Tracy, "Narrative Theology," 196.
110. Owen Thomas points this out, also in *Divine Action*, 38.
111. Sallie McFague, *Models of God: Theology for an Ecological, Nuclear Age* (Philadelphia: Fortress, 1987), 70.
112. Ibid., 71.
113. Ibid., 72.
114. Cited by Thomas in *Divine Action*, 46.
115. John Cobb, "Natural Causality and Divine Action," in Thomas, ed., *God's Activity in the World*, 112.
116. Ibid.
117. Ibid., 103.
118. Ibid., 104–6.
119. Ibid., 107.
120. Ibid.
121. Ibid., 111–12.

Chapter Three

1. See for instance Carl F. H. Henry, *God, Revelation, and Authority* (Waco, Tex.: Word, 1976), 1:237–38. Henry criticizes the "resort to analogy as the preferable basis for 'a sound theology'" which results in "forfeiting both logical coherence and univocal knowledge or literal truth about the Divine." It is clear here that, like Gilkey and so many others we have noted, Henry regards "univocal knowledge" as synonymous with "literal truth." If it is to be literal truth, then, revelation must take (or be reducible to) the form of propositional utterances. "Christian theology . . . consists essentially in the repetition, combination, and systematization of the truth of revelation in its propositionally given biblical form." This view displays little appreciation for literary diversity, placing genres themselves on a scale of truth. Contrast the preceding, for instance, with Tremper Longman III: "Which communicates more powerfully, 'Speak righteously' or 'The mouth of the righteous flows with wisdom, but the perverted tongue will be cut out' (Prov. 10:31 NASB)? Which speaks more vividly, the statement 'love your neighbor as yourself' or the story of the Good Samaritan?" ("Storytellers and Poets in the Bible: Can Literary Artifice Be True?" in Harvie M. Conn, ed., *Inerrancy and Hermeneutic: A Tradition, A Challenge, A Debate* [Grand Rapids: Baker, 1988], 149). Somewhat like the positivists, Henry at this point falls prey to the descriptive (or what Austin calls the "constative") fallacy, regarding all statements as reports.
2. Calvin, *Institutes*, 1.16.7.
3. My colleague S. M. Baugh pointed out to me the parallel with the ancient Cynics and atomists.
4. Ian Barbour, *Science and Religion: New Perspectives on the Dialogue* (Harper & Row, 1968), 5.
5. Ibid., 6.
6. Polkinghorne, *Quarks, Chaos, and Christianity* (New York: Crossroad, 1996), 82.

7. John Searle, *Speech Acts: An Essay in the Philosophy of Language* (Cambridge: Cambridge University Press, 1969), 52.
8. Polkinghorne, *Belief in God in an Age of Science* (New Haven: Yale, 1998), 80.
9. Ibid., 51.
10. Ibid.
11. Ibid., 52.
12. Ibid.
13. Ibid., 54.
14. Ibid. Ironically, some physicists see such a clearing for the role of God in the world that they see physics rather than religion as the most appropriate future discipline for the study of God. See, for instance, Paul Davies, *God and the New Physics* (New York: Simon & Schuster, 1983).
15. Ian Barbour, *Issues in Science and Religion* (Englewood Cliffs, N.J.: Prentice-Hall, 1966), 122.
16. Cf. A. Funkenstein, *Theology and the Scientific Imagination from the Middle Ages to the Seventeenth Century* (Princeton, N.J.: Princeton University Press, 1986); Christopher Kaiser, *Creation and the History of Science* (Grand Rapids: Eerdmans, 1991).
17. This is a highly debated topic in studies of scholastic theology and late medieval/early modern philosophy. Cf. Heiko Oberman, *The Harvest of Medieval Theology: Gabriel Biel and Late Medieval Nominalism* (Durham, N.C.: Labyrinth Press, 1983), 30–56, 192, 207–10; Philotheus Boehner, "On Recent Presentation of Ockham's Philosophy," *Franciscan Studies* 9 (1949): 443–56; E. M. Buytaert, ed., *Collected Articles on Ockham* (St. Bonaventure, N.Y.: Franciscan Studies, 1958); Michael Allen Gillespie, *Nihilism before Nietzsche* (Chicago: University of Chicago Press, 1995). Calvin's reaction against Ockham's position supports Gillespie's thesis that modernity begins with Ockham's radical severing of the *potentia Dei absoluta* from the *potentia Dei ordinata* when the reformer sides with "the sounder Schoolmen" over "the more recent Sophists" (Ockham and Biel) in the matter of predestination (*Institutes* 2.2.6). Calvin directly attacks the practical rejection of the *potentia Dei ordinata* and obsession with God's absolute power, "that absolute will of which the Sophists babble, by an impious and profane distinction separating his justice from his power" (*Institutes* 1.17.2). Elsewhere he adds, "What the Sorbonne doctors say, that God has an absolute power, is a diabolical blasphemy which has been invented in hell" (*CR* 34: 339 ff.).
18. John Calvin, *De aeterna Dei praedestinatione* (*CR*, 8:361).
19. For Paul Feyerabend, for instance, "there is only *one* principle that can be defended under *all* circumstances and in *all* stages of human development. It is the principle: *anything goes.*" We must proceed in science "counterinductively," he says, invoking the sophists. Accordingly, he concludes his piece, "Always remember that the demonstrations and the rhetorics used do not express any 'deep convictions' of mine. They merely show how easy it is to lead people by the nose in a rational way," "Science without Scientism," in *The Truth about the Truth: De-confusing and Re-constructing the Postmodern World*, ed. Walter Truett Anderson (New York: G. P. Putnam's Sons, 1995), 200–203.
20. Polkinghorne, *Belief in God in an Age of Science*, 55.
21. Ibid.
22. Ibid., 56.
23. Ibid.
24. Ibid., 57.
25. Ibid.

26. Ibid., 58.
27. Ibid., 63.
28. Ibid., 67.
29. Ibid., 70.
30. Ibid.
31. Ibid., 71–72.
32. Barth, *CD* III/3: 163, where Calov is quoted as admitting that we can speak popularly of chance *respectu nostri*, "and in consideration of *causae secundae*, but not *respectu Dei*."
33. Calvin, *Institutes*, 1.16.9: "[H]owever all things may be ordained by God's plan, according to a sure dispensation, for us they are fortuitous. Not that we think that fortune rules the world and men, tumbling all things at random up and down, for it is fitting that this folly be absent from the Christian's breast! But since order, reason, end, and necessity of those things which happen for the most part lie hidden in God's purpose, and are not apprehended by human opinion, those things, which it is certain take place by God's will, are in a sense fortuitous. For they bear on the face of them no other appearance, whether they are considered in their own nature or weighed according to our knowledge and judgment."
34. Calvin, *Institutes*, 1.16.2.
35. Acts 17.
36. Calvin, *Institutes*, 1.16.8.
37. Ibid.
38. William P. Alston, "How to Think About Divine Action," in Hebblethwaite and Henderson, eds., *Divine Action*, 53.
39. Ibid., 54.
40. Ibid., 60–61.
41. Ibid., 63.
42. William P. Alston, *Perceiving God: The Epistemology of Religious Experience* (Ithaca, N.Y.: Cornell University Press, 1991).
43. Even Pannenberg appears to have revised his thesis somewhat on this point. Taking presuppositions more seriously, he argues, "In other words, the Christian belief in the event of the resurrection of Jesus Christ presupposes an outlook on reality in general that is not shared by everybody." Many "will be inclined to accept almost any alternative explanation of the course of events, no matter what the historical evidence might be, whenever claims to such an occurrence are raised." There are no established "criteria and tools of historical judgement [that] are not beyond dispute" ("History and the Reality of the Resurrection," in *Resurrection Reconsidered*, ed. Gavin D'Costa [Oxford: One World, 1996], 62–63).
44. David R. Griffin, "Relativism, Divine Causation, and Biblical Theology," in Thomas, ed., *God's Activity in the World*, 120.
45. Eugene TeSelle, "Divine Action: The Doctrinal Tradition," in Hebblethwaite and Henderson, eds., *Divine Action*, 80.
46. Thomas F. Tracy, *God, Action, and Embodiment* (Grand Rapids: Eerdmans, 1984), 59–65.
47. Rodger Forsman, "'Double Agency' and Identifying Reference to God," in Hebblethwaite and Henderson, eds., *Divine Action*.
48. Ibid., 131.
49. Ibid.
50. F. Michael McLain, "Narrative Interpretation," in Hebblethwaite and Henderson, eds., *Divine Action*, 151: "A basic action is one that is performed not by or in simultaneously performing some other action. A non-basic action is done *by* performing a basic action. . . . By this route we arrive at the not implausible

view that bodily movement is part of the meaning of *human* action concepts. Does it follow that things must be this way *in general* with action concepts? Intuitively, no. We can readily distinguish the questions: (1) How do human beings bring about the actions they perform, and (2) Is movement of an agent's body part of the concept of action?"

51. Alston, "How to Think About Divine Action," 57.
52. Frank Dilley, "Does the 'God Who Acts' Really Act?" 57.
53. Ibid., 58.
54. Barth, *CD* III/3: 164–65.
55. Westminster Confession, chap. 5, *Book of Confessions* (Louisville, Ky.: Presbyterian Church [U.S.A.]), 6.024–6.
56. See B. A. Gerrish, "'To the Unknown God': Luther and Calvin on the Hiddenness of God," in *The Old Protestantism and the New* (Chicago: University of Chicago Press, 1982).
57. Calvin, *Institutes*, 1.16.9.
58. Ibid., 1.17.1.
59. Ibid., 1.17.2.
60. Ibid., 1.17.9.
61. Charles Hodge, *Systematic Theology* (Grand Rapids: Eerdmans, 1946, from the Charles Scribner & Co. edition, 1871), 1:598.
62. Ibid., 599.
63. Ibid., 600.
64. Calvin, *Institutes*, 1.18.1.
65. Owen Thomas, "Recent Thought on Divine Agency," in Hebblethwaite and Henderson, eds., *Divine Action*, 47: "[Thomas] Tracy's analogy of two people pulling on a rope to ring a bell is clearly not a case of double agency, since each agent contributes part of the action. The same applies, I believe to Thiemann's analogies of the sister passing on the mother's message about dinner, the town crier reading the royal decree, and the minister reading the presidential proclamation. In each case the agents are performing distinct actions or distinct parts of one action. They would be valid analogies of double agency only if the passing on or reading were in fact the very occasion on which the message, decree, or proclamation became a reality or became effective, such that there was an identity of the actions of the two agents. For example, in the case of the royal decree, if the context were such that it actually became effective in an official proclamation, say, by a magistrate before the parliament, then this might be a fairly good analogy of divine-human double-agency. Both agents, the crown and the magistrate, would be active in the one event of the proclamation of the decree. Furthermore, Rahner's analogies (two and three dimensional space, the laws of inorganic matter and biology) and some of Polanyi's analogies (the laws of mechanics and machines, vocabulary and grammar) are also not analogies of double agency since no intentional action is involved. However, Polanyi's other analogies (physiology and purposive action, the rules of chess and the player's strategies) are possible analogies of divine-creaturely double agency. But they are analogies of double agency between God and sub-human agents rather than between God and autonomous agents."
66. Ibid. 48–49.
67. Charles Hodge, *Systematic Theology*, 603.
68. For instance, David Brown writes, "Thus one needs divine distance in order to preserve room for independent human decision-making" ("God and Symbolic Action," in Hebblethwaite and Henderson, eds., *Divine Action*, 106).
69. Ronald Thiemann, *Revelation and Theology: The Gospel as Narrated Promise* (Notre Dame, Ind.: University of Notre Dame Press, 1985).

70. Thomas, "Recent Thought on Divine Agency," 48.
71. Austin Farrer, "Grace and Free Will," in Thomas, ed., *God's Activity in the World*, 196–97.
72. Ibid., 200.
73. Dilley, "Does the 'God Who Acts' Really Act?" 57.
74. Thomas, "Recent Thought on Divine Agency," 49.
75. Barth, *CD* III/3: 133.
76. Vernon White, *The Fall of a Sparrow: A Concept of Divine Action* (Exeter: Paternoster, 1985), 55.
77. John Searle, *Speech Acts: An Essay in the Philosophy of Language* (Cambridge: Cambridge University Press, 1969), 57.
78. Once more I find Frank Dilley to be a terrific source for an apt summary of the problem: "If God could send an east wind to rescue the people of Israel, then he could have sent one to melt the iceberg that sank the Titanic, and he could have sent a disease germ to destroy Hitler as he sent a plague to rout the armies of Sennacherib. It would take very little interference to make the world considerably better. Liberalism, by confining God's actions to general ones, reduced the problem of theodicy considerably by affirming that there are many evils which result from the general order and hence are not preventable. Once it is said that God can act selectively, then it is legitimate to raise the question 'why' about every preventable natural evil, and many preventable human evils" ("Does the 'God Who Acts' Really Act?" 55).
79. Barth provides a useful summary of the scholastic Lutheran-Reformed debate in terms of breaking chiefly with Stoicism or with Epicureanism, although both rejected either position: *CD* III/3: 162.
80. Jeffrey Eaton, "Divine Action and Human Liberation," in Hebblethwaite and Henderson, eds., *Divine Action*, 213.
81. Ibid., 214.
82. Ibid., 222.
83. Ibid., 223.
84. Ibid., 224.
85. Ibid., 225.
86. Ibid., 228.
87. It seems surprising that many radical feminist theologies should turn to neo-pagan resources or to process-panentheistic models, since it is difficult to know how one could identify "God" with "the way things are" more than by thinking of all events in relation to God as body to soul. By contrast, Latin American and African liberation theologies have tended to concentrate on the prophetic mode, proclaiming God's intervention in history. Here, apocalyptic irruption of transcendent judgment and redemption, not steady evolution or immanent progress, is the motivating paradigm for criticism and action. See for instance Alan Boesak, *Black and Reformed: Apartheid, Liberation, and the Calvinist Tradition* (Maryknoll, N.Y.: Orbis, 1984). See also Gustavo Gutiérrez: "Human history, then, is the location of our encounter with God, in Christ," in *Essential Writings*, ed. James B. Nickoloff (Maryknoll, N.Y.: Orbis, 1996), 91. Not only God's activity in the world, but God's grace, is necessary for genuine liberation: "Nothing, no human work however valuable, merits grace, for if it did, grace would cease to be grace. This is the heart of the message of the Book of Job. Paul will repeat it no less forcefully" (172).
88. Serene Jones, from a lecture on Calvin at Yale Divinity School in the fall of 1996.
89. Calvin, *Institutes*, 1.17.8.
90. McFague, *Metaphorical Theology*, 10.

91. Ibid., vii.
92. McLain, "Narrative Interpretation," 143.
93. We will discuss this in greater depth in connection with canonicity.
94. Ernst Bloch, *Man on His Own: Essays in the Philosophy of Religion*, trans. E. B. Ashton (New York: Herder & Herder, 1971), 76.
95. Although the traditional understanding of God as "supreme being" has been much misunderstood, especially since Heidegger, perhaps it would make more sense in the light of our proposal to concentrate on action rather than ontology. Perhaps instead of "supreme being," we should think of God along the lines of a "supreme agent" for whom intention and enactment are one, parallel to Aquinas's identification of being and act, essence and existence as one in God.
96. Depending on how one reads him, Duns Scotus anticipates either a Spinozan drift toward pantheism (and is thus a predecessor to process thought) or untangled the problems in Thomas's notion of the *analogia entis* in order to provide a firmer basis for it. In either case, he does discuss the univocity of being and hints at Jesus Christ as the univocal core, but does not develop it. See, for instance, C. R. S. Harris, *Duns Scotus*, vol. II: *The Philosophical Doctrine of Duns Scotus* (Bristol, England: Thoemmes Press, 1994), 62–67; Alexander Broadie, *The Shadow of Scotus: Philosophy and Faith in Pre-Reformation Scotland* (Edinburgh: T. & T. Clark, 1995), esp. chap. 4.
97. Hans Frei, *The Identity of Jesus Christ: The Hermeneutical Bases for Dogmatic Theology* (Eugene, Ore.: Wipf & Stock Publishers, 1997), 132–74.

Chapter Four

1. Paul Ricoeur, *History and Truth*, trans. Charles A. Kelbley (Evanston, Ill.: Northwestern University Press, 1965), 120.
2. Calvin, *Corpus Reformatorum* (*CR*) 55, 219.
3. Julius Schniewind, "A Reply to Bultmann," in *Kerygma and Myth: A Theological Debate*, ed. Hans Werner Bartsch and trans. Reginald H. Fuller (London: SPCK, 1953), 50.
4. Paul Ricoeur, *Figuring the Sacred: Religion, Narrative, and Imagination*, trans. David Pellauer and ed. Mark I. Wallace (Minneapolis: Fortress, 1995), 40.
5. Ibid.
6. Wolfhart Pannenberg, *Basic Questions in Theology*, trans. George H. Keim (Philadelphia: Westminster, 1971), 1:103–4.
7. Francis Watson, *Text and Truth: Redefining Biblical Theology* (Grand Rapids: Eerdmans; Edinburgh: T. & T. Clark, 1997), 10.
8. Ibid.
9. Norman Malcolm, *Wittgenstein: A Religious Point of View?* edited with a response by Peter Winch (Ithaca, N.Y.: Cornell University Press, 1994), 42.
10. Pannenberg, *Basic Questions in Theology*, 1:100.
11. Ibid., 131.
12. Cf. Richard B. Gaffin Jr., *Resurrection and Redemption: A Study in Paul's Soteriology* (Philipsburg, N.J.: Presbyterian & Reformed Publishing Co., 1987), 23.
13. Carl Braaten, "The Resurrection Debate Revisited," *Pro Ecclesia* 8, no. 2: 155. Braaten quotes Robert W. Funk's account of a meeting of the Jesus Seminar in which the latter "tells about how once he formulated the proposition, 'The resurrection was an event in the life of Jesus,' and presented it to members of the Jesus Seminar.'" The response? According to Funk himself, "My proposition was received with hilarity by several Fellows. One suggested that it was an oxymoron. . . . Others alleged that the formulation was meaningless, since we all assume, they said, that Jesus' life ended with his crucifixion and death. I was

surprised by this response. I shouldn't have been. After all, John Dominic Crossan has confessed, 'I do not think that anyone, anywhere, at any time brings dead people back to life.' That's fairly blunt. But it squares with what we really know, as distinguished from what many want to believe. Sheehan is even blunter: 'Jesus, *regardless of where his corpse ended up*, is dead and remains dead'" (emphasis added) (147).

What is remarkable is the extent to which this group, with a peculiar attraction to media attention, claims to be proceeding along scientific principles while being explicit in their a priori dismissal of the very possibility of the anomalous. While science itself has advanced beyond the Enlightenment, it would seem that certain quarters of theology have some catching up to do.

14. Gareth Jones, "The Resurrection in Contemporary Systematic Theology," in *Resurrection Reconsidered*, ed. Gavin D'Costa (Oxford: One World, 1997), 42.

15. In addition to the Reformers, Blaise Pascal also picked up on the "hiddenness" motif: "What can be seen on earth points to neither the total absence nor the obvious presence of divinity, but to the presence of a hidden God. Everything bears this mark," *Pensées* 449. Preferring earlier formulations, we reject the hypertranscendence/hyperimmanence implicit in Barth's "wholly hidden"/"wholly revealed" dialectic. In our view, God is full of secrets, though not caprice.

16. Ricoeur, *Figuring the Sacred*, 162.

17. Thucydides, *History of the Peloponnesian War*, trans. Rex Warner (Baltimore: Penguin Books, 1954), 24.

18. Cf. F. F. Bruce, *The Acts of the Apostles: The Greek Text with Introduction and Commentary* (Grand Rapids: Eerdmans, 1984), 15.

19. See also, for instance, 2 Peter 1:16–25.

20. This is to be distinguished from a bare chronology on one hand and historical fiction on the other. Luke himself acknowledges his own creativity in arranging the reports to serve an evangelistic purpose. Compare with John's stated objective, "[T]hese are written so that you may come to believe that Jesus is the Messiah, the Son of God, and that through believing you may have life in his name" (John 20:31).

21. C. Stephen Evans, *The Historical Christ and the Jesus of Faith: The Incarnational Narrative as History* (Oxford: Clarendon Press, 1996), 6.

22. Ibid., 7.

23. Immanuel Kant, *Religion within the Limits of Reason Alone*, trans. Theodore M. Greene and Hoyt H. Hudson (New York: Harper & Bros., 1960), 56. Kant was well aware of the scholastic distinction between archetypal and ectypal theology. In fact he accepts it in his *Lectures on Philosophical Theology*, trans. Allen Wood and Gertrude Clark (Ithaca, N.Y.: Cornell University Press, 1978), 23. Nevertheless, in *Religion within the Limits of Reason Alone* (approximately five to eight years later), archetypes are present in the human mind. This is a perfect example of how inappropriate it is to describe post-Reformation scholasticism as rationalistic.

24. Ricoeur notes that Kant's interpretation of Rom. 5 "is certainly a Pelagian interpretation of the phrase 'in Adam,' but it has as much right as does Augustine's in the conflict of interpretations" (*Figuring the Sacred*, 81).

25. Kant, *Religion within the Limits*, 55.

26. Ricoeur, *Figuring the Sacred*, 84: "The only thing that is important philosophically is the Christ of faith elevated to an idea or an ideal. Second, Kant admits that, as regards this archetype of a good intention, 'we are not the authors of this idea, . . . and it has established itself in man without our comprehending how human nature could have been capable of receiving it.' . . . This is why 'it

is more appropriate to say that this archetype has *come down* to us from heaven
and has assumed our humanity.' . . . Joining these two points together, we can
say the following: '[W]e need, therefore, no empirical example to make the idea
of a person morally well-pleasing to God our archetype; this idea as an archetype is already present in our reason."

27.   Ibid.
28.   Ibid., 85.
29.   Ibid.
30.   Cf. book 3 of Kant's *Religion*, 85.
31.   Kant, "Religion within the Boundaries of Mere Religion," in *Religion and Ratio-
      nal Theology*, trans. and ed., Allen W. Wood and George Di Giovanni (Cam-
      bridge: Cambridge University Press, 1996), 148, 150.
32.   Ricoeur, *Figuring the Sacred*, 86.
33.   Once more we are faced with the *theological* a prioris of philosophy determin-
      ing what one can and cannot allow to even come before the bar. And all of this
      is known deductively, so Kant can know quite a bit about the noumenal realm
      after all.
34.   Ronald Thiemann, *Revelation and Theology: The Gospel as Narrated Promise*
      (Notre Dame, Ind.: University of Notre Dame Press, 1985).
35.   It is not surprising that on the basis of his universal religion of pure morality,
      Kant (in the span of ten pages) dispenses with the absolute necessity and
      unsubstitutability of Jesus Christ, his deity or resurrection, and of the insepa-
      rability of Christianity from the particular history of Israel. Christianity repre-
      sents "a total abandonment of the Judaism in which it originated . . . at a
      juncture when much foreign (Greek) wisdom had already become available to
      this otherwise still ignorant people, and this wisdom presumably had the fur-
      ther effect of enlightening it through concepts of virtue and, in spite of the
      oppressive burden of its dogmatic faith, of making it ready for revolutions
      which the diminution of the priests' power, due to their subjugation to the rule
      of a people indifferent to every foreign popular faith, occasioned—it was from
      a Judaism such as this that Christianity suddenly though not unprepared arose"
      (*Religion and Rational Theology*, 156).
36.   Cf. Ernst Benz, *The Mystical Sources of German Romantic Philosophy*, trans. Blair
      R. Reynolds and Eunice M. Paul (Allison Park, Pa.: Pickwick Publications,
      1983); Cyril O'Regan, *The Heterodox Hegel* (Albany, N.Y.: SUNY, 1994).
37.   James Robinson, *A New Quest for the Historical Jesus* (London: SCM Press,
      1959), 31.
38.   Pannenberg, *Basic Questions in Theology*, 1:242.
39.   Anthony Thiselton, *The Two Horizons* (Grand Rapids: Eerdmans, 1980), 242.
40.   Martin Heidegger, *Being and Time* (Oxford: Basil Blackwell, 1962), 432.
41.   Thiselton pointed out the circularity of Heidegger's argument: "'History' can
      never be reduced to the status of what is merely present-at-hand; hence history
      can only concern *Dasein* in the present. But this is only to say that the kind of
      'history' which relates to *Dasein* in the present can only concern *Dasein* in the
      present. It is in practice a value judgment about the relative worth of different
      ways of using the word 'historical.' In practice, we sympathize with what Bult-
      mann and Heidegger wish to affirm, although we have reservations about what
      they seem to be denying. It is true that, as Dilthey and Collingwood saw, what
      is important about history is its disclosure of the self in the present. However,
      this does not in itself give an exhaustive account of what history is. We may
      agree with Bultmann and Heidegger that certain aspects of history are *primary.*
      The question yet to be further explored is to what extent the singling out of
      some aspect of history as primary devalues other aspects and leads to their

neglect. David Cairns goes so far as to describe Bultmann's position as 'the flight from history'" (*The Two Horizons*, 250).

42. Gadamer, *Truth and Method*, 2nd revised ed., trans. revised by Joel Weisenheimer and Donald G. Marshall (New York: Continuum; 1994), 301–2.

43. Pannenberg writes, "The nineteenth-century quest for the historical Jesus based itself on the history of Jesus, but in such a way that the connection between Jesus and the apostolic proclamation of Christ became obscured. The kerygmatic theology of our century countered this approach by declaring that the historical attempt to go behind the texts was theologically irrelevant, and that the texts are theologically binding only in their witnessing character. Today, it is becoming apparent that this is no solution. For the unified 'essential content' of Scripture which, for Luther, was the basis of its authority, is for our historical consciousness no longer to be found in the texts but only behind them, in the figure of Jesus who is attested in the very different writings of the New Testament in very different and incongruent ways" (*Basic Questions in Theology*, 1:7).

Pannenberg shares Hegel's Enlightenment view of authority as inherently repressive, despite his own perceived dogmatism, as well as other Hegelian assumptions, as we note below.

44. Pannenberg, *Basic Questions in Theology*, 1:8.

45. Ricoeur, *History and Truth*, 48.

46. Ibid., 75.

47. Pannenberg, *Basic Questions in Theology*, 1:69.

48. Ibid., 71.

49. Ibid., 74, n.142.

50. In some respects the advance guard of renewed interest in the Trinity for solving the one and many problem of modernity, Colin Gunton has addressed this point thoroughly in *The One, The Three, and the Many*.

51. Pannenberg, *Basic Questions in Theology*, 1:78. Pannenberg, of course, acknowledges Herodotus and Thucydides, but argues that their histories are not "historical" in their consciousness.

52. As we note elsewhere, the Hebrew-vs.-Hellensitic paradigm, though well worn in modern theology, has occasioned a great deal of reductionism. Ancient Greek thought is notoriously resistant to general description, given the variety of its competing schools and claims. Perhaps Platonism is ordinarily implied as the contrast to Hebrew thought, yet even here we must be aware of the influence of Philo on Jewish thought. That said, there does appear to be a general set of presuppositions and problems that preoccupies Greek in contrast to biblical thought. General contrasts may then be made in the light of that caveat.

53. Ricoeur, *History and Truth*, 84–85.

54. Ibid., 90.

55. Ibid., 92.

56. In saying this, we must distinguish between Hellenistic historiography and the appropriation of Greek language and conceptualities. Taking our cue from the use of *Logos* in the fourth Gospel, we can subvert the Greek narrative by redescription. This is what the New Testament writers did so well and, at least at their best, what the patristic, medieval, and post-Reformation systematizers did as well.

57. Ricoeur, *History and Truth*, 191. It is worth noting that Ricoeur himself periodically acknowledges his Reformed theological heritage, and this is also observed (even critically) by others. Despite his general sympathy for Paul Tillich's thought, Ricoeur's distinctive approach, combining Jewish and Christian sensitivities in interpreting scripture, has been remarkably suggestive for our own proposal.

58. Rudolf Bultmann, *Jesus Christ and Mythology* (New York: Charles Scribner's Sons, 1958), 32.
59. Gaffin Jr., *Resurrection and Redemption*, 35.
60. It is remarkable that Bultmann and New Testament scholars under his sway on this point seem to overlook such a fundamental motif in Johannine and Pauline thought. Pannenberg is surely justified in concluding, "If he had not been writing as a New Testament scholar, we might have imagined that Bultmann was unaware of what other New Testament scholars have regularly called the double polarity of eschatology in the New Testament, according to which both the 'now' and 'not yet' have weight and importance" (*Basic Questions in Theology*, 1:265).
61. Pannenberg, *Basic Questions in Theology*, 1:66.
62. Ibid.
63. Ibid.
64. Ibid., 67.
65. While a secular historian might be looking for mention of significant figures in Israelite history attested in extrabiblical literature, the biblical writers select those individuals—some obscure, others villainous in its history—who are links to the human ancestry of Jesus. Some perhaps are selected in the genealogy for theologically subversive reasons: even before we get to the good news proper, here we notice a host of unsavory characters, as far as moral perfection and social mores. First, women are not usually mentioned at all in ancient genealogies, but here five are mentioned, including Tamar. Judah's daughter-in-law, Tamar was soon widowed, but, as was the custom, she was promised Judah's youngest son when he came of age. He came of age, but the promise was not kept, so Tamar appeared on the road in the apparel of a prostitute, and Judah paid her with a signet ring and cord, and a staff. Upon receiving news that his daughter-in-law was pregnant and had been engaged in prostitution, Judah called for her to be burned, but Tamar produced the signet, cord, and staff. "So Judah acknowledged them and said, 'She is more in the right than I, since I did not give her to my son Shelah'" (Gen. 38:1–29). Tamar is selected out of all the myriad possibilities in Jesus' ancestry because already the content of scripture is determining its form. There are Rahab the prostitute who rescued the spies, Ruth who, as a Moabite, belonged to an outcast ethnic community; and Bathsheba, Uriah's wife who was seduced by King David. The list of men is not so exemplary either. But the point was not to herald an ancestry of moral heroism; it was to link Jesus genetically to Israel's throne, contrasting divine faithfulness to the covenant with human failure.
66. William Dennison's *Paul's Two-Age Construction and Apologetics* (Lanham, Md.: University Press of America, 1985) argues this contrast more fully: "My task is to demonstrate that Plato's view of two worlds is antithetical to the Christian's view of two worlds as constructed by the Apostle Paul and that the history of Christian thought should never have synthesized Paul and Plato" (2). As a student of Gaffin's, Dennison advocates the redemptive-historical school's aversion to Platonism.
67. Ricoeur, *History and Truth*, 111.
68. Cf. Ligon Duncan III, "The Covenant Idea in Ante-Nicene Theology" (Ph.D. diss., University of Edinburgh, 1995).
69. Calvin, *Corpus Reformatorum* (*CR*) 55, 219.
70. Adolf von Harnack, *What Is Christianity?* (New York: G. P. Putnam's Sons, 1904), 160–61.
71. Ricoeur, *History and Truth*, 120.
72. Evans, *The Historical Christ and the Jesus of Facts*, 183.

Chapter Five

1. So Schleiermacher writes to his cultured despisers, "What is revelation? Every original and new communication of the Universe to man is a revelation, as, for example every such moment of conscious insight as I have just referred to. Every intuition and every original feeling proceeds from revelation. . . . What is inspiration? It is simply the general expression for the feeling of true morality and freedom" (*On Religion: Speeches to Its Cultured Despisers*, trans. John Oman [New York: Harper Torchbooks, 1958], 89).

2. Karl Rahner, *Foundations of Christian Faith*, trans. William V. Dych (New York: Crossroad, 1986), 116.

3. Ibid., 117.

4. See George Lindbeck, *The Nature of Christian Doctrine: Religion and Theology in a Postliberal Age* (Philadelphia: Westminster Press, 1984).

5. See especially *How to Do Things with Words*, 2d ed., ed. J. O. Urmson and Marina Sbisa (Cambridge: Harvard University Press, 1975); *Philosophical Papers*, 3d ed., ed. J. O. Urmson and G. J. Warnock (Oxford: Oxford University Press, 1979); *Sense and Sensibilia*, ed. G. J. Warnock (Oxford: Oxford University Press, 1964).

6. See especially *Speech Acts: An Essay in the Philosophy of Language* (Cambridge: Cambridge University Press, 1969); *Intentionality: An Essay in the Philosophy of Mind* (Cambridge: Cambridge University Press, 1983). Particularly in *Speech Acts*, Searle fleshes out some of the most interesting suggestions in Austin's *How to Do Things with Words* and in some ways improves on Austin's arguments.

7. Ibid., 100.

8. Ibid., 102–3.

9. Ibid., 102.

10. Searle, *Speech Acts*, 16.

11. Ibid., 22.

12. Austin, *How to Do Things with Words*, 4. Examples of such performative utterances, says Alston, include the following:
    "'I do (sc. Take this woman to be my lawful wedded wife)'—as uttered in the course of the marriage ceremony. 'I name this ship the Queen Elizabeth'— as uttered when smashing the bottle against the stem. 'I give and bequeath my watch to my brother'—as occurring in a will. 'I bet you sixpence it will rain tomorrow.' In these examples it seems clear that to utter the sentence (in, of course, the appropriate circumstances) is not to describe my doing of what I should be said in so doing or to state that I am doing it: it is to do it. . . . When I say, before the registrar or altar, &c., 'I do,' I am not reporting on a marriage: I am indulging in it."

13. Ibid., 24.

14. Ibid., 25.

15. Ibid., 39.

16. Ibid., 35–37.

17. Ibid., 57–61.

18. Ibid., 60.

19. Ibid., 20.

20. Kevin Vanhoozer draws on speech-act theory for a general hermeneutic, in *Is There a Meaning in This Text?* (Grand Rapids: Zondervan, 1998), where he refers to a "covenant of discourse" between author/speaker and reader/hearer. While sympathetic to this project, I am interested here in using "covenant" in its specifically biblical context.

21. Walther Eichrodt, trans. J. A. Baker, *Theology of the Old Testament* (Philadelphia: Westminster Press, 1951), 1:36.
22. Ibid., 37.
23. Ibid., 38, 42. Gerhard von Rad writes along similar lines, arguing that canonical saving history receives its time divisions through its covenant theology: "Focal points in the divine action now stand out in relief from parts of the history that are more epic in character, and as a result of the division perfectly definite relationships between the various epochs, of which the old summaries as yet gave no hint, are now clear. The most striking decisive moments of this kind are the making of covenants by Jahweh" (*Old Testament Theology*, trans. D. M. G. Stalker [San Francisco: Harper San Francisco, 1962], 1:129).
24. Eichrodt: "This type of popular religion, in which the divinity displays only the higher aspect of the national self-consciousness, the national 'genius,' or the mysterium in the forces of Nature peculiar to a particular country, was overcome principally by the concept of the covenant. Israel's religion is thus stamped as a 'religion of election,' using this phrase to mean that it is the divine election which makes it the exact opposite of the nature religions" (*Theology of OT*, 43).
25. Ibid., 46.
26. For the connections to the ancient Near Eastern "suzerainty treaty," see Meredith Kline, esp. *Treaty of the Great King* (Grand Rapids: Eerdmans, 1961).
27. Meredith Kline, *The Structure of Biblical Authority* (Grand Rapids: Eerdmans, 1975), 14. This volume explores the relationship of canon and covenant.
28. Cited by Kline, *Structure of Biblical Authority*, 29, from the treaty of Tudhaliyas IV with Ulmi-Teshub.
29. Von Rad, *Old Testament Theology*, 130.
30. Ibid.
31. Emmanuel Levinas, *Basic Philosophical Writings*, ed. Adriaan T. Peperzak et al. (Bloomington, Ind.: Indiana University Press, 1996), 106.
32. Philip Melanchthon, *Loci communes (1543)*, trans. J. A. O. Preus (St. Louis: Concordia Publishing House, 1992), 81.
33. Ibid., 82–83.
34. Theodore Beza, *The Christian Faith*, trans. James Clark (Lewes, England: Focus Publishing, 1992), 40. This is a fairly recent translation of Beza's *Confession de foi du Chrétien* (Geneva, 1558).
35. Ibid., 41.
36. Ronald Thiemann, *Revelation and Redemption* (Notre Dame, Ind.: University of Notre Dame Press, 1985), 95. Anyone who accepts a high Christology will surely appreciate Thiemann's logic. But while Jesus is God's speech in a univocal sense, scripture is divine speech in a more complicated, though not less true, manner.
37. As will become more apparent in the next chapter, I am indebted to Nicholas Wolterstorff, for both his Wilde Lectures at Oxford University and their published result, *Divine Discourse* (Cambridge: Cambridge University Press, 1995). The quote here is from page 225.
38. Ibid., 283.
39. Ibid. Wolterstorff embraces the notion of inspiration, but insists that it must not be taken to mean that "the phenomenon of X inspiring Y to say such-and-such is . . . the same as X saying such-and-such—nor, indeed, the same as Y saying such-and-such. Divine inspiration and divine discourse are distinct, albeit inter-related, phenomena."
40. Ibid., 284.
41. As I mention in the next chapter, Protestant dogmatics traditionally distinguished between revelation and inspiration on the basis of just such instances.

Given the sophistication with which they handled this topic, it is not surprising that such distinctions allowed them to interpret scripture for divine discourse without either rendering all of scripture divine "revelation" or regarding that which was obviously not intended to be divine discourse as extraneous to the process of inspiration.

42. Cited by Wolterstorff, 285.
43. Ibid., 288.
44. Ibid., 290.
45. Ibid., 291.
46. Ibid. They were witnesses: that is their identity. But were they also commissioned to speak on God's behalf, as his proxy? "Quite clearly Ireneaus regarded them as so commissioned; for he applies to them the words which Jesus, in Luke (10:16), is recorded as applying to the 'seventy' whom he sends out . . . And indeed . . . it's hard to see why the apostles would not have been so commissioned if 'the seventy' were" (293).
47. Ibid., 295.
48. Ibid.
49. Meredith Kline's *The Structure of Biblical Authority* remains the most succinct and illuminating study of this topic. See especially part 1, Canon and Covenant.
50. Brevard Childs, "Interpreting the Bible amid Cultural Change," *Theology Today*, 54/2 (July 1997): 210–11.
51. Ibid., 296. Wolterstorff is no doubt referring to the "Office of the Keys," as it is understood in classic Reformed and Lutheran confessions and dogmatics. Specifically with reference to the preached word, these traditions insist that it is in this way that the kingdom of heaven is opened and closed here and now, as well as there and then. This is the encounter that dialectical theology rightly emphasizes, but without the horizontal-historical side of the vector.
52. This is Wolterstorff's term throughout *Divine Discourse*.
53. Gabriel Fackre, *The Doctrine of Revelation: A Narrative Interpretation* (Grand Rapids: Eerdmans, 1997), 18.
54. Ibid.
55. Especially in reference to E. Fuchs, Thiselton's description is a terse summary and is cited here in Anthony Thiselton, *The Two Horizons: New Testament Hermeneutics and Philosophical Description* (Grand Rapids: Eerdmans, 1980), 345.
56. Gadamer, *Truth and Method*, 309. Agreement here should not imply acceptance of Gadamer's whole analysis of "fused horizons."
57. G. C. Berkouwer, *Studies in Dogmatics: General Revelation* (Grand Rapids: Eerdmans, 1955), 73.
58. Paul Ricoeur, *Figuring the Sacred: Religion, Narrative, and Imagination*, trans. David Pellauer and ed. Mark I. Wallace (Minneapolis: Fortress, 1995), 55.
59. Ibid., 56.
60. Ibid.
61. Ibid.
62. Ibid., 57.
63. Fackre, *Doctrine of Revelation*, 3.
64. Ernst Fuchs, *Studies of the Historical Jesus* (London: SCM, 1964), 30.
65. Gerhard Ebeling, *Theology and Proclamation: A Discussion with Rudolf Bultmann* (London: Collins, 1966), 38.
66. These sentiments are elaborations of similar arguments advanced by Geerhardus Vos, Herman Ridderbos, Meredith Kline, and others.
67. Richard Gaffin Jr., *Resurrection and Redemption* (Phillipsburg, N.J.: Presbyterian & Reformed Publishing Co., 1978), 22.
68. George Hunsinger, "What Can Evangelicals and Postliberals Learn from Each

Other?" in *The Nature of Confession*, ed. Timothy R. Phillips and Dennis L. Ockholm (Downers Grove, Ill.: InterVarsity Press, 1996), 150. Throughout the chapter, Hunsinger interacts favorably with Kuyper, Bavinck, and Richard Gaffin.

69. G. E. Wright, *God Who Acts: Biblical Theology as Recital* (London: SCM, 1952), 107.
70. Umberto Eco, *Six Walks in the Fictional Woods* (Cambridge: Harvard University Press, 1994), 32 ff.

Chapter Six

1. Paul Ricoeur, *History and Truth*, trans. Charles A. Kelbley (Evanston, Ill.: Northwestern University Press, 1965), 218.
2. Ludwig Wittgenstein, *The Wittgenstein Reader*, ed. Anthony Kenny (Oxford: Blackwell, 1994), 304.
3. Paul Ricoeur, *Figuring the Sacred: Religion, Narrative, and Imagination*, trans. David Pellauer and ed. Mark I. Wallace (Minneapolis: Fortress, 1995), 305.
4. Hans-Georg Gadamer, *Truth and Method*, 176; I am indebted to Professor Wolterstorff, the Virgil who escorted me through this profound work (Theological Hermeneutics, spring 1997, Yale University).
5. For a fascinating analysis of this factor, see Stephen Toulmin, *Cosmopolis: The Hidden Agenda of Modernity* (Chicago: University of Chicago Press, 1990).
6. Gadamer, *Truth and Method*, 182.
7. Mark C. Taylor, *Erring: A Postmodern A/Theology* (Chicago: University of Chicago Press, 1984).
8. Kevin Vanhoozer, *Is There a Meaning in This Text? The Bible, the Reader, and the Morality of Literary Knowledge* (Grand Rapids: Zondervan, 1998); Brian Ingraffia, *Postmodern Theory and Biblical Theology* (Cambridge: Cambridge University Press, 1995).
9. John Webster, "Hermeneutics in Modern Theology," *Scottish Journal of Theology* 51, no. 3 (1998): 315.
10. Kurt Mueller-Vollmer, ed., *The Hermeneutics Reader* (New York: Continuum, 1994), 4.
11. Ibid., 9.
12. For an intriguing discussion of mimesis in relation to Romanticism, see Hans-Georg Gadamer, "Poetry and Mimesis," in *The Relevance of the Beautiful and Other Essays*, ed. Robert Bernasconi (Cambridge: Cambridge University Press, 1986), 116 ff.
13. Schleiermacher writes, "Indeed, a person thinks by means of speaking. Thinking matures by means of internal speech, and to that extent speaking is only developed thought. But whenever the thinker finds it necessary to fix what he has thought, there arises the art of speaking, that is, the transformation of original internal speaking, and interpretation becomes necessary. Hermeneutics and rhetoric are intimately related in that every act of understanding is the reverse side of an act of speaking, and one must grasp the thinking that underlies a given statement. . . . [U]nderstanding a speech always involves two moments: to understand what is said in the context of the language with its possibilities, and to understand it as a fact in the thinking of the speaker" (Mueller-Vollmer, *Hermeneutics Reader*, 12).
14. Ibid., 83.
15. Ibid.
16. Ibid., 19. Wilhelm von Humboldt (1767–1835) moved away from Schleiermacher's individualism somewhat by underscoring the sociability of linguisticality. Mid-century historical hermeneutics divided sharply between Leopold von Ranke and Johann Gustav Droysen, the latter arguing that the historian's goal was not to reconstruct the past in an objective history, but to recognize the

current effects of the inaccessible events. For Droysen—and this will be influential for Bultmann—an utterance or inscription not only discloses the rational content of what is said, but is "an expression of something 'internal' which discloses to the historian—besides its obvious meaning—the attitude, intention, or state of mind of its originator." What are we to do with the inner life of another? Our intersubjectivity warrants this. In every human act, we mirror the inner life of others and historical events.

17. Gadamer, *Truth and Method*: "We think we understand when we see the past from a historical standpoint—i.e., transpose ourselves into the historical situation and try to reconstruct the historical horizon. In fact, however, we have given up the claim to find in the past any truth that is valid and intelligible for ourselves. Acknowledging the otherness of the other in this way, making him the object of objective knowledge, involves the fundamental suspension of his claim to truth" (304).

18. Mueller-Vollmer, *Hermeneutics Reader*, 36.

19. Ibid., on Bultmann: "There are, therefore, no historical facts or phenomena *per se* out of which knowledge could be fashioned. In formulations which echo those of Droysen in his *Historik*, Bultmann states emphatically that facts of the past turn into historic phenomena only 'when they become significant for a subject which itself stands in history and is involved in it'" (37).

20. This rather well-attested historical fact has never been faced in any direct way by Derrida or deconstruction in the criticism of Christianity as platonically oriented to thought (the best) or speech (one step removed from thought), but generally suspicious of writing. At the very least, Protestantism cannot be liable to that charge.

21. As Nicholas Wolterstorff has put it in discussions, "If Sally repeatedly asserts that she is a bison, I stop interpreting her discourse and begin to interpret Sally!"

22. Gadamer, *Truth and Method*, 183.

23. Ibid., 292.

24. Ibid. Given this statement, it is ironic that Gadamer could be engaged for purposes of criticizing Christian theology on the basis of his general hermeneutics.

25. Anthony Thiselton, in *New Horizons in Hermeneutics* (Grand Rapids: Zondervan, 1992), cites Bultmann: "Earlier attempts at demythologizing [include] . . . allegorical interpretation [which] . . . spiritualizes the mythical events so that they become symbols of processes going on in the soul" (162).

26. Francis Watson, *Text and Truth: Redefining Biblical Theology* (Grand Rapids: Eerdmans, 1997).

27. Calvin, *Institutes*, 1.8.10.

28. Cf. Christopher R. Seitz, "The Old Testament as Abiding Theological Witness," *Theology Today* 54, no. 2 (July 1997).

29. For instance, Thiselton replies, chiefly to Derrida, "The text is more than a 'docetic' or disembodied system of signifiers," and he, Colin Gunton, and Kevin Vanhoozer are among a growing chorus insisting on the relation of Christology to hermeneutics (cf. Vanhoozer, *Is There a Meaning in This Text?* 229).

30. Stanley Hauerwas, *Unleashing the Scripture: Freeing the Bible from Captivity to America* (Nashville: Abingdon, 1993), 20–21. Vanhoozer, *Is There a Meaning in This Text?* 278–79, provides a useful critique of Hauerwas on this point.

31. Chap. 1 is provocatively titled, "Taking the Bible Away from North American Christians." It would take an entire chapter just to analyze Hauerwas's arguments in this volume. For our purposes here, suffice it to say that its weakness in grasping the nuances of Reformation positions vis-à-vis modern individualism is matched only by its sentimental appeal to ecclesiastical authority.

32. Vanhoozer, *Is There a Meaning in this Text?* 314.
33. Since this is a project in theological prolegomena, we have neither the space nor the expertise to wade in the deep end of the hermeneutical pool. This chapter, for good or for ill, will have to assume at the beginning that certain key tenets of radical hermeneutics are irreconcilable with Christian theology. Cf. Francis Watson, *Text and Truth:* "In each case, a genuine and valuable hermeneutical insight is converted into a more questionable hermeneutical dogma. The insight that 'meaning' is more than the transference of a given content from the mind of the author to the mind of the reader is incorporated in a radical hermeneutic that proclaims the death of the author and the openness of texts to an unlimited plurality of readings. The insight that textual interpretation takes place within particular communal contexts is converted into the dogma that autonomous readers and reading-communities create their own meaning out of inert textual raw material. The insight that different approaches to interpretation can further the interpretative task, rather than hindering it, becomes the dogma that all interpretations can lay claim to equal 'legitimacy' and 'validity'. . . . In this black-and-white world, the new can only be successfully marketed if its relation to the old can be summed up in a few simple slogans" (96).
34. Webster, "Hermeneutics in Modern Theology," 309.
35. Ibid., 322.
36. Ibid., 329.
37. Ricoeur, *Figuring the Sacred,* 2.
38. "The Critique of Religion," in *The Philosophy of Paul Ricoeur: An Anthology of His Work,* ed. Charles E. Reagan and David Stewart (Boston: Beacon, 1978), 219.
39. Ricoeur, *Figuring the Sacred,* 7.
40. Paul Ricoeur, *Interpretive Theory: Discourse and the Interpretation of Meaning* (Ft. Worth: Texas Christian University, 1976), 95.
41. Paul Ricoeur, "The Narrative Function," in *Hermeneutics and the Human Sciences,* ed. and trans. John B. Thompson (Cambridge: Cambridge University Press, 1981), 274.
42. Wallace, intro. to Ricoeur, *Figuring the Sacred,* 11.
43. Ricoeur, *Figuring the Sacred,* 113.
44. Ibid., 37.
45. Ibid., 39.
46. Ibid., 45.
47. Ibid., 47.
48. Ibid.
49. Ibid.
50. Ibid., 71.
51. Ibid., 72.
52. Ibid., 238.
53. The published papers of Nicholas Wolterstorff's 1993 Wilde Lectures at Oxford University, *Divine Discourse* (Cambridge: Cambridge University Press, 1995).
54. Cited by Wolterstorff, *Divine Discourse,* 133.
55. Ibid., 191.
56. Ibid., 199.
57. Ibid., 205.
58. Ibid., 206.
59. Ibid., 207.
60. Ibid., 209.
61. Ibid., 210.

62. Ibid., 211.

63. For instance, when Nathan tells David a story of an unjust man, he is accusing David of doing this same thing. This is an example of what Wolterstorff calls *transitive discourse*. This is the sort of thing that happens when the same person produces a locutionary act (producing word-tokens) that generates an illocutionary act (promising, commanding, asking, accusing, asserting), which, in turn, generates another illocutionary act. In the case of the Song of Songs, then, "the *allegorizing* discourse belongs to the divine author, the *allegorized* discourse, to the human author. We don't take the human author to have been speaking of the love of God for the Church; and we don't take God to be speaking that sensuous love song which is the Song of Songs all by itself" (214).

64. Ibid., 215. The locus classicus for this sort of thing is 1 Timothy 2:12: "I permit no woman to teach or to have authority over a man; she is to keep silent." Is this what God was saying to the early church, or is God still saying this to us today? Rather than simply discarding this as if it were not divine speech, Wolterstorff suggests that we plumb the deeper intention of this discourse. Is God "issuing to all of us a deeper and more general point, whose application in that particular kind of situation yielded the injunction that women be silent, but whose application in our situation yields a rather different injunction"?

65. Ibid., 205.

66. John Searle, *Speech Acts: An Essay in the Philosophy of Language* (Cambridge: Cambridge University Press, 1969), 43.

67. Ibid.

68. Ibid., 45.

69. Wolterstorff, *Divine Discourse*, 239.

70. Once more, discourse analysis will assist us greatly in this task of distinguishing noematic and designative content. Strong views of inspiration do not require the affirmation that scripture is "without error," plain and simple, but that scripture is "without error in what it affirms." That is the designative content. While I think Wolterstorff's examples here are strained, there are probably others—for instance, when Jesus says that the mustard seed is "the smallest seed" (Mark 4:31, NIV). Is Jesus in error here? Since he is obviously referring to the range of experience available to his hearers, Jesus is most likely *designating* an analogy with their experience. Those who see biblical writers and speakers as intending by their speech to offer general geological or horticultural information will miss the designative content. While, strictly speaking, the mustard seed is not the smallest seed in existence, it is (for Jesus' hearers) "the smallest seed *you* [first-century Israelites] plant in the ground." Therefore it would seem unnecessary to call such examples errors in any sense, noematic or designative, since the designative is the discourse's intent.

71. Calvin, commentary on Genesis 1:6.

72. Wolterstorff, *Divine Discourse*, 195–99.

73. Watson, *Text and Truth*, 121.

74. Wolterstorff, *Divine Discourse*, 226.

75. In the same way Jesus' resurrection not only secures or proleptically anticipates the final resurrection, but is the beginning of that single eschatological event, in Pauline language, "the firstfruit" of the full harvest. Richard Gaffin Jr. elaborates this in *Resurrection and Redemption: A Study in Paul's Soteriology* (Phillipsburg, N.J.: Presbyterian & Reformed, 1978).

76. On this point see especially Meredith Kline's *Structure of Biblical Authority* (Grand Rapids: Eerdmans, 1975): "The New Testament, though not legislatively codifying these [Mosaic] life-norms, does presuppose them and didactically confirm them. But the Old Testament's community life-norms for Israel

are replaced in the New Testament by a new polity for the church." Taking a more nuanced interpretation of the notion of "canon," Kline concludes that although all scripture is faithful and embraced by Christians, not all of scripture is canonical, in the strict relationship that this concept has with "covenant" in Kline's work.

77. Despite structuralist tendencies, Frei (like Searle and Wolterstorff) affirms that, according to *sensus literalis* interpretation, authorial intentions (those intentions actually floating about on the surface of speech/writing) are accessible: "The intention may be that of the human author, in which case the construal of the text by the original audience has to be added. Or it may be the intention of the divine 'author' or 'inspirator' in the community's construal of the text as sacred or the coincidence of human and divine intention. If there is a theory of divine inspiration, the 'literal' sense may be extended to overlap with the figurative or typological sense that may be part of the literal sense for God, though not for the human author" (*Theology and Narrative: Selected Essays*, ed. George Hunsinger and William C. Placher [New York: Oxford University Press, 1993], 102). It is precisely that *implication* of divine inspiration that I want to indicate below.

78. Ibid., 103–4; cf. Augustine, *Later Works*, 198–99.

79. Ibid., 102.

80. For a more general theory of literal sense, see John Searle: "The notion of the literal meaning of a sentence only has application relative to a set of background assumptions, and furthermore these background assumptions are not all and could not all be realized in the semantic structure of the sentence in the way that presuppositions and indexically dependent elements of the sentence's truth conditions are realized in the semantic structure of the sentence" ("Literal Meaning," in *Expression and Meaning: Studies in the Theory of Speech Acts* [Cambridge University Press, 1979], 120).

81. See, for instance, Brevard Childs's provocative article, "Interpreting the Bible amid Cultural Change, *Theology Today* 54 (July 1997): 200–11.

82. Cf. Hans Frei's "Response to 'Narrative Theology: An Evangelical Appraisal," in *Theology and Narrative: A Critical Introduction* (Philadelphia: Trinity Press International, 1991), chap. 9.

83. Michael Goldberg, *Theology and Narrative*, 47.

84. Ibid., 56.

85. Ibid., 192.

86. It is perhaps worth noting, as a popular expression of this tendency in evangelical circles, that the movement's most famous evangelistic tract is called "The Four Spiritual Laws" and opens by comparing the spiritual laws governing the spiritual world to the physical laws governing phenomena.

87. I would concur with George Hunsinger's analysis of the cleavage between American fundamentalist/evangelical and orthodox Reformed hermeneutics. Following Richard Gaffin Jr.'s summary of the Amsterdam theology, rather than that of Jack Rogers and Donald McKim, Hunsinger concludes, "The likes of Kuyper and Bavinck therefore emerge as more fruitful dialogue partners, it seems to me, than the likes of Henry for any future discussion between evangelicals and postliberals. . . . [Kuyper] does [not] try to present Scripture's unity, as Henry does, as a 'logical system of shared beliefs' or as a comprehensive 'rational unity.' Instead Kuyper stresses that 'Christ is the whole of Scripture, and Scripture brings the esse of the Christ to our consciousness.' . . . By contrast, when Henry writes of scriptural unity, he does not (to my surprise) concentrate on a Christ-centered reading. Rather, he comes close to postulating a dichotomy between propositional content and personal encounter with Christ

(as though they somehow failed to form a unity)" ("What Can Evangelicals and Postliberals Learn from Each Other?" in *The Nature of Confession*, ed. Timothy R. Phillips and Dennis L. Ockholm (Downers Grove, Ill.: InterVarsity Press, 1996), 134–61.

88. Ricoeur, *Figuring the Sacred,* 220.
89. Ricoeur: "Following Gadamer, I call this 'the "thing" or issue of the text.' This issue of the text is the object of hermeneutics. It is neither behind the text as the presumed author nor in the text as its structure, but unfolded in front of it" (Ibid).
90. Ibid., 221.
91. Ibid.
92. Cf. Richard Gaffin Jr., *Resurrection and Redemption*: "From the perspective of the history of redemption believers today are in the same situation as was Paul. Together with him they look back upon the climactic events of Christ's death, resurrection, and ascension, while together with him they 'wait for his Son from heaven' (1 Thess. 1:10), the one event in that history which is still outstanding. . . . Thus the continuity between Paul and his interpreters is clear. Specifically, they are related in terms of a common redemptive-historical index" (23). This rests on the argument that "the Messiah's coming is one (eschatological) coming which unfolds in two episodes, one already and one still to come, that the 'age-to-come' is not only future but present," most definitively in the resurrection of Jesus as "the firstfruits of them that sleep" (91).
93. Ricoeur, *Figuring the Sacred,* 43.
94. David Tracy, *Blessed Rage for Order: The New Pluralism in Theology* (New York: Seabury Press, 1975): "To what aspects of reality, ordinary or perhaps extraordinary, do these texts refer the reader? These referents of the text do not refer to the meaning 'behind' the text (such as the author's real intention or the social-cultural situation of the text. Rather, . . . the referent of the text expresses the meaning 'in front of' the text. More exactly, we can determine both an object-referent of some existential import (viz., that way of perceiving reality, that mode of being-in-the-world which the text opens up for the intelligent reader) and a subject-referent (viz., the personal vision of the author implied by the text). In the latter case, one can establish the meanings present in the vision of the world of that 'implied author' (for example, the vision of the 'world' of Jesus as referred to by the parabolic texts" (78).
95. The hypothetical character of this reading event leaves response at bay, at least for the moment, giving priority to the text. Ricoeur's eagerness to avoid the subjectivism and psychologism of Romantic hermeneutics energizes his argument. It is the world that unfolds in front of the text, not the intentions or meaning of the author behind the text, that is of concern. On this point (viz., leaving response at bay), Ricoeur's appropriation of Heidegger is quite different from Bultmann's: "The theological implications here are considerable: the first task of hermeneutics is not to give rise to a decision on the part of the reader but to allow the world of being that is the 'issue' of the biblical text to unfold. Thus, above and beyond emotions, disposition, belief, or nonbelief, is the proposition of a world that in the biblical language is called a new world, a new covenant, the kingdom of God, a new birth. These are the realities unfolded before the text, which are certainly for us, but which begin from the text. This is what one might call the 'objectivity' of the new being projected by the text. A second implication is this: to put the 'issue' of the text before everything else is to cease to ask the question of the inspiration of the writings in the psychologizing terms of an insufflation of meaning to an author that projects itself into the text. If the Bible can be said to be revealed, this ought to be said of the 'issue' that it

speaks of—the new being that is displayed there. I would go so far as to say that the Bible is revealed to the extent that the new being unfolded there is itself revelatory with respect to the world, to all of reality, including my existence and my history. In other words, revelation, if the expression is meaningful, is a trait of the biblical *world*" (44).

96. Cf. Paul Ricoeur, "Toward a Hermeneutic of the Idea of Revelation," *Harvard Theological Review* 70 (1977): 26.

97. Wallace, introduction to *Figuring the Sacred*: "While Ricoeur consistently appropriates these insights into the truth-value of art and the dynamics of horizon-fusion, he enters a caveat against a certain romanticist bias against *explanation* in the German hermeneutical tradition from Friedrich Schleiermacher and Wilhelm Dilthey to Heidegger and Gadamer. This tradition has labored against the importation of reductionist methods from nonhumanistic disciplines for the understanding of literary texts and other works of art. While this prohibition has rightly preserved the truth-bearing integrity of creative works, it has wrongly insulated the interpretation of these works from a full and critical evaluation of their origins and interactions with structures of domination and oppression. Ricoeur has learned from Jürgen Habermas that a pure conversational model for textual understanding is not enough in the light of the systematic distortions that undermine open dialogue and understanding" (9–10).

98. For an excellent analysis of this point, see Miroslav Volf's "Theology, Meaning, and Power," *in The Future of Theology: Essays in Honor of Jürgen Moltmann*, ed. Miroslav Volf, Carmen Krieg, Thomas Kucharz (Grand Rapids: Eerdmans, 1996).

99. Tracy, *Blessed Rage for Order*, 100.

100. Ricoeur, *Figuring the Sacred*, 244. However, Ricoeur concludes that the biblical stories, however "history-like," do not constitute history: "It is not history because the purpose of history writing according to documentary evidence is also not part of the writer's intention" (ibid.). This is an astonishing claim, especially in the light of the quite explicit self-description in Luke 1:1–4 and Acts 1:1–3.

101. George Lindbeck, *The Nature of Christian Doctrine: Religion and Theology in a Postliberal Age* (Philadelphia: Westminster Press, 1984), 64–69. Although I find Lindbeck's cultural-linguistic model illuminating, especially in its analysis of religious conversion, William A. Christian (among others) has provided a satisfying defense of truth claims that *The Nature of Christian Doctrine* does not seem to treat adequately: "Truth Claims in Religion," *Journal of Religion* 42, no. 1 (Jan. 1962). Lindbeck is among many who appeal to Wittgenstein's "language game" analysis to argue for the incommensurabilty of religious systems. Space does not allow us to pursue this, but in a paper delivered at the American Academy of Religion in 1998, Keith Ward correctly noted that while the Wittgensteinian analysis would suggest that religions *have* language games, they are not themselves language games.

102. H. Richard Niebuhr, *The Meaning of Revelation* (New York: Macmillan, 1941), 44 ff., where he compares and contrasts Lincoln's "insider" version of American history and that of the Cambridge Encyclopedia: "The inspiration of Christianity has been derived from history, it is true, but not from history as seen by a spectator; the constant reference is to subjective events, that is to events in the lives of subjects. What distinguishes such historic recall from the private histories of mystics is that it refers to communal events, remembered by a community and in a community. Subjectivity here is not equivalent to isolation, nonverifiability, and ineffability; our history can be communicated and persons can refresh as well as criticize each other's memories of what has happened to

them in the common life; on the basis of a common past they can think together about the common future" (53).

103. I realize that this is an assumption, revealing my own bias for ultimate narrative or dramatic coherence (along with the reversals, complications, and other interesting but off-putting elements). I would suspect that even Derrida and Rorty would in their off-hours want to see a "meaningful" stage play after spending a lot of time in the "theater of cruelty."

104. For instance, in relation to the reports, especially in the Gospels, one would expect there to be no discrepancies in a text that was the product of collusion. The apostles and their circles meet at a conference for several days until they come up with identical accounts of the details and chronology of events, and the result is four Gospels (at least three) that basically reiterate each other. But instead, what we actually find in the Gospels is not a chronology, a simple reporting of the facts, but distinct theological treatises—or better yet, *sermons*—on the dramatic fulfillment of redemptive history in Jesus Christ. Even journalists will provide differing accounts of the same facts, depending largely on their angle, and Gospels scholarship has long labored over the different strategies and interests motivating each Gospel's production.

105. Johannes Quasten identifies Theodore's nonextant volume *De obscura locutione*, in addition to his extant five-volume *Adversus allegoricos*, his attack on Origen's allegorizing, *Patrology*, vol. 3 of the Golden Age of Greek Patristic Literature (Westminster, Md.: Christian Classics, 1990), 414.

106. *Recognitions of Clementine*, in *The Ante-Nicene Fathers*, eds. Alexander Roberts and James Donaldson (Edinburgh: T. & T. Clark/Grand Rapids: Eerdmans, reprinted 1989), 8:202–4.

107. Ibid, 203.

108. *Literal Postill on the Bible*; cited by Beryl Smalley, *The Study of the Bible in the Middle Ages* (Oxford: Basil Blackwell, 1952), 46–66. Mickey Mattox notes that this *Literal Postill*, a commentary on the whole Bible based on the literal sense, had a tremendous impact on Luther: "Indeed, Lyra's influence on Luther has been thought by some to be so pervasive that it was said, 'Had Lyra not lyred, Luther would not have danced' (*si Lyra non Lyrasset, Lutherus non saltasset*)" ("Recovering the Riches of Premodern Exegesis," *Modern Reformation* (July/Aug. 1999): 16–20.

109. Mattox, "Recovering the Riches of Premodern Exegesis," 20.

110. Calvin, *Institutes* 2.5.19.

111. Thomas Aquinas, *Summa Theologica*, trans. Fathers of the English Dominican Province (Westminster, Md.: Christian Classics, 1981), 1:1a.1.10.

112. Martin Luther, *Answer to the Hyperchristian, Hyperspiritual, and Hyperlearned Book by Goat Emser in Leipzig* (1521), Luther's Works (American Edition) (Philadelphia: Fortress Press, 1957), 39:176–79.

113. Ibid., 178.

114. Irenaeus, "Against Heresies," in *The Ante-Nicene Fathers*, ed. Alexander Roberts and James Donaldson (Edinburgh: T. & T. Clark/Grand Rapids: Eerdmans, reprinted 1989), 1:330.

115. Kevin Vanhoozer, *Is There a Meaning in This Text?* 120. Vanhoozer cites Ronald Hall: "The spirit of writing is essentially disembodied, essentially a break with the world," and concludes that it is an incarnational Christology that challenges modern/postmodern Gnosticism (121 ff.).

116. Hans Frei, *Eclipse of Biblical Narrative* (New Haven: Yale University Press, 1974), 25. Frei alludes to the connection between eucharistic and linguistic directions: "From what I have said about the verbal, narrative rendering of reality, and given Calvin's own stress on the importance of preaching and action

specifically connected with the words of institution, it is evident that for him the linguistic performance of celebrating the Lord's Supper not only fitly signifies but verbally embodies the spiritual reality it represents" (ibid.).

117. Calvin, *Institutes* 3.4.4.
118. Ibid., 4.16.15. The context of this discussion is the defense of infant baptism against a tendency to separate the two testaments of one covenant of grace.
119. Calvin, *Institutes*, 2.10.23.
120. For example, see Calvin's comments on Gen. 1:16; 3:8; 1 Cor. 2:7; Jer. 18:11.
121. Wolfhart Pannenberg, *Basic Questions in Theology*, trans. George H. Kehm (Philadelphia: Westminster Press, 1970), 1:197.
122. For instance, George Lindbeck charges that while evangelicals are to be applauded for reading the Bible, they are "often fundamentalistic and almost always precritical in their hermeneutics" ("Scripture, Exegesis, and Community," in *Biblical Interpretation in Crisis*, ed. Richard J. Neuhaus (Grand Rapids: Eerdmans, 1989, 101). Lindbeck, of course, has no problem with premodern, classical exegesis, and has a high regard for the traditioning community's example in reading the texts. Nevertheless, he cannot adopt a premodern, classical view of biblical inspiration, although an enormous classical consensus on the nature of that inspiration is clearly exemplified in tradition. Like Marx's remark that one had to pass through the "fiery brook" of Feuerbach, Lindbeck seems to think that any theology worth its muster must first pass through liberalism. Hardly an abandonment of liberalism, postliberalism is, as the term implies, a matter of moving beyond. It is not a matter of repudiation, but of progress.
123. Watson, *Text and Truth*, 105.
124. Ibid.
125. Thus, for instance, Stanley Hauerwas writes, "When this distinction [between text and interpretation] persists, sola scriptura becomes the seedbed of fundamentalism, as well as biblical criticism. It assumes that the text of the Scripture makes sense separate from a Church that gives it sense" (*Unleashing the Scripture: Freeing the Bible from Captivity to America* [Nashville: Abingdon Press, 1993], 27).
126. *The Book of Confessions* (Louisville, Ky.: General Assembly of the PCUSA, 1991), "The Westminster Confession" 2.7.
127. Francis Watson, *Text and Truth*, 123.
128. Wolfhart Pannenberg, *Systematic Theology*, trans. Geoffrey W. Bromiley (Grand Rapids: Eerdmans, 1991), 1:59ff.
129. Herman Ridderbos, *Redemptive History and the New Testament Scriptures*, trans. H. De Jongste (Phillipsburg, N.J.: Presbyterian & Reformed Publishing Co., 1963), 9.
130. Cited ibid.
131. Cited ibid.
132. Cf. Vern Poythress, "What Does God Say through Human Authors?" in Harvie M. Conn, ed., *Inerrancy and Hermeneutic: A Tradition, A Challenge, A Debate* (Grand Rapids: Baker, 1988), 81–99.
133. Cf. N. T. Wright, *The New Testament and the People of God* (Minneapolis: Fortress, 1992), esp. 280–388.
134. Francis Watson, *Text and Truth*, 73–74.
135. Despite the divisions and often heated polemics involved, the creeds and confessions of the various communions of Christendom actually testify to a remarkable unity. While serious and important differences are clearly stated, wide agreement is also evident across the landscape of ecclesiastical symbols. Couldn't this be anecdotal evidence of the Bible's basic clarity and unity and, therefore, its capability for being summarized, when so much agreement exists between otherwise divided camps?

Chapter Seven

1. Hans-Georg Gadamer, *Truth and Method,* 299.
2. Ibid., 297.
3. John Milbank, *Theology and Social Theory: Beyond Secular Reason* (Oxford: Blackwell, 1993), 105.
4. Ibid.
5. Francis Turretin, *Institutes of Elenctic Theology,* vol. 1 (first through tenth topics), trans. G. M. Giger, ed. J. T. Dennison Jr. (Phillipsburg, N.J.: Presbyterian and Reformed Publishing, 1992), 16.
6. See F. L. Battles, "God Was Accommodating Himself," *Interpretation* 31 (1977): 19–38.
7. Calvin, *Institutes,* 1.8.11; 1.13.21.
8. For criticism of the "translation" paradigm, see David H. Kelsey, *The Uses of Scripture in Recent Theology* (Philadelphia: Fortress, 1975); cf. Deut. 29:29.
9. Calvin, *Institutes,* 1.14.3.
10. Ibid., 1.17.12.
11. Ibid., 2.16.2.
12. Ibid., 1.6.3.
13. Kevin Vanhoozer, *Is There a Meaning in This Text?: The Bible, the Reader, and the Morality of Literary Knowledge* (Grand Rapids: Zondervan, 1998), 18.
14. I am borrowing this analogy from Luther's *Preface to the Old Testament* (1545), in Timothy Lull, ed., *Martin Luther's Basic Theological Writings* (Minneapolis: Augsburg Fortress, 1989), 119.
15. Richard Rorty, *Philosophy and the Mirror of Nature* (Princeton: Princeton University Press, 1979), 38–39.
16. Colin Gunton, *Enlightenment and Alienation* (Grand Rapids: Eerdmans, 1985), 34.
17. Ibid.
18. This is not to deny the formula, *finitum non capax infiniti,* or the so-called *extra-calvinisticum,* since it affirms that God was fully present in Jesus Christ—only that he was not *contained* by this hypostatic union, but continued to fill the heavens and the earth.
19. Interestingly, exegesis probably reveals a decided preference for the former type of statement over the latter.
20. Francis Turretin, *Institutes of Elenctic Theology,* 16.
21. Rom. 1:16–17: "For I am not ashamed of the gospel; it is the power of God for salvation to everyone who has faith, to the Jew first and also to the Greek. For in it the righteousness of God is revealed through faith for faith; as it is written, 'The one who is righteous will live by faith.'"
22. Pannenberg still wants to find a nonanalogical discourse and locates this in doxology. However, this language is (a) equivocal rather than univocal and (b) an ascription of something univocally true of God's inner being: "[I]n the act of adoration specific attributes are ascribed to God 'in himself,' but only in such a way that they are handed over to him and thereby undergo a change in their meaning which is no longer determinable by us." So such doxological speech does make assertions "about God himself, about his eternal essence," but argues that "the analogy exists only in the language, not between the language and God himself." Thus, such "analogy" is really "equivocation" (*Basic Questions in Theology,* trans. George H. Kehm [Philadelphia: Fortress, 1970], 1:216–17). Consistent with his proleptic eschatology, Pannenberg concludes that the correspondence of this equivocal speech to divine reality will be revealed at the

end: "Judged from our standpoint, the concepts by which we praise God's essence become equivocal in the act of the sacrifice of praise. At the same time, however, we utter them in the hope of a fulfillment which by far overcomes the distance fixed in the analogy" (238). But is this not an underrealized eschatology? Has not God already, by inspiring and authorizing scripture and raising Jesus from the dead, judged the appropriateness of our praise by how closely it conforms to the analogical discourse in scripture?

23. Calvin, *Institutes*, 1.13.5.
24. Carl F. H. Henry, *God, Revelation, and Authority* (Waco, Tex.: Word, 1979), 4:118. Henry does not do justice to the tradition on this point. This question was in fact at the heart of the debates, and Scotus and Aquinas among others knew that their formulation had to account for this objection. Cf. Allan B. Wolter, ed. and trans., *Duns Scotus: Philosophical Writings* (New York: Thomas Nelson & Sons, 1962); Allan B. Wolter, *The Philosophical Theology of John Duns Scotus*, ed. Marilyn McCord Adams (Ithaca, N.Y.: Cornell University Press, 1990), 98–122; Thomas Aquinas, *Summa Theologiae*, esp. part 1, questions 12 and 13.
25. Ibid. Cf. Gordon Clark, *A Christian View of Man and Things* (Grand Rapids: Eerdmans, 1952); *Three Types of Religious Philosophy* (Nutley, N.J.: Craig, 1973).
26. Henry, *God, Revelation, and Authority*, 119.
27. Ibid.
28. Ibid., 120.
29. Ibid., 121.
30. Quoted by Berkouwer in *Studies in Dogmatics: Holy Scripture* (Grand Rapids: Eerdmans, 1955), 74.
31. Cf. Kevin Vanhoozer's very insightful christological-hermeneutical parallel: *Is There a Meaning in This Text?*, 303–6.
32. Rudolf Bultmann, *Jesus Christ and Mythology* (New York: Charles Scribner's Sons, 1958), 20.
33. M. G. Kline observes, "So, for example, in the Canaanite epic of Baal and in the Babylonian Ennuma Elish, Marduk being the hero-god in the latter, the theme of divine house-building follows that of victory over draconic chaos. This mythical literary tradition quite clearly lies behind the mode of representation of Israel's redemptive history as recorded in the Book of Exodus. . . . Then, after his victory over the dragon, Yahweh proceeds to build a house for himself" (*Structure of Biblical Authority* [Grand Rapids: Eerdmans, 1975], 79). The difference in the case of Israel's narrative is that the only God who is God actually did do these things, mocking the gods that are no gods.
34. I. M. Crombie, "The Possibility of Theological Statements," in *Religious Language and the Problem of Religious Knowledge*, ed. Ronald E. Santoni (Bloomington, Ind.: Indiana University Press, 1968), 101.
35. Ibid., 103.
36. John Calvin, *Institutes*, 1.5.8.
37. Ibid., 1.6.14.
38. Paul Ricoeur, *The Symbolism of Evil* (Boston: Beacon Press, 1969), 101.
39. Gadamer, *Truth and Method*, 189.
40. Ibid., 191.
41. Ibid., 192.
42. Richard Rorty, *Objectivity, Relativism, and Truth: Philosophical Papers* (Cambridge: Cambridge University Press, 1991), 1:81.
43. H. A. Hodges, *The Philosophy of Wilhelm Dilthey* (London: Routledge & Kegan Paul, 1952), 120.

44. bell hooks, an African American herself, makes a good case for questioning postmodern commitments to "otherness," in "Postmodern Blackness," in *The Truth About the Truth: De-confusing and Re-constructing the Postmodern World*, ed. Walter Truett Anderson (New York: G. P. Putnam's Sons, 1995), 117 ff. For instance, "Postmodernist discourses are often exclusionary even as they call attention to, appropriate even, the experience of 'difference' and 'Otherness' to provide oppositional political meaning, legitimacy, and immediacy when they are accused of lacking concrete relevance. Very few African-American intellectuals have talked or written about postmodernism" (117).

45. Gabriel Vahanian offers a striking observation: "Imperialism feeds on space, on the distance between us and them. It breaks down as soon as language obliterates the distance. Language obliterates what separates us from one another, what separates me from the other, from that alone in relation to which not only I am but I am faced with the question . . . to be where not to be. . . . That is, through communication, through communion with others, rather than through their annexation and oppression by means of that abuse of power that consists in abusing language, albeit by sacralizing it" ("Ontotheology and the Future of Theology," in *Religion, Ontotheology, and Deconstruction*, ed. Henry Ruf [New York: Paragon, 1989], 162–63).

46. David Tracy, *The Analogical Imagination* (New York: Crossroad, 1987), 113.

47. Ibid. To be sure, Tracy would not want to be identified with our proposal, and his notion of analogy is not ours.

48. Among the numerous examples of the lawsuit form are Isaiah 59 and Hosea 4.

49. Serene Jones, *Calvin and the Rhetoric of Piety* (Louisville, Ky.: Westminster John Knox Press, 1995), 133.

50. Austin Farrer, "Inspiration: Poetical and Divine," in *Interpretation and Belief*, ed. Charles Conti (London: SPCK, 1976), 56.

51. Austin Farrer, "Prologue: On Credulity," in *Interpretation and Belief*, ed. Charles Conti (SPCK, 1976), 5.

52. Barbara Brown Taylor, "Face to Face with God," *Christian Century*, February 28, 1996.

53. Gadamer, *Truth and Method*, 47: "Faith is the attitude of one who accepts being interpreted at the same time that he or she interprets the world of the text. Such is the hermeneutical constitution of the biblical faith. In thus recognizing the hermeneutical constitution of the biblical faith, we are resisting all psychologizing reductions of faith. This is not to say that faith is not authentically an *act* that cannot be reduced to linguistic treatment. In this sense, faith is the limit of all hermeneutics and the nonhermeneutical origin of all interpretation. The ceaseless movement of interpretation begins and ends in the risk of a response that is neither engendered nor exhausted by commentary. It is in taking account of this prelinguistic or hyperlinguistic characteristic that faith could be called 'ultimate concern,' which speaks of the laying hold of the necessary and unique thing from whose basis I orient myself in all my choices. . . . Or it could be called 'unconditional trust.'"

54. Although his analysis is too eager to read Luther through the eyes of existential theologians, Gerald L. Bruns does pick up on a legitimate aspect of the Reformation's hermeneutic and its contrast with much of modern Protestantism, conservative and liberal: "Here the text is not so much an object of understanding as a component of it; what one understands when one understands the Scriptural texts is not anything conceptual and extractable as a meaning." But apart from some identifiable content (*die Sache*), how can there be any contact between speaker/text and hearer/reader? Bruns continues: "Rather, what one understands (that is, enters into) is the mode of being or life of faith

informed by the text in much the way a plot informs a work as its soul or shaping spirit. This emphasis on experience as against formal exegesis or the construction of meaning helps us to get clear about what it might be for a text to be self-interpreting in the sense that Luther understands this term" ("*Scriptura sui ipsius interpres*: Luther, Modernity, and the Foundations of Philosophical Hermeneutics," in *Hermeneutics Ancient and Modern* [New Haven, Conn.: Yale University Press, 1992], 146).

55. Ibid. Again, I think that Bruns overinterprets Luther in the direction of encounter, but its general contours are not without support from the primary sources.

56. Calvin, *Institutes*, 3.15.4; cf. 2.11.22.

57. Calvin writes, "Therefore, since we are barred from law righteousness, we must betake ourselves to another help, that is, to faith in Christ. For this reason, as the Lord in this passage ["the rich young ruler"] recalls to the law a teacher of the law whom he knew to be puffed up with empty confidence in works, in order that he may learn he is a sinner, subject to the dreadful judgment of eternal death, so elsewhere he comforts with the promise of grace without any mention of the law others who have already been humbled by this sort of knowledge: 'Come to me all who labor and are heavy-laden, and I will refresh you . . . and you will find rest for your souls' (3.19.9)."

58. I would maintain that instead of the two horizons being fused, the eschatological/redemptive-historical horizon mediated through scripture (especially through preaching) actively converts, transforms, reconfigures one's horizon.

59. David Tracy, *The Analogical Imagination*, 433.

60. Ibid.

61. Cf. Gadamer, *Truth and Method*, 181.

62. Miroslav Volf, "Theology, Meaning, and Power," *in The Future of Theology: Essays in Honor of Jürgen Moltmann* (Grand Rapids: Eerdmans, 1996). Agreeing with Foucault's point that one is never outside of power, Volf writes, "The answer, I suggest, is neither 'worldly power' nor 'no power,' but 'the power of the crucified Christ.' . . . Notice that the crucified Christ is not a messiah without power; he is a messiah with a new kind of power—the power of 'the weak,' which puts to shame 'the strong,' the power of 'the things that are not' which 'nullify the things that are.' Theology as reflection on the word of the cross must be embodied in the community of the cross whose particular kind of weakness *is a new kind of power inserted into the network of the powers of the world*" (emphasis added) (61).

63. Mark C. Taylor, *Erring: A Postmodern A/Theology* (Chicago: University of Chicago Press, 1984).

64. Friedrich Nietzsche, *The Will to Power*, trans. Walter Kaufmann and R. J. Hollingdale (New York: Random House, 1967), 71.

65. Calvin, *Institutes*, 1.6.1.

66. Ibid., 1.6.2.

67. Calvin writes, "In this ruin of mankind no one now experiences God either as Father or as Author of salvation, or favorable in any way, until Christ the Mediator comes forward to reconcile him to us" (1.2.1).

68. Calvin, *Institutes*, 1.7.4.

69. Ibid.

70. Ibid. In its place "value" and "fact" have been inserted in modern thought, including theology, so that, for instance, they correspond to *Geschichte* (the sense in which Christianity is true) and *Historie* (the sense in which it is not).

71. Ludwig Wittgenstein, "Ethics, Life and Faith," in *The Wittgenstein Reader*, ed. Anthony Kenny (Oxford: Blackwell, 1994), 300.

72. *Institutes*, 1.7.4.
73. Ibid., 1.8.1–2.
74. John Webster, "Hermeneutics in Modern Theology," *Scottish Journal of Theology* 51, no. 3 (1998): 317.
75. George Lindbeck, *The Nature of Doctrine: Religion and Theology in a Postliberal Age* (Philadelphia: Westminster Press, 1984), 64.
76. J. L. Austin, *How to Do Things with Words*, 2d ed., ed. J. O. Urmson and Marina Sbisa (Cambridge: Harvard University Press, 1975), 15.
77. Ibid., 16.
78. Gottlob Frege, *The Basic Laws of Arithmetic: Exposition of the System*, trans. and ed. Montgomery Furth (Berkeley, Calif.: University of California Press, 1964). A pioneer in the analytic tradition, Frege was critical of idealism, the interlocutor for this work.
79. Martin Luther, "The Freedom of a Christian," in *Reformation Writings of Martin Luther*, translated from Weimar Edition by Bertram Lee Woolf (London: Lutterworth Press, 1952), 1:356ff.
80. Ibid., 379.
81. Iris Murdoch, *The Sovereignty of Good* (London: Routledge & Kegan Paul, 1970), 95. It is interesting that Murdoch herself does not believe in God.
82. John Calvin, "Calvin's Reply to Sadoleto," in *A Reformation Debate*, ed. John C. Olin (Grand Rapids: Baker, 1996), 59.
83. Kevin Vanhoozer, *Is There a Meaning in This Text?* 402.
84. But a Christian realist does believe that reality is constructed, not self-interpreting. This larger reality is the construction of the same one who has addressed the world in history. But because this reality is constructed already by God, and is given to creatures, it should be regarded as neither a given (naive realism) nor as a creation of the self (constructivism as hyperidealism). Thus this reality is accessible ultimately only by means of the "spectacles" that scripture provides, to borrow Calvin's well-known metaphor (*Institutes* 1.6.1).
85. Friedrich Nietzsche, *The Will to Power*, 34.
86. Auguste Lecerf is correct when he argues that, while the Scotist and nominalist doctrine of divine omnipotence can lead only to skepticism and capriciousness, Calvin's notion stands in marked contrast: "Calvinism, on the contrary, maintains that God is so powerful that the more really He acts, the more reality the creature has in his being, his action, and his liberty: *Providentia Dei causas secundas non tollit sed ponit*" (*An Introduction to Reformed Dogmatics* [London: Lutterworth Press, 1949], 114); the Latin citation is from Wollebius.
87. Martin Heidegger, *Being and Time* (Oxford: Basil Blackwell, 1962), 31.
88. For instance, he writes, "The face enters into our world from an absolutely foreign sphere, that is, precisely from an ab-solute, which in fact is the very name for ultimate strangeness" (*Emmanuel Levinas: Basic Philosophical Writings*, ed. A. T. Peperzak et al. [Bloomington, Ind.: Indiana University Press, 1996], 53). Although I have some reservations concerning Ricoeur's analysis of selfhood, he has probed the self-and-other problem in a richer way than Levinas. "In a philosophy of selfhood like my own," says Ricoeur, "one must be able to say that ownership is not what matters. What is suggested by the limiting cases produced by the narrative imagination is a dialectic of ownership and of dispossession, of care and carefreeness, of self-affirmation and of self-effacement. Thus the imagined nothingness of the self becomes the existential 'crisis' of the self" (*Oneself as Another*, trans. Kathleen Blamey [Chicago: University of Chicago Press, 1992], 168). It is precisely this dialectic that I want to affirm in my own account. In fact, it is particularly evident in scripture and theology as the com-

mand-promise (law-gospel) dialectic. We also affirm the shift from the ontology of selfhood to existential crisis.

89. See for instance Pannenberg, *Systematic Theology*, 1:242 ff.

90. Walter Brueggemann, *The Bible and the Postmodern Imagination: Texts under Negotiation* (London: SCM, 1993), 54.

91. Cf. Anders Nygren, *Agape and Eros*, trans. Philip S. Watson (London: SPCK, 1982). I know that there is considerable debate over Nygren's interpretation, particularly his surrender of *eros* to the "dark side." My reference here is purely illustrative and should not be taken as a serious stand on this debate.

92. Brueggemann, *The Bible and Postmodern Imagination*, 55.

93. Francis Watson, *Text and Truth: Redefining Biblical Theology* (Grand Rapids: Eerdmans, 1997), 104.

94. Ricoeur says, "To read a narrative is to redo with the text a certain 'line' or 'course' (*parcours*) of meaning. . . .This is, as I said, a semiotic approach completely distinct from the historical-critical method. It takes the text in its last state, just as it has been read by generations of believing and non-believing readers, and it attempts to reconstruct the codes that govern the transformations at work in the narrative" (*Figuring the Sacred*, 151).

95. Ibid., 161.

96. Ibid., 162.

97. Ibid., note.

98. Ibid., 176.

99. As Meredith Kline observes in *The Structure of Biblical Authority* (Grand Rapids: Eerdmans, 1975), examples of this can be found in Deut. 4:2; 27:2 ff; Josh. 8:30. The sanction is renewed in the new covenant (Rev. 22:18–19).

100. Ronald Thiemann, *Revelation and Theology: The Gospel as Narrated Promise* (South Bend, Ind.: University of Notre Dame Press, 1985), reminds us of the inevitably soteriological character of hermeneutics and, more specifically, the notion of revelation, by underscoring divine prevenience as the sine qua non of any genuinely Christian view.

101. Cf. Gerhard von Rad, *Old Testament Theology*, trans. D. M. G. Stalker (San Francisco: Harper San Francisco, 1962), 2:235.

102. For instance, despite one's objections to traditional Roman Catholic formulations, it is important to note that this body's official position is not that the magisterial church created the canon, but that, once closed, the church provides the certainty that this was in fact *the canon* of scripture. Cf. "Canon of Scripture," in *Sacramentum Mundi: An Encyclopedia of Theology* (New York: Herder & Herder, 1968), 1:252–54.

103. M. G. Kline, *Structure of Biblical Authority*, 88–89.

104. Ibid., 90.

105. Calvin, *Institutes*, 1.19.1.

106. With Romans 10:17 as its source, the Heidelberg Catechism declares that "The Holy Spirit works faith in our hearts by the preaching of the Holy Gospel, and confirms it by the use of the holy sacraments" (Q. 65).

107. Cited by G. C. Berkouwer, *Studies in Dogmatics: Holy Scripture*, trans. Jack Rogers (Grand Rapids: Eerdmans, 1975), 44.

108. Ibid.

109. Ibid., 45.

110. "When the Advocate comes, whom I will send to you from the Father, the Spirit of truth who comes from the Father, he will testify on my behalf" (John 15:26). "And when he [the Spirit] comes, he will prove the world wrong about sin and righteousness and judgment. . . . When the Spirit of truth comes, he will guide

you into all the truth; for he will not speak on his own, but will speak whatever he hears, and he will declare to you the things that are to come. He will glorify me, because he will take what is mine and declare it to you" (John 16:8, 13–14). "And the Spirit is the one that testifies, for the Spirit is the truth. There are three that testify: the Spirit and the water and the blood, and these agree. . . . Those who believe in the Son of God have the testimony in their hearts. . . . And this is the testimony: God gave us eternal life, and this life is in his Son" (1 John 5:6–11). "[T]hese things God has revealed to us through the Spirit; for the Spirit searches everything, even the depths of God. . . . Now we have received not the spirit of the world, but the Spirit that is from God, so that we may understand the gifts bestowed on us by God. . . . 'For who has known the mind of the Lord so as to instruct him?' But we have the mind of Christ" (1 Cor. 2:10, 12, 16). "When we cry, 'Abba! Father!' it is that very Spirit bearing witness with our spirit that we are children of God" (Rom. 8:15–16).

111. Berkouwer, *Studies in Dogmatics*, 49.
112. Calvin, *Institutes*, 3.2.6.
113. Harold Bloom, *The American Religion: The Emergence of the Post-Christian Nation* (New York: Simon & Schuster, 1992). Throughout this work Bloom approvingly observes the ways in which American religion across the landscape, from fundamentalist to secularist, exhibits "gnostic" habits.
114. See, for instance, Irenaeus, "Against Heresies," in *Ante-Nicene Fathers* (Edinburgh: T. & T. Clark/Grand Rapids: Eerdmans, reprinted 1989), 1:441.
115. Calvin, *Institutes*, 1.9.1.
116. It seems obvious from the passage that it is not the heart or the Spirit that is being substituted for the word and the letter, since the promise is that in the new age the Spirit will engrave the word on the hearts of the people.
117. Calvin, *Institutes*, 1.9.3.
118. For instance, the Second Helvetic Confession interprets "letter" not as the written scriptures in general, but as "the doctrine of the law which, without the Spirit and faith, works wrath and provokes sin in the minds of those who do not have a living faith. For this reason, the apostle calls it 'the ministry of death'" (chap. 13). And it goes on to add that this is diametrically opposed to the spirit-matter dichotomy of the sects. Later, it warns against opposing "the Spirit" to the church's ordinary ministers, "inasmuch as God effects the salvation of men through them," not in their person but in the exercise of their ministry. "Hence we warn men to beware lest we attribute what has to do with our conversion and instruction to the secret power of the Holy Spirit in such a way that we make void the ecclesiastical ministry" (chap. 18).
119. See chap. 1 in this work, where this point is made at greater length.
120. Gabriel Fackre, *The Doctrine of Revelation: A Narrative Interpretation* (Edinburgh: Edinburgh University Press, 1997), 206.
121. George Barna, *Marketing the Church* (Ventura, Calif.: Regal, 1992), 41, 145. As a *Newsweek* article describes evangelical as well as other churches, "They have developed a 'pick and choose' Christianity in which individuals take what they want . . . and pass over what does not fit their spiritual goals. What many have left behind is a pervasive sense of sin" (September 17, 1984), 26. William Willimon has pointed out the ironies of evangelical secularity in his article "Been There, Preached That," *Leadership* (fall 1995): 75–78.
122. Wolfhart Pannenberg, "Theological Table Talk," *Theology Today* 54, no. 2 (1997): 213. He adds, "In 2 Cor. 3:6–8, Paul opposed the apostolic proclamation in terms of the ministry of the spirit to the ministry of the letter of the law in the old covenant. The authority of the gospel, and therefore that of the apostolic writings and even that of the Old Testament writings in their Christian

usage, is not one of the 'letter,' corresponding to the letter of the law, but is to be understood in terms of the content of the gospel. That does not exclude that the gospel itself has to be taken literally in its affirmations and that the apostolic writings need literal interpretation. It is only by literal interpretation that the gospel they contain can be discerned."

123. An interview with Edgar V. McKnight, *Modern Reformation* 8, no. 4 (July/August 1999): 39.

124. Kevin Vanhoozer, *Is There a Meaning in This Text?* 410. He criticizes Donald Bloesch in this connection. Related also are the conclusions of Stephen Fowl and his influence in the work of Richard Hays. Vanhoozer comments, "Hays agrees and adds that Paul too opts for the 'hermeneutical priority of the Spirit-experience' as over against the text of Scripture" (ibid.).

125. Ibid., 411.

126. Ibid.

127. And this question concerns not only the major traditions or even denominations of Christianity, but the many schools within each communion.

128. Calvin, commentary on 2 Cor. 3:6.

129. Willem Balke, *Calvin and the Anabaptist Radicals*, trans. William J. Heynen (Grand Rapids: Eerdmans, 1981), 326–27.

130. Robert Louis Wilken, review of Andre LaCocque and Paul Ricoeur, *Thinking Biblically: Exegetical and Hermeneutical Studies*, trans. David Pellauer, in *First Things*, May 1999, 68.

131. Calvin, *Institutes*, 1.5.9.

132. It is "obviously absurd to assert that Scripture can be self-interpreting," says Hauerwas, and yet, "You do not have or need 'a meaning' of the text when you understand that Church is more determinative than text," *Unleashing the Scripture: Freeing the Bible from Captivity to America* (Nashville: Abingdon Press, 1993), 23.

133. Ibid., 27. The irony is that Hauerwas differs from his fundamentalist nemesis on this important point only in sophistication. Where the fundamentalist blurs the lines between text and interpretation implicitly by often concluding that a refusal to accept every interpretation is tantamount to rejecting biblical authority, more ecclesiastically "communitarian" groups draw on cultural-linguistic, sociology of knowledge, and poststructuralist theory to make the point explicitly. In both cases, however, the church can easily cease to function as a summoned community and instead confuse itself with the speaker and the content of revelation. Cf. Karl Rahner, *Foundations of the Christian Faith* (New York: Crossroad, 1978), 370–80. Even the postliberal narrative school's renewed focus on the *sensus literalis* seems to be somewhat undermined when an obvious point (viz., the ecclesial context of the Christian language game) is turned into an all-absorbing metaphor. For instance, Kathryn Tanner defines the *sensus literalis* as "what a participant in the community automatically or naturally takes a text to be saying on its face insofar as he or she has been socialized in a community's conventions for reading the text of Scripture" ("Theology and the Plain Sense," in *Scriptural Authority and Narrative Interpretation*, ed. Garrett Green [Philadelphia: Fortress Press, 1987], 63). I am all for appreciating our socio-historical rootedness in interpretive communities, but does this definition not reduce interpretation to the activity of the reader? The classical notion of the plain sense had far more to do with the meaning in the text, without denying the uses put to it by the church.

134. Quoted in Kevin Vanhoozer, *Is There a Meaning in This Text?* 411.

135. Johann Adam Mohler practically places text and church in isomorphic identity: "The Church is . . . his eternal revelation" (*Symbolism: Exposition of the*

Doctrinal Differences between Catholics and Protestants [New York: Dunigan, 1844], 350).

136. I have in mind not only traditional images of the magisterium, but of the new magisterium, which we call "the academy." Christian theologians are not a magisterium or a caste of cognoscenti with no obligation but to their own career in the academy. They are fellow parishioners who must, like all believers, come to their theological task as assembled hearers of the word of God.

137. For instance, in a full and concise passage G. C. Berkouwer writes, "It is clear that here we find ourselves on a level completely distinct from that of a formalistic conception of the canon. For here we do not approach the canon in its structure out of merely formal criteria, but rather out of its basis, its foundation in the history of salvation. *In the canon the church, in faith, found its redemptive-historical foundations.* This can only be understood when we pay attention to the kerygma, martyria, or didache, that is, the content of the New Testament witness. Confronted by this testimony as the apostolic witness regarding God's one complete act of salvation, the church did not create the canon, but, indubitably assured regarding the content of this witness, subjected herself to it" (emphasis added), 84.

138. Calvin, *Institutes*, 1.7.1.

Chapter Eight

1. Francis Watson, *Text and Truth: Redefining Biblical Theology* (Grand Rapids: Eerdmans; Edinburgh: T. & T. Clark, 1997), 4.

2. G. E. Wright, *God Who Acts: Biblical Theology as Recital* (London: SCM Press, 1952), 110.

3. Ibid., 111.

4. Ibid.

5. Carl Braaten, "The Resurrection Debate Revisited," *Pro Ecclesia* 8, no. 2 (1999): 147–58.

6. Cf. Heb. 11:1: "Now faith is the assurance of things hoped for, the conviction of things not seen. Indeed, by faith our ancestors received approval."

7. Jürgen Moltmann, "The Resurrection of Christ: Hope for the World," in *Resurrection Reconsidered*, ed. Gavin D'Costa (Oxford: One World, 1997), 76–77.

8. Cf. Heb. 1:3: "[The Son] is the reflection of God's glory and the exact imprint of God's very being, and he sustains all things by his powerful word."

9. Cf. especially Rom. 8:18–25; 1 Cor. 15:20–28; 2 Cor. 5:1–5.

10. See also 2 Pet. 1:20–21: "First of all you must understand this, that no prophecy of scripture is a matter of one's own interpretation, because no prophecy ever came by human will, but men and women moved by the Holy Spirit." Note that it is the origin of the speech that is not "a matter of one's own interpretation." Perhaps this is some indication of that elusive and often speculative topic "inspiration" (a term that frequently causes more confusion than clarity). The Synoptic Gospels, for instance, report, but they do not just report—they interpret. They are the writings of evangelists, after all, with an agenda in mind (as is always the case in all discourse). Both testaments can be best described as divine utterance and divinely inspired interpretation (designative content) of God's attributes, works, and words.

11. Wolfhart Pannenberg, *Basic Questions in Theology* (Philadelphia: Westminster Press, 1970), 1:24.

12. Walther von Loewenich, *Luther's Theology of the Cross* (Minneapolis: Augsburg Publishing House, 1976), 69.

13. Ibid., 70.

14. Hans Frei writes, "The Christian community is gathered in hope, and that extends to as ordinary a task as that of a common way of reading its sacred text. One may take the Church through time and space to be, among other things, not a babble of voices talking completely past one another, but a groping and imperfect community of interpretation possessing a common language sufficient for people by and large who do biblical interpretation seriously, whether as technicians or simply as adherents looking for help in life and belief" (*Eclipse of Biblical Narrative* [New Haven: Yale University Press, 1974], 56).
15. Ibid., 59.
16. Ibid., 90–91.
17. George Lindbeck, *The Nature of Doctrine: Religion and Theology in a Postliberal Age* (Philadelphia: Westminster Press, 1984), 122.
18. C. Stephen Evans, *The Historical Christ and the Jesus of Faith: The Incarnational Narrative as History* (Oxford: Clarendon Press, 1996), 183.
19. Richard Gaffin Jr., *Resurrection and Redemption: A Study in Paul's Soteriology* (Phillipsburg, N.J.: Presbyterian & Reformed Publishing Co., 1978), 121.
20. H. Richard Niebuhr, *Resurrection and Historical Reason* (New York: Macmillan, 1957), 27.
21. Cornelius Van Til, *The Great Debate Today* (Nutley, N.J.: Presbyterian & Reformed Publishing Co., 1971), 40–41.
22. Ibid.
23. Oscar Cullmann, *Salvation in History* (London: SCM Press, 1965), 22.
24. Geerhardus Vos, *Biblical Theology: Old and New Testaments* (Grand Rapids: Eerdmans, 1959), 80.
25. See Calvin's criticism of Augustine on this point: "Augustine according to his custom showing himself to be far too much of a Platonist, is enraptured with I know not what ideas, namely, that God before he made the world had the form of the entire work projected in his mind and that in this manner things lived in Christ which as yet had no existence" (Commentary on John 1:3).
26. Cf. Heb. 6:16–20; Gal. 3:15–25.
27. Gaffin, *Resurrection and Redemption*, 35.
28. Ibid., 38.
29. Herman Ridderbos, *Paul: An Outline of His Theology*, trans. John R. W. De Witt (Grand Rapids: Eerdmans, 1975), 56.
30. Julius Schniewind, in *Kerygma and Myth: A Theological Debate*, ed. Hans Werner Bartsch, trans. R. H. Fuller (London: SPCK, 1953), 56.
31. Geerhardus Vos, *Redemptive History and Biblical Interpretation: The Shorter Writings of Geerhardus Vos*, ed. Richard Gaffin Jr. (Phillipsburg, N.J.: Presbyterian & Reformed Publishing Co., 1980), 5.
32. Ibid., 6.
33. Ibid., 6–7.
34. Gaffin, *Resurrection and Redemption*, 22.
35. Richard Lints, *The Fabric of Theology: Toward an Evangelical Prolegomenon* (Grand Rapids: Eerdmans, 1993), 264.
36. Ibid. As mentioned early in this volume, I owe a profound debt to Richard Lints's *The Fabric of Theology* for trailblazing many of these areas.
37. Abraham Joshua Heschel, *God in Search of Man* (New York: Farrar, Straus and Giroux, 1955), 7.
38. David Cairns, *Scottish Journal of Theology*, 21, no. 2 (June 1968): 223.
39. From the *Glaubenslehre*, 12.3, cited by Francis Watson, *Text and Truth: Redefining Biblical Theology* (Grand Rapids: Eerdmans, 1997), 139.
40. James Barr, "The Old Testament and the New Crisis of Biblical Authority," *Interpretation*, 25, no. 1 (Jan. 1971). The arrogance of modernity, evidenced

here in a typical liberal claim, is far more aggressive and expansive than anything in the period of confessional orthodoxy.

41. Watson, *Text and Truth*, 141.
42. Ibid., 143.
43. Cited, ibid.
44. Cited, ibid., 160.
45. Rudolf Bultmann, "The Significance of the Old Testament for the Christian
    Faith," ed. B. W. Anderson, in *The Old Testament and Christian Faith* (New
    York: Harper & Row, 1963), 31.
46. Ibid., 29, n.6.
47. While few evangelical scholars identify themselves as dispensationalists without
    qualification, dispensationalism's penchant for identifying law and gospel with
    Old and New Testaments, respectively, continues to have significant hermeneu-
    tical consequences for most evangelicals. Furthermore, as Moltmann and oth-
    ers have complained, such an approach shifts the focus of revelation from the
    redemptive-historical field, centering on Christ and his cross and resurrection,
    to the correlation of prophetic texts to current and future events in the world
    generally. More recent developments in certain dispensationalist quarters have
    indicated a willingness to rethink at least the sharpness of these contrasts.
48. See for example Robert L. Saucy, *The Case for Progressive Dispensationalism*
    (Grand Rapids: Zondervan, 1993).
49. Christopher R. Seitz, "The Old Testament as Abiding Theological Witness,"
    Theology Today, 54, no. 2 (July 1997): 216–23.
50. Ibid.
51. Hans-Georg Gadamer, *Truth and Method*, 131.
52. Geerhardus Vos, *Biblical Theology*, 7.
53. Ibid., 8.
54. Francis Watson, *Text and Truth*, 6.
55. With this group one ordinarily associates Herman Bavinck, J. A. C. Van
    Leeuwen, Klaus Schilder, Herman Ridderbos, and Princeton's Geerhardus Vos,
    the ranking representative of this impressive school. Declining Abraham
    Kuyper's invitation to occupy the first chair in biblical theology at the Free Uni-
    versity of Amsterdam, Vos taught at Calvin Seminary (which he had also
    attended, fresh from the Netherlands) until he finally accepted Princeton's offer
    to become Professor of Biblical Theology in 1893, remaining there until his
    retirement in 1932. As Richard Lints notes, "Vos is the first evangelical propo-
    nent of what has come to be called 'biblical theology.' Although there is no indi-
    cation that Vos understood his task to be in conflict with traditional systematic
    theology, his methodology nonetheless looks very different" (*Fabric of Theol-
    ogy*, 182). Happily, this redemptive-historical school is enjoying an ever-
    expanding audience at present.
56. An outstanding example would be Johannes Cocceius (1603–69). See especially
    his *Summa doctrinae de foedere et testamento Dei* (1660), most notably chap. 16.
    Pannenberg traces the interest of the Roman Catholic Tübingen school in the
    kingdom of God to Cocceius (*Systematic Theology*, trans. G. W. Bromiley
    [Grand Rapids: Eerdmans; Edinburgh: T. & T. Clark, 1998], 3:26). Further,
    "Only in the federal theology of Johannes Cocceius does the kingdom of God
    come into view again as a dominant theme of salvation history and eschatol-
    ogy" (530). Similarly, Moltmann, in *The Coming of God: Chris-tian Eschatol-
    ogy* (Minneapolis: Fortress Press, 1996), says that the "initial form" of the
    "transposition of eschatology into time can be found in the 'prophetic theology'
    of the seventeenth century. . . . Prophetic theology tacitly assumes that history
    and eschatology, experienced present and predicted future, lie along one and

the same temporal line," a position that Moltmann rejects (7). Nevertheless, he does appreciate this movement's "rebirth of messianic eschatology," although Moltmann exaggerates both the antiapocalypticism of the confessional writings and the chiliasm of the "prophetic theology" (157). In *Theology of Hope* (Minneapolis: Fortress Press, 1993), he notes that the ideas of "progressive revelation" in history and of redemptive history as eschatological "go back to late federal theology (J. Cocceius). . . . In contrast to Orthodoxy's supranaturalistic and doctrinaire view of revelation, the Bible was here read as a history book, as the divine commentary upon the divine acts in world history. . . . It was the start of a new, eschatological way of thinking, which called to life the feeling for history" (70). Despite the unwarranted contrast with orthodoxy (Cocceius was a leading Reformed scholastic), Moltmann is certainly accurate in his account of where things went wrong, when, especially in pietism and a renewed millenarianism of a certain type, "eschatological progressiveness of salvation history" was no longer read off of the cross and resurrection, "but from other 'signs of the times,'" which led to either optimism or despair, depending largely on world and ecclesiastical conditions (71). M. Douglas Meeks, in *Origins of the Theology of Hope* (Philadelphia: Fortress Press, 1974), observes the influence of Otto Weber on Moltmann's thought: "Weber was a representative of the Reformed tradition and its emphasis on covenant, theocracy, election, and continuity in history. . . . In large part the theology of hope is a contemporary exegesis of Calvin's view of the faith-hope dialectic" (20–21).

57. Cf. Richard Muller, *Post-Reformation Reformed Dogmatics,* vol. 1: *Prolegomenon* (Grand Rapids: Baker, 1987).
58. Geerhardus Vos, *Biblical Theology,* 16.
59. Gaffin, *Resurrection and Redemption,* 26.
60. Ibid.
61. Ibid., 17.
62. Geerhardus Vos, *Redemptive History and Biblical Interpretation,* 23.
63. Ibid., 18.
64. Geerhardus Vos, *Redemptive History,* 21.
65. Ibid.
66. In the *Institutes* alone, see, for instance, 1.6.2; 1.14.20; 2.6.1; 3.20.23.
67. Clifford Geertz, *Local Knowledge: Further Essays in Interpretive Anthropology* (New York: Basic Books, 1983), 35–40.
68. Cited by Kevin Vanhoozer, "The Voice and the Actor," in John G. Stackhouse Jr., ed., *Evangelical Futures: A Conversation on Evangelical Method* (Grand Rapids: Baker, 2000), from Bernard Ramm, *The Evangelical Heritage: A Study in Historical Theology* (Grand Rapids: Baker, 1973), 131.
69. Ibid., 91.
70. Jehuda Halevi, "Kuzari," in *Three Jewish Philosophers,* ed. Hans Lewy, Alexander Altmann, Isaak Heinemann (New York: Atheneum, 1969), 33.
71. Ibid., 35.
72. Gaffin, *Resurrection and Redemption,* 113.
73. Francis Turretin, *Institutes of Elenctic Theology,* trans. G. M. Giger; ed. J. T. Dennison Jr., vol. 1 (Phillipsburg, N.J.: Presbyterian & Reformed Publishing, 1992), 16.
74. Calvin, *Institutes,* 3.2.1. Muller's own comparison is found in his *Post-Reformation Reformed Dogmatics,* 202–3.
75. Turretin, *Institutes of Elenctic Theology,* 16.
76. Ibid., 17.
77. Richard Muller: "We note, again, that theological prolegomena are never *vor-dogmatisch* [for these scholastics]: they are an integral part of dogmatic system

that develops in dialogue with basic dogmatic conclusions after the system as a whole has been set forth" (*Post-Reformation Reformed Dogmatics*, 81).

78. Hans Urs von Balthasar, *A Theology of History* (New York: Ignatius Press, 1994), 20.

79. James Barr, "The Old Testament and the New Crisis of Biblical Authority," *Interpretation*, 25, no. 1 (Jan. 1971): 24–40, esp. 26: "The purging of this Greek thought and a rethinking in Hebrew categories would, it was supposed, revivify the whole corpus of Christian thinking and enable its content to be made relevant for the modern world; for—it was, rather vaguely, supposed—the Hebrew way of thinking had much in common with modern trends in science, in psychology, and in history; and it was the presence of Greek elements in traditional Christianity which had caused blockages of communication."

80. Paul Ricoeur, *Oneself as Another*, trans. Kathleen Blamey (Chicago: University of Chicago Press, 1990), 41.

81. Geerhardus Vos, *Redemptive History*, 8–9.

82. Abraham Joshua Heschel, *God in Search of Man*, 98.

83. Paul Ricoeur, *History and Truth*, trans. Charles A. Kelbley (Evanston Ill.: Northwestern University Press, 1965), 5.

84. Calvin, *Institutes*, 3.20.2.

85. This does not, however, mean that an impious or unregenerate theologian cannot produce sound theology, as Turretin argues against the enthusiasts: "Although an impious theologian does not carry his system into practice, it does not cease to be practical in itself because the abuse of the subject does not overthrow the legitimate use of the object" (*Institutes*, 23). This underscores the clarity of scripture even apart from divine illumination.

86. John Calvin, *A Reformation Debate*, ed. John C. Olin (Grand Rapids: Baker, 1966), esp. 58.

87. Cf. Charles S. McCoy and J. Wayne Baker, *Fountainhead of Federalism: Heinrich Bullinger and the Covenantal Tradition* (Louisville, Ky.: Westminster/John Knox, 1991). The seminal contributions of such Reformed scholastics as Johannes Althusius (especially his *Vindiciae contra tyrannos*) and Philippe Duplessis-Mornay to political philosophy is quite evident. In applying covenant theology to social ethics, say McCoy and Baker, they provided "the first systematic articulation of a federal political philosophy" (49). A concluding chapter, "Federalism and the U.S. Constitution of 1787," provides an interesting analysis of the literature on this subject.

88. José Miguez Bonino, *Doing Theology in a Revolutionary Situation* (Philadelphia: Fortress, 1975), 9.

89. Ibid.

90. Ibid., 11.

91. Gustavo Gutiérrez, *Essential Writings*, ed. James B. Nickoloff (Maryknoll, N.Y.: Orbis Books, 1996), 30.

92. Ibid., 31.

93. Ibid., 31–32.

94. John de Gruchy, *Liberating Reformed Theology: A South African Contribution to an Ecumenical Debate* (Grand Rapids: Eerdmans, 1991), xviii. Cf. John de Gruchy and Charles Villa-Vicencio, ed., *Apartheid Is a Heresy* (Grand Rapids: Eerdmans, 1983), especially de Gruchy's chapter "Toward a Confessing Church," which draws on the Confessing movement of Lutheran and Reformed churches in Nazi Germany.

95. Alan Boesak, *Black and Reformed* (Maryknoll, N.Y.: Orbis, 1982). John de Gruchy makes this point also: "Yet it was under the dominance of such evangelicalism, rather than the strict Calvinism of Dort, that the Dutch Reformed

Church agreed at its Synod of 1857 that congregations should be divided along racial lines" (de Gruchy, *Liberating Reformed Theology*, 23).

96. Walter Brueggemann, "Texts That Linger, Words That Explode," *Theology Today* 54, no. 2 (July 1997): 191–92.

97. Ibid., 192.

98. Gabriel Fackre has suggested some lines of discussion regarding the Noahic covenant in *The Doctrine of Revelation: A Narrative Interpretation* (Grand Rapids: Eerdmans, 1997), 61–100.

99. Abraham Joshua Heschel, *God in Search of Man*, 31.

100. Michel de Certeau, "How Is Christianity Thinkable Today," in *The Postmodern God: A Theological Reader* (Oxford: Blackwell, 1997), 150.

101. Francis Watson, *Text and Truth*, 13.

102. David Tracy, *The Analogical Imagination* (New York: Crossroad, 1987), 19.

103. Ibid., 20–21.

104. William Willimon, "Formed by the Saints," *Christian Century*, Feb. 7–14, 1996.

Chapter Nine

1. Richard Lints, *The Fabric of Theology: Toward an Evangelical Prolegomenon* (Grand Rapids: Eerdmans, 1993), 5–6.

2. Nietzsche, *The Portable Nietzsche* (New York: Viking, 1954), 40.

3. Mark C. Taylor, *Erring: A Postmodern A/Theology* (Chicago: University of Chicago Press, 1984), 6.

4. Ibid., 73.

5. Ibid., 156–58.

6. For instance, Peter's Pentecost sermon in Acts 2 exegetes Joel 2, with Christ's death and resurrection as securing the certainty of this fulfillment among them. In his next sermon, Peter proclaims, "The God of Abraham, the God of Isaac, and the God of Jacob, the God of our ancestors, has glorified his servant Jesus" who, despite their rebellion, "God raised from the dead." . . . In this way God fulfilled what he had foretold through all the prophets, that his Messiah would suffer" (Acts 3:13–18). Stephen's moving sermon begins with Abraham and moves through the patriarchal period, the exodus, Israel's rebellion in the wilderness, and Jesus Christ as God's true tabernacle in the world (Acts 7). These are typical of the sermons summarized for us in Acts.

7. Martin Luther, "The Holy and Blessed Sacrament of Baptism," *Luther's Works* (American Edition), vol. 35, *Word and Sacrament*, ed. E. Theodore Bachmann (Philadelphia: Fortress Press, 1960), 33.

8. Ibid., 36.

9. Philip Melanchthon, *Loci communes* (1543), trans. J. A. O. Preus (St. Louis: Concordia Publishing House, 1992), 142.

10. Herman Ridderbos, *Paul: An Outline of His Theology*, trans. John R. W. DeWitt (Grand Rapids: Eerdmans, 1975), 411.

11. Wilhelm Pauck, ed., *Melanchthon and Bucer*, Library of Christian Classics (Philadelphia: Westminster Press, 1969), 237.

12. Ibid.

13. See especially Christopher Elwood, *The Body Broken: The Calvinist Doctrine of the Eucharist and the Symbolization of Power in Sixteenth-Century France* (New York: Oxford University Press, 1999).

14. The Book of Common Order of the Church of Scotland Commonly Known as John Knox's Liturgy and the Directory for the Public Worship of God Agreed Upon by the Assembly of Divines at Westminster (Edinburgh: William

Blackwood & Sons, 1886): "In the name and authority of Jesus Christ, I, the minister of His blessed Evangel, with consent of the whole Ministry and Church, absolve thee, N., from the sentence of Excommunication, from the sin by thee committed, and from all censures laid against thee for the same before, according to thy repentance; and pronounce thy sin to be loosed in heaven, and thee to be received again to the society of Jesus Christ, to His body the Church, to the participation of His Sacraments, and, finally, to the fruition of all His benefits: In the name of the Father, the Son, and the Holy Spirit. So be it" (69).

15. Clement Greenberg, "Modernist Painting," in *The New Art*, ed. Gregory Battcock (New York: Dutton, 1966), 101–2.

16. Kenneth Frampton, "Towards a Critical Regionalism: Six Points for an Architecture of Resistance," in *Postmodern Culture*, ed. Hal Foster (London: Pluto Press, 1985), 20.

17. Paul Ricoeur, *History and Truth*, trans. Charles A. Kelbley (Evanston, Ill.: Northwestern University Press, 1965), 276–77.

18. I have in mind here especially the Ancient Christian Commentaries project launched by Thomas Oden, but also a growing circle of evangelical students of these writers.

19. 2 Pet. 3:1–9.

Index of Names

striking similarities between Reformation and the present, 151

Van Til, Cornelius, 229

Volf, Miroslav, 14, 43–44, 198

von Balthasar, Hans Urs, Jesus as center of redemption and revelation, 249

von Humboldt, Wilhelm, 57, 305n. 16

von Rad, 133, 143, 232, 233

von Ranke, Leopold, 100, 305n. 16

Vos, Geerhardus, 12, 29, 30, 37, 116, 230, 252, 278n. 10, 278n. 20
  canonical disunity, 237–38
  distinguishing biblical and systematic theology, 241
  eschatological process, 31
  first evangelical proponent of biblical theology, 324n. 55
  view of history, 39, 40
  integration of word-revelation and act-revelation, 233
  "new thing" present in resurrection, 286n. 91
  progress of biblical story, 237
  proof-texting, 241–42

Wallace, Mark I., 153

Ward, Keith, 311n. 101

Watson, Francis, 100, 151, 162, 173, 177, 239
  fragmentation leading to neo-Marcionite tendency of New Testament scholarship, 235
  fragmentation of theology, 220
  literal sense, 177
  objections to convert narratives into parabolic/metaphorical interpretation, 180
  practice of theology, 262

readers only receiving meaning, 205
modern theology as new Marcionism, 236

Webster, John, 148, 152, 201

White, Vernon, 91

Whitehead, Alfred North, 69, 74

Wieman, Henry Nelson, 74

Wilken, Robert Louis, 215

William of Ockham, 78

Willmon, William, 263

Wittgenstein, Ludwig, certainty and redemption, 10, 101, 184, 200

Wolff, Christian, 148

Wolterstorff, Nicholas, 3, 103, 137, 168, 173
  authorial discourse interpretation, 156–65
  canonicity, 138
  disciples as witnesses concerning Jesus, 138
  divine discourse model, 140
  God speaking in Jesus Christ, 139
  notion of inspiration, 303n. 39
  preference for discourse over manifestation, 143
  reflecting on Calvin's *testimonium Spiritus Sancti*, 137
  relating speech-action theory to theological hermeneutics, 156
  transitive discourse, 308n. 63

Wright, G. E., 49, 67–70, 125, 220
  criticism of traditional dogmatics, 220–21
  biblical theology project, 96
  faith seeing miraculous in nonmiraculous events, 83

Zwingli, Ulrich, 165, 270

Index of Subjects

certifying New Testament narrative, 116
crisis surrounding, 106
demythologizing, 66
eschatological implications, 231
historical and subjective, 102
last stand for divine intervention in history,
    113
meaning of in context of Old Testament
    expectations, 102, 105
two episodes of same event, 37–38, 116
revelation, 225
coordinated with redemption, 146
from divine actions, 232
as final cause of divine communication, 103
from history, 232
in history, embodiment of, 233–34
interpretation of redemption, 233
models of, 125, 140–41
as narrated promise, 137
not universally given, 132
servant of redemption, 5
subservient to redemption, 145, 226
viewed in manifestational over historical
    terms, 36
witness to and interpretation of redemption,
    103
revelational theologies, 36
Revelation and Redemption (Thiemann), 137
rhetorico-conceptual structure, 157
rhetoric of piety, 193
righteousness of faith, 267
righteousness of works, 267
romantic hermeneutics, 193
Romanticism, 28, 124, 148–49, 169, 227
root metaphors, 10

sacrament
gracious character of, 270
objective means of grace and ratification of
    covenant, 271
performative sign and seal, 269–71
performative utterances, 270
retaining essence regardless of faith, 211
sign and seal, 270
sacramental theology, relation of "sign" and
    "thing signified," 8
sacraments, signs of God's goodwill, 269–70
sacred, Jewish-Christian suspicion of, 144–45
salus historicus, 102
salvation, individual, 7
salvation history, 166
sanctification, 224
saving acts, God's witness to, 6

scandal of particularity, 124
Schwärmerei, 210
science
boundaries with theology, 53
communication with theology, 3, 85
scientific progress, 50
scriptural discourse, intent of human author,
    182
scripture
allegorical use of, 258–59
antithetical to Spirit, 211
approaching as one narrative, 164
as covenant, 204, 207
as divine interpretation of reality, 15
communal interpretation, 253
danger in treating as end in itself, 244
equal weighting with culture, 13
fit between *signum* and *res significata,* 186
illocutionary force, 195
interpreted in light of universal conscious-
    ness, 100
interpreting humans, 195
move from indicative to imperative, 258
personal commitment to, 264
preceding individual, 209
relationship to Spirit, 210–15
representing redemption, 185
single, unified meaning, 171
speculative theory of, 2
unity around, 5
Second Helvetic Confession, 89–90, 320n. 118
secular analysis, 15
secundum agens, 91
self
birth and death of, 23–24
dissolution of, 151
master of reality, 124
selfhood, 225, 266
self-identity, decentering of, 196
semiotic analysis, 205
sensus allegoricus non est argumentivus, 172
sensus communis, 216
sensus historicus, 176
sensus literalis, 75, 103, 152, 158, 164, 172,
    189–90, 195, 216, 309n. 77, 321n. 133
sensus normalis, 75
sensus plenior, 103, 179
sermon
climax of word event, 268
reenactment of covenant, 269
shalom, goal of covenant, 133
sign, 271
sign-events, 144

Printed in the United States
43885LVS00007B/100